TOM CUNLIFFE

THE COMPLETE YACHTMASTER

SAILING, SEAMANSHIP AND NAVIGATION
FOR THE MODERN YACHT SKIPPER

11TH EDITION

ADLARD COLES

LONDON • OXFORD • NEW YORK • NEW DELHI • SYDNEY

ACKNOWLEDGEMENTS

The author gratefully acknowledges the assistance of Alan Watson and the late John Hart, whose wisdom on the subject of radar was freely shared for the benefit of us all.

ADLARD COLES
Bloomsbury Publishing Plc
50 Bedford Square, London, WC1B 3DP, UK
Bloomsbury Publishing Ireland Limited,
29 Earlsfort Terrace, Dublin 2, D02 AY28, Ireland

BLOOMSBURY, ADLARD COLES and the Adlard Coles logo are trademarks of

Bloomsbury Publishing Plc
First edition 1994
Second edition 1997
Third edition 2000
Fourth edition 2003
Fifth edition 2006
Sixth edition 2008
Seventh edition 2010
Eighth edition 2014
Ninth edition 2017
Tenth edition 2021
This edition published 2025

Copyright © Tom Cunliffe, 1994, 1997, 2000, 2003, 2006, 2008, 2010, 2014, 2017, 2021, 2025

Photographs © Tom Cunliffe, 2021, 2025

Tom Cunliffe has asserted his right under the Copyright, Designs and Patents Act, 1988, to be identified as Author of this work

All rights reserved. No part of this publication may be: i) reproduced or transmitted in any form, electronic or mechanical, including photocopying, recording or by means of any information storage or retrieval system without prior permission in writing from the publishers; or ii) used or reproduced in any way for the training, development or operation of artificial intelligence (AI) technologies, including generative AI technologies. The rights holders expressly reserve this publication from the text and data mining exception as per Article 4(3) of the Digital Single Market Directive (EU) 2019/790

Bloomsbury Publishing Plc does not have any control over, or responsibility for, any third-party websites referred to or in this book. All internet addresses given in this book were correct at the time of going to press. The author and publisher regret any inconvenience caused if addresses have changed or sites have ceased to exist, but can accept no responsibility for any such changes

The publishers and author accept no responsibility for any errors or omissions, or for any accident, loss or damage (including without limitation any direct, consequential, special or exemplary damages) arising from the use or misuse of, or reliance upon, the information contained in this book

A catalogue record for this book is available from the British Library

Library of Congress Cataloguing-in-Publication data has been applied for

ISBN: HB: 978-1-399-42215-4; ePub: 978-1-399-42214-7; ePDF: 978-1-399-42217-8

2 4 6 8 10 9 7 5 3 1

Typeset in Minion by Carr Design Studio
Printed in UAE by Oriental Press

To find out more about our authors and books visit www.bloomsbury.com and sign up for our newsletters

For product safety related questions contact productsafety@bloomsbury.com

Note: while all reasonable care has been taken in the publication of this book, the publisher takes no responsibility for the use of the methods or products described in the book

This product has been derived in part from material obtained from the UK Hydrographic Office with the permission of the UK Hydrographic Office, Keeper of Public Records

Charts and tidal information on pages 112, 130, 131, 134, 137, 138, 145, 146, 147, 165, 168, 177, 191, 193, 205, 227, 231, 235, 254, 255 © British Crown Copyright, 2025. All rights reserved

THIS PRODUCT IS NOT TO BE USED FOR NAVIGATION.

Notice: The UK Hydrographic Office (UKHO) and its licensors make no warranties or representations, express or implied, with respect to this product. The UKHO and its licensors have not verified the information within this product or quality assured it

Yachtmaster™ is a trademark of the Royal Yachting Association registered in the United Kingdom and selected marketing territories. For information on RYA qualifications and RYA approved training courses for both power and sail, please visit the website: www.rya.org.uk/courses-training/Pages/hub.aspx or telephone: 0844 556 9528 (from overseas telephone +44 23 8060 4100), or write to: RYA Training, RYA House, Ensign Way, Hamble, Southampton SO31 4YA

CONTENTS

INTRODUCTION	**1**
1 THE SKIPPER	**4**
2 THE THEORY OF SAILING	**7**
Sails	8
3 EFFICIENT SAILING	**13**
Shaping the headsail	14
Shaping the mainsail	17
Sail combinations	18
Hull balance	19
Shortening sail	19
'Code Zero' sails	22
Cruising chutes	22
4 BASIC SEAMANSHIP UNDER SAIL	**23**
Tacking	23
Gybing	24
Poling out a genoa	26
Painless sail reduction	28
Heaving to	28
Reefing	30
Single-line reefing	32
In-mast mainsails	32
In-boom mainsails	32
Headsail changes	33
5 BOAT HANDLING UNDER SAIL	**35**
No brakes	35
Wind awareness	36
Tide awareness	36
Sailing slowly	37
Mooring under sail	38
Anchoring	42
Berthing	42
6 BOAT HANDLING UNDER POWER	**44**
Pivoting	44
Blowing off	44
Rudder effect	45
Propeller effects	46
Moving ahead	47
The set piece short turn	47
Motoring astern	48
Berthing	49
Coming alongside	54
Leaving an alongside berth	58
Bow thrusters	59
7 ROPES AND ROPEWORK	**60**
Types of rope	60
Wire halyards	61
Knots, splices and whippings	62
Eyes and ends	65
Rope handling	66
Securing the yacht	68
Coming alongside	68
Towing	70
Towing with the dinghy	72
8 ANCHORING	**73**
Holding ground	74
Types of anchor	74
Types of cable	76
Weighting the cable	77
Selecting an anchorage	78
Laying an anchor	79
Weighing anchor	82
Fouled anchors	83
Anchoring stern- or bow-to	85
Kedging off	86
Storm anchoring	86
9 YACHT ENGINES	**88**
Basic maintenance	88
Trouble shooting	90
Fuel problems	92
10 SAILING IN HEAVY WEATHER	**95**
Preparing the boat	96
Sails	96
Steering in waves	98
Survival tactics	100

THE COMPLETE YACHTMASTER

11 NAVIGATION - AN INTRODUCTION		**103**
12 CHARTS, PUBLICATIONS AND CHART TABLE TOOLS		**107**
Latitude, longitude and the globe		107
Chart projections		108
Direction		110
Paper and electronic charts in practical perspective		110
Chart symbols		111
Other information on the chart		113
Chart datums		113
Privately produced paper charts		113
Electronic charts		114
Chart corrections		115
The Nautical Almanac		116
Pilot books and sailing directions		116
Chart table tools		118
13 AIDS TO NAVIGATION		**119**
Lighthouses		120
Offshore marks		123
Inshore marks		124
14 TIDAL HEIGHTS		**127**
Tide tables		129
Times		129
Secondary ports		129
Tidal definitions		132
Intermediate tidal heights		134
Tidal curves		136
Non-astronomical factors in tide movements		139
The essence of a tidal height question		139
Using tidal height calculations safely		142
15 TIDAL STREAMS		**143**
Tidal gates		143
Tide-induced sea states		144
Information on tidal streams		144
16 TRADITIONAL NAVIGATIONAL INPUTS		**150**
The compass		150
Variation		151
Deviation		153
Heeling error		156
Local magnetic anomalies		156
Compass dip		156
The log		157
Depth		159
17 THE ESTIMATED POSITION		**162**
Leeway		163
Plotted vectors		164
The tide vector		164
The echo sounder		165
Plotting		166
The log book		166
The end is nigh!		167
18 CLASSICAL POSITION FIXING		**168**
The eyeball fix and the position line		169
Sources of position line		171
Preplotting and use of ship's heading		175
The running fix		176
Evaluation of fixes		177
19 SATELLITES AND RADAR		**180**
Global Positioning System (GPS)		181
Chart datums		182
Beyond the fix		183
Electronic chart plotters		187
Plotting on the screen		194
Marine computers		194
Radar		195
20 COURSE SHAPING		**200**
Course to steer at the turn of the tide		202
The longer passage		203
Leeway		204
Cross-tide sailing with GPS		205
21 NAVIGATIONAL STRATEGY		**207**
Wind, tide, light and darkness		207
Wind shifts		207
Beating in water free of currents		208
The favoured tack		208
Unpredicted wind shifts		209
Anticipated wind shifts		210
Beating in a cross-current		211
Beating in a cross-tide		211
Tacking downwind		212
22 PASSAGE PLANNING		**214**
Charts and overall distances		215
Passage planning with chart plotters		215
Alternative destinations		216
Waypoints		217
Waypoint lists		217
Weather		218
Tidal streams		218

Traffic Separation Schemes (TSS)	219
Tidal heights	219
Daylight	219
Fuel	220
Courses to steer	220
Tactics and strategy	221
Pilotage plan	221

23 PILOTAGE 222
Safe track	223
Further thoughts on piloting with a plotter	226
Forward planning	227
Cockpit-mounted plotters	229

24 PASSAGE NAVIGATION 230
The passage plan	231
The passage without electronics	232
The same passage using GPS and a paper chart	235
The passage with a plotter	238

25 DOMESTICS OF A PASSAGE 240
Food	240
Sleep	241
Warmth	242
Space	242
Seasickness	242

26 FOG 244
Maintain your plot	244
Fog seamanship	245
Fog tactics	246

27 COLLISION AVOIDANCE IN POOR VISIBILITY 250
Responsibility for lookout	250
AIS	251
Digital radar	254
Display options	254
Simple collision avoidance	258
MARPA	259
Top tips for radar collision avoidance	263

28 TACTICS AND NAVIGATION IN HEAVY WEATHER 266
Navigation in poor conditions	267
Position fixing	268
Course steered and estimated position	268

29 DAMAGE CONTROL 271
Tool kits and spare parts	272
Fire prevention and fighting	276
Jury rigs	276
Ropes around the propeller	278
Steering failure	278
Dismasting	280
Loss of electronics	280

30 EMERGENCIES 281
Lifeboat rescue	282
Helicopter rescue	283
First on the scene	285
Taking to the liferaft	286
Pyrotechnics	288

31 MAN OVERBOARD 290
The reach-turn-reach	291
Crash stop	292
Bringing the casualty aboard	294
Search and rescue	295

32 WEATHER 297
The frontal depression	298
Mutually exclusive air masses	298
Air circulation	298
Depression formation	299
Depression tracks	301
Frontal anatomy	301
Occlusions	303
Secondary depressions	303
Locating a low-pressure centre	304
Wind strengths in depressions	304
Cyclonic winds	304
Depressions in the southern hemisphere	304
High pressure	304
Fog	305
Sea breezes	306
Significant local winds	306

APPENDIX 1: Stability in Sailing Yachts 307
The GZ curve	307

APPENDIX 2: Commercial Endorsement of the RYA/MCA Yachtmaster Certificate 310
Professional Practices and Responsibilities (PPR)	311

INDEX 312

THE COMPLETE YACHTMASTER

Colours are up. Time to rouse out the crew and get under way.

INTRODUCTION

The sailor's market-place is well stocked with books on every topic to do with salt water. I ought to know, I've written a number of them myself. There are two groups of specialist sailing texts. One deals with matters such as navigation, boat handling and meteorology, with which every skipper must have more than a nodding acquaintance. The other caters for the ever-enlarging number of subjects relating less directly to the essence of moving a yacht safely from one location to another. The volume you are about to read is designed specifically for skippers and potential skippers. Its purpose is to gather together all those vital areas of expertise to be found in the first group of books, place them in a systematic order between two covers, and discuss them in a practical way. The book should therefore not only prove useful as a companion to a sailing course, either hands-on or theoretical, but will also provide a long-term reference for the boat's bookshelf.

I make no claim that *The Complete Yachtmaster* is the only work you will require in order to take charge of a yacht. Certain items, such as the use of radio communications, require a specialist volume in their own right, and it is not insignificant that teaching the VHF syllabus is a separate subject in most mainstream training systems.

Likewise, the wider aspects of boat maintenance and general husbandry are barely touched here. People's needs in such departments vary enormously, as do their talents for servicing them. If you own a classic wooden vessel you will have no desire to read about the application of epoxy coatings to a blistered GRP hull, but whatever type of craft you sail, you should know how to calculate the rise of tide at a given time and location. You may be such a congenital mechanical duffer that the finest manual on boat electrics will be no more than an incubus on your chart table, while the acquisition of the same work could change your neighbour's life. Both of you, however, share an imperative demand for the skill to bring your vessels alongside crisply, cleanly and without fuss.

It is to such primary questions that this book is dedicated. In it, you will find the basic information that, when mastered and practised, will enable you to skipper a well-found yacht on coastal and offshore passages, taking due account of night and day, and whatever weather may betide.

In earlier editions this policy led to omitting comment on the International Regulations for Preventing Collisions at Sea (Colregs). The rules themselves are straightforward; they must be learned largely by rote, and reprinting them here would be a waste of paper. In the days before radar, AIS and other electronic aids became widely used, implementing them was plain sailing, so the subject was avoided. Today, interpreting the readouts from modern yacht electronics has rendered the subject of collision avoidance more complex, rather than less. Used to their full potential, these instruments can provide a remarkable degree of protection against collision. Abused or misunderstood, they are well documented as having led to increased rather than diminished danger, so a full chapter is now dedicated to dealing with these issues.

Throughout the world, cruising training schemes have been set up by national and private authorities. The contents of these are more or less the same, forming the core of what all skippers should have at their fingertips. The British-based RYA Yachtmaster program is the oldest and among the best established. It has been used as a loose framework for this book. However, the RYA's navigation policy is now based on 'electronics first'. While accepting and applauding the universal take-up of GPS-based systems, it is my belief that traditional, time-honoured methods should be fully understood and practised. The navigator with this philosophy will know what questions to ask the electronic plotter and will get more from the answers. In uncertain times, the possibility of GPS being interfered with by those who wish us ill is rising. The ability to switch seamlessly from electronics to classical methods is therefore a vital safety factor and remains the mark of a complete Yachtmaster.

Fortunately, most examiners are of a similar point of view, so my own early experience with the scheme is more relevant than the 'electronics first' approach might suggest.

I turned up at the appointed hour, aged 30, to take an at-sea examination in my own yacht. She was a 13-ton cutter which, at the time, had no engine. I had recently completed a cruise from the UK to Brazil and home again via the Caribbean, the USA and Canada. I was annoyed at the need to have a 'ticket', but I was driven into the arms of the establishment because I had lost a plum delivery job to a man who had one. My expectations were for needless red tape, a desk sailor as an examiner, and a lot of stupid questions. I couldn't have been more wrong. The list of things I was supposed to know was comprehensive and entirely sensible. My examiner proved far more interested in whether I could sail than if I knew the Morse code (now mercifully discontinued from the scheme), and his probing revealed one or two gaps in my armour of which I was justly ashamed. He passed me, but with a stiff talking-to.

I thought about my exam for six months, then I gave up delivering yachts to become a sailing instructor.

Since those days, I have spent enough time voyaging and working with trainers in other countries to recognise that while such details as buoyage and the format of tide tables may vary, the essentials of seafaring emphatically do not. Sailors are travelling more than they used to. Ever greater numbers of us are taking to the oceans in our own vessels, or as crew for others, while the ready availability of charter craft in the best cruising grounds worldwide is tempting more of us to try something different. For these reasons, though the spelling follows British rather than North American forms, *The Complete Yachtmaster* is produced without bias to the specific arrangements of any one nation. I wrote this edition while my boat was resident in the Baltic. Some of the photos, therefore, represent activity in Sweden, Denmark or Finland, but the action could take place anywhere.

You'll notice that the business of sailing and boat handling is explored in the early chapters of the book. The reason for this is simple. When we go down to our boats for the weekend, we tell our neighbours we are 'going sailing'. No one ever says, 'Oh, I'm off for a

INTRODUCTION

spot of navigation. See you on Sunday night.' The sailing is the most important thing. Of all the facets of cruising, it requires the most practice and, for many people, it is the most difficult thing to learn.

All books have to start somewhere and throughout this text the assumed entry level of knowledge is around the RYA's Day Skipper qualification. The 'Introduction to Yachting' course could also serve a proactive student. What this means to non-RYA readers is that to get the best from this book you need to know port from starboard, north from south, and what constitutes a latitude/longitude position. If you're a sailor, it will also help if you understand the basic principles of tacking and gybing, because it's assumed you have these on board when we go into details of how to make the manoeuvres painless. Should you be concerned that the book may be pitched beyond your present level, buy *The Complete Day Skipper* instead. If you've already read this work, you'll find a certain amount of recap here. This serves to revise as well as to provide a springboard for more advanced studies of the same subjects.

The first edition of this book was written in the early 1990s in a different climate of gender discussion to that prevalent today. The sea, were it to be asked, would probably be disinclined to spend time justifying political correctness. Nevertheless, a note is called for to explain why, throughout the text, the skipper, the cook, or any other individual is normally awarded the masculine singular form of the personal pronoun. The plain fact is that anything else is too cumbersome to read and to write. However, absolutely no suggestion of male ascendancy is to be implied. If I were to note that, 'When the skipper has navigated the yacht on to the rocks, it is he who must bear the blame,' there is no implication that a female skipper would not be just as capable of so dismal a denouement, but to write 'he or she' every time is a non-starter. Therefore, I have followed the convention adopted by the classical languages. The masculine form is used to refer to a person whose sex is, for the purposes of the text at least, indeterminate or irrelevant. Likewise, and without apology, a boat is always referred to as 'she'.

Tom Cunliffe

The author's boat alone in a snug anchorage. Perfect peace.

1 THE SKIPPER

Skippering a yacht is one of the most satisfying recreations known. For many of us, it grows into more than a mere pastime, with our jobs becoming only the means to finance our boating lives.

Yachting is uniquely gratifying because, if it is practised to the full, it engages every facet of our being. It can be as physical as we care to make it. It is intellectual, with the problems posed by navigation often requiring solutions of great accuracy. It is also aesthetic: there are few more beautiful human creations than a sailboat carving her way through the sea. Lastly, and probably most important of all, there are times when it asks serious questions about the core of our characters. The net result is that the captain's role becomes so absorbing as an end in itself that it leaves little time for worrying about other things.

This only works, though, if you are at one with the whole boating environment. The sort of skipper who gets the balance of his duties wrong tends to find his own performance less than satisfactory. Poor results, especially if they seem inexplicable, lead to a general lack of well-being, and before long the business of yachting begins to lose its lustre, not only for the skipper, but also for those who have chosen to sail with him.

A glance at the chapter headings of this book gives a rough idea of the number of definable skills that must be at the disposal of the Yachtmaster. These subjects are not individual streams of learning. Each spills over into the others, by varying amounts under different circumstances. The good skipper is not only master of every discipline, he is able to evaluate the amount of time that should be devoted to each in a given situation. This sense of proportion comes best with experience, but education and a degree of self-training in the objective assessment of a task can be an enormous help.

On an average passage in coastal waters, even if the area is unfamiliar to the skipper, the amount of time spent navigating should be small. After all, what is there to do? You have only to ascertain your position from time to time, make sure that you are on track for your destination, or if not, then at least check that you are making decent progress to windward, and that your yacht is maintaining an adequate clearance from any dangers. That is all there is to it. So long as you are at home with the simple techniques required to achieve this end, you should have to spend only a few minutes each hour at the chart table. The remainder of your time is then available for other chores such as getting the best from the boat, making sure the crew are fed, watered and happy, cheering up cousin Bert who is turning green in the aft lee corner of the cockpit, noting the squall galloping down out of the wind's eye, and avoiding

THE SKIPPER

the supertanker trying to expunge you and your team from the face of the ocean blue. So it is with a skipper who is comfortable with the job.

Sadly, life isn't always like that. There is a strong tendency for sailors who are less than perfectly sure of themselves to spend far too much time at the navigation station. To say that they 'over-navigate' is not strictly true because, often, 20 minutes of effort results only in a spidery mess of indeterminate lines on the chart, followed by an undignified scurry to the lee rail. The skipper who falls into this trap isn't lacking in a sense of responsibility, he is indicating a shortage of competence in extracting the essence of his navigational requirements.

At sea, the skipper's place may be in the cockpit, in the galley, or even in his bunk. The one place where he is not required for anything but the minimum of time is in the navigatorium. Numerous people fail their hands-on Yachtmaster examination for making this mistake. To come back at the examiner and say, 'But I thought that is what you would have expected of me,' indicates a dangerously low degree of self-confidence. The real seaman says to himself, 'I know what I'm doing, and if this character doesn't like it, the whole system is out of order.' In fact, the system is in a fair state of health, so a capable person with such an approach will probably get the ticket, always provided there is no shortfall in sailing skills.

There is more to good skippering than maintaining a sense of proportion at sea. Even at the planning stage, one area of knowledge integrates with others to produce a smooth-running result. You can't think out a ten-day cruise, or even a 12-hour beat to windward, without the tactical capacity to make the most of any projected weather changes. A mathematically accurate tidal height calculation can be a dangerous item of data if no allowance is made for sea state, while a difficult piece of night pilotage is often rendered less traumatic by noting the time of moonrise and making use of the light available an hour or so later.

There are some skippers with whom people come back to sail over and over again. Others have constant problems persuading their victims to return on board. The difference is never coincidence, though it may occasionally result from a genuine personality clash. Far more often, disharmony on board a small vessel is the direct fault of the person in charge.

Where a skipper is of marginal technical competence, his best chance of maintaining the morale of his team lies in a 'let's tackle this problem together' approach. If the sea spares him and he possesses interpersonal skills of a high order, he and his crew may yet have an enjoyable time. Even an able autocrat who delegates few

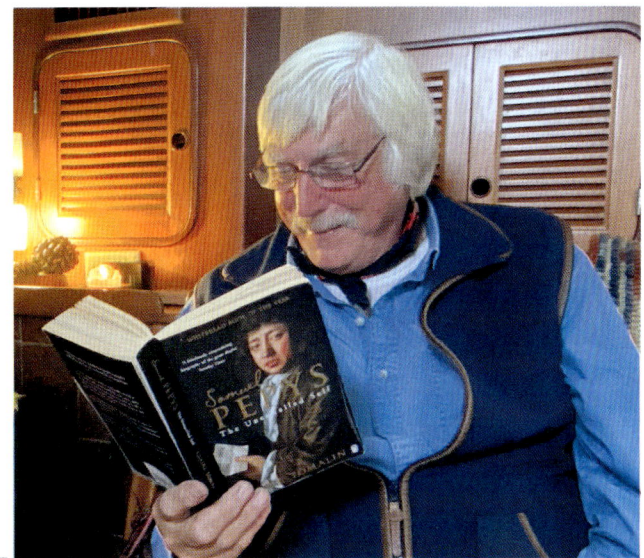

Staying relaxed while on or off watch creates an atmosphere of general confidence.

of his duties is liable to finish up with a crew whose only function aboard is to further his ends, rather than a group working under his overall guidance towards a goal they all seek. So long as the skipper knows his business, the success and the happiness of the crew depend largely upon thoughtful delegation and calm, positive communication. If all hands are clear about what is expected of them and no one is asked to perform a task that is unsuitable to his ability, morale starts out on a sound footing. The skipper can then work with the crew to sort out watch systems, apportion the less pleasant duties, and ensure that the food and drink departments are running smartly.

A capable navigator, or even a trainee, can be detailed to keep an eye on the yacht's position. Given that his appointment is not then repeatedly compromised by an insecure skipper, the navigator's sense of achievement will make him a better companion than if he had been used merely as an autopilot and winch-winder.

A skilled leader can pass a surprising amount of responsibility to people of limited qualification. He does this by being well on top of the task himself, assigning a function that may be demanding to the person concerned, but over which he can keep a controlling eye. If all goes well, a word of praise will work wonders for the atmosphere aboard. If things begin to go awry, the situation can be nipped in the bud by a deft, tactful intervention, after which the delegate can continue, better informed, but not chastened. Even small children can have their active place in the ship's company; taking charge of fenders and flags makes an excellent start to a seafaring career. Pride in a task, however small, needs encouraging. It results in a happy ship whose objectives are successfully achieved with no fuss at all.

The inherent, quiet authority of able skippers often place them in the position of a parent with the family that their crew rapidly becomes. Age does not enter into this, nor does sex. I have seen 25-year-olds slip smoothly into this role when some of their crew have been twice their years. This state of affairs is natural and entirely beneficial to the well-being of all on board. It is also widely precedented. Arguably the most successful skippers the sea has ever known were on the China clippers of the 1850s. One imagines such men as being hoary greybeards gazing aloft with eyes left bloody by half a century of wind-burn. In fact, many were under 30. But every one of them was referred to by his crew as 'The Old Man'.

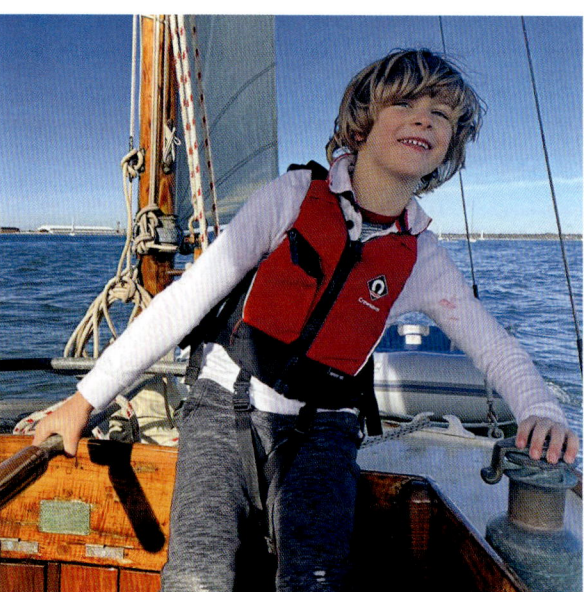

Getting the kids involved from the start brings families together and pays handsome dividends in the long term. This lad will be taking his parents sailing one day.

THE THEORY OF SAILING

2

I had been sailing for many years before my first opportunity arose to skipper a powerful motorboat. She was not fast, but she was seaworthy and had a more than adequate supply of horses harnessed to the inboard end of her propeller shaft. Making passages in her was a revelation. I could shape cross-tide courses accurately because my boat speed was a known factor. ETAs could be predicted with uncanny accuracy by simply dividing the distance to run by the number of knots I had decided to dial up. Unless the weather was of hooligan status, it bothered my progress little, if at all, and by keeping the watch from inside the wheelhouse, crew fatigue became an inconsequential factor.

The sailor's world may be theoretically greener than that of his brothers and sisters in motor yachts, but it is complicated in the extreme. Many of us mitigate this by judicious use of a reliable auxiliary power unit, but not many of these are beefy enough in small sailing craft to motor effectively straight into the eye of a strong wind in the open sea. Even if yours is among

The stack-packed main remains as good an option as one can find for mainsail management. The skipper has slacked away the lazy jacks with the sail set so as not to compromise shape.

THE COMPLETE YACHTMASTER

the few that can, you probably choose to sail her to her destination if at all possible. It's often more like hard labour and the end result is less predetermined, but the satisfaction is in inverse proportion to the uncertainty. What is more, there is a mystical pleasure that flows from the way a sailing craft converts the passing air into forward motion. That's why we all do it.

There is no secret about how a yacht sails downwind. If you sat in a buoyant bath tub and spread a few square feet of cloth to the breeze, you'd increase your wind resistance enough to blow away to leeward. The directional stability of your vessel might leave something to be desired, but up to a point, the more sail you set the faster you would go.

Non-sailors can never grasp how a boat manages to sail across the wind, or work her way towards a point from which it is blowing. Yachtsmen accept this apparently illogical phenomenon as a matter of daily course, but not all of us understand the mechanism by which it occurs. Unless you are one of the small number of instinctive sailors, a knowledge of what is going on will help you to operate a boat more effectively.

Sails

Contrary to what you might assume, a sail isn't a bag for collecting wind, it is an aerofoil that operates on the same principle as the wing of an aeroplane. If an aerofoil is presented at the correct angle to a stream of air, it causes the air to bend, with the result that the air on the convex side of the foil is accelerated. It is a law of the universe that if a flowing gas can be induced to travel more quickly it will exert less pressure. This means that there is a pressure difference between the two faces of a functioning aerofoil. Low pressure is on the convex side, and comparatively high pressure opposes it. In the case of an aircraft, the convex side of a basic wing is uppermost. The wing is therefore sucked upwards into the area of lower pressure, just as surely as the dust on your carpet is drawn into the bag of your vacuum cleaner. The wing rises in defiance of gravity. If its lift is sufficient, it carries the rest of the airframe along with it into the sky.

Fig 2.1 The force generated by a sail acts at right angles to a line joining luff and leech.

THE THEORY OF SAILING

Fig 2.2 Resolving the force of a sail. The diagonal force of a sail can be reduced to two component forces, one forward and one athwartships.
a Closehauled, the sideways force outweighs the forward one.
b Freed off, with the sail sheeted well out, the forward component is the greater.

A sail experiences the same forces as a wing, but in order to translate its effect into the desired result, something happens that is more complicated than flight. In order to fathom what is going on, we need to take a closer look at the sail as an aerofoil.

As the photographs on p. 16 and p. 17 show, a well-cut sail that is properly set cuts the air cleanly. The lift it is generating acts at an angle of 90° to a line joining its luff and its leech (Fig 2.1). Its maximum curvature, or camber, is about 40% of the way aft. This latter factor can vary, as we will be discussing in the next chapter, but it must never be in the after half of the sail. If that is allowed to occur, the aerofoil effect is disastrously impaired.

So far so good, but we still haven't answered the question as to why the boat is not simply sucked into the direction of the lift of her sail. The reason lies in her keel, which supplies the vital element of lateral resistance.

A well-designed sailing craft has absolutely no interest in going sideways. When the diagonal force from the rig arrives at the keel, it undergoes a process of resolution into two basic components. One pulls athwartships; the other forwards (Fig 2.2). Depending on the set of the sail, the forward component is frequently much smaller than its athwartships counterpart, but because the capacity of the keel for resisting this is so great, and any reluctance to move ahead is diminutive, the vessel slides forward through the water.

Basic sail trim

As the sail is trimmed progressively further from the fore-and-aft line of the yacht, the forward component of its lift increases. It is therefore easier to sail fast while reaching than it is closehauled. The system only works properly, however, so long as the sail is cutting the wind cleanly.

Fig 2.3 (p. 10) indicates that a sail that has been let out too far is backwinded. If it is sheeted in too hard, it stalls. The trick of setting a sail correctly on a reach is, therefore, to ease the sheet until the luff shows signs of backwinding, then pull the sail in just far enough to put it to sleep, and no further. You'll know then that it is not stalled, and that it is delivering as much forward drive as it is able.

THE COMPLETE YACHTMASTER

Running

When the boat has turned far enough from the wind to place it on her quarter, you won't be able to ease the sheets any more on a conventional yacht. The main is pressed against the shrouds, and the headsail will flop about in its wind shadow. At this point the mainsail is beginning to stall. There is nothing to be done about this, but you can console yourself with the knowledge that, because it is squared right away, whatever drive it is managing to deliver will be entirely in a forward direction. Coping with the jib on a run will be described in Chapter 4.

You should resist the temptation to oversheet the main in order to 'keep it clear of the shrouds'. It isn't doing itself any measurable damage. So long as it is vanged well down, the small amount of chafe will be an acceptable trade-off for not spoiling the trim of the boat.

As you steer her further downwind, there comes a time when the breeze will be aft. The boat is now on a dead run. No vessel has ever enjoyed this point of sail, not even one with a single squaresail, because there is now no aerofoil effect left at all. Unless there is a lot of breeze, this leaves the rig feeling sloppy and makes for slow progress with heavy, unrestrained rolling thrown in as a bonus. In spite of the negative features of running, there are times when it is unavoidable. Techniques for surviving it are discussed in Chapter 4.

In a fore-and-aft-rigged craft such as a modern yacht, the danger of an accidental gybe

Fig 2.3 Airflow across a sail.

THE THEORY OF SAILING

must be appended to the list of miseries endured on a run. Even with the boat dead before the wind, her main boom must be over one side or the other. Nominally it must be to leeward, except that there is no lee side on a run. If the boom is to starboard and you allow the wind to creep around towards the starboard quarter, the boom will then be on the weather, or windward, side. This is an unstable state, and unless the boom is restrained by a preventer it may slam violently across the boat, settling the account for the treatment you have given it.

From time to time you will be obliged to turn the boat's stern through the wind. A gybe will then be inevitable, but since you will have planned it, it can be controlled (see Chapter 4) and need be no more dangerous than your morning coffee. Swallow that in one gulp and you'll burn your throat. Sip it, and it'll set you up for the rest of the day.

Closehauled sailing

If you start out with your boat sailing on a beam reach and bring her up steadily towards the wind, you'll be trimming your sails progressively towards the fore-and-aft line. Somewhere around 45° from the wind you'll find that the sails won't come in any further. At this point you are closehauled. If you try to steer above a closehauled course the luffs of your sails will collapse, or lift, and the yacht will slow down. She will also begin to go sideways as the forward component of her sails diminishes to near zero. Conversely, if you sail the boat below (or downwind of) a closehauled course with the sails sheeted hard in, she will heel excessively and slow down.

It is therefore up to the helmsman to steer a closehauled boat precisely in the correct 'groove'. It is he who presents the rig at the desired angle to the wind, or who causes it to lift or stall. This is what defines the difference between closehauled sailing and any other situation. Once the sheet trimmers have set the sails closehauled they can do no more, except in terms of detail, which we'll consider later on.

Sailing to windward

When you are presented with a destination to the windward side of a closehauled course, you won't be able to fetch it directly. The answer is well known. You must tack, or beat towards it. The art of carrying out this basic process of zig-zagging, however, takes a lot of learning, and the variation in performance between a skilled operator and a novice can be remarkable. Fortunately, with a modern yacht as your vehicle, there need be no doubt that you will achieve your end. The only question will be how long it takes you to get there.

Sailing to windward, Baltic-style.

Fig 2.4 Simple beating to windward.

At its simplest, the process goes like this: sheet in your sails, then see which tack offers the greater gain towards where you hope to go. Steer the yacht so that she is as near the 'closehauled groove' as you can get her. Sail on until your destination lies abeam. This is as close as you will be able to approach on that tack, so you should now go about. If your boat is performing well you will find that you can sail right to your chosen spot closehauled (Fig 2.4).

Often, you'll be congratulating yourself that you'll arrive shortly, only to find that a wind shift leaves you groping. When this happens, don't pinch the boat too close to the wind. It almost never pays. Just keep steering so as to present the rig at the correct angle to the breeze, as before: bring the boat slightly too close to the wind (sails lifting) and bear away a degree or two. If you fail to make it on this tack, 'flop over' again when your harbour mouth, or buoy, or that continent somewhere over the horizon, is abeam. You'll get there in the end. The strategies for tacking towards a distant windward objective will be discussed in Chapter 21.

Sailors used to talk of working a boat to windward. This was a description they instinctively bestowed on the business, and they were right. The fact that a vessel can be moved in direct opposition to the source of her motion is a miracle that should never be taken for granted, even though it is far easier to execute in a modern yacht than ever it was in the working craft from which they are ultimately derived. Nonetheless, as soon as our evening watering hole slips tantalisingly into the windward sector of the horizon, we are on our mettle. Any fool can reach around the seas, but it takes a sailor to beat efficiently.

EFFICIENT SAILING   3

Sails today are very different from their ancestors in the period before the polyester revolution. Shape has always been the most important factor in sail efficiency, and time was when you chose your most suitable canvas for the conditions, pulled it up and sheeted it in. Some cruising sails are still made like this. They work well enough, but the cloth from which they are cut often means that their performance potential is nowhere near that of a modern sail whose geometry can be modified to suit the wind and sea. Such equipment has worked its way into cruisers following the lead set by racing yachts, whose hi-tech vanguard have now moved on to cloths of such sophistication and stability that the shape cut into their sails is barely compromised until they literally burst.

We have seen in Chapter 2 that the maximum camber of a sail should be somewhat forward of the middle of its cross-section. In practice this varies to a degree with what sort of sail it is and how hard the wind is blowing. The power of an aerofoil depends upon its depth of curvature, so a baggy sail will drive you along in light airs far more effectively than a flat one. As the breeze hardens, the power of the full-cut sail will become too great for the boat. It must then be flattened or reefed, if either is possible, or changed for a different sail if not. This requirement is underlined by the fact that as the wind increases, a sail naturally becomes fuller and the point of maximum camber is blown aft towards the leech. Both these results are the opposite of what is desirable, and something must be done to mitigate them.

In addition to the question of camber control, there is also the matter of twist. Most sails twist away from the wind in their upper sections. This tendency is built into them deliberately and can be controlled so that it works to your advantage.

Twist is a shut book to many sailors, but to ignore it will measurably compromise your boat speed. The reason for its importance is this: wind blows more strongly aloft than near the deck, because surface friction with the sea slows it down. When a boat sails along, the wind she actually experiences is a composite known as *apparent wind* (Fig 3.1, p.14). She may be powered by a true wind from abeam, but she is making a ghost breeze from dead ahead in an equal and opposite direction to her own progress through the flowing air. This phantom combines with the true wind to generate the actual breeze across the sails. The apparent wind that they form comes from further ahead and is stronger than the true wind, so long as it is not blowing from well abaft the beam.

Clearly, the faster the true wind for a given boat speed, the less will be the interference caused by the boat's movement. Because the true wind aloft is a little stronger than at

Fig 3.1 Apparent wind. The apparent wind is greater than the true wind and blows from further ahead.

deck level, the apparent wind up there is somewhat more 'free' than the air lower down. If the upper part of the sail can be twisted to take advantage of this, its resultant force (Chapter 2) will produce a larger forward component than that being delivered by the lower section of the same area of canvas. Furthermore, the whole of the sail will be setting cleanly, with no part either lifting or stalling.

In the case of a fractional-rig, the upper section of the mainsail cuts undisturbed air, while the lower parts receive their wind already bent further aft by the headsails. Twist control is vital if the top of the sail is not to be stalled completely.

Too much twist can generate a fearsome loss of power if it is allowed to go unchecked while you are reaching on a windy day. The boom kicks up in disgust, while the upper third of the mainsail dumps its air unceremoniously to leeward over its tortured leech.

Shaping the headsail

In most boats, the primary tool for headsail camber control is the halyard winch. Some traditional craft are equally well-served by a tack downhaul, but whatever method is employed, the crucial feature of the sail at any given time is its luff tension.

Hoist the sail, then steer the boat on, or nearly on a closehauled heading. Now look up at the mid-part of the sail. If it has a 'go-fast stripe' your task is made easier. If not, you'll have to judge its shape by looking at the seams. The camber should swell out to a maximum 35–40% of the way aft from the luff. If it is too far aft, tension up the halyard and watch the draught move forward. If the luff is too 'hard' (ie, the camber is too far forward), slack away a few inches and keep looking.

If the sail seems susceptible to this treatment, check it again once your boat speed has built up. The apparent wind will now be greater and the sail may require some adjustment. It's important to do this with your fully open roller reefing genoa as well as a hanked-on sail.

As the wind picks up, keep hardening the luff until your efforts to maintain a good camber become fruitless. The sail should now be overpowering the boat if the sailmaker and the designer got their sums right. Change it for a smaller one, which should also be flatter cut, or roll some away.

The converse of keeping your sails reasonably flat as the wind hardens is that a sail can sometimes be set up to be too shallow-cambered. It will then lack the power to drive the boat in light airs. If the sail seems lifeless, ease the halyard, and the sheet too if necessary, so as to power up the canvas.

Attention to the luff of the sail may cause the leech to require service. The leech-line, if fitted, is a light piece of small stuff sewn into the trailing edge of the sail. It should be gently 'tweaked' just far enough to stop the leech beating, *and no further*. Too much tension causes a hooked leech, which is hateful to behold. If the leech is already hooked, slack away the line as far as the sail will let you.

The twist of a headsail is determined mainly by the position of the sheet leads. Most boats have these on sliders. If yours doesn't, the sail must be cut to the position of the fixed leads.

Sheet-lead positions are crucial (Fig 3.2). When the helmsman brings the sail a little too close to the wind from closehauled or a close reach, the luff should lift evenly all the way up. If the bottom of the luff lifts first, the genoa sheet-lead car is too far forward on its track, making the leech too tight so that the sail is not twisting enough. If the top goes first, there is too much twist, caused by the sliding car being too far aft. The best position can only be found by experiment, but luff 'tell-tales' are a tremendous help. If you don't have any, install them now. All you need are three 8in (20cm) lengths of wool pushed through the sail with a sail needle, about 6in (15cm) abaft the luff (in a 35-footer) and knotted on both sides. The windward ones will always flick up just before the sail lifts. If the leeward ones go dancing they tell you without room for argument that the sail has stalled either from oversheeting on a reach, or because the person steering the boat to windward is driving her to leeward of her best course.

It's critical to inspect the position of the sheet lead after you've pulled a reef or three into a roller genoa. Chances are the car will need to be moved forward. Failure to take this simple step will depower the genoa by letting the top twist away. The sail is already struggling because it's been rolled. Don't be fooled. Not even the smartest will set as well with six rolls in, so you can help it give its best by making sure it's led properly.

Fig 3.2 Genoa twist.

THE COMPLETE YACHTMASTER

  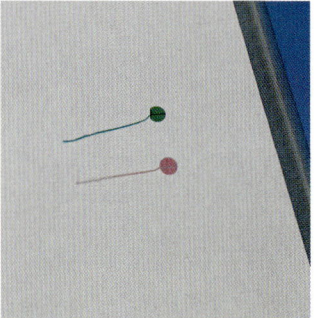

Tell-tales in the genoa luff make all the difference when it comes to setting sail.

1 Windward side tell-tale lifting – either not sheeted tight enough or sailing too close to the wind.

2 Leeward side tell-tale lifting – the sail is stalled, either oversheeted or steering too far off the wind.

3 Spot on!

The clew on this sophisticated headsail has been allowed to rise a little to induce twist in the upper portions to mirror that of the mainsail.

EFFICIENT SAILING

A well-found yacht will have a small tackle led aft to the cockpit on either side to control the car's movements. A non-sailor's boat may well see you stumbling down a heavily heeled side deck after dark to fiddle around with a nasty fitting under substantial load – the very thing a roller sail is meant to avoid – so don't spare the pennies. Rig a tackle and give the boat and her crew their best chance.

Shaping the mainsail

As in a headsail, mainsail camber is largely controlled by luff tension. However, sails on boats with any pretension to performance generally also offer a clew outhaul. The effects of this will extend approximately to the lower third of the sail. Haul it out to flatten the sail as the breeze fills in.

A mainsail set together with a genoa will emphatically not require a hard entry. Such a form will often result in the backwinding of the main luff when the boat is closehauled. Instead, a gentle curve aft to a maximum camber virtually in the centre of the sail will work well if the boat is masthead-rigged. The more powerful sail of a fractional-rigger should carry its maximum camber somewhat further forward, but still with a flat, gentle entry.

Mainsail twist is highly controllable on a modern yacht. Leech tension, the essential element, is determined by the mainsheet when closehauled. With the kicking strap (or kicker, or centre boom vang) let off, juggle the sheet tension until the top batten of the sail lines up with the boom when viewed from directly underneath. There is no need to lie in the bottom of the cockpit, a glance will suffice.

Once you have the twist you are after – and if the sails are well cut, the leech of the main will now sweetly follow that of a well-trimmed genoa – the mainsail's angle of attack can be determined by using the mainsheet traveller, so long as the wind is well forward of the beam. This means in practice that when you are beating or close-reaching you shape the sail with halyard, outhaul and sheet, then trim it with the traveller. If you are far enough off the wind to want to ease the sheet, set up the kicker to maintain leech tension when the sheet can no longer supply it.

The crew of this large, professionally run yacht has adjusted the twist of the mainsail to mirror that of the jib whose clew has risen when the sheet was eased.

On a race boat, the powerful kicker may be brought into service even closehauled to help flatten the sail. Such fine tuning is a waste of effort on most cruising mainsails, but the basics should never be neglected. I've heard people complain along the lines of 'All this sail shape nonsense is for the boy racers. Who cares about ¼ knot?' I do, for one. At 6 knots it is worth 6 miles over 24 hours. To be an hour later than you might have been could lose you a tide, resulting in a further three hours' delay. It may also be the last straw for a fatigued crew, causing a fatally bad decision in the face of a rising gale which you would otherwise have missed. Or you might merely get in after the shops have closed.

Whatever the result, not to give your boat her best chance to perform well is unseamanlike. You don't have to thrash a boat to extract that extra ¼ knot, yet carried to its logical conclusion, 6 miles lost in a 24-hour passage is the best part of two days wasted on the average ocean crossing, though in fairness I have met people who don't press on because they seem to like it out there.

Sail combinations

Una-rigged craft often sail excellently. A single, well-shaped aerofoil set from a lightly stayed or unstayed mast can be shaped with great precision and can be remarkably closewinded. Two notable examples of the truth of this are the Finn dinghy and the North American cat boat. As yachts become larger, a single sail becomes a worse proposition for reasons of handling and of shipping a spar of sufficient proportions to carry it. From time immemorial, therefore, sail plans have been divided.

In addition to the benefits above, split rigs offer two further advantages. Because individual sails are set forward and abaft the centre of lateral resistance (CLR) about which the boat effectively pivots, they can be sheeted so as to balance her steering characteristics. At speeds too low for the rudder to be useful, the sails can even be used to persuade the vessel to point where you want her to go. Secondly, the slot between two sails produces a Venturi effect, accelerating the air that is squeezed through it. This raised velocity increases the power not only of the rig as a whole but also of its individual components. Those who doubt that this is happening have only to stand in the slot of a yacht sailing to windward in 15 knots of breeze. Tell them to hang on to their hats, though. It's breezier in there than they'd ever have believed back in the cockpit.

As skipper, you have the balance of the boat's rig at your fingertips, and assuming that she is well designed, there is plenty you can do about it (Fig 3.3, p. 19). The yacht should be easy and light to steer, showing a gentle tendency to turn into the wind if left to her own devices. If she has too much mainsail on and only a small jib, a sloop will want to round up. The result is weather helm. This tires the unfortunate who must steer, as well as slowing the vessel down through the drag of the rudder. The dreaded lee helm, on the other hand, is the lot of the sailor whose boat is carrying too much canvas forward and too little aft.

Lee helm is a dismal condition. It makes manoeuvring difficult, steering frustrating, and it has a debilitating effect on the yacht's capacity to sail close to the wind without making excessive leeway. A touch of weather helm holds the rudder a degree or two to leeward, which diverts the flowing water, just enough to help the keel lift the vessel in opposition to the sideways forces. Lee helm achieves the converse effect.

EFFICIENT SAILING

Effective sail area too far forward = lee helm

Effective sail area too far aft = weather helm

Sails balanced = balanced helm

Fig 3.3 Sail balance.

Hull balance

In addition to the disposition of her sail plan, a yacht's helm balance varies depending on how much she is heeling. As she heels to leeward, any tendency to weather helm will increase. Rolling to windward generates lee helm. This makes sense when you consider that the whole outfit is being pulled along by the rig. As the boat heels, the centre of effort of the mast and sails moves outboard. If you dragged the boat through the water by a rope on the end of a beam lashed athwartships across her deck, she would try to swing away from that side. The same thing happens with the rig.

Boats with flat, beamy midships sections, such as are found in many high performance modern cruisers and racers, suffer from a more subtle source of heel-induced weather helm. As they lean over, the leeward side of the immersed hull becomes rounded to a point of exaggeration. The weather side is correspondingly flattened. The imbalance produces weather helm which, in certain cases, appears suddenly and uncontrollably above a critical angle of heel. You need to watch out for this in such a vessel, particularly if you are sailing in a river on a gusty day, surrounded by expensive moored yachts.

Shortening sail

Shortening sail as the wind strengthens is part of the sailor's everyday life. It is not something to be put off. The process should be as natural as shifting gears in the family car. Not only does carrying the right canvas for the conditions give you a drier ride and increase your chances of arriving with the boat in one piece, it keeps the yacht more upright. As we have just discussed, the less a boat is heeling, the easier she will be on the helm. This benefit is assisted by the

A single reef in the main as the wind starts to rise will ease the helm and take off little speed, if any.

fact that the centre of effort of a smaller headsail or a reefed genoa is further forward than that of a larger one. Similarly, a reef in the mainsail moves the leech inboard along the boom. The sails are therefore generating less weather helm than if the yacht were spreading everything she carried. With a sensible awareness of the principles of sail balance in your mind, it isn't difficult to reduce your canvas in such a way that the boat's behaviour remains docile.

It would be unwise to generalise about where to begin sail reductions. A masthead cruising sloop will usually set out by tying one reef into the mainsail. This may be followed by a few rolls in the genoa before going for the second reef, and so on. A fractional-rigger often reduces the size of her headsail first. A ketch or yawl has a mizzen to consider as well, but the principles remain the same.

The years since the mid-1970s have seen the rapid rise and general acceptance of patent reefing systems. The best of those offered for headsail roller reefing have by now achieved high reliability and are able to reef the sail to a moderate degree without too much sacrifice in shape. Poorer gears produce a dismally reefed sail that looks more like a flour bag than a number 3 genoa. With the canvas rolled away to storm jib size, the result is execrable. Nonetheless, all such arrangements give the benefit of instant sail area adjustment. In a short-handed craft this sometimes more than compensates for what is lost in pure performance. No boat must go to sea, however, without making at least some arrangements for the day when the gear fails. The most satisfactory answer is a separate forestay that can be readily set up and to which a storm jib may be hanked. Indeed, this produces the best of all worlds because such a jib will invariably set better than the deeply rolled genoa. It can therefore be used routinely for heavy weather sailing.

By far the simplest and best way to reef the main is with 'slab' reefing, as described in Chapter 4, but if you are disinclined to leave the cockpit to shorten sail, in-mast and in-boom systems can be bought off the shelf. In-mast gears put considerable weight aloft and add to the awful sum of the rig's windage. They may or may not be reliable, and many a sail built for

EFFICIENT SAILING

A modern in-boom reefing system produces a well-shaped sail easily from the cockpit.

such a set up will have a straight or even a hollow leech with no battens. On a contemporary rig this looks downright sad and it's certainly less powerful than the elliptical trailing edge of the conventional mainsail, although vertical-batten systems are now going some way to dealing with this drawback. A better solution is a modern in-boom mainsail reefing system. The best of these are way in advance of the old 'round-the-boom' roller reefing. Such a method was never ideal on the Bermudan rig, though it remained in use for decades, but the latest arrangements produce a highly controllable sail with a proper vang, a full roach and no extra weight aloft.

Mainsail reefing options therefore subdivide into three main choices: in-mast roller, in-boom or round-boom roller, and traditional gear for reducing the sail in 'slabs' at the foot. Slab and quality in-boom both produce a satisfactory sail shape; both are extremely reliable, although if anything should go wrong, slab is usually more readily repaired at sea. Mainsails of under 500sq ft (46sq m) are easily handled by two healthy adults and slab-reefing variants can be dealt with singlehanded without major inconvenience. The latest fully battened mainsails and lazy-jack stack packs make the job of stowing child's play.

Nonetheless, the roller alternatives do have a place. They help huge yachts to be run without numerous deck-hands. They also enable the elderly or the unfit to keep on enjoying their cruising, but if these options are to be chosen, it's important to be aware of their limitations in sail shape and the horrors that may result should some component of an in-mast system fail. A good in-boom sail with full battens can deliver a proper aerofoil so long as it has a fully operational vang or kicker. Such systems are proving reliable in the second decade of the 21st century. Even if they fail, the components are within easy reach to work on. At worst, the halyard can simply be let go to drop the sail. Although in-mast systems have improved greatly, they still represent a total commitment to the dependability of the gear. A trip to the masthead in a gale holds little appeal for any of us.

'Code Zero' sails

Light weather, and the Code Zero headsail has got the boat moving against all the odds.

For a cruising boat to be non-intimidating to sail in moderate to heavy going, she will probably be a little short of sail area in light winds. That's the way of the world, and with the wind blowing from forward of any angle the chute can take care of, something else is needed if you are to stay clear of the engine start button. The answer today is the 'Code Zero' sail. Dating from race boats some decades back, these headsails are set flying. Although originally developed for close-reaching, they can be carried with the boat almost close-hauled, yet will still perform with the wind a long way aft. A 'Code Zero' brings the boat to life in light going and is easy to set and furl if combined with a so-called 'top-down furler'. This rolls it away without fuss, to be bagged and stowed below as the breeze picks up.

Cruising chutes

Today's Bermudan-rigged yachts have much in their favour, but sailing downwind in light and moderate going is not one of them. Ideally, this endemic shortfall is cured by using a spinnaker, but this lies beyond the comfort zone of many cruising sailors. The answer is a 'cruising chute'. This has been developed from the modern asymmetric racing spinnaker and is really a light, extra-full genoa that only attaches at tack, head and clew. It works in airs too gentle for a multi-purpose genoa, and can be set on a very broad reach without a pole. Sailmakers will deliver them complete with a 'snuffer' – a sort of sleeve that rolls down over the sail, spilling its wind miraculously. This removes the worry from using so powerful a tool. In short, a downwind passage in light weather without a chute is like the proverbial day without sunshine.

Sorting out the cruising chute snuffer while still in harbour is a good idea.

BASIC SEAMANSHIP UNDER SAIL 4

If you were looking for a definition of seamanship, you could say that it is the art of making the sailor's skills look easy.

It is tempting to imagine that a simple task like winding a sheet in on a cockpit winch will be much the same under any skipper, or that heaving down a reef is a nuisance whoever is driving the boat. In fact, neither proposition is true. One master may soak a foredeck crew while they are changing a headsail; another will go out of his way to keep them dry and safe. The task of setting up a yacht for a long run downwind can be soft and gentle, or it can be a dice with death at the wrong end of a 10ft booming-out pole. It all depends on the captain.

The two basic rules are to keep all the gear under control so that nothing can be strained or broken, and never to put a crew member in the position of having to tackle an item that is not well within the person's physical capabilities. It is rarely necessary to fight the boat or her equipment. Handled properly, they can usually be made to turn their strength in your favour.

Tacking

In my years as a Yachtmaster examiner I have perched on the sterns of numerous craft to watch their crews put them about. In a protracted short-tacking session, such as occurs when beating up a river, a poor helmsman can exhaust the winch-winders after a few turns. The way he does it is this: as the riverbank comes galloping up he bawls, 'Ready about … lee-ho,' in his saltiest voice, then he jams the helm hard over. The boat flips through the wind with the crew struggling to clear a jammed sheet. The boat is allowed to go on turning until she is well below a closehauled course on the new tack. The crew haven't even begun to wind in the sheet, so they are now left with a genoa full of wind. By the time they have laboriously ground it in, the skipper is singing out again, 'Ready about.' They groan, and the sloppy proceedings are repeated over and over until Hadrian on the port winch feels a bad twinge in his thoracic region.

'I say, skipper,' he mutinies, already blue in the face, 'if we don't start motoring shortly you'll be hearing from my executors.' The mistake, of course, is that the boat is not being creatively steered. It isn't enough just to bang her over from one tack to the next. The helmsman should sail her as quickly as possible from full on one tack, through the wind and begin bearing away, but he should stop her turning a degree or two before she fills on the new tack. On all but the largest vessels the crew can then whip most of the sheet in using the winch

THE COMPLETE YACHTMASTER

Tacking – as the boat comes through the wind, the crew is watching the leech of the genoa, waiting to sheet in hard as soon as it passes the new lee shrouds.

as no more than a snubbing device. The last foot or two is wound home as the helmsman bears away on to his course.

Tacking like this requires little energy and loses far less ground than the other method, but it does need a thinking person on the helm. Watch the crew, encourage them to hit the sheet at just the right moment, and don't let the yacht slow down too much. If you do, she'll stall, and you'll end up with the dreaded lee helm until she's worked up enough pace to slot back into the groove.

It shouldn't be necessary to back a headsail in a normal tack on a well-designed boat. Doing so slows her down and usually makes sheeting-in more like hard work as well. The technique should only be employed as a last resort, or when to miss stays would have such truly catastrophic results that you need to be 100% certain of getting her round.

Gybing

Gybing has a bad reputation. Some people will even turn through 270° to avoid it. The reasons for this are obvious, yet so long as the manoeuvre is decently executed, they need carry no weight. In a modern yacht, a gybe should be an innocuous affair.

There is an essential difference between gybing from one tack to the other and going about to achieve a similar end. In the gybe, the stern passes through the eye of the wind. Since a fore-and-aft rigged mainsail will not 'feather' with the wind aft, it must be full throughout the manoeuvre. At some point, it changes instantaneously from being full on one side to being full on the other. At this moment, if it is uncontrolled, it will fly across the boat, carrying its boom with it. There are three possible consequences of this, and none are desirable. The least damaging is that no harm comes to the ship, but the crews' nerves are shredded. The middle ground, depending on your point of view, is that some part of the vessel – usually the boom, the gooseneck, or a running backstay – carries away. The greatest horror is that the boom cracks a skull that it finds in its path; very likely it will complete the job by dunking its victim overboard. The bigger the vessel, the greater the dangers accruing from an unintentional gybe – unintentional, mark you, and therefore uncontrolled.

The good skipper lays all these nasties to rest by the simple expedient of hauling the mainsheet in before gybing. Put your best helmsman on duty and get him to run dead downwind. Now heave the sheet in until the boom is more or less amidships. Take a turn on the cleat, winch or, if the sheet is jammed off to a cam-cleat in its bottom block, make it fast with that. If the yacht has running backstays, make them both up, then let off the new leeward one. The helmsman now carefully brings the stern of the yacht through the wind so that the leech of the main flops across. As it does so, the sheet is surged quickly away. The helmsman will do well to apply a momentary dose of weather helm the instant after the boom comes across, because the whole steering geometry of the boat will be reversing, and if he doesn't, the yacht will try to gripe up towards the wind. All boats do this, though some are much worse than others.

Once the boom is squared away, then, and only then, can you order up your new course. During the whole gybing process, the vessel should have deviated from a dead run only by the few degrees it took to bring the breeze from one side of the stern to the other.

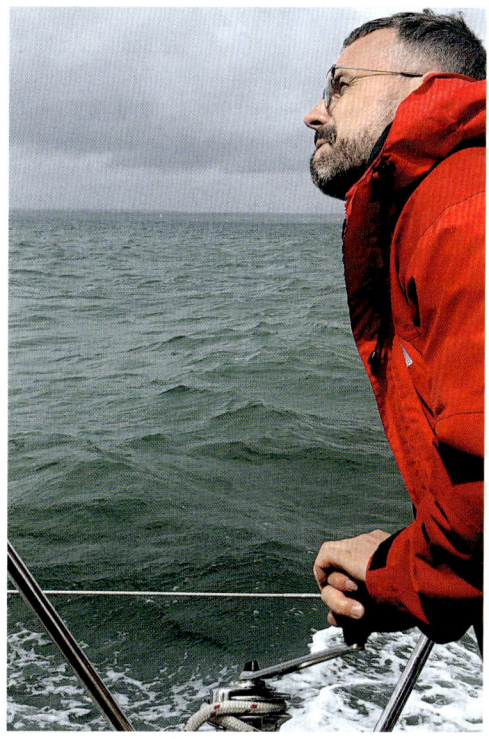

If you have more than one sail set on a boom, as you would on a ketch, for example, you should obviously deal with both sails as you would with the main on a sloop or cutter. What you elect to do with any headsails (except a spinnaker) is less critical, *so long as you do not let them blow around the forestay.* If you are short-handed, by far the best answer to a head-sail that is not poled out (see overleaf) is to do nothing with it at all until the mainsail is well and truly gybed. Once that is out of the way, you can attend to the genoa by passing it across the boat from sheet to sheet. By maintaining some tension on the old sheet until the new one has taken over, the whole business will pass so smoothly you'll wonder what all the fuss was about – and quite rightly too.

Watch the sail, not the winch, while you are trimming.

SKIPPER'S TIP

Traveller safety

It's easy to become lazy about cleating off the mainsheet traveller, if you have one. When the boom comes across in a gybe, the car will crash across the boat like a guillotine if its progress is not checked. Should anyone's fingers be in the way, there will be only the skipper to blame for the resulting amputation. Before you set up for a gybe, check the traveller.

Poling out a genoa

One of the first things discovered by the neophyte sailor is that when a fore-and-aft rigged vessel is well off the wind, her headsail will no longer draw on the same side as the mainsail because the latter canvas robs it of its wind. You now have three choices. You can closehaul it behind the main to stop it banging around; you can drop it or roll it away so as to put both the sail and the crew out of their misery; or you can pull it across to the windward side of the boat and fill it by goose-winging.

The bad news about goose-winging is that in any but the flattest of water the roll of the boat renders the headsail's state so unstable that it cannot be relied upon to remain full. Instead of banging about in the lee of the mainsail, it bangs around on the weather side of the foredeck, driving all hands frantic and wearing out your gear.

The answer is to stabilise the sail by rigging a pole between its clew and the mast. In tiny craft this can often be achieved by shoving the sail out with a boathook, or even a broom handle. In a yacht of any size at all, a proper pole must be used if both it and the crew are to survive. Rigging the pole is easy if done in a seamanlike manner. Give the beast even an inkling that it could take charge, however, and you are exposing your foredeck people to hardship and real danger. Here's how to do it safely:

- Closehaul the genoa behind the mainsail to keep it quiet while you are on the foredeck, or roll it away if it's that sort of sail.
- Go forward and fix the heel of the pole to the mast fitting.
- Attach the pole topping lift and downhaul (or foreguy), with the lazy (windward) genoa sheet passing over and outboard of the topping lift.
- Pass the bight of the lazy sheet through the jaws at the outboard end of the pole.
- Hoist the pole until it is parallel with the deck (trial and error will determine the best subsequent overall height). Keep the outboard end to windward of the forestay.
- Lay aft and clear all personnel off the foredeck.
- Haul in on the lazy sheet, slacking away the lee sheet as you do so. In due course the sail will gybe and can be trimmed with what has now become the working sheet. If you've rolled it up, simply unroll it on to the pole.
- Take up the slack on the downhaul to ensure that the pole does not 'sky'.
- If you have a long way to run, it pays to rig an afterguy on the pole as well as the topping lift and the foreguy. The pole is then entirely independent of the sheets.

BASIC SEAMANSHIP UNDER SAIL

Poling out in light weather, the pole may be stable enough with just a topping lift to steady it. In heavier going, full pole guys will be called for. Setting the heel of the pole higher than the end discourages it from kicking up.

Notice that this has been achieved without anyone having to handle the pole with any weight on it. When gybing the sail off the pole again you should apply the same principles. Even if you can't roll it, there are still one or two ways of succeeding. You can bring the boat up to a beam reach if the wind is not too strong. The headsail will come aback and can be eased through the foretriangle on to the lee sheet once more. Once the sail is off it, the pole can be brought down and stowed at your leisure.

If it is windy and you don't fancy this manoeuvre, you can gybe the mainsail so that the genoa 'dies' in its lee. The pole can then be unhitched from the mast and smartly tripped from the sheet. Alternatively, in modest conditions, you can just ease away on the weather sheet and take up slack to leeward until the sail works its way over to the lee side. This method is simple, but often untidy, creating problems with the clew of the sail falling foul of the forestay.

> **SKIPPER'S TIP**
>
> **Making the roller pay its way**
> Remember, when the sail is a roller furler, the skipper can make full use of its capacity for diminution (or even disappearance) on demand, to transform slow-speed manoeuvres into a piece of cake.

Painless sail reduction

Except during races, it is only in the rarest of circumstances that a good skipper sends anyone on to the foredeck of a yacht that is sailing hard to windward. Even on a close-reach the deck can be a wet and dangerous place when travelling at speed. The first consideration before either reefing or changing down headsails must therefore be to *slow the boat down*, or even to stop her. Even if you don't like your crew, it pays to consider their feelings. They'll be worse company still if they are cold, wet and have had a fright.

Achieving your ends in this case is surprisingly little trouble. If you want to keep some way on the boat for tactical reasons, she will slow down dramatically yet remain under control if you steer somewhere between a close-reach and closehauled, easing your sheets so that the forward thrust of the sails is greatly diminished. By juggling helm and sheets you can now persuade her to go as slowly as the sea state will allow.

There is only one snag with using this method to keep the foredeck hands dry. It needs someone to steer the boat. An efficient autopilot can offer some sort of substitute for the real thing, but because it can neither feel the boat nor see the wave to which she must luff to retain equilibrium, it will never be as good at this particular skill as you are. If you are short-handed, or even if you aren't, there is always the option of heaving to.

Heaving to

When you heave to, you manoeuvre your boat so that she loses all way, yet keeps her sails full for most of the time. There are all sorts of misapprehensions about heaving to. Some boats do it more successfully than others, but the basic principles are the same for any vessel. A sloop is brought to rest with the wind on whichever side is most expedient. Her headsail is sheeted aback and her mainsail is pinned well in to leeward. The headsail tries to push the bow off the wind while the main has an opposing effect. In a perfect world, the keel would balance one against the other so that equilibrium was attained. Unfortunately, life is not quite so simple.

Left entirely to her own devices, a boat set up in this way will fall so far off the wind that the mainsail fills and begins to drive her ahead. If the rudder were left amidships she might gather enough way to be a nuisance, so the helm is lashed to leeward to ensure that if she makes any way at all, she will try to head up into the wind. As soon as she is close enough for the mainsail to begin spilling, the push of the backed headsail stops any tendency to go ahead and she falls away until the main balances things up (Fig 4.1). The boat is now in a state of dynamic equilibrium and the helmsman can walk away from his job.

A yacht with a large mainsail, a small jib and a deep forefoot, such as a traditional gaff-rigged craft, will often heave to pointing 45° from the wind, and hence the seas. A short boom and a big genoa militate against such an ideal state of affairs, though by adjusting the sheets and understanding the effect each sail is likely to have, most boats can be persuaded to 'point up' tolerably well.

Although a vessel with no forefoot to speak of may not be able to use the manoeuvre as a heavy weather survival tactic, the practice of heaving to may still be helpful in short-handed cruising, particularly if the boat is not fitted with an autopilot.

By now you'll probably be asking what possible use heaving to can be during a sail change, since the very act of reducing mainsail area, or even temporarily removing a headsail, will destroy the balance on which everything depends. In the case of changing jibs, things may go awry, but at least you won't need a helmsman and the boat will lose

Fig 4.1 Heaving to.

The author's cutter hove to on a windy day with staysail sheeted aback and a reef in the main.

all her liveliness once the jib is down. While you are reefing the main, your vessel may tend to fall off the wind, but the security of knowing that she isn't under way can sometimes make up for this disadvantage.

Reefing

Slab reefing has been in use for hundreds of years and hasn't ever been bettered. Today's gear has made what was a heavy task into a lightweight procedure which can, with practice, be executed in less than a minute (Fig 4.2). A method is the answer to getting it right. Fix the system in your mind and you'll reef like clockwork, even on a dark night.

- Ease the sheet and let off the kicking strap or boom vang.
- **A)** Take the weight of the boom on the topping lift.
- **B)** Ease the halyard and hook the reef tack cringle on to the reefing horn at the forward end of the boom. If there is no horn, lash the cringle down with a few turns of line. A safer arrangement where the reef clew pennants are led aft is to rig a Dyneema tack line from the forward cringle of each reef and lead it aft to the cockpit via some sort of fairlead at the gooseneck. The whole operation can then be performed in security and nobody need venture into the wild world on deck.
- Set up the halyard.
- **C)** Pull down the clew pennant so that the leech cringle is snugly down on the boom and the foot of the sail is well hauled out. Yachts of any size are usually equipped with a winch for this job. It may be at the mast, on the boom, or in the cockpit (in which case the pennant will lead to it via a series of turning blocks). Some older boats use a tackle. If the pull is too hard for comfort, let the sheet right off for a few seconds so that the sail spills all its wind.
- **D)** Ease the topping lift, sheet in the sail, then set up the vang or kicker. You can now tie in the reef points if you feel it's necessary. On a short-boomed masthead sloop you could sail round the world without ever doing this. On a long-footed traditional mainsail, failure to tie in the points is not merely untidy and unseamanlike, it may sometimes compromise the security of the boom itself. Generally speaking, points should not be tied around the boom. Under the foot of the sail is better, if the canvas is attached to the spar by using a track and slides. Many of today's craft carry the sail in a groove in the boom. If yours is one of these, you've no choice but to tie up the points around the whole affair. Just be doubly careful when shaking out your reef that you never release the pennant without first taking off the ties. If you do, the weight of the sail and boom will come on to the eyelets of the reef points which were never designed for this purpose. They may survive if they are tied round the foot of the sail, but if they are round the boom the extra rigidity can damage the cloth.
- Trim the jib (or let draw if you have been hove to) and sail on.

The process of reefing is carried out in about 20 seconds on a 38ft (11.5m) racing yacht. In a family cruiser it should not take more than a minute or so if you are not tying in the points.

BASIC SEAMANSHIP UNDER SAIL

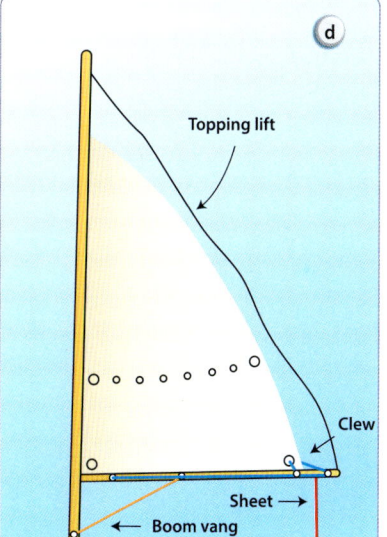

Fig 4.2 Reefing.

🗨 SKIPPER'S TIP

Reefing safely
Never try to tie in points with the boom banging about; always sheet in first.

Single-line reefing

This is slab-reefing refined by sophisticated gear inside the boom, so that by easing the halyard and winching down a single line in the cockpit, tack and clew are hove down together. Fine in theory and grand at its best, such arrangements are often let down by cheap rope and poor turning blocks, resulting in a no-win stretch binge that precludes a decent sail shape in high winds. Shaking reefs out can be akin to a session in the gym because the friction hinders the pennant running out of the boom end. Single-line reefing also leaves you with an unconscionable length of rope in the cockpit, and it usually means you can't have three reefs in the mainsail. Despite these unarguable truths, the system remains popular with certain manufacturers. Why these misguided folk don't rig simple, non-stretch tack lines through turning blocks, then aft to the cockpit, and leave well alone with the clew pennants is beyond me. This simple refinement allows reefing without going forward and doesn't involve any of the horrors inherent in a typical single-line reefing system. Say no more...

In-mast mainsails

The secret of happiness with an in-mast mainsail is boom angle. Although this can vary from boat to boat, a good starting point is with the outboard end somewhere around 8° above the horizontal. Mark the vang and topping lift to achieve this and always pre-set them before reefing, furling or unfurling. This isn't hard to do and it makes all the difference. These sails are usually cut to allow the lower edge of the sail to rise as it is rolled in. With everything set just right, a nice tight spiral should result.

To unfurl the sail, maintain some outhaul tension while the foil rotates; never let the sail get sloppy inside the spar. If the system has a power or winch-driven furler, ease away no more than a turn or two, then heave it out with the outhaul. When reefing or furling, it's vital to maintain some outhaul tension. It also helps to steer the boat a few degrees off head-to-wind. As the sail winds itself up, you'll see a bigger gap on one side of the groove than the other. Keep this larger gap on the weather side and you will have an easier life.

In-boom mainsails

A good in-boom system can be hoisted, lowered or reefed with the wind as far as 45° off the yacht's centreline. Head-to-wind will always be best, but this is often not realistic in practice. So long as the sail can spill wind, good results can be achieved. As with in-mast systems, vertical boom angle is critical. Many manufacturers patronise their customers by pre-setting the vang to the desired angle for hoisting and furling, then fixing this angle permanently. No real sailor should accept this situation because it kills the sail by robbing the user of the vital element of leech tension control, especially when reefed well down. If this is what you are given, bin it now and install a powerful adjustable vang instead. The line from this will usually run aft to the cockpit. Mark it, and the topping lift too, with a turn of tape when you have the angle you want. Usually, 2 or 3 degrees less than a right-angle between boom and mast is ideal, but you can only really tell by experimenting.

BASIC SEAMANSHIP UNDER SAIL

If your system incorporates a controllable downhaul, as is found on the excellent Leisure Furl arrangements, hold a little tension on this when hoisting. When reefing or furling, maintain some halyard tension to keep the roll tight while the downhaul is on the winch. The tight roll is the key.

Headsail changes

With the establishment of the roller reefing genoa, headsail changes are less of a daily chore than they used to be for most people. Nonetheless, some sailors still prefer to keep a selection of well-setting jibs and genoas. Switching from one to the next is such a simple, logical process that no comment is required, except to reiterate the necessity for taking off way before venturing out of the cockpit and the desirability of changing down in good time.

If you have a large headsail set and you anticipate trouble in dropping it, the final solution is to run the boat downwind for a few seconds at the crucial moment (Fig 4.3):

- Bear away on to a broad-enough reach to place the genoa into the lee of the mainsail. This will neutralise all its homicidal tendencies.
- Sheet the genoa in hard behind the main to make certain that it cannot kick around and endanger the foredeck brigade.
- Go forward, drop the sail and secure it.
- You can now bring the boat back on course if you have a mind to. She won't go nearly so fast under mainsail only, and her motion will be considerably eased.

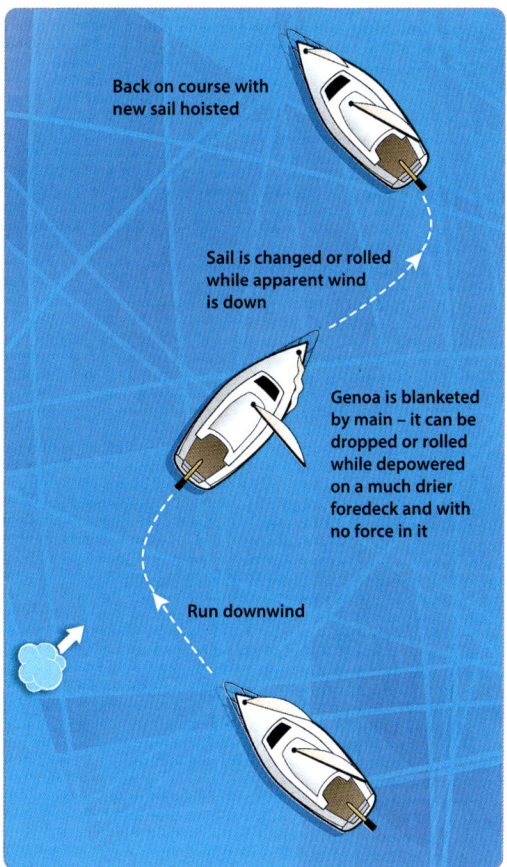

Fig 4.3 Running off to change headsails.

THE COMPLETE YACHTMASTER

A sweet, straight lead makes all the difference to a furling line's effectiveness. These on the author's yacht have expensive lead blocks that have paid their way many times over. There is no hard angle at the aft end leading into the cockpit. Although the yacht is 44 feet length overall (LOA), it is rarely necessary to lead the furling lines to a winch, so clean is their route aft to the crew.

 SKIPPER'S TIP

Killing the roller

If you are struggling to roll away a genoa with a furling gear, steer right off the wind to hide it in the lee of the mainsail as though to change a genoa. It will come in like a lamb. If the problem persists, look critically at the blocks leading the furling line aft. Ten to one these are creating friction. With a straight run, a masthead genoa on a 45-footer can be furled without a winch by a moderately fit person.

BOAT HANDLING UNDER SAIL 5

If you are a comparative newcomer to the world of sailing, you may think it odd that a chapter on handling under sail should precede one explaining how best to benefit from auxiliary power. Should you have come to cruising from dinghy sailing, however, it will seem entirely natural. There are even a few of us left who learned our sailing in cruisers without any power unit at all, save a sweep or a quant pole. In fact, sailing a yacht of moderate tonnage in close quarters can be as easy as motoring, so long as one or two rules are borne in mind.

No brakes

The most important elements of boat handling revolve around the various circumstances in which you may want to stop, or get under way.

The only thing that can stop a sailing vessel – other than the undesirable intervention of a rock, shoal or quay wall – is her own skin friction and air resistance. Acting against these are two forces that induce her to keep moving: the forward drive of her sails and her own momentum. You can shed the first of these easily enough if you think about what you are doing. Momentum depends upon such variables as how fast you are going when the power comes off, and how much air resistance is stacking up against it. It also depends upon the displacement and hull form of your vessel. For a given craft these latter two criteria are, of course, fixed. Their effects are predictable once you know her habits, and they are generally referred to as the manner in which she 'carries her way'.

An old-fashioned, heavy yacht seems to keep going for ever if she is luffed up to a lightish breeze from 5 or 6 knots. I have seen an Eight Metre carry her way, head-to-wind, for more than 100 yards (91m). She finally stopped with her mooring right under her spoon bow. The bowman was lying on the foredeck ready to stretch down, pick it up and secure it. At the other end of the scale come ultra-light trailer-sailers. I once luffed one of these up to a mooring in a strong breeze during a period of my life when I was usually sailing a 6-ton fin-keeler. I didn't expect the boat to go far, but she stopped dead miles short of the buoy so that I had to tack back up to it for my next try.

Clearly, judgement is required to bring your yacht to a standstill right where you want her. Fortunately for most of us who are blessed with a higher degree of mortality than my Eight-Metre skipper, we can keep the judgement factor to a minimum by making sure that before we take the power off, by dropping the sails, easing the sheets, or luffing head-to-wind, we line up with rule number one:

- When manoeuvring under sail, always go as slowly as you possibly can without losing control.

However, we'll go into this in more detail later in this chapter. Before even beginning to think about the boat, you must be aware of what is going on around her. You need an accurate lead on the wind direction, and it's important to determine the relationship between this and any tidal stream or current. Get either of these wrong and you may as well have bought a motorboat. Happily, being right is just a matter of informed observation.

Wind awareness

We have seen in Chapter 3 that when the true wind is blowing across a moving boat, the apparent wind that results is affected not only in strength but also in direction. It always comes from forward of the true wind until the boat is on a dead run. With the wind well aft, the apparent wind speed will be less than the true wind. As it approaches a point just abaft the beam they may become similar, and as the true wind comes on to or forward of the beam, the force of the apparent wind will always exceed it.

It follows that if you want any accurate information about the true wind, it is no good looking at the burgee, the wind indicator or any instrument that cannot read out wind direction as 'true' or 'apparent'. You are sailing (or motoring) in the apparent wind that is being experienced by every item on board, from the ensign through your own senses right up to the fanciest electronic transducer. Other than a linked function computer, only your eyes can tell you what you want to know, which, when you consider that they didn't cost you a cent, represents remarkable value.

Where there is no current, moored yachts will be lying head-up to the true wind. If there is a flag ashore, you can check that, but a far more accurate device is available at all times when there is light to see it. As the wind blows on the face of the water, it marks it with tiny ripples which run at right angles to its direction. Don't use the waves to judge. They may be being bent by other forces. Just use the ripples. Train yourself to be aware of them at all times. They'll never let you down.

Wind ripples are unmistakable in light or hard weather, once you've learned to spot them.

Tide awareness

When it comes to boat handling, the one thing you do not do if you want to gauge the tide is consult the tide tables. Look at any fixed object with water flowing past it, including a moored or anchored vessel, and you'll see a bow-wave. That tells you all you need to know.

If you are running up a river and there's nothing around that will indicate whether or not the tide has turned, you can often put the boat beam on to the direction of the river and see which way she is being set by observing the bank dead ahead of you. The answer should be immediately obvious, even if you are turning in your own length. If it's not, you can only conclude that it is slack water.

Sailing slowly

Shortening sail

If you're going to sail into a crowded harbour, or up a narrow river on a breezy day, it will probably pay to shorten sail before you get there. Manoeuvrability is severely restricted by a large genoa, as is visibility. So get rid of it, either by rolling half of it away, or by changing it for a smaller, higher-cut sail. Reef the main if necessary, but have nothing to do with your genoa, except on the gentlest of days.

Although shortening down can be helpful, it doesn't pay to be overzealous. The wind may be lighter in the harbour than out at sea and a boat that is grossly undercanvassed can be a disappointment to handle. She may even let you down.

Dropping one sail altogether is often a winner if your rig will balance without it. A gaff cutter will sail slowly without her all-powerful staysail, so long as there is a jib on the end of the bowsprit. Ketches and yawls may go well enough with main or mizzen stowed, and so on. The only way to know is to experiment with the boat in question.

Sailing under main only

Often, it can be handy to execute a manoeuvre under mainsail only. It'll be no help if you have to stop with the breeze abaft the beam, of course, because you won't be able to spill wind (see below), but when approaching a mooring, a man overboard or an anchorage in slack water it can be a winner.

To succeed under main only, a boat must have a reasonably sized sail. Yachts with huge genoas and artificially small mains will not perform well, but a boat with a more balanced rig will sail beautifully, if slowly, so long as the sheet is eased well off when closehauled. The tendency is to oversheet, because, with a jib set, the main is often not far from the centreline. With no jib to bend the air on to it, the main can be set much further out. This increases forward drive and balances the helm, so don't fall into the trap of pinning it in.

Spilling wind

So long as the wind is forward of the beam, you can control your speed perfectly by easing sheets until the sails spill wind. If you try this closehauled you'll go sideways as your speed drops, so be careful. When the breeze is on or abaft the beam, a conventional yacht can't lose any way with her mainsail set. The boom presses on the shrouds even with the sheet slacked right off, and the sail fills just the same. In marginal cases it helps to dump the kicking strap or boom vang, allowing the upper part of the leech to fall away. The result of this feature of mainsails is that if you ever need to stop with the wind from aft, you have no choice but to drop the mainsail and proceed under headsails, spilling wind as necessary. This becomes important when manoeuvring in tides.

Oversheeting

As a temporary expedient in light or moderate airs, you can sometimes shed way by sheeting the sails in so hard that they lose all drive. This technique can be quite useful, but it must be treated with caution because it can play havoc with the balance of your helm.

Scandalising

Another way of ditching drive from a main or mizzen is to scandalise it. This shocks the sail into a state of refusal by doing something really horrible to it. Let the kicker or vang right off, overhaul the mainsheet to the knot, then drag the boom end skywards with the topping lift.

Mooring under sail

No tide

However slowly you approach the buoy, you'll usually have to come head-to-wind at the end to luff off the last of your way. A skilled skipper in a boat that is well known to him can luff from quite a distance and come to rest at the buoy. For most of us, this is simply too much to ask, but the matter does not have to finish there. If you set up the approach so that you are close-reaching towards a point a few yards downwind of the buoy, your task is extremely easy (Fig 5.1).

Fig 5.1 Mooring under sail – no tide. Approach on a close-reach, spilling wind to control speed. Luff off the last of your way and pick up the buoy on your lee bow.

BOAT HANDLING UNDER SAIL

Having ditched the last of her way by topping up her boom, this training boat is making a neat job of picking up a mooring buoy.

Spill wind to slow down when you are still some distance away. Proceed, making as little way as you can, but watching all the time for signs of the keel stalling, which can happen with the wind forward of the beam if you go too slowly. As the keel stops functioning properly, the boat's head falls off the wind and you find yourself pushing the tiller to leeward (vice versa with a wheel) to correct her. What you should be doing if you feel this starting to happen is heaving in the mainsheet. The extra drive from aft will usually put the boat back on to the rails so that you can soon ease the sail out with the boat under control once more.

When you arrive immediately downwind of the buoy, let the sheets off altogether and luff, ensuring that the person on the foredeck knows which side to pick up. Actually, the ideal state is to remain slightly 'below' head-to-wind and pick up between the stem and the leeward chainplates. Don't forget that if you have lost rather too much way the boat may refuse to luff if asked with the helm alone. If this happens, be ready to haul in the mainsheet to give her a leg up.

Some craft will execute this manoeuvre under mainsail only. This is a desirable characteristic because the people on the foredeck won't be beaten around the ears by an unruly jib clew.

THE COMPLETE YACHTMASTER

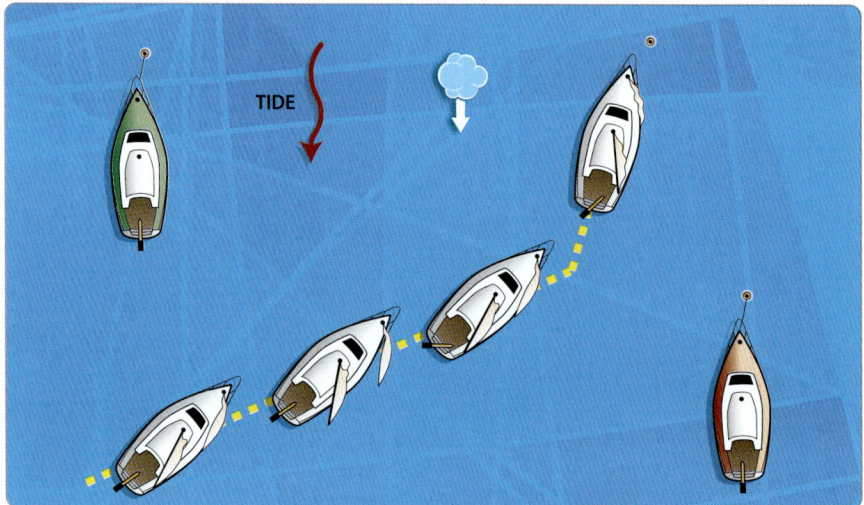

Fig 5.2 Mooring under sail – wind with tide. Approach the buoy on a close-reach, crabbing across the tide and checking way by spilling wind. Use transits to ensure you are not swept downtide. Come head to tide for the pick-up.

Wind with tide

The principle is the same here as where there is no stream, except that when the boat is moored she will still be moving relative to the water flowing by. You don't, therefore, have to luff to a standstill. You have only to bring your speed down to that of the tide, which makes life considerably easier, as you retain control of the boat throughout the manoeuvre (Fig 5.2). With the no-tide situation, control diminishes to zero when you lose the last of your way.

The only drawback is the requirement to exercise more judgement in order not to end up hopelessly downtide of your destination, but this possibility can often be obviated by making use of a transit. Line the mooring buoy up with a suitable object in its background, so that the two remain in line as you approach on your close-reach. You are then guaranteed to arrive at the right place. If they start moving relative to one another, you can correct with sheet, helm or both.

This system of observing and rectifying any sideways motion holds good right across the whole boat-handling agenda. As we shall see, it is also of vital importance in pilotage, collision avoidance and, to a lesser extent, navigation. A sailor without a transit, or 'range', to assist his daily chores is like a radio with a broken aerial.

Wind against tide

The only satisfactory way to stop a boat in relation to a mooring, a dock or just the seabed (if you were coming to anchor) is to bring her in uptide. If you approach a buoy with the tide behind you, it will be necessary to make a sternboard equal to the speed of the stream before you can stop. Even if you were able to achieve this, the effort involved far outweighs any conceivable benefits.

BOAT HANDLING UNDER SAIL

Fig 5.3 Mooring under sail – wind against tide. Come on to a close-reach and drop the mainsail. Approach the buoy from an upwind/downtide position, controlling way by spilling wind or rolling away part of the headsail. Lose the last of your way alongside the buoy.

The result of this immutable fact is that, when you are picking up a buoy with the wind blowing against the stream or current, you must approach it *downwind*. Since you cannot control downwind boat speed with the mainsail up, you have no choice but to stow it and come to the mooring under headsail alone. The manoeuvre is now a pushover. You can work the headsail sheet like an accelerator pedal in your car and produce whatever speed you need to creep along (Fig 5.3). The only complication comes if it is blowing hard. Then you may find that the flogging sail is generating so much windage that it drags you along too quickly, even with the sheet eased right away. If so, you'll have to roll up most of the sail and use the furling line as well as the sheet. If you don't have a roller reefer, drop the sail well down the stay, then have the foredeck crew hold its leech out to catch as much wind as you need. If even that is too much sail, you have no choice but to blow down on to the buoy under bare poles and grab it as you go by. You can do no more...

Wind across tide

If you're lucky you'll find yourself in a position to close-reach up to your mooring with the tide right on your nose. This is the best of all possible worlds. Often, though, the facts confronting you are less ideal. With the breeze somewhat abaft the beam, it may be obvious that you must treat the manoeuvre as a 'wind against tide' pick-up. Sometimes, the situation is just plain ambiguous. Whenever you are not clear which it is, or on any occasion when the wind is unsteady in direction and may shift so as to embarrass you, apply the second great maxim of boat handling: *When in doubt, drop the mainsail.*

Most modern yachts will jog along merrily enough without it, and once it is stowed, your chances of a serious debacle are reduced by a quantum jump.

SKIPPER'S TIP

Leaving a mooring

If you treat leaving a mooring with the same logic as when picking it up, all will be well. Beware of the wind against tide situation and, if in doubt, don't hoist the main until you are clear of the buoy and sailing free. If you can do it, sail away with main only, so as to give the foredeck crew an easier ride, but if there is a necessity to be on a particular tack when you leave, hoist the jib and be ready to back it if need be, to enable the boat to pay off the way you want her to go. And remember, there's no rule against simply dropping the buoy with no sails up and drifting clear of the neighbours if that's the safest thing to do!

Anchoring

The same principles apply to the boat handling side of anchoring. There is, however, considerably more to it, so anchoring will be discussed separately in Chapter 8.

Berthing

There is nothing magical about sailing alongside. The only difference between this and picking up a mooring is that in the former case you grab a buoy that you hope is within reach on the lee bow, while in the latter you grab a dock or pontoon beside which the yacht is more or less stopped. The same systems are utilised for coping with various combinations of wind and current, with the added complication that if the wind is blowing strongly towards the dock, you will not want to sweep the quay with your main boom. The answer is: when in doubt, drop the main.

Have plenty of fenders rigged, and make sure you have a 'stopping rope' ready (Chapter 7) in addition to the normal dock lines. Go slow, don't be shy, adhere to all the basic rules and never forget boat handling maxim number three, which states: *Never enter any tight corner without having an escape route ready in case things do not develop as you hoped they might.*

If the wind is blowing either along or off the berth, sailing out will present no difficulties.

BOAT HANDLING UNDER SAIL

Sternboarding is perfectly possible in surprisingly large yachts. Ease the main sheet right off, shove the boom as far out as you can, and steer away downwind just as if going astern under power.

Just sort out the wind and tide combinations and use the jib alone if the mainsail won't spill wind while you are still tied up. It may even pay to turn a smallish yacht end-for-end in order to present her to the conditions at a more desirable angle.

All of this is perfectly straightforward. The time you may experience difficulty is if the wind is blowing on to the dock, making it a lee shore. No boat can ever pull herself off a lee shore under sail alone. It is a physical impossibility. If you find yourself in this position, there is nothing for it but to haul out using external assistance. This may be from a friend who will give you a pluck off the wall, or you may be able to manage from your own resources. Ideally, you will tie your bow to a mooring or stake situated to seaward. You may even be able to warp yourself across the river, if your boat is tied to one bank. If none of these tidy solutions presents itself, you must lay out your kedge and haul off using that. Once you are clear of the lee shore, sailing out the anchor is usually an easy matter.

6 BOAT HANDLING UNDER POWER

As soon as you install a propeller on a boat, you enable her to do two things that she cannot do under sail. She can make way for an unlimited period into the eye of the wind or in no wind at all, and she can stop more quickly than ever she could by virtue of the natural forces that otherwise prevail. It so happens that these two items are often critical, particularly the former. They enable an indifferent power-assisted seaman to succeed where the finest sailor in the world could resort only to warping his vessel into her berth.

It is easy to drive a boat under power. To drive her well is another matter altogether, though doing so need not involve virtuoso performances. Indeed, all that most of us would ever ask is to be able to slide so quietly into our berths that no one on shore notices our arrival, and our crews never realise quite how it was done.

What then happens to a boat when she is under power?

Pivoting

Unlike a motor vehicle, a boat is not guided by the movement of anything at her front end. Whatever force is making her turn, as we have seen when discussing sail balance, she pivots about her centre of lateral resistance. This is just as true under power as it is under sail. It means, among other things, that if your vessel is lying alongside a dock you will never work her off it tidily by shoving the helm over and motoring ahead. Before her bow can swing out, her stern must swing in. Somehow, the bow must be persuaded to come off the wall. Pushing off is the obvious way but there are others which we shall explore later.

If the yacht is moving ahead and you need to steer close around an obstruction, or avoid an imminent collision, it is vital to remember the question of pivoting. Many buoys or piles have been struck by the stern of a vessel as her helmsman turned the helm the wrong way, thinking that he was steering away from the danger, when all the time he was swinging the stern inexorably into it.

Blowing off

When you bring a yacht to rest beam-on to the wind, her bow will invariably blow off downwind, as the boat pivots around her keel (Fig 6.1). How fast or how far this happens varies from boat to boat, but you can bank on it with complete certainty.

With the boat moving well through calm water there will be no discernible tendency to blow off except in the hardest cross-winds because the keel is biting the water and doing its job, just as it is when she is sailing. It is only as the vessel slows down to stalling speed that the keel loses its dynamic efficiency and the bow blows away. If you are losing way in a final approach, it's important to realise that this will happen and make any arrangements that may be necessary – either to allow for it or to counteract it – before the effects become embarrassing.

Fig 6.1 Turning.

Rudder effect

When a boat is moving ahead, the action of the rudder is obvious. On moving astern, however, the situation is less clear. Theoretically, you should stand looking aft when steering, then operate the wheel or tiller so that the *rudder* is pointing in the direction you want the stern to swing. As any owner of a long-keeled yacht will tell you, life is not often that simple. A fin-keeler with a deep spade rudder will sometimes steer beautifully astern at very low speeds. Sadly, some boats refuse to steer astern at any price at all. The majority will agree to a compromise, but in order to give them a chance you must bear in mind all the forces that are acting upon the boat. The rudder is only one of them.

If the propeller is placed immediately forward of the rudder (it should be and often is), you can enjoy the benefit of being able to pivot your yacht around her turning point when she is not moving ahead at all. Put the helm hard over so that the rudder is acting as if you were going ahead. Now give her a solid blast full ahead for a few seconds. Unless she is very light, the yacht won't gather any appreciable way, but the surge of water thrown aft by the propeller will be hurled out sideways by the rudder blade. The stern will be thrown in the opposite direction.

Because propellers are situated abaft the rudder in only the rarest of cases, this effect cannot be reproduced by giving the engine a burst astern. Nonetheless, a strong kick in reverse will usually shunt the stern of a boat predictably one way or the other, but it is the propeller that is doing the work, not the rudder. The phenomenon goes under various names. We shall refer to it as 'propwalk'.

THE COMPLETE YACHTMASTER

Fig 6.2 The short turn.

Propeller effects

Water being driven off a revolving propeller comes away in a spiralling vortex. At all times this creates a certain amount of sideways force, though it becomes negligible when the boat is moving ahead above stalling speeds. When she is not under way, the results are noticeable and sometimes dramatic, particularly with the engine in reverse. Ahead, they are always masked by the effect of the rudder; astern, the rudder is ineffective until some speed has been built up, and even then the blade does not react on the water being thrown from the propeller.

If you have the more common 'right-handed' propeller, you will find that when the engine is put astern, the stern of the yacht will shunt across to port, and vice versa with a left-handed prop. On some craft this can be so positive that it becomes a primary manoeuvring tool; in others it is barely perceptible. What you need to determine by experiment is which way the stern will go and how hard.

The best means of finding this out is to run the engine astern while you are tied up. A glance over both quarters will be enough to indicate on which side the turbulence is greatest. Freed of the dock, the boat would naturally shimmy her stern away from the disturbance.

If you forget to find out while you are still in your berth, steer straight ahead in calm water, put the engine out of gear and let your way fall off. When you are nearly stopped, but before your head starts blowing about, put the propeller half astern and observe in which direction the boat tries to swing. Once you've stitched up the details of your propwalk, you have gone a long way to producing tidy power handling.

Moving ahead

If you want to turn tightly when you are moving ahead, you have two choices: either you make the turn while carrying way or you do it with the gears engaged and the propeller throwing water over the rudder blade. The latter will generate a shorter turning circle – the more power on, the smaller it will be – but since you will probably find your vessel accelerating as you go round, you'll need good nerves if you are surrounded by expensive yachts. Should you 'bottle out' halfway round you may not make it, but carry on regardless and the bill will be heavier if your judgement proves shaky. The power turn is not for the faint-hearted, but in competent hands it can be a problem-solver.

The set piece short turn

Sometimes a need arises to spin a vessel in her own length, or not much more. If your boat is unusually athletic and you are of the sort of disposition that peers unflinchingly into the cannon's mouth, you may still get away with a power turn, particularly if you can arrange your affairs so that she is swinging *with* the propeller. Most times, such a bold approach is better turned down, either to ease the strain on your heart or, more usually, because the yacht simply won't swivel tightly enough without help. In either case the answer is the short turn (Fig 6.2, p. 46).

- Decide whether to turn to port or starboard. This will be determined by which way your stern goes with the engine in reverse. If the stern shunts to port, you should set up to turn the boat to starboard, or vice versa.
- Having decided which way you're going, position the boat so as to capitalise on what space is available.

Let's now assume that you have a right-handed propeller and that the yacht therefore wants to make her turn to starboard, with her stern swinging to port:

- Put the rudder hard to starboard (tiller to port) and leave it there.
- Give the engine a strong burst ahead. The stern will swing to port and her head to starboard.
- As soon as she shows signs of gathering way, put the engine into neutral, then into astern (gently – be kind to the gearbox). Run it at about half revs, and watch the propwalk pull her round. Unless you are proposing to gather sternway in order to reposition the boat, you won't need to move the rudder (to do so could well be counterproductive). It isn't the rudder that is turning the boat when the engine is astern like this; it is the propeller.
- Watch the ship's head carefully. When the rate of swing diminishes, give her another few seconds ahead (duration: several seconds).
- Repeat as necessary until you are round. Practice works wonders for perfecting this manoeuvre, but note that yachts with a sail drive may disappoint because the propeller is often too far ahead of the rudder to reproduce the spectacular results of

THE COMPLETE YACHTMASTER

the conventional drive train. There is no ready answer to this, but all is not lost. Yachts with these systems are often of the fin-and-spade profile variation, which steers at low speeds far better than any other form.

Checking over the side for propwash with engine astern and boat tied up securely – one of the surest ways of spotting the throw of the propeller.

Motoring astern

As we've noted already, some vessels do this readily while others seem determined to refuse. Generally, the longer the keel, the more difficult steering becomes when you are going the wrong way. The same, incidentally, holds good if you are trying to sail backwards (sternboard) with your mainsail held aback by a muscular crew member. Moving astern successfully brings all your skills into play. You need to be aware of whether or not the yacht's head will try to blow off and, if so, whether this effect will work with or against your propwalk. Propwalk is the overriding consideration. It affects all boats until they have built up sufficient sternway for the rudder to counteract it. This can be anything from 1 to 5 knots. When it is over 3, my advice is to avoid going astern if at all possible. Once again, you need nerves like backstays to stick to your guns until you finally gain control, while an awkward gust of wind across the bows could leave you terminally embarrassed, for all your guts and bravado.

The one thing you should always be able to predict is which way the yacht will swing. You may not be able to stop her doing it, but at least you won't be disappointed, and there's another point: if you know what she'll do, you can often control circumstances to minimise, or even neutralise, the effects of her wickedness. If you know your boat will go on shoving her stern to starboard for 30 yards (27m or so), try to give her a solid sheer the other way before you start. The two may have cancelled out by the time the rudder gets a grip. You can also sometimes turn a cross-wind into an ally, be it ever so fickle. A yacht whose stern gallops to port will try to throw her bow to starboard. When there is a stiff breeze on the starboard bow, her head will be trying to blow off to port. One force will help to neutralise the other. Try going astern in that boat with a gale on the port bow, however, and you'll spin in your own length, do what you will.

If the yacht is one of the many awkward ones, but is equipped with a bow thruster (see p. 59), the steering astern issue is resolved. Simply set the helm amidships, start moving astern and steer by using the bow as a rudder. Thrust it to starboard if you want the stern to swing to port etc, and if the boat ought to be making a straight line, keep an eye on whether the bow is drifting to one side or the other. If it starts swinging, use the thruster in good time to stop it happening. It works beautifully.

Twin rudders

Ten years before this edition of the book was published, twin rudders were still the exception. Now, more and more yachts are being fitted with them to minimise the effects of the very wide sterns currently in favour. An offset rudder stays in the water when a wide, flat stern heels over. A central rudder soon comes half-out, with potentially nasty results. This is all very well, but there is a downside. A central rudder is a critical element in slow-speed manoeuvring by means of throwing prop-wash against it, as already described. This doesn't work with twin rudders, so more thought is needed before entering a tight situation. A bow thruster helps, and these are often standard fittings on larger twin-ruddered yachts, but the basic problem remains. On the positive side, such yachts generally steer beautifully going astern, so, given a bit more space and due attention to any cross-winds, a 'three-point turn' can still be achieved. Forewarned is forearmed. Nothing at sea comes without a price, and twin rudders are typically win-lose. The important thing is to be aware of their shortcomings as well as their obvious advantages for a certain type of yacht.

Berthing

Mooring

Picking up a mooring under power is the easiest of all manoeuvres. All you need remember is to head up into the tide, if there is any. If there isn't, head up into the wind. When in doubt, favour the tide.

Looking at the other boats already moored will help decide which way to approach, but make sure they are of a similar configuration to yours. A light catamaran will scuttle about head-to-wind at the same time as a deep-keeled yacht seems unaware that the breeze is blowing at all.

Anchoring

As with the 'under sail' chapter, you will find what you need to know about anchoring in Chapter 8.

The Mediterranean stern- or bow-to mooring

It's easy for sailing instructors in Britain to become obsessed with the techniques of bringing boats alongside (see p. 53), but it doesn't do to forget that a large proportion of the world's sailors rarely find themselves in this position. Instead, they operate in harbours and marinas with no finger jetties, preferring to lie with one end to the quay and the other held securely 'off' by a submerged mooring line. The system has two great advantages. It maximises the use of space and it is much cheaper to set up. It only works, however, in conditions of zero or minimal rise and fall of tide. In the Mediterranean, such conditions are commonplace. When I was a young yacht skipper in the south of France, longer ago than I'd care to admit, the arrangement was invariably that you let go a bow anchor somewhere in the middle of the port, then went astern into your berth, paying out cable. This technique is dealt with in the next section, but charterers in the sun will be relieved to learn that such sophistication is now rarely required. Moorings for holding off are ubiquitous, for which we can all be truly thankful.

Here's how it works:

- As you approach the quay, you need to find out how to pick up the hold-off mooring. Occasionally, you'll see a buoy, in which case grab it and use the line provided. If there's no buoy, approach the quay carefully and look for some sort of light line, or chain disappearing from it into the depths.
- Back up to the wall (or nose up if you don't want the dockside loafers checking out your dinner), get a couple of lines ashore, one either side, and have your strongest crew pick up the light messenger line.
- While the stern is being secured to the wall, Mr Muscle follows the messenger line out to seaward, walking along the deck as he does. In due course, he'll be rewarded by a stronger line which he leads in over the bow roller, or fairlead.
- By now, the stern should be secure and within jumping space or passerelle distance of the dock. Heave up hard on the haul-off line until there is no chance of a passing wash or an on shore breeze smacking you into the stonework, and the job is done.
- Rig the sunshade, plug the boat in, and pour yourself a cool one. The fridge will be working again as soon as that electricity is hooked up.

Almost everybody contrives, at some stage of their life, to allow the mooring messenger to get sucked into the propeller. The answer to this is to keep it in hand, use your commonsense, and never, ever, forget that a moment's inattention will mean your time has come.

Box berths

These are a somewhat more refined method of securing yachts 'bow- or stern-to' a dock or wall. They proliferate in the Baltic and in the USA. Once again, a critical factor is modest tidal movements. Box berths come in all sorts of variations, but the common factor is that rather than the mooring line of the Mediterranean system, the boat is held away from the dock by two lines leading generally to piles set a little over a boat's length to seaward. The conventional arrangement in box berths is usually, but not always, to come bows in. If you're lucky there will be some sort of small jetty to let you climb on board amidships. Typically, however, you'll have to scramble ashore over the pulpit, unless you're stern-to.

To get into a box berth, here's what you do:

- Your boat is at risk from graunching one pile or the other as you come in. It can be quite difficult to avoid this, especially in a cross-wind. Many boats built in the Baltic have rubbing bands to allow you to slide along even a steel pile without damage. If you don't have such a luxury, rig a heavy rope fore-and-aft high up on the topsides. Rig fenders ready to kick over as soon as you're through the piles if there are neighbours.
- Drive in with one line ready on each bow and one line led forward from each quarter.
- As your midships passes between the piles, either loop the stern lines over them as slip ropes, lasso them with a bowline, or secure in some other way that seems appropriate. Always secure the weather side first in a crosswind.
- Letting the stern lines run, but keeping them out of the propeller, proceed up to the dock and get someone ashore with the bow lines.
- Even up, and with one eye on the price of liquor in the far north, brew yourself a health-promoting herbal drink.

Pile moorings

Tying up between a pair of piles is a peculiarly British way of carrying on. Mercifully, it is now rare. However, the advice holds good for any situation where a yacht is to be moored fore-and-aft. Piles provide a stable and very safe way of keeping large numbers of boats lying fore-and-aft in the crowded, tide-swept rivers of the south.

Getting into a Baltic box berth isn't always easy. This yacht is attempting to come in stern first. The crew is hanging onto the post with one hand while trying to get a rope on with the other. The skipper, meanwhile, is maintaining control as best he can and preparing to back up to the dock where the photographer is standing ready to take his stern lines.

Once you're all secure in a box berth you're very safe indeed with the boat supported at all four corners.

Piles psyche out the inexperienced operator in a big way. I kept my boat on piles for years and more often than not approaching strangers would attempt to tie up to me rather than pick up the empty visitors' piles next door. I'm afraid I gave them short shrift, not because I'm a naturally unwelcoming sort of chap, but because it was unreasonable for my privacy to be invaded because of so needless a misconception. It is far easier to pick up a set of 'bare' piles than it is to raft up to some unfortunate who got there first. All you have to do is to contrive two ropes in the right places. To tie up to another boat you need at least four lines, probably six. You must rig fenders, and after all that, you must still go through the usual social nonsense: 'Mind if we come alongside you?' 'Sure, you won't be bothered if we leave at 0400, will you?'

So how do you perform this miracle on bare piles? Mirrors? The dinghy? A passing carrier pigeon? No. What you do is a running moor. Basically, this means that you drive up to the first pile, tie on to it, then drive up to the second, paying out rope from the first. When you're secured to that one as well, you shorten up aft and ease out forward until the boat is centred, and then you make fast.

In practice there are one or two pitfalls into which the unwary may blunder. To avoid these, use the following step-by-step guide to the piles (Fig 6.3):

- Piles are invariably sited more or less along the axis of any tidal stream. They also carry mooring rings which can slide up and down a large, vertical iron horse.
- Make your approach uptide, if there is any; if there isn't, make it upwind. If the wind is blowing across the piles, approach from the downwind side of the first pile.
- Prepare your lines, paying particular attention to the stern line, which must be good and long. Some people like to run the ropes through the mooring rings and back on board, so as to be ready to let go by slipping them when the time comes to leave. If this is your choice (it isn't usually mine) you'll need an even longer stern line. Nothing fouls up the whole business like running out of this vital rope. Watching people try to remember how to tie a double sheetbend as steam erupts from the skipper's ears is good value, but is rarely rewarded with a successful result. Both ropes must be flaked clear to run.
- Your best knotter should now carry the working end of the stern line, correctly led through the aft guard rails, forward to the shrouds.
- Approach the downtide pile and stop with the shrouds alongside the mooring ring. You may feel you need a fender handy, but if you sail a black fishing boat you can forget about such finesse. It is axiomatic that you don't let this pile get abaft your boat's pivot point while the crew are working on it. If you do, the boat will swivel round, the tide will come under her quarter, and all will be lost. Your only answer then is to abort and start again.
- Keep the boat fore-and-aft with the tide while your crew ties the stern line on to the ring on the pile. If they are not threading it through and back, the best knot for this is a round turn and a bowline (see Chapter 7 to find out why).
- With the stern line secure, motor slowly to the uptide pile, stop with your lee bow alongside (lee bow because then any wind will blow you on rather than off), secure, and drop back, evening up the lines as you go.

BOAT HANDLING UNDER POWER

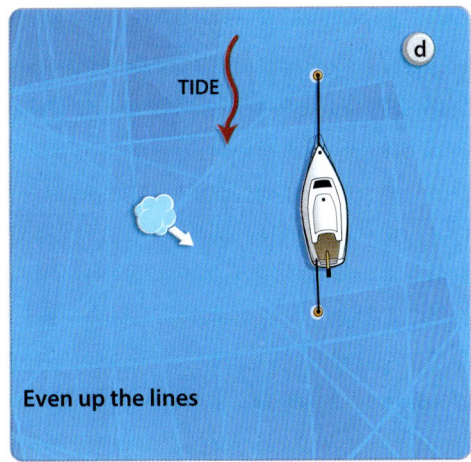

Fig 6.3 Pile moorings.

- The job is extremely easy in a boat of any size at all but if you don't feel you can cope with the dynamics, or your crew are all low on rope literacy, an equally safe alternative is to launch your dinghy, with the stern line aboard. The dinghy crew attach one end of this to the downtide pile in their own sweet time. You drive the yacht past it and secure her to the uptide pile, which presents no challenge at all. While you are doing this, the dinghy comes alongside and hands up the other end of the stern line. Even up when the bow is fast and that's the job.

Piles should pose no problem to a reasonably competent skipper. Anyone who chickens out by rafting up needlessly should have his club tie snipped off immediately south of the knot.

Securing to the rocks in the northlands provides a surprisingly safe mooring. The skipper has already deployed a stern anchor. As the boat nudges up to the shore, still in deep water, the mate hops off with two bow lines and secures them to whatever is convenient – often handy pine trees.

Coming alongside

Coming alongside a berth is an everyday affair for most of us, yet it's surprising how wired up people become about it. The answer is to analyse the various aspects, address each one in turn, form a simple plan of action, brief your crew carefully, then execute the manoeuvre steadily and positively. Proper use of warps is crucial to tying up alongside, so before we go any further, we'll take a look at exactly what each does, and why. The nuts and bolts of how they should be handled and made fast are dealt with in Chapter 7.

Under most circumstances, a yacht of any size below 55ft (17m) or so is best tied up with four ropes (Fig 6.4). These are the bow line (or head rope), the stern line, the bow spring (or head spring) and the stern spring. Assuming the boat is 'head up' to the tide or the wind is blowing along the dock, she will be secure enough lying to a bow line only, but she will not be tidy. She will lie bows-in to the dock, risking damage to her pulpit, and bow in general. Putting on a stern line that leads away aft will do little to remedy this situation. However, if you rig a stern spring from well aft to run out parallel to the bow line she will settle back on the pair of ropes and lie sweetly beside the dock.

That is the theory. Of course, life is not so simple. She would lie adequately to the two lines so long as the tide were very strong, or if she were left motoring astern against them. Since the former is rarely the case and the latter is an undesirable long-term state of affairs, the position can be firmed up by rigging a stern line to hold the boat back against the other two warps. Should she now ride forward, of course she will hang from the stern only and will finish up

BOAT HANDLING UNDER POWER

Fig 6.4 Berthing alongside: four ropes for four jobs (ends on the dockside, the slack coiled up aboard). Bow line is parallel to stern spring. Stern line is parallel to bow spring. Fenders are in place.

grinding her aft toerail against the wall, but this situation is neutralised by deploying a bow spring to act as a pair with the stern line.

When you are coming alongside, it is important to decide which are the first lines to run ashore. Often, in moderate circumstances of wind and tide, you will opt for bow line and stern line, then rig the springs immediately afterwards. Sometimes, however, you may opt for a 'pair'. If there is a strong stream running along the dock, you will be well advised to choose bow line and stern spring. Get these ashore and secure, then let the boat settle back to them while you rig a stern line, followed, at leisure, by the bow spring. If you are in doubt about how snugly she'll lie, motor gently astern against the first pair until the stern line is rigged.

Stern-to with a rough-and-ready passerelle contrived out of a simple plank of wood. Such an arrangement is no substitute for a professional passerelle, secure at the inboard end and supported by a topping lift.

Having worked our way through the theoretical functions of warps, let's get back to the order of service for coming alongside:

- Assess wind and tide conditions on the berth to decide which way to come in. Like pile moorings, you will of course choose to arrive uptide or upwind, whichever is the stronger.
- As you come in, you may want to put your engine astern to drag off the last of your way. If this seems at all likely, bear in mind what your propwalk will do. If it is going to pull your stern into the dock, so much the better. If the contrary will be the case, be ready to check the stern with your warps, and don't use reverse at all if you can avoid it. If there is no tide and not much breeze, you should always choose to put the side to the dock which the boat naturally favours (Fig 6.5). A right-handed propeller will slide you sweetly into a port-side to berth, for example.

Fig 6.5 Coming alongside – no tide. If you have a choice, always dock on the side to which your propeller throws you when going astern. Boat **a** is fighting the propwalk; boat **b** is letting it work for her.

- Tell your crew 'which side to' you are coming in, detail off hands for the different jobs, then briefly outline your plan and each person's part in it. Don't make a pedantic meal of this; just tell them what's going on.
- Prepare your lines in good time, and have your crew standing by in way of the shrouds to step neatly ashore as you bring up alongside. Crew hanging around in the bows with a head rope in their hands are doomed to disappointment, and you won't be able to see where you're going either.
- Make sure that you have at least three generously sized fenders rigged around the centre of the boat. If you have a spare, be ready with a roving fender also.
- As slowly as you can, bring the yacht into the berth. Watch transits on the dock, slip or pontoon to make sure that you are going where you think you are, just as you did when mooring under sail. If there is a strong tide, you may even be able to ferry-glide in sideways under the tightest control imaginable. As the fenders touch the dock, the line handlers should step ashore, walk crisply to the designated cleat or bollard and make fast the ends of their lines. Slack is now taken up on board, and the remaining lines rigged as soon as possible. So long as you stick to one rope for one job, with no ropes doubled up on cleats aboard or ashore, the business of tying up is simplicity itself. As soon as you err from this principle, chaos – or at best, an unseamanlike lash-up – is the inevitable result.

If you are short-handed and the yacht has a well-sited midships cleat or fairlead, rig a line from this as you come in, but have the others ready for action. So long as the fairlead is in approximately the same transverse plane as the centre of lateral resistance, or pivot point of the boat, all will be well unless there is a ripper of a tide or a gale of wind. Bring the yacht alongside so that the point of attachment on board is adjacent to a cleat on the dock. Step ashore and make the rope off short. Lasso it if the topsides are too high to hop off. That will hold the boat well enough while you run your four mooring lines out. Once the yacht is properly secured the short line can be retrieved.

SKIPPER'S TIP

Rafting manners

Sometimes you will have to raft up to one or more other vessels. If so, the conventions are clear and universally applied:

a Ask permission before coming alongside.

b The most recent arrival supplies the fenders.

c Secure to the yacht inside you, then rig shore lines (or pile ropes) to take your own weight without waiting to be asked. Very occasionally, if your boat is small compared with your host's, it can make sense to lie to the larger craft's lines, but you must always ask if this will be in order. Not to do so is equivalent in rudeness to helping yourself to a stranger's beer without so much as a 'by your leave'.

If the onboard attachment point is not ideally situated – ie, forward or abaft the pivot point of the boat - it is often possible to modify the plan accordingly. Where the cleat is abaft the ideal point, rig as short a line as you can, then motor slowly forward against it. Steering the stern into the dock (this means steering the bow out) will usually help, and this should guarantee reasonable temporary stability. If the cleat is forward of the pivot point, you'll have to motor astern against the short line and see how you manage. Robbed of the useful shove of the rudder when going ahead, this is unlikely to be as effective, but on some boats, it works fine. On others, it's a non-starter. Only testing will tell the truth.

Leaving an alongside berth

At the beginning of the chapter we noted that you can't just 'drive' a boat from an alongside berth. This is because if you try to steer out, the dock prevents her stern from pivoting in, with the result that you bash your stern along the dock and don't succeed. Shoving the bow off is the simplest solution to this difficulty, but this isn't always practical, particularly in strong onshore winds, or where larger yachts are concerned. What you require is a method that falls between pushing off and hauling the bow out using a kedge. The answer is to spring off, as shown in Fig 6.6.

Fig 6.6 Springing off.

Springing off involves removing all your lines except one spring line, then motoring against it so that the opposite end of the boat is levered off the wall.

To spring the bow out, motor astern against the stern spring and the bow will waltz round to seaward as if by magic. If this doesn't work, springing the stern out is even more effective.

BOAT HANDLING UNDER POWER

Leave the bow spring on, motor ahead against it, and turn your rudder in towards the wall as though you wanted to steer your bow in. The propeller wash is blown inwards by the rudder. The bow spring levers the stern out as well and, before you know it, you are far enough out to let go and motor astern into open water.

Don't forget to use your fenders intelligently while springing off, and always be sure that you can let go the spring line without leaving one of your crew on the pontoon.

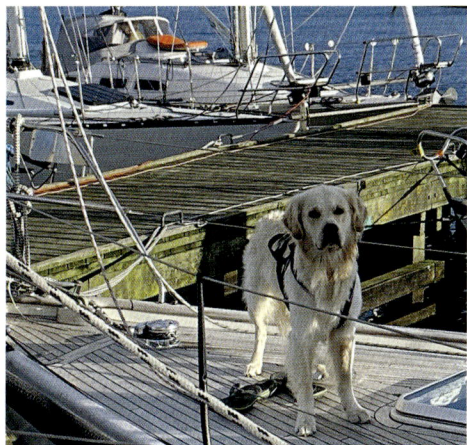

A proper sea dog keeping port watch for his owners. Note the starboard bow line on the yacht, which is rigged as a slip rope. Almost universal in European waters.

The downside of slip ropes. It's unusual but it can happen. This one chafed through overnight on a mooring ring.

Bow thrusters

Modern boats handle superbly under power compared with their predecessors, but they have one great weakness. Because they have little or no forefoot, they blow about easily. At slow and sub-stalling speeds, they are therefore victims of the wind and need any help they can get. This often comes in the form of a bow thruster. As well as shoving boats into and out of some improbable berths, bow thrusters can be used to overcome heavy propwalk. For a boat that does not steer readily astern, they can solve the problem by having the helm set amidships and literally guiding her along stern-first with bursts of the thruster. The secret of successful use of a thruster is to give it a long, sustained burst at the critical time, rather than a series of frantic blips. This really gets the bow swinging. A typical electrically driven unit will overheat if left running for minutes, but this rarely happens in practice. In case it does, make sure you know how the fuse works. Some can be cajoled back into life immediately; others have no external switch and cannot. If yours does not, you'll just have to grit your teeth until it cools down sufficiently to wake up again. Nothing you can do will speed this up, so if a refusal of duty seems a possibility, try to leave a get-out plan for the awful contingency of losing it at a critical moment.

7 ROPES AND ROPEWORK

Today's yachts are such marvels of technical sophistication that they only really have two things left in common with craft from the days of Noah. Both float most of the time, and both use rope.

Rope has been the primary tool of the sailor since the dawn of sail. The material from which it is now constructed, however, would be unrecognisable to a sailor of even the mid-20th century. The natural fibre ropes, now consigned to history, deteriorated after a short life through a rapidly advancing process of weakness and decay. They were also brutal to handle when wet. By contrast, most of today's high-class yacht cordage is light in weight, pleasant to use, impervious to damp and strong beyond what seem the bounds of reason. The only thing to be said against it is that most forms resist the ancient art of splicing, which was so easily executed in traditional materials. Working an eye into a piece of 22mm (⅞in) prestretched polyester leaves most operators with aching palms and an untidy result. The only answer is to invest in a Swedish fid, stop off each strand with tape while you splice, and take your time.

Types of rope

Various types of rope are now available, and it is important that the right one is used for a particular job. *Polyester* is strong, pleasant to handle and long-lived even in sunlight. In its prestretched forms it is often distinguished by a black fleck, or 'rogues yarn'. It is stable enough for sheets and some halyards. Polyester rope is available in either three-strand (traditional) or braided versions. The braided variety is extremely easy on the hands and is generally unwilling to tangle. This makes it ideal for sheets, as well as halyards that are to be led aft. For other uses it may be considered too prone to chafe. Polyester rope can be utilised for anything, but it is somewhat expensive so is often substituted by polypropylene for such items as dock lines.

Polypropylene is strong, low on stretch, but rough to handle, and degrades seriously in the ultraviolet rays of the Sun. For this reason it becomes unreliable after a few years of constant exposure. It is cheap, however, and easy to splice. This makes it excellent for dock lines, where its low price encourages you to go a few sizes bigger than the minimum. Large ropes are easier to pull and less prone to chafe damage. Polypropylene can be used for running gear in an emergency, but is otherwise not recommended.

Nylon is the strongest traditional rope of all, in its three-strand or its plaited versions. Its salient property, other than good chafe resistance, is that it is exceedingly elastic. This

ROPES AND ROPEWORK

It's a calm day so the crew will get away with this unseamanlike bunch of rubbish they're throwing across to the other boat. In a hard offshore wind, by the time the crew on the inside boat had sorted it all out and hove it back again, the boat arriving would have blown halfway to Christmas.

feature suits it ideally for anchor work. All anchor rodes or kedge warps should be of nylon. The stretch cushions the pull on the hook and lessens the chances of it being jerked from the bottom by a sudden surge of motion from the boat.

More and more hi-tech materials are appearing in yacht cordage under trade names such as Spectra and Dyneema. Super-strong, low-stretch and ultra lightweight, these ropes were once found more commonly on racing yachts, but their obvious benefits are making them common in cruising boats where their considerable expense is generally agreed to be justifiable. Typically, a single-line reefing system would be well served by them. Polyester halyards are far better rigged with these miracle, high-stretch-modulus materials.

Wire halyards

In spite of the excellent stability of prestretched polyester, it is not really rigid enough to set up a Bermudan sail that makes any pretence at performance. To neutralise this menace, cruiser-racers or fast cruisers were once rigged with wire halyards terminating in rope tails for ease of handling. These may still be found, but today's superior solution is to use Dyneema or some other near-zero stretch cordage instead. When any residual wire halyard starts to 'jag' and show signs of getting to the end, replace it with Dyneema. It's a cruel cut financially, but if the boat still has one of those ghastly captive-reel wire winches with a brake, that has to go along with the halyard. Replace it with a self-tailer and you'll be in with a chance of making it to the

THE COMPLETE YACHTMASTER

boneyard with all your fingers intact. Don't be tempted to skimp and use polyester rope. It will stretch for sure. Such a halyard leaves a sail with a leading edge like a crinkle-cut potato chip and a yacht that goes to windward like a haystack.

Knots, splices and whippings

Ropework in a yacht today is simple compared with what went on aboard even a small trading schooner of a hundred years ago. Unlike the crew of a traditional gaff cutter, most of us can get away with a sparsity of knowledge that would have left our forebears thunderstruck. Some skills we must retain, however, and being adept at them is not just a question of pride in a job well done. The wrong knot jamming up at an inconvenient moment can still result in embarrassment, or even the loss of the vessel.

You can buy excellent books and DVDs on knots. Indeed, I recommend wholeheartedly that you do so. Some are as big as a modest encyclopaedia, and mastering their contents offers a pastime for life. If this seems rather beyond the call of duty, you can get away with knowing only seven, but I do mean *know*. Total familiarity is what you want. Don't scrape around until you finally manage to get one right, breathe a sigh of relief, and then go on to the next. Once you've come to grips with a knot, practise it until you can tie it in the dark, first time, the following morning. Take to work – in your pocket or your bag – on Monday morning a length of ¼in (6mm) diameter line. When the client's back is turned, flash off a quick bowline. Bang the two ends into a double sheet-bend under the boss's desk while you are receiving the hard word about last week's sales figures, and take it to the bathroom to improve the shining hour. Only then will there be no fumbling on the foredeck – after all, if the skipper is struggling to bend on the jib sheets, what can he expect of the crew?

The *figure-of-eight* (Fig 7.1) is a simple but effective stopper knot. Its usual application on a yacht is in the ends of the sheets, so that if left untended they cannot come unrove.

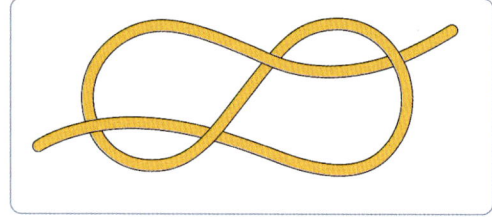

Fig 7.1 The figure-of-eight: a simple stopper knot.

The *clove hitch* (Fig 7.2) is extremely quick to tie. Its official use is to attach the bight of a line around another rope or a bar. Unofficially it is convenient for hitching fenders to guard rails and dinghy painters to pushpits – on a short-term basis. However, if it is used for this sort of job, it *must* be backed up by at least one half hitch, otherwise it is capable of working itself loose.

The *rolling hitch* (Fig 7.3) is the only knot for securing to the bight of another rope, then administering a sideways pull. A typical

Fig 7.2 The clove hitch.

62

application would be when you contrive a set of riding turns on your sheet winch with a sail full of wind and the clew out of reach. Rolling hitch a line to the sheet, between the winch and the sail, lead it to a spare winch, then wind on enough tension to give you some slack on the offending sheet, which can then be freed with no trouble at all. The knot can also be used to secure the fall of a tackle around its own parts – neat and effective. To tie a rolling hitch, you use the same technique as for a clove hitch, but the first turn is taken twice around instead of once.

Fig 7.3 The rolling hitch.

A *reef knot* (Fig 7.4) has only one official job on board, though it is sometimes seconded for making off a lashing. It is used, as its name suggests, for tying in reef points. In order not to jam up it must be symmetrical and, as every boy scout can tell you, it is tied in the 'left over right, right over left' manner. If you slip both ends as loops, you have a knot suspiciously like the bow we all tie in our shoes. To undo a reef knot, pull the opposite ends of each side. It will usually capsize for you.

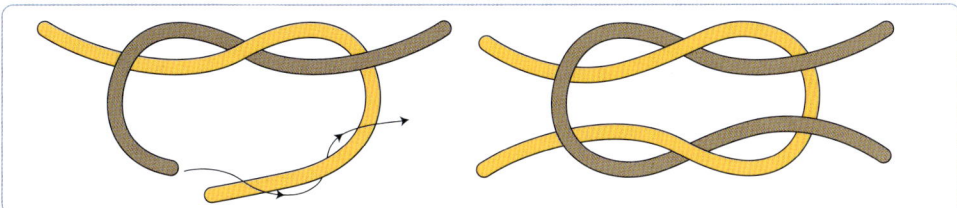

Fig 7.4 The reef knot.

The *bowline* (Fig 7.5) is the most important knot of all. It supplies a loop that will never slip and never lock up under the most enormous loadings. It is used for numerous jobs, but bending on the jib sheets to the clew ring of the sail is now a universal application. You can use it to tie up your dinghy or to loop a dock line over a bollard. You can even employ two interlocked to join a couple of ropes together.

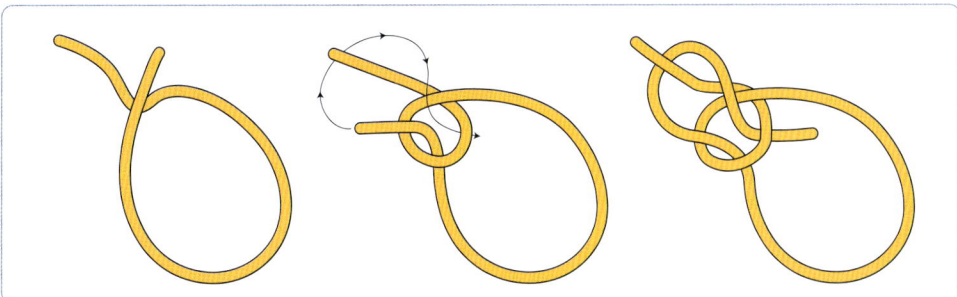

Fig 7.5 The bowline: the most important knot of all. Don't go sailing until you can tie this in the dark, backwards or forwards, every time.

How you tie it is up to you. Just remember this: Nelson, John Paul Jones, and every other serious seaman never heard of rabbits and holes. Indeed, the very mention of the furry creature with long ears on board was held to be bad luck. So try to master the quick twist method, the sleight of hand, the smooth, foolproof system that won't let you down when the foredeck is plunging bows under and you are sick and dog-tired.

The *sheet bend* (Fig 7.6) is extremely quick to tie and is a reliable way of joining two ropes, so long as they both remain under steady strain. If they are to be subject to snatching, take the working end round again (twice more if you feel it needs it) and make a double (or treble) sheet bend.

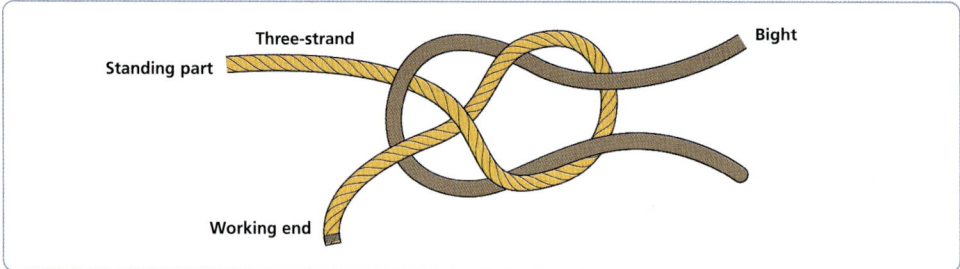

Fig 7.6 The single sheet bend: useful as a 'quickie knot'. For the double form, take an extra turn of the three-strand rope around the bight and tuck it in under its own standing part.

The *round turn and two half hitches* (Fig 7.7) is the absolutely sure way of tying up your dinghy, or your mooring rope to a ring in the quay wall. It is also the conventional means of securing fender lanyards to the guard rails. The knot has the advantage that, within reason, it can be let go under load, particularly if you have slipped the hitches into a 'bow' form. Its other great recommendation is that it is the most obvious knot in the world to tie. You can teach it to a two-year-old as his or her first knot.

Fig 7.7 The round turn and two half hitches.

These seven knots will see you safely around the seas. There are several more that have genuine applications in today's sailoring world, but if you are entirely familiar with the ones we have discussed, you need never be stuck with a loose end.

ROPES AND ROPEWORK

Eyes and ends

A scraggy rope's end, or cow's tail, is an abomination. It looks vile; but more importantly, it will foul whenever it is given half a chance. Furthermore, it often proves impossible to reeve. If a length of three-strand begins to splay at the end, it can be stopped off momentarily with a thumb knot (single overhand 'granny') to keep it from going any further. It must then be attended to straight away, because it certainly won't reeve with a knot in the end.

With most man-made fibres it is possible to melt the ends of the strands together. This can be quite successful with some braidlines. It has been known to work with three-strand, but whipping is more secure, neater and, let's face it, more satisfying.

A *common whipping* is made as shown in Fig 7.8. This will serve after a fashion, but if you need to be certain, you can convert it to a *sailmaker's whipping* by the following expedient. Begin as though you were performing a common whipping, but when you reach the end of the rope, pass the whipping twine between two strands of the rope at the crown of the whipping and bring it down the outside, following the lay of the rope, to the bottom. There, you open the lay of the rope and pass the twine through to the next strand; bring it back up to the crown, across the top to the next strand, back down, through, up again and so on until you have two passes at each strand (pulling each tight as you go). When you reach the crown for the last time, pass the twine through the bight (or loop) which you left up there, right at the beginning, and pull it tightly under the whipping to finish off, just as you did with the common job.

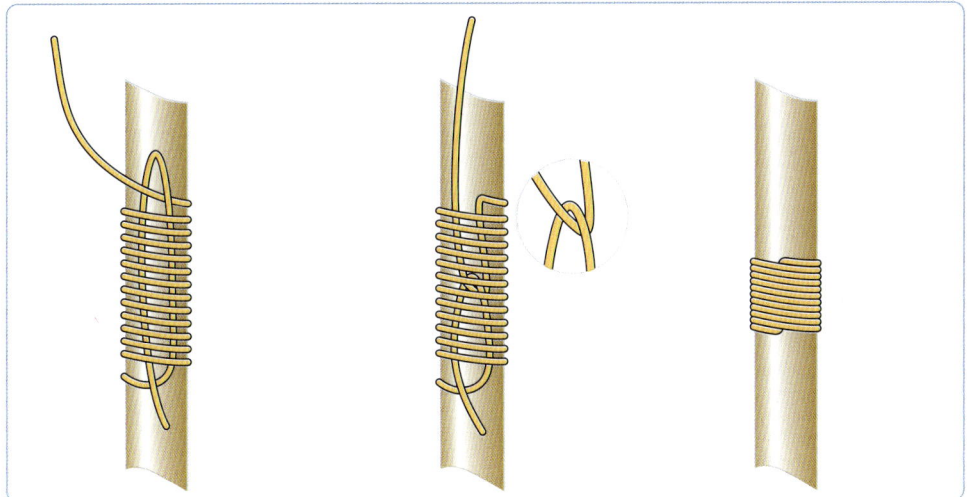

Fig 7.8 A common whipping. Every sailor should be able to execute one of these quickly and without referring to a textbook.

You'll hear people saying that this type of whipping must be done with a palm and needle, and so it must if you are putting one on the end of a braided rope; otherwise, fiddle-de-dee! I have whipped ropes like this for 25 years and they have crossed oceans in such vulnerable sites as under the bowsprit of a schooner where they served to finish off the permanent gaskets. Take it from me, they do not let go, and they are quick and easy to execute.

THE COMPLETE YACHTMASTER

> **SKIPPER'S TIP**
>
> **Splicing pint by pint**
>
> The art of splicing three-strand rope is dying out among amateur sailors, more is the pity. The only splice you really need is the eye-splice. The short splice, used for joining two ropes permanently if untidily together, is useful for fixing up chafed-through dock-lines which are otherwise full of life. The eye-splice is not illustrated here because there is more than one correct way to do it, and besides, there are some things you just can't learn from books. I was taught by a shipmate in a pub.
>
> The deal was that I bought the beer. It took him three pints to get me squared away. I practised until the landlord called 'time'. We had to carry my tutor back to the ship, but it was cheap at the price. I never forgot how to make that vital first tuck.
>
> If you want to learn to splice, find yourself a thirsty sailor and do the job properly, or visit my website and download instructions from the videos: tomcunliffe.com/product-category/video.

Rope handling

Making fast

Whatever you are making fast a rope to, in whatever circumstances, you should always ask yourself the same questions: could conditions conceivably arise in which I will require to ease or release this rope under load? If so, have I made it fast in such a way that this will be readily possible? If not, will I be able to slack up sufficiently by easing the other end?

Reading between the lines, you'll be able to see that a rope should never be made up in such a way that neither end can be eased under control. Now walk round any yacht marina and cast a critical eye on the way the boats are tied up. They'll get away with their folly in a nice antiseptic marina berth, but if those skippers tie up like that on a tidal wall on a windy day…

Extrapolating this proposition one notch further, you'll see that when you tie up a boat, each rope (bow line, stern spring, etc) must be a separate entity, and each must have its own separate point of attachment on board. If you secure one on top of another, sooner or later you'll want the bottom one when the top one is loaded up. Similarly, if you use the other end of the bow line for the bow spring, you'll end up with a lubber's muddle that would sink a sailor's heart. Get it right: *One rope, one job, half the work, no problem.*

Securing to a cleat

There are various seamanlike ways of securing to a cleat. The important thing is to ask yourself: is the way I am doing this absolutely foolproof against jamming or locking up, and will I be able to ease the rope away under control if I want to? Answer 'yes' and you are doing it right.

It's important to lead the rope properly in the first instance or you are on a loser. Once the first half turn is on, plenty of figures-of-eight works well, though some folk prefer a full round turn first. 'Suit yourself,' is what I say, so long as it can't lock up and won't work loose.

When a rope is made up on a cleat, or belayed to a pin, it is the friction of the turns that holds it fast. Theoretically, therefore, there is no need for any sort of 'back turn' or locking hitch to finish the job. This is true in a perfect world. Unfortunately, there are circumstances where a locking hitch is desirable for total security, for example where a cleat is too small to accept the required number of figures-of-eight, or if the rope is so springy and slippery that you cannot trust it to stay put. Sometimes, a locking hitch is useful on a mooring line if you are leaving the boat, but wherever you use one, always be sure that there are sufficient turns underneath it so that it cannot jam up, whatever chance may come along. So long as you obey that rule, what harm can there be in a locking hitch? None, I believe, yet die-hards will fix you with their glittering eyes and state that he who uses a back turn is no sailor. He wasn't, in the days of hemp and manila ropes, which shrink-wrapped themselves on to a cleat when they were soaked in water. But that was half a century ago.

All I ask is that you consider the principles, then think each case out for yourself.

Coiling

All three-strand ropes are right-hand laid. As a result, they coil clockwise. Cable-laid hemp hawsers didn't, but I haven't seen one of those on a yacht since 1969, and then it was so old it snapped under the most modest of loads. Try to force a right-handed rope the other way and it will hate it. So will you, especially when it runs off the coil in a series of block-shattering kinks. You shouldn't have it in you to coil against the lay, whether you are tidying up your washing line or coiling a 50 fathom (91m) kedge warp on the deck.

Most braidlines and plaited ropes can be turned either with or against the clock because they have no 'handed' lay. This is useful, but try not to get into the habit of coiling them against the sun, even though you can. Once you've set yourself into the habit of always coiling clockwise, going against the grain will be almost impossible and you'll never be caught out coiling a laid-up rope backwards by mistake. Interestingly, as an examiner, I could see someone committing this primary sin from the corner of my eye. They had a lot of ground to make up afterwards if they were to pass their certificates.

If you want a long rope to run clean for all its length, it isn't always a good idea to rely on a coil. Flaking, or faking, is usually more reliable. Simply lay the rope down in a suitable fashion, passing it through your hands the whole way, so that when it is called to run, *not a single inch of it will be under the inch that precedes it*. There are prescribed patterns for flaking ropes out, but any pattern, even disorder, will do, so long as the principle above is adhered to.

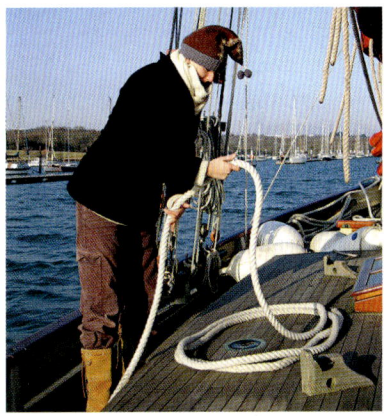

When a rope's too big or long to coil in hand, coil it on the deck like this. Make it up with a clove hitch around itself.

Working a Brummel eye splice into the end of a Dyneema halyard isn't nearly as hard as it looks. It may not be in the syllabus, but it's a job any complete yachtmaster should take pride in tackling.

Securing the yacht

Which knot?

Most of the time it is obvious which knot should be used in a particular case; sometimes there is a choice; occasionally, it genuinely doesn't matter which one you select. As always, the answer is to take a moment to think through what you expect of the knot, and what could go wrong. A typical example is how to tie the yacht up to a ring. Do you use a round turn and two half hitches, or is a bowline preferred?

The first question is: will I have to let the rope off from the dock under load? And the reply should be: not necessarily, because the other end of the line will be made fast to a cleat aboard, and I can always ease that away.

This leaves the use of the bowline open. If, for some reason, you may not be able to ease the line from the deck, a bowline should never be used. The main advantage that may be won by employing a bowline is that you can make the loop as long as you like. Sometimes, when tying up to a box berth post, for example, it is handy to be able to untie the rope without actually getting close to the ring because it may be submerged at High Water. If you do use a bowline for any mooring purpose, however, always lay a round turn on the ring before making the knot. This will treble the bearing surface and eliminate any tendency to chafe.

Coming alongside

The chances are that your crew will be less experienced than you. Watching someone who doesn't really know what to do step ashore with a dock line is rarely edifying. It's up to you to tell the hands what is required. Here is a rule-of-thumb method for a fully crewed boat. It covers most regular situations:

- State 'which side to', and rig fenders. (Don't put them over until you're nearly there, though. Nothing looks more sloppy.)
- Prepare all four dock lines. Have two ready for instant action.
- Lead the lines out correctly (through pulpit/pushpit, etc), decide how much you'll need ashore, then allow half as much again for contingencies.
- Coil each up in hand, ready to take on to the dock. Then make the bight fast aboard, on the cleat designated for the line – just in case it is necessary to 'take a turn' ashore in order to stop the boat.
- As the boat comes alongside, the two lines are carried ashore and *the ends* made fast on the dock. The slack is pulled in and made fast aboard.
- Unless you specifically tell them to do so, the crew should not snub any lines. The helmsman is in complete charge at all times.
- As soon as possible, send out the remaining two lines.
- Note that the ends of all four lines are made off ashore; and all slack rope is on board the yacht. This discourages thieving. It also looks tidy, and passers-by who have come to admire your vessel won't trip and fall into the harbour.

ROPES AND ROPEWORK

> **SKIPPER'S TIP**
>
> ### Chafe
>
> On the question of chafe, you should always be aware that a single line led through a ring and back on itself – such as you might use when picking up a mooring – is extremely vulnerable in this respect. Lying to such an arrangement is fine for a short stop in calm weather. Overnight, by all means leave the doubled line on for convenience, but secure the main weight with a heavier rope attached by a round turn and two half hitches, or a round turn and a bowline. If things look really grim on an exposed mooring buoy, you can always go for the final solution and shackle on your anchor cable. It'll be noisy for the denizens of the fo'c'sle, but you're the skipper so you'll have shrewdly selected the quarter berth for your own watch below.

If you are short-handed, you won't be able to achieve this ideal state of affairs. Then you must step ashore with the two lines, take up the slack on the dock and make the bight fast there and then. Once you've got the other lines on, you can tidy up so that everything is left in the approved manner.

The same rules apply if you are alongside another yacht. Always make your ends fast on her. Her skipper doesn't want a great heap of your old rope dumped in his cockpit – and don't ask her crew to pull in your boat. Why should they? If you were coming alongside the harbour wall, you'd have to manage alone. To throw the other owner's wife a bunch of tanglies and ask her to heave away is to add insult to injury. If it were me, I'd make the end off, chuck the rest into the sea with a friendly 'All fast', and let them get on with it, assuming they'd rigged their fenders adequately, that is.

Preparation with the lines makes all the difference when approaching a potentially tight situation.

Slip lines

Sailors who cruise in Northern Europe will find that locals invariably secure their yachts using slip ropes – that is, one end is secured on board, the bight is led ashore, around the cleat, then back on board again where it is made fast. There are pros and cons to this method. The big 'pro' is that when the time comes to leave, the crew can slip the line from on board and nobody has to be ashore. A 'con' promoted by traditionalists is that the rope can chafe where it goes around the cleat or bollard on the dock. In practice, I have found that with modern cordage this is rarely the case. A small-diameter ring is another matter and must always be suspect, particularly on a mooring buoy where I have seen a single slip line part overnight due to chafe at the ring. A second downside is that passing the slip line is a lot more trouble than dropping a bowline onto a cleat and taking up the slack on board, particularly on a windy day. For a slip rope, a long length of line is typically carried or passed ashore. While the slack is being hove past the cleat and handed back, the yacht has blown away and the skipper is left with a red face. All this being said, there is much to recommend the system. In any case, if this is how they all do it, perhaps it's best to go with the flow.

The slip rope really comes into its own when a short-handed yacht is leaving a berth, off which she is being blown by a stiff wind. Nobody wants to be left behind, so the trick is to rig a bow and a stern slip rope to replace the single lines already there, bring all the rest on board, then slip the last two when everyone is securely on deck. Rigging slip ropes when the yacht is being blown on is a total waste of time. When an examiner sees this, he starts to wonder about the candidate's real-life experience.

Stopping the vessel

Sometimes, you need to stop the boat with a rope:

- Always lead the rope from abaft your pivot point, otherwise your stern will swing out as your way comes off.
- Make fast the bight on board, and step ashore with a reasonable supply of line as the boat goes by.
- Snatch a turn around a strong cleat and let the line surge around it, applying steadily more pull as the boat slows down. You can stop quite a heavy vessel in a few yards like this, but if you attempt to stop her dead, something will break. The potential energy of 7 tons proceeding at 3 knots is phenomenal. Dissipated over a short distance it is readily controlled by a competent infant, but if you snub the line off short, the energy available would comfortably lift an automobile. It will lift your cleats as well, if the rope doesn't snap first.

Towing

Ideally, you should attach a tow rope to the towing vessel in the vicinity of her pivot point. Only in this way can full manoeuvrability be retained. If you are supplying the tow with your yacht, this is probably going to be impossible, because of your backstays and the general lack of strong points in the desired area. Towing is therefore best done from the stern, but it must be from the centre. You are usually left with no choice but to rig a strop between the quarter cleats or fairleads and attach the tow line to the bight of this, normally with a bowline. If the sea is rough, you may find your cleats taking severe punishment. If so, take lines from them to the primary winches and grind them forward against the pull. That will firm them up enough to cope with most circumstances. Suspending a weight from the bight of the tow line may help take out some of the snatch.

ROPES AND ROPEWORK

Rigging a bridle to take a tow line serves not only to carry the attachment clear of any encumbrances, it also divides the load between two attachment points. The system works well for a dinghy, but is even more important when towing another yacht.

When you, yourself, are under tow, you should arrange to lead the line over the bows, but watch out for chafe. You'll certainly have to rig some sort of chafing gear.

A long plastic pipe is best, but on an extended tow this may disintegrate. If the chips are really down and you are running out of gear, you may have to sacrifice your plumbing system. Toilet piping is the best chafing gear yet devised by man. Second-hand it leaves something to be desired socially, but by this time such fine considerations will have been left behind.

If you are being towed by a powerful vessel, your cleats or foredeck samson posts will soon be under the severest strain. Just as when you are towing, they should be winched up tight; indeed, anything you can do to spread the load round the ship will be desirable. If you have a keel-stepped mast, you can put your tow line round that. Don't try this in a seaway, though, if your spar is stepped on deck, or you may join the ranks of those who aggravated their misfortune with a rapid dismasting.

Make fast the tow line (yours, for preference, or you may come in for a more serious salvage claim), and settle down to steer the boat straight at the stern of the towing craft. If your vessel is small enough, keep any movable weight (like your crew) as far aft as possible, and maintain communication – even if it's only visual – with the towing vessel at all times.

Towing in harbour is best done with both craft alongside one another, tied together with good spring lines (see overleaf). Steering may not be ideal, but at least the tug can stop without receiving the tow in his cockpit.

If you are involved in a rescue operation, try to agree a fee beforehand, if payment seems appropriate. Failure to do so could involve you or your insurers in some very heavy expense.

Towing with the dinghy

In harbour, it pays to tow alongside so you can stop the yacht. Secure the dinghy tightly under the quarter (four ropes, complete with springs) with the outboard motor propeller abaft the yacht's rudder. That way the dinghy can steer the yacht by shoving her stern around until she has enough way on to gain control herself. If the prop is forward of the rudder, this won't happen. Towing ahead, use a bridle as usual, but bear in mind that the yacht has huge inertia compared with the dinghy. This creates some odd situations. Don't think about steering with the dinghy as such. Just point the outboard propeller in the way you want to turn and don't worry where the dinghy seems to be pointing. Once you have good way on, keep in line with the yacht's bows and let her helmsman do the steering.

SKIPPER'S TIP

Living with the neighbours

Make sure your crew always cross another boat forward of the mast, and tell them to be aware of noise. A twanged shroud or a clumsy boot on a stowed booming-out pole when you creep back aboard at closing time will not endear your team to anyone. Keep it quiet is the watchword!

Locks can seem hairy places – and some are! However, careful line tending generally keeps things in order.

ANCHORING

8

The onset of large-scale marina development has led to a decline in anchoring as an everyday occurrence. Serious cruising yachts still do it regularly, but a growing number of marina-hoppers from the Western world's great yachting centres hardly anchor at all. This is an unmitigated blessing because it keeps the wilder harbours, rivers and roadsteads clear of gleaming fleets.

During our time ocean cruising, my wife and I spent literally hundreds of nights and days lying to various types of ground tackle in different boats. I can count on one hand the occasions on which we dragged, and they were all predictable. The right tackle well deployed is always a better bet than a mooring of unknown quality.

Anchors do not work by virtue of their weight alone. They sink their teeth into the seabed, and won't let go until you are ready to wrest them clear. Their mass is built up largely to assist them in doing this. All anchors dig in by being pulled along the bottom in as horizontal a direction as can conveniently be achieved. Heaving the hook over the bow and tying off the rode when the ironmongery hits the ground serves no purpose at all. The minimum effective length of chain cable for all practical anchoring is three times the depth of the water (Fig 8.1). This is known as a 3:1 scope; ideally it should be increased to at least 5:1 if you are

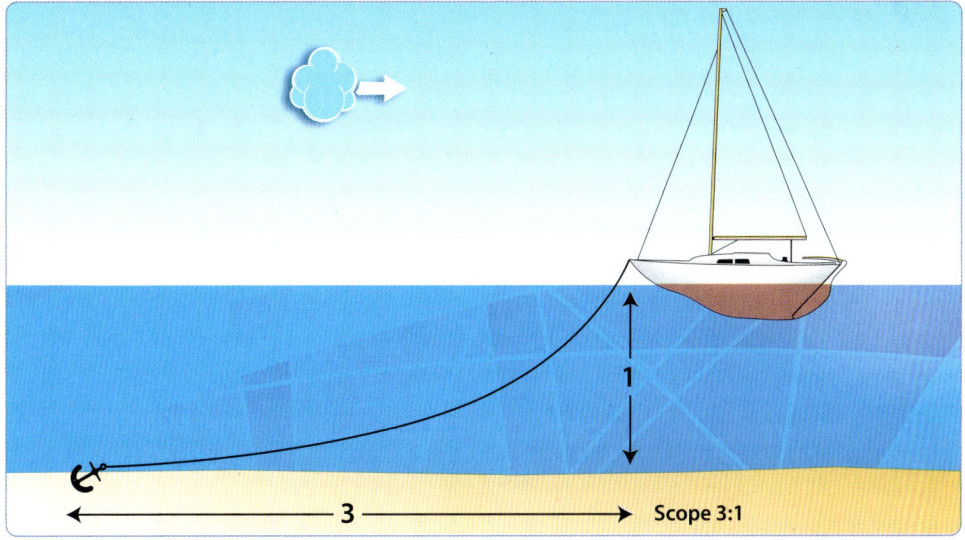

Fig 8.1 Classical anchoring.

anchoring on a nylon warp. If circumstances allow it, longer scopes are a first-class insurance against dragging. If the water is shallow, it's worth adding the height of the bow to the water depth before calculating how much cable to let go. A 5ft freeboard in 10ft of water makes a substantial difference.

A big anchor well dug in on a 10:1 scope of chain is virtually unshiftable, especially if you weight the cable, but more of that later.

Holding ground

An anchor is only as good as the substrate you are asking it to take hold of. Firm sand promises a fair grip and offers the advantage of clean ground tackle when you come to weigh. Don't expect the world from soft sand, and don't attempt to anchor on rock unless your life depends upon it and no other option is available. Your hook either won't hold at all or, if you are lucky (or perhaps unlucky, depending upon your circumstances), it will become irreversibly jammed in a crevice. There it will stay, and you will stay with it if you are using chain cable. If a rode is allowed to touch a rock, or a coral bottom particularly, it will chafe through in short order and you'll be on your way.

Mud and clay, or clay and sand, are the best holding grounds of all. I once sat out a very serious blow at the end of a long scope of chain with my CQR (see below) working its way steadily deeper and deeper into blue clay. It worked so well that when we wanted to leave, nothing we could do would pluck the hook out. The diver subsequently hired assured me that he had to dig to find it!

Always beware of foul ground. It is sometimes given a mention on the chart, but often you must use your commonsense. Any ancient harbour, or areas in the vicinity of long-term boatyards, should not be used for anchoring. The bottom will be cluttered up with all sorts of rubbish, including redundant mooring cables. If you must anchor there, always use a tripping line (see p. 84).

Types of anchor

The CQR or plough

When the plough anchor made its apocryphal first appearance aboard seaplanes before World War II, it was the best burying anchor ever seen. It remained the hook of choice for cruising sailors for many decades and is still a sound option today. It is fairly easy to stow and in its 'genuine CQR' form (try running the letters together; they stand for 'secure') it is superbly forged, richly galvanised and will give a lifetime of trouble-free service as a best bower. It isn't as good as a fisherman anchor in kelp, but otherwise it is only beaten by some of the modern penetrating and burying anchors. Beware fake CQRs. There are lots of these around. They are false gold, and may prove equally treacherous.

ANCHORING

The Bruce anchor

This fine piece of hardware was developed for oil platforms. It holds as well as a CQR when things are going its way, and works better than most on a short scope. It is, however, a brute to stow, except in a permanent bow roller arrangement. You may feel that this is unsatisfactory for a number of reasons, including the stowage of a considerable weight exactly where no sane person would want it, but many reasonable folk find the compromise is worth it. At least you don't have to totter around the foredeck carrying 50lb (22kg) of muddy old iron every time you get under way. For my own 14-ton long-keeled yacht I use a 30kg Bruce and 45 fathoms of ⅜in (10mm) chain. It may sound a lot of tackle and it is, but the hook stows perfectly on the bow and I never worry as I tuck myself into my bunk with the wind howling.

The author's Bruce anchor shows its hand as it brings up a clawful of good, solid mud. It was never going to drag, dug in like that.

The Danforth anchor

This exhibits the obvious property of stowing flat. It also holds well in sand of indifferent quality. For these reasons it is a useful extra anchor to keep aboard. Some people favour it as a kedge. The Fortress anchor looks similar to a Danforth, but is forged from a light alloy and has a good reputation for holding power. It is thus ideal as a kedge, because these are often stowed in awkward places and nobody wants to put his back out struggling with a heavy anchor when things are hectic.

The spade anchor

The spade anchor as a generic term represents a shopful of patent anchors that have arisen to challenge the CQR and Bruce as the champions. I like the actual proprietary 'Spade', because, while it does have amazing holding power for its weight, it has the additional benefit that you can readily remove the shank from the business end. This makes it ideal for anyone sensible enough to want a really useful kedge but who is strapped for space to stow it. Other variants are solid and include the highly recommended 'Rocna', the 'Bugel', the 'Mason Supreme' from New Zealand and the 'Sword' from the makers of Spade. Some are better than others, but all claim to supersede the plough and the Bruce.

The fisherman anchor

The fisherman anchor is much maligned, yet much misunderstood. So long as it is well designed, this traditional anchor form is still one of the finest anchors available for larger craft of the heavy displacement persuasion. It doesn't work very well at much less than 60lb (27kg) and it needs to be used with chain, but given these parameters, it can grab amazingly well in normal holding grounds, as well as having the edge over all other forms in weedy, kelpy bottoms.

When unstocked, it takes up an unexpectedly small amount of space. The 20-ton traditional cutter I sailed from 1998 to 2010 favoured an 85lb (approx 40kg) fisherman and ⁷⁄₁₆in (11mm) chain. With plenty of scope, the arrangement has never been known to let her down.

Conclusions

My own subjective experience of other types of anchor may be of interest. The combination of a 35lb CQR or Bruce and plenty of ⅜in (10mm) chain has worked flawlessly on cruising yachts of up to 35ft (10.6m). A 30kg Bruce and ⅜in chain has delivered similarly peerless performance on my current 44-footer. One can only speak as one finds, and while the modern Rocna and the rest may score more points in magazine tests, I have found no reason to doubt my rather older-style arrangements. I may add that when asked recently how many nights I had spent at anchor, I lost count at 1,000. Bigger anchors work better than smaller ones of a given type, because their weight helps them to dig in, and all cruising vessels should carry at least two. Speak to the anchor manufacturer rather than the boat-builder to determine the correct size for your requirements. Many of today's production craft are delivered with ground tackle that couldn't be expected to hold a sailboard, let alone 5 tons of yacht.

Types of cable

Chain

The great advantage of chain over nylon rope is its weight. When a boat is riding to a chain, the cable sags into a curve called a *catenary*. As a result, the pull delivered to the hook is more horizontal. A spin-off from this is that you can lie to the shortest possible scope. The weight of the chain also produces a damping effect on the boat's tendency to surge around. This not only keeps her quiet, it also reduces her capacity for plucking the anchor out of the bottom. Magazine tests in the new millennium have suggested that these benefits are illusory and that catenary has no effect on holding power. I would rather set my years of experience in the school of hard knocks against these apparently empirical studies. In real life, chain undoubtedly damps a boat's tendency to surge from side to side with a tug on the hook at the end of every swing. The catenary might occasionally be pulled out straight in lighter cable in shallow water (⁵⁄₁₆in or 8mm is marginal for any serious boat of over 30ft), but it happens rarely and only in big winds. The rest of the time, the catenary is doing its job. Chain cable is, of course, totally chafe-resistant, both at the seabed and at the bow fairlead. It also self-stows if the locker is deep enough, and is comparatively easy to scrub clean.

To set against all these plus factors, chain is heavy to carry on board and expensive. It also requires regalvanising every ten years or so. While its strength is normally above suspicion, it can allow snubbing to occur in extreme conditions. This will be considered under 'Storm anchoring' (see p. 86).

The final drawback of chain is that it is noisy at the stemhead. Long-term cruisers often solve this problem by rigging a short nylon rope 'snubber' hooked into the bight of the cable 'between wind and water'. This is made fast on deck so as to take the strain.

The cable above the hook is allowed to droop in a short bight, while it is left made fast on deck so that in the event of the strop chafing through, nothing is lost but a short piece of rope.

Nylon rope

The strength of nylon rope, together with its remarkable elastic properties, makes it ideal for anchor rode. The tendency it has to chafe, as noted above, must be kept constantly in mind. At deck level a dedicated length of plastic hose, cut to allow it to slip on to the bight, often does the trick. At the business end, a minimum of 2½ fathoms (4.5m) of chain should be rigged between the rode and the anchor – the more chain the better. The weight of the chain will improve the angle of pull, and chafe at the seabed will be neutralised.

Scopes of rode should be as long as convenient at all times, and the light weight of the material increases your incentive to do the right thing. Unless you have a good windlass, the opposite is true with chain, where the far-sighted mariner often ends up compromising what he knows should be laid on account of the joys in store when the time comes to lug it all back in again.

The loss of the damping effect of chain is to some extent compensated by the extreme spring of the nylon, which keeps snatching loads on the anchor to a minimum.

Weighting the cable

Sometimes there simply isn't enough room to lay the scope you'd otherwise choose. This can happen in a tight river where 2:1 or 2½:1 is the best you can safely manage, or it may occur in a gale in an open anchorage, when you would like to lay out 8:1 or 9:1, but to do so would bring you too close to another boat.

In such cases it is well worth weighting down the bight of your cable, be it warp or chain (Fig 8.2, p. 78). Proprietary chunks of custom-made gear used to be available under such imaginative brand names as 'chum' or 'angel'. If you can't lay your hands on a modern 'Anchor Buddy', rig a 56lb (25kg) scale weight to a big shackle and lower that down the cable until it is about halfway to the seabed. Beware of chafe if the cable is nylon. Visit www.youtube.com/watch?v=ZPskVtbIrfg for more on anchor weights.

In the absence of any prepared heavy item, you can always press that broken-down outboard engine into service, or lash together half a dozen house-bricks.

Preparing the anchor weight on the author's yacht. You may not be lucky enough to have one of these wonderful 1930s devices, but any heavy weight slung down the chain will work as well.

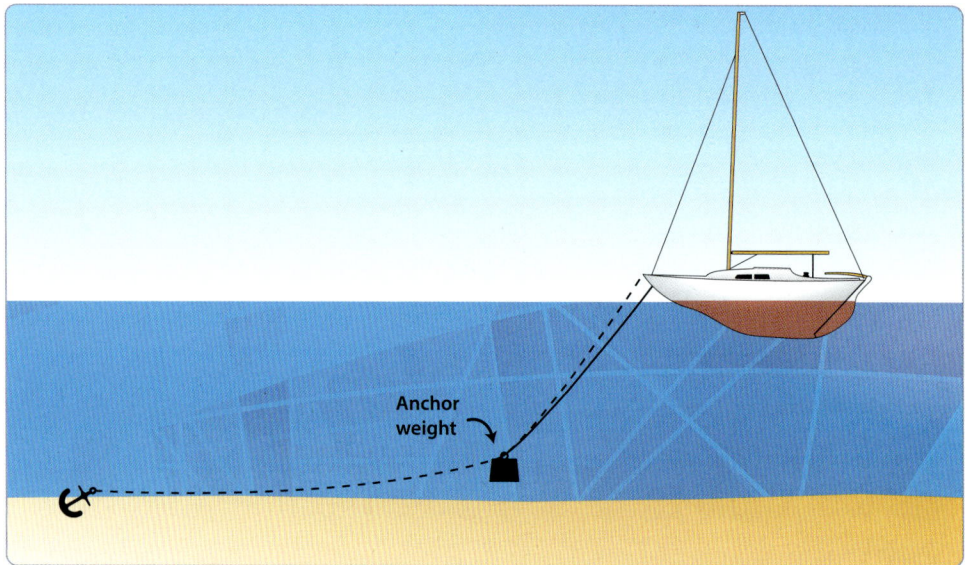

Fig 8.2 Weighting the cable. The weight depresses the catenary of the cable, giving the anchor a better angle at which to take hold.

Selecting an anchorage

Shelter is the prime consideration when selecting an anchorage, closely followed by good holding ground (Fig 8.3). Since the right tackle will hold the boat in any wind within reason, it is the sea from which you require protection. I have lain in comfort with a whole ocean blowing two and a half thousand miles of tradewind sea my way, with no more protection than a coral reef, just awash, a hundred yards to windward. Apart from the thrumming of the breeze in the rigging, it was so calm you could have been on the Thames.

A bay with a couple of good headlands provides fine shelter in an offshore breeze, but always be sure that what begins as 'offshore' is going to stay that way. The last thing you want is to find your idyll turned into a breaking lee shore at two in the morning.

The ideal depth for anchoring would be sufficient to float you with at least half your draught for a safety margin all round. This is often not practicable. Nevertheless, you should avoid anchoring in deeper water than is absolutely necessary because your scope options will be less if you do. Besides, it will mean more gear to lift when the time comes. Considerations of tidal rise will often enter into this decision, but those are dealt with in Chapter 14.

When picking your spot to let go, bear in mind your probable swinging circle. This is more important with regard to shoals than it is to other boats. Unless they are of a radically different form from your own, you should swing in some sort of unison unless some are anchored on rope. Don't take chances, even so, particularly in tidal rivers. With the wind against the tide, anything can happen, and it often does.

ANCHORING

Fig 8.3 A safe anchorage – perfect shelter in winds from NNW to SSW; safe from N to S through W. (Note the useful transit to check the anchor is holding.)

Laying an anchor

The success of anchoring rests in the way the cable is laid, the manoeuvring of the boat and the relationship between the two. The crucial thing to remember about setting an anchor is that it doesn't do the job by itself. Its shape has been developed so that when pulled along the seabed it will roll over and get cracking, but if no one gives it a tug it can only lie there until a real strain is exerted. Then it may dig in, or it may not, depending upon the sort of pull the boat delivers, and by that time you are probably tucked up in your bunk, hoping for the best.

Under power

Nowadays most people anchor under power. Easy enough. First, head the boat up to the wind, the tide, or to seaward if she finds herself in an open roadstead where an onshore breeze may become a contingency. As soon as she has lost way over the ground, drop the anchor, or lower it if it's light enough. When it's on the bottom, check the run of the cable and steer away astern, laying cable in a straight line as you go. Because an anchor won't generally dig in at high speeds, put the engine out of gear when the chosen scope has nearly all run out over the roller, and let the boat just carry her way astern.

Next snub the cable and let the yacht's weight pull out any bights that may have been laid on the seabed as she goes. Once the cable has been straightened, the foredeck crew will see it rising from the water. This demonstrates that the anchor is taking a nibble at the substratum.

Now comes the magic. Rather than allowing the yacht to imagine she's anchored, and ride forward under the effect of the weight of cable, put the engine half astern as the last of her way comes off. After a few seconds she will begin to move slowly astern again as the hook works into the bottom. If she travels any distance, the anchor is skating over the ground, and the yacht must be slowed down to give it a chance. In all probability, however, it will take; if it doesn't, heave it up and try again. The yacht will come to rest with the propeller still turning astern and the cable stretching out ahead at a shallow angle.

At this point you should take a critical look around you to see if you're dragging the pick through the clay. The best method of being sure is to use beam transits. Any two items will do. A tree and a courting couple will serve beautifully, so long as the human element isn't moving around too much. At night, a star can profitably be lined up with an illuminated public convenience or anything else nearer to you than the star itself.

If your transits are stationary, put on a few more revolutions to make sure. The couple will slide away from the tree slightly as the boat leans harder on her cable, then they may well creep back into the shade as the yacht springs back a few feet under the weight of the catenary. As soon as you are convinced, you can throttle down the engine and hoist the anchor ball. You'll sleep soundly now, because if the anchor can stand the pull of your engine, it can certainly cope with most of what the weather can throw at you.

Under sail

Sailing the anchor in at the end of a passage is particularly satisfying, especially if the whole trip has been made without groping for the diesel. However, if you are at all tight for space, you'll have to sum up your options carefully, because unlike the mariner anchoring under power, the sailor may only have a single chance.

The shrewd operator will already be aware that tidal stream often poses the question, 'Will the mainsail fill or spill when I am lying to my anchor?' Just as in a mooring situation, the answer dictates whether or not the main can be carried through the manoeuvre. However, when the current does not command your actions, the most positive method is to approach

When anchoring in Mediterranean harbours, note the angle of everyone else's anchor chains/warps and lay yours in the same direction, as far out as you can.

Tight for space. Everything looked fine when the second yacht anchored, but by not allowing enough swinging room for all eventualities, these two are now drifting together – just what nobody wants at midnight!

sailing downwind under headsail only, with the main stowed. This method is more hairy than some sailors have stomach for. I can understand this, but if you want to be sure, and you've space enough to do it, why not give it a go?

Approach from upwind, let go the anchor where you want it to lie, then sail on, spilling wind from the jib to keep your speed within sensible bounds. After the cable has been snubbed off you'll be in no doubt that the hook is holding because the yacht will suddenly swing round and lie head up to the breeze with the jib flogging.

If you can't cope with the sudden-death qualities of this method, the truly civilised technique for digging in the hook, if conditions allow, is this: lower your headsail early, luff exactly head-to-wind, drop anchor as the boat loses the last of her way, then physically push out the main boom on a slack sheet and sternboard dead downwind until you have laid out your desired scope of cable. The yacht's bows will dip as this is snubbed off and the anchor takes hold, leaving you confident of success. It's elegant, it needs skill and practice, but as with Alice's Thanksgiving Dinner, 'it can't be beat'.

Should neither of these methods prove practicable, you will need to rely upon the inertia of the boat alone to dig in the anchor. If this is going to be the way of things, you'll manage better if you drop all sails as the anchor is let go. This is because your bow could well fall far enough off the wind to fill the main before the hook has dug in, resulting in an embarrassing cruise round the anchorage with 20 fathoms of chain hanging over the bow.

In circumstances where you can't risk lowering all your canvas, bear in mind that the windage of a flogging headsail will aggravate any tendency to blow off. So, even if it seems more prudent to leave the main up, you are still better off dropping the jib. The folks assembled on the foredeck to handle the ground tackle will love you for your care and consideration, and if things do go wrong, rehoisting it in a hurry is easy. Again, a certain amount of space is required.

Anchoring under sail in the brave new world of the reliable auxiliary has one significant difference from laying a hook with no certainty of available power. If your engine doesn't work, or you are a real sailor who doesn't have one at all, ignore the following advice.

For the rest of us, there will always be occasions when light airs have made it impossible to sail in the hook to our satisfaction. If serious wind is expected in the near future, it is worth swallowing your pride and digging the beast in under power just before bedtime. Otherwise you'll wake at 0400 to the first flurry of rain and lie there wondering whether or not you should go on deck, 'just to make sure'.

SKIPPER'S TIP

'Backing off' in a sailing yacht

Some boats will keep their heads up to the wind while 'backing off' from an anchor if you sheet the main hard in. The foredeck crew can help hold her head-to-wind by carefully checking the cable as it runs out. This works well under mizzen alone in a ketch or a yawl. It's a treat in a schooner under mainsail. Don't forget that as soon as the boat begins to sternboard, she is steering astern as surely as if she were under power, so her rudder operates in reverse.

Weighing anchor

Under power

When there is no wind or tide to speak of, you can pull most yachts up to their anchor either by using the windlass or by manual heave-ho. If you opt for 'Armstrong's patent', take the strain steadily to get the boat moving. Once her inertia is overcome, the cable will rattle in merrily enough. On occasions when you have wind, tide or sea to contend with, motoring carefully towards the hook will ease life remarkably for the foredeck gang. A windlass can also benefit from some gentle assistance from the propeller.

When the cable is 'up and down', the vertical pull will normally lift the anchor clear of its hold. If it doesn't, and neither you nor your windlass can heave it clear, try motoring half astern. This does the trick on most occasions. Sometimes, however, the pick is so firmly in that you must use the whole boat to break it out. Ease away enough cable to enable you to take a run at the hook, then go full ahead, gathering slack as you approach the anchor. When the cable is nearly up and down, snub it off, either with the windlass or around a cleat or post. The inertia of the whole boat plus her engine power is now brought to bear on the anchor, which will come clear unless it is fouled.

ANCHORING

Sailing out your anchor

The usual criteria of wind and tide apply. If you are lying to the tide, with the wind abaft the beam, the job is easy. Pull up a headsail, sheet in, then sail up to and over the anchor, gathering slack as though you were breaking it out under power. As you sail over it, snub the chain and let the boat do the work.

When there is no tide, or the tide is with the breeze, you'll have to hoist the main, letting it spill wind until you've hauled the boat up to the hook and broken it out by main force. If you've no windlass and the pick won't budge, hitch a spare halyard on to the bight of the cable (rolling hitch) and lead it to a winch. If your cable is of rope, lead it to your biggest sheet winch. When the anchor breaks out, run up a headsail and off you go.

There is nothing to stop you having a jib hoisted as you weigh anchor, except the fact that it gets in the way. If instant control is critical, you'll just have to put up with this.

Finally, where you have searoom in abundance, there is no reason not to heave the anchor up with all your sails stowed. It's neat, and it totally defuses the traumas associated with flogging sails. After the hook is aboard and you have washed down, set a genoa, bring the boat up on to a close-reach, hoist the main and away you go.

Fouled anchors

So long as it stays shackled to its cable, which it will if you have wired the shackle properly, there are only two things that can go wrong with an anchor on the seabed. It can become fouled, either by its own cable around a spare fluke (as can happen with a fisherman) or by some foreign body neutralising its effectiveness (such as a large baked-bean can impaled on the fluke of a CQR). These difficulties, together with excess of seaweed, will cause the anchor to fail in its duties. The only cure is to heave it up, clear it, and try again.

The other type of fouling has the opposite effect. An anchor is designed to grab the ooze, but given half a chance it will grab an undersea cable even more efficiently. Anchors are also prone to embracing wrecks, bedsteads, drowned motor cars and anything else they can lay their flukes on. These problems are best avoided by not anchoring in foul ground, but should you be caught out, or just plain unlucky, your actions are as follows:

- Heave up using any available power to try and bring the anchor, plus its obstruction, within reach from deck or dinghy. When you can grapple the ground-chain, pass a rope around it and make both ends fast on board.
- Lower away the anchor until the weight of the ground-chain comes on to your rope and the hook falls clear. You are now moored to the ground-chain by a doubled-back rope.
- Let go one end of your rope, pull it aboard from the other, and you are on your way. This method is especially useful when you foul someone else's anchor in a crowded harbour.

If the above doesn't work, your last hope – short of a swim – is to use the dinghy to lower a bight of chain down your anchor cable with both ends aboard. When the chain reaches the anchor it will sometimes slide down the shank until it reaches the crown. If it is then pulled vertically upwards it will, in ideal circumstances, 'capsize' the anchor, lifting it clear of the obstruction. Don't expect the world from this, but it's worth a try before you call in the diver.

If the water is reasonably warm and less than about 20ft (6m) deep, a fit person equipped with mask, snorkel and flippers has an excellent chance of clearing his own anchor. Every yacht should carry this equipment. If you don't have it, or you can't swim well enough, you'll have to pay for the professionals.

> **SKIPPER'S TIP**
>
> ### Trip lines
>
> When in doubt, rig a trip line from the crown of your anchor. The other end is either secured to a small buoy (an old fender from the local skip will do) or brought back on board. Rig the line before you anchor, then if your pick fouls you can pull it clean by capsizing it with the tripping line. Be careful about the length of the line. Be aware of the danger of wrapping it around your propeller shaft, and if you decide to bring it back to the stem to avoid the messiness of an anchor buoy, watch out for it winding itself round the anchor chain as you swing. If it does this too many times, it won't work when you want it. I've even known one shorten itself so much through this that it self-tripped.
>
> Tripping lines are a thorough-going nuisance, but occasionally it is sensible to rig one despite the trouble they can bring.

Recovering an anchor that has been well and truly fouled on an underwater cable. Note the tripping line, which is rigged to capsize the anchor and free it.

Anchoring stern- or bow-to

In small harbours, or exceptionally steep-to anchorages, it can save space and increase security if boats lay an anchor and moor between it and the harbour wall – or a convenient rock or tree. A lot of this goes on in Scandinavian anchorages in areas of little tidal rise, and it was the standard method in Mediterranean harbours before the arrival of haul-off moorings (see p. 50). Baltic and Norwegian yachts often carry a dedicated kedge warp on a reel aft for this alone.

End-on anchoring:
1 Bow-to Baltic berthing is a breeze with a pulpit ladder.
2 Anchoring stern-to in the Med, it's critical to establish clear communication between bow and stern. Nothing disappoints a skipper so much as having the hook snubbed when he's backing in and still 10 feet short of the dock.
3 A webbing reel makes a useful kedge warp where the kedge is used on a regular basis to lie bow- or stern-to. It is especially favoured in the Baltic.

Given a convenient kedge set up, 'bow-to' is far easier to execute. Just drive in, bung the kedge over when you're a few boat's lengths out – the further the better – and set it up after the bow is secured to the tree. 'Stern-to' mooring is a real test of your combined seamanship skills, but has the potential safety benefit of using the bower anchor. The only advice I would offer is general: don't forget your fenders if other yachts are involved, think creatively about the effect that propwalk and cross-winds are likely to have on your manoeuvre, station competent people at the windlass, and communicate with them all the time. They can help keep you in line on your approach by carefully surging the cable, but they can ruin your chances utterly by snubbing it too soon.

Kedging off

When you've run aground and you can't get off any other way, lay out the heaviest anchor you can handle, as far to seaward as you can manage to propel the dinghy. Lead the warp to your most powerful winch from either bow or stern, depending upon which way you think you're most likely to come off, and haul her back into deep water. In extreme cases, you may need to reduce draught by lightening the boat (carrying stores ashore, emptying water tanks, etc) or by inducing a heel. The most dramatic way of reducing draught is to send a snatch block aloft on a halyard (the spinnaker halyard for preference, because of its universal swivel), with the bight of the kedge warp through it. The warp is then led through turning blocks to the winch (the genoa fairlead block is often ideal). When you start winding, the boat will be laid over as well as hauled away. It often works and the drama is tremendous value for any onlookers.

Storm anchoring

When you fear your best bower and your maximum scope aren't going to be enough, you'll have to lay out your number two anchor on the end of your kedge warp. Lay it from the dinghy, or use the yacht if time and circumstances permit. Take it as far out as you can, so that the yacht is at the apex of a 'V' formed by the two anchor cables.

Anchored in perfect shelter in a hard breeze. Plenty of scope on the cable. No worries at all.

Sailing out your anchor

The usual criteria of wind and tide apply. If you are lying to the tide, with the wind abaft the beam, the job is easy. Pull up a headsail, sheet in, then sail up to and over the anchor, gathering slack as though you were breaking it out under power. As you sail over it, snub the chain and let the boat do the work.

When there is no tide, or the tide is with the breeze, you'll have to hoist the main, letting it spill wind until you've hauled the boat up to the hook and broken it out by main force. If you've no windlass and the pick won't budge, hitch a spare halyard on to the bight of the cable (rolling hitch) and lead it to a winch. If your cable is of rope, lead it to your biggest sheet winch. When the anchor breaks out, run up a headsail and off you go.

There is nothing to stop you having a jib hoisted as you weigh anchor, except the fact that it gets in the way. If instant control is critical, you'll just have to put up with this.

Finally, where you have searoom in abundance, there is no reason not to heave the anchor up with all your sails stowed. It's neat, and it totally defuses the traumas associated with flogging sails. After the hook is aboard and you have washed down, set a genoa, bring the boat up on to a close-reach, hoist the main and away you go.

Fouled anchors

So long as it stays shackled to its cable, which it will if you have wired the shackle properly, there are only two things that can go wrong with an anchor on the seabed. It can become fouled, either by its own cable around a spare fluke (as can happen with a fisherman) or by some foreign body neutralising its effectiveness (such as a large baked-bean can impaled on the fluke of a CQR). These difficulties, together with excess of seaweed, will cause the anchor to fail in its duties. The only cure is to heave it up, clear it, and try again.

The other type of fouling has the opposite effect. An anchor is designed to grab the ooze, but given half a chance it will grab an undersea cable even more efficiently. Anchors are also prone to embracing wrecks, bedsteads, drowned motor cars and anything else they can lay their flukes on. These problems are best avoided by not anchoring in foul ground, but should you be caught out, or just plain unlucky, your actions are as follows:

- Heave up using any available power to try and bring the anchor, plus its obstruction, within reach from deck or dinghy. When you can grapple the ground-chain, pass a rope around it and make both ends fast on board.
- Lower away the anchor until the weight of the ground-chain comes on to your rope and the hook falls clear. You are now moored to the ground-chain by a doubled-back rope.
- Let go one end of your rope, pull it aboard from the other, and you are on your way. This method is especially useful when you foul someone else's anchor in a crowded harbour.

If the above doesn't work, your last hope – short of a swim – is to use the dinghy to lower a bight of chain down your anchor cable with both ends aboard. When the chain reaches the anchor it will sometimes slide down the shank until it reaches the crown. If it is then pulled vertically upwards it will, in ideal circumstances, 'capsize' the anchor, lifting it clear of the obstruction. Don't expect the world from this, but it's worth a try before you call in the diver.

If the water is reasonably warm and less than about 20ft (6m) deep, a fit person equipped with mask, snorkel and flippers has an excellent chance of clearing his own anchor. Every yacht should carry this equipment. If you don't have it, or you can't swim well enough, you'll have to pay for the professionals.

 SKIPPER'S TIP

Trip lines

When in doubt, rig a trip line from the crown of your anchor. The other end is either secured to a small buoy (an old fender from the local skip will do) or brought back on board. Rig the line before you anchor, then if your pick fouls you can pull it clean by capsizing it with the tripping line. Be careful about the length of the line. Be aware of the danger of wrapping it around your propeller shaft, and if you decide to bring it back to the stem to avoid the messiness of an anchor buoy, watch out for it winding itself round the anchor chain as you swing. If it does this too many times, it won't work when you want it. I've even known one shorten itself so much through this that it self-tripped.

Tripping lines are a thorough-going nuisance, but occasionally it is sensible to rig one despite the trouble they can bring.

Recovering an anchor that has been well and truly fouled on an underwater cable. Note the tripping line, which is rigged to capsize the anchor and free it.

ANCHORING

Anchoring stern- or bow-to

In small harbours, or exceptionally steep-to anchorages, it can save space and increase security if boats lay an anchor and moor between it and the harbour wall – or a convenient rock or tree. A lot of this goes on in Scandinavian anchorages in areas of little tidal rise, and it was the standard method in Mediterranean harbours before the arrival of haul-off moorings (see p. 50). Baltic and Norwegian yachts often carry a dedicated kedge warp on a reel aft for this alone.

End-on anchoring:
1 Bow-to Baltic berthing is a breeze with a pulpit ladder.
2 Anchoring stern-to in the Med, it's critical to establish clear communication between bow and stern. Nothing disappoints a skipper so much as having the hook snubbed when he's backing in and still 10 feet short of the dock.
3 A webbing reel makes a useful kedge warp where the kedge is used on a regular basis to lie bow- or stern-to. It is especially favoured in the Baltic.

Given a convenient kedge set up, 'bow-to' is far easier to execute. Just drive in, bung the kedge over when you're a few boat's lengths out – the further the better – and set it up after the bow is secured to the tree. 'Stern-to' mooring is a real test of your combined seamanship skills, but has the potential safety benefit of using the bower anchor. The only advice I would offer is general: don't forget your fenders if other yachts are involved, think creatively about the effect that propwalk and cross-winds are likely to have on your manoeuvre, station competent people at the windlass, and communicate with them all the time. They can help keep you in line on your approach by carefully surging the cable, but they can ruin your chances utterly by snubbing it too soon.

Kedging off

When you've run aground and you can't get off any other way, lay out the heaviest anchor you can handle, as far to seaward as you can manage to propel the dinghy. Lead the warp to your most powerful winch from either bow or stern, depending upon which way you think you're most likely to come off, and haul her back into deep water. In extreme cases, you may need to reduce draught by lightening the boat (carrying stores ashore, emptying water tanks, etc) or by inducing a heel. The most dramatic way of reducing draught is to send a snatch block aloft on a halyard (the spinnaker halyard for preference, because of its universal swivel), with the bight of the kedge warp through it. The warp is then led through turning blocks to the winch (the genoa fairlead block is often ideal). When you start winding, the boat will be laid over as well as hauled away. It often works and the drama is tremendous value for any onlookers.

Storm anchoring

When you fear your best bower and your maximum scope aren't going to be enough, you'll have to lay out your number two anchor on the end of your kedge warp. Lay it from the dinghy, or use the yacht if time and circumstances permit. Take it as far out as you can, so that the yacht is at the apex of a 'V' formed by the two anchor cables.

Anchored in perfect shelter in a hard breeze. Plenty of scope on the cable. No worries at all.

Once the blow is really happening, even up the strain on the two hooks. If the wind is expected to shift significantly, buoying the anchors is a useful sophistication because then you can see where they are. This helps you to think creatively about how best to use them from the other end of the warp and the cable.

Alternatively, you can rig two anchors in tandem by attaching an extra one to the bower on the end of a short length of chain. I have no personal experience of this method, but sound commentators have been recommending it for many years.

Chain and rope combinations

In really extreme circumstances, I have known yachts to snub at chain cable even on a 10:1 scope. Snubbing is unacceptable. The answer, if this rarest of situations looks like developing, is to rig a longish length of nylon warp into the bight of the final 50ft (15m) or so of chain. The slack is taken up on the warp and the chain eased out into a bight. The stretch of the nylon now acts as a spring to which the boat lies comparatively quietly. She also benefits from the ultimate security of the chain, which is still there, and the warp is assisted in its job by the weight of the bight, which it must straighten out before its elastic limit is reached. A suitable length of warp ready-equipped with a chain hook should be carried for this. It can also double as the fair-weather 'snubber' mentioned on p. 76.

Keeping the windlass in good shape is vital. I'm grabbing the chance on a quiet day. The anchor cable is secured by a stopper while I'm working.

9 YACHT ENGINES

The most dramatic of the remarkable revolutions in yachting brought about by the great technological advances of the second half of the 20th century is the establishment of the light, totally reliable diesel auxiliary. Gone are the days when we pressed the starter button, hand in mouth, more in hope than in expectation. The petrol marine engine with its vulnerable electrics and lethal fuel is in full retreat. It may be cheap, and it does weigh next to nothing, but its vices are no longer considered acceptable by the majority, at any price.

Today's marine diesels and automotive conversions are the wonder of the age, and nobody should take them for granted. They are the biggest single safety feature on the boat. They will drive us to windward, helped by a deep-reefed mainsail, in the most difficult weather. They will drag our boats off a weather berth that would otherwise smash them to matchwood. They allow us access to marinas and quays where to sail in would be inconvenient in the extreme. They propel us at a useful speed through calms. They lighten our darkness with their associated electrical systems, and they power the electronics that, lamentably, are becoming necessities of life for some sailors. They can even heat the washing-up water. And all they ask is the minimum of tender, loving care.

Basic maintenance

A diesel engine will give year after year of trouble-free running so long as it is regularly supplied with clean fuel, lubricated with clean oil, and cooled by clean water. It will start every time if there are enough amps in the battery to turn it at the required speed and the starter motor and battery have bright, dry terminals.

Routine maintenance as recommended by the manufacturer should therefore be attended to in an attitude of religious dedication. All these tasks will be of a minor nature and are easy for a non-technical person to perform – assuming the boat-builders have used their brains with regard to the engine installation. Acid levels in non-sealed batteries require regular checks to ensure all is well. When this type of accumulator starts needing regular top-ups, it is often a sign that the end of its life is near; engine and gearbox oil levels are simplicity itself to monitor, but bear in mind that some units give a higher reading when the oil is hot than when it is cold.

The engine oil must be changed at the designated intervals. An extra change is recommended immediately before winter if the boat will not be used much, so that the engine rests with clean oil inside. Most yards make life even easier by supplying a dumping point for used oil. The oil filter should be renewed at each oil change and this, too, ought to be a five-minute job.

> **SKIPPER'S TIP**
>
> ### Oil spills
> Be ready and well prepared for oil spills when servicing your engine. If you don't have a drip tray that catches everything, use absorbent pads under the oil and fuel filters if in any doubt at all. The days of acceptable oily bilges are over and discharging oil into the environment is actually illegal in many countries.

Every year, change the seawater pump impeller whether it needs it or not. This too is easy to do. The practice is useful, and too many engine overheats have been caused by old impellers starting to break up just when the unit was supposed to be giving its all. Every two or three years the starter can be removed, checked over, and serviced if required. That should be all it needs.

If you have an old-fashioned stern tube which has a greaser, give it a turn every couple of hours when the engine is running. With the boat at rest and the engine off, turn the greaser down until you feel resistance. You'll be surprised how rarely you need to tighten your stern gland. Many modern boats have zero-maintenance 'deep-sea' or 'drip-free' seals. These feature a rubber bellows that is a vital component of the waterproof integrity of the shaft/hull interface. While generally reliable, the bellows has a finite life, and if it were to fail the results could be drastic. Therefore keep an eye on the unit and check it periodically for elasticity.

Watch your alternator drive-belt tension, and keep all your electrical connections clean and dry, particularly the heavy ones to the starter motor. It's a good idea to remove all these once a year, brighten them up if necessary, then remake them. If there have been any signs of corrosion, a smear of Vaseline after the terminal is tightened up will help. Earth connectors are especially important in this respect. A bad earth can cause no end of intermittent problems, including a starter motor that clicks impotently when all the indications are that it should be turning the engine over.

Whether your engine is cooled by 'raw seawater' or a heat exchanger with a fresh water/antifreeze mixture maintained at the right temperature by seawater, keep an eye on the seawater intake filter. If the engine ever stops ejecting cooling water through its exhaust pipe, or whatever other arrangement it uses, the first place to look for a fault is here. Shut the engine intake seacock, take the lid off the filter or strainer, and withdraw the perforated basket that does the work. This may be clogged with weed, or even mud if you have inadvertently taken the ground in soft stuff. If the filter is clean, suspect a plastic bag or jellyfish sucked into the inlet, but not having reached the filter unit. Open the seacock carefully, and see if water comes in. If it doesn't rush through, remove the pipe at the seacock and try again. If it's still reluctant to gush, open the cock wide and poke a suitable prodder straight through. Be ready to shut it smartly when the excellence of your result manifests itself in a two-foot fountain.

Clean fuel is a vital element in a reliable diesel engine. Make sure that what goes into the tank is pure, with no water content. If in doubt, filter the fuel using a good-quality funnel with a water-stopping gauze trap. Clean out your tanks every so often, and maintain at least two filter units between the tank and the injector pump. These filters should be spruced up regularly, at least a minimum of once a season, and one of them should have a glass bowl to facilitate an instant visual check on the state of affairs. Dirty fuel over a period of time will stop an engine as surely as running the tank dry. Any boat not carrying at least two sets of spare fuel filters is not 'ready for sea'.

Trouble shooting

Flat batteries

All properly organised cruising yachts carry a dedicated engine-starting battery, isolated from all the prodigal extravagances of the domestic supply. In theory it should be impossible for this battery to be flattened, since it will use little of its potential capacity starting a healthy engine, and it is always rapidly topped up to full charge. Any decent battery of suitable size will have more than enough 'starts' in it for all normal and most abnormal circumstances. If the engine won't go after cranking it for ten seconds, then something is wrong and should be investigated. Don't flatten your battery to no purpose. It pays to ship a 'cheap and cheerful' automotive starter battery that is always fully charged. Its dedicated purpose is to start the engine with jump leads when all else has failed. Alternatively, small yachts with only a single battery can ship an automotive emergency car starter pack as a bomb-proof back-up.

A comprehensive, modern battery monitor is an important addition to every yacht's dashboard.

Hand-starting

Theoretically, any engine up to 30 or so horsepower can be hand-started by a healthy adult who means business. Some engines seem to be designed to make this difficult, while certain notable yacht manufacturers install the hardware so that the handle either cannot be inserted, or cannot move through a full circle. The compression of a diesel motor is so great that it cannot normally be turned by hand, much less started, unless the exhaust valves are lifted. Therefore most small engines have decompressors, or valve lifters, fitted to their cylinder heads.

Ideally, an engine is arranged so that its decompressors can be addressed individually, but by no means all manufacturers see the wisdom of this. If all the cylinders of a multi-pot unit have to be brought into compression at the same time by throwing a single lever, even a powerful athlete may find starting the engine from stone-cold something of a struggle. However, in an ideal world, this is not the case, and the sequence of events goes like this:

- All the cylinders are decompressed. Half throttle, or more as recommended, is selected, and any cold-start mechanisms are activated.
- Start winding the handle. If there are two of you, the stronger should wind with both hands, giving it all he's got (like handling the anchor, this is not a job for sexual equality); the other stands by the decompressors.
- When the engine is spinning as fast as you are going to make it, one cylinder is compressed, while you keep winding at full tilt. Any cylinder will do, and it should fire up, though it may not generate enough 'oomph' to turn the engine alone.
- Keep winding, and throw the second decompressor. A three-cylinder engine will almost certainly run by now. The third cylinder (and the fourth if there is one) can be activated at leisure, while the ship's strong man is being resuscitated beside the drinks locker.

Fortunately, such a monumental effort is not always required. It is only rarely that the starter battery is absolutely flat. As soon as the engine makes clear its unwillingness to start, you must stop trying with the starter motor and conserve those residual volts. They are going to save you considerable exertion.

Let's suppose there is no human powerhouse available, or that the engine is a registered recalcitrant. Muscle-power alone won't be enough, but the battery may still be delivering the best part of 12 volts; it's just that it doesn't have that extra kick to cause the diesel vapour to explode in the cylinder. Try this:

- When the decompressed engine is turning as fast as you can make it by hand, activate the starter motor.
- Immediately, throw the decompressors over, while you continue to give both methods of turning the engine all you've got. You'll achieve a result nearly every time.

If your engine cannot be hand-started by you, or anyone else in the probable vicinity, you should always carry a can of ether spray of the type known imaginatively as 'Easistart'. As soon as it becomes clear that the engine is unwilling, desist from wearing out the starter and deploy the chemical weapons. Squirt the stuff into the air intake, preferably while the motor is turning. The combustion chambers will receive such a dangerously explosive mixture that the pistons are belted back down the bores with shocking force. If you don't blow off the cylinder head, the engine will have an excellent chance of doing the honest thing for you. If you can decompress it to help it build up revolutions before going for broke, so much the better.

Overheating

This stops an engine with horrible efficiency. What is worse, it can stop it on an unpleasantly permanent basis given the full opportunity. An overheated engine may seize, or run a bearing, resulting in serious and expensive disintegration. The usual reason for overheating is a failure of seawater circulation, nearly always caused initially by a blockage at the supply end. If your exhaust is water-cooled, you'll know the water supply has failed by the change of tune. Even so, you should always check visually after starting the engine. The most common blockage source is a seacock left off.

If the water stops circulating, refer to the final paragraph on page 89. When water is passing as far as the pump, but not circulating, you probably have a damaged pump impeller. This usually occurs either as a result of overheating following failure to turn on the cock, or a blocked filter. Never go to sea without a spare. They are easy to change, but you may need a pump gasket as well. If you haven't got one, don't despair; cut one out from a piece of stout paper which you have first waxed by rubbing with an old candle.

If water still doesn't circulate, you have a more serious problem. Call in the yard, or buy a book on engine repairs.

Fuel problems

Bleeding the engine

If a diesel engine pegs out under load and it hasn't overheated, there is probably air in the fuel system. The only other likely explanation is that it has suffered some major mechanical failure. There'll be no doubt if that is the cause, because there will be dramatic manifestations in the form of noises, fumes and smells. Fortunately, air in the fuel is far more common. It is also readily dealt with.

Your fuel system usually becomes air-locked because either you have run out of fuel, or you have clogged-up filters as a result of dirty diesel.

It's simple to ascertain whether or not air is your problem. At the end of the fuel chain are the injectors, which are easily recognised. They are on the side of the cylinder head and look something like all-metal spark plugs. Follow the pipes back from them to the fuel injection pump, which is generally bolted to the side of the engine. Inspect this and you'll find one, or possibly two, bolt heads apparently doing nothing much at all. These are the bleed screws. Ease them off a turn or two. If the system is choked with air, bubbles will froth out. The airlock that they indicate must now be systematically expunged. This is achieved surprisingly easily by following the fuel in its pipe all the way from the tank to the cylinders of the engine.

The first filter is usually positioned between the tank and the body of the engine. This filter does most of the work and is often the one that is clogged up. Turn off the fuel tap at the bottom of the tank and take the filter apart, cleaning it out and replacing the disposable element – if there is one – from your well-stocked engineer's stores. This won't take you long if the filter is accessible. Have an old towel by you to mop up the excess diesel, as well as a small plastic container to collect the main spillage. If the filter is inaccessible, I suggest that you either move it or buy a new yacht from a more caring manufacturer, because sooner or later you're going to have to do the job when it really matters.

The top of the filter will have a bleed screw like the one on the pump. Reassemble the filter, turn on the fuel, then ease this away until bubbles start foaming out. If the tank is lower than the filter, you may have to work the small lever on the side of the fuel lift pump (see next paragraph) to induce a flow. When clear diesel runs out, tighten down the screw. The system is now bled this far. If by any chance there is no bleed screw, crack the feed pipe union at the side away from the tank.

YACHT ENGINES

Fig 9.1 Bleeding a diesel engine.

The fuel pipe's next stop is at the lift pump, unless there is more than one pre-filter. The engine usually operates this by mechanical means, but when the main power unit is not functioning, you must turn the engine with the starter motor or by hand (a decompressor helps). If this is unattractive on account of anxiety about your battery or your heart, you can activate it perfectly well with the small lever on one side of it, which enables you to pump fuel manually.

There is usually a final filter between the lift pump and the injector pump. This filter is not often dirty if the first one is working well, but if you have any doubts, strip and clean it anyway. Whether or not you do so, you will certainly have to bleed it in the usual way. From here, the fuel pipe runs to the all-important injector pump. Bleed this as well. Now you are ready to start her up. The injectors will bleed themselves, but it may take some seconds of engine-cranking before they are doing their work successfully.

If you are imprudent enough to run out of diesel, you must go through the same process. You may think you'll never be so stupid as to let this happen, but sooner or later everyone is caught out. In my case it resulted from a blocked-up sight gauge. I knew I had enough diesel to get back to my mooring – until the engine stopped. I was left drifting around the English Channel in a glassy calm until a passing Frenchman exchanged 5 gallons of the finest for a quantity of good English ale.

THE COMPLETE YACHTMASTER

Check that you know how to clear your fuel lines before you put to sea. The filter on this engine has a particular size nut to let air out of the fuel. Do you have a spanner that fits it?

Try to make sure that when your turn comes, bleeding the fuel through after you have filled the tank from your carefully carried emergency cans is mere routine. Don't wait for a moment of life and death to find out whether or not you can do it. Try it first in your berth on a foul day when you don't feel like going for a sail. You only need the simplest tool kit. Ultimately, you'll be glad you did, because there are no mechanics offshore waiting for your call. And if the engine ever stops on a dark and stormy night, you'll be confident that you know exactly what to do, regardless of what boat you are on.

SKIPPER'S TIP

A final word of warning

If a bleeding operation looks like resulting in a long period of cranking, close down the water intake seacock. This is because the cooling water being deposited in the exhaust system is not being blown out the back by gases from a running engine. It is possible for the build-up to trickle down into the cylinder head with disastrous results. So, if in doubt, shut the seacock, but don't forget to re-open it as soon as she fires up.

SAILING IN HEAVY WEATHER

10

With modern weather forecasting, it is possible to sail for a lifetime on short passages and avoid the worst of bad conditions. However, anyone who ventures across the North Sea, the Bay of Biscay, the Gulf of Maine, or any other true offshore passage, must be ready to take what comes. This is particularly so at the beginning and end of the season. In winter, anything can happen, anywhere.

The question of what constitutes heavy weather varies from boat to boat, from crew to crew, and may well depend on the wind direction. A 22ft (6.7m) cruiser trying to work to windward in 25 knots of breeze in open water will afford little pleasure to her people. On a broad reach they will be having a rattling good sail. A 40ft (12m) ocean racer of mid-1970s vintage with a strong team of sailors can make fast, safe passages in 35 knots of wind, while a 30ft (9m) cruiser with a family crew including young children could well be ill-advised to leave harbour in such a blow.

In heavy weather, living on board becomes extremely difficult, with an increased need for a strong lead from the skipper. If you are sailing with ship's rules about such items as safety harnesses, keep to them religiously yourself, and be sure that others do too.

Meals must be served regularly if it is humanly possible, even if they only consist of canned soup and a sandwich. Morale, as well as the continuing physical strength of your crew, demands this. People will need telling that they should turn in to their bunks for rest periods. If you don't insist on them doing this, they'll stay in 'the fresh air' until apathy and hypothermia reduce them to liability status.

We all imagine that going below will induce seasickness, and so it will if we stand around down there doing nothing but feeling sorry for ourselves. I discovered at an early age that the best way to combat this scourge is to 'get your head down' as quickly and as often as possible. The question of seasickness is considered in greater detail in Chapter 25, and it should never be forgotten that most crews fold up before a well-found yacht gives in, so looking after them is your prime consideration. Everything else there is to say on the subject of hard weather is merely writing on the waves if the crew is unfit to execute your good ideas.

Preparing the boat

A boat should be secured both on deck and down below at any time she is going to sea. Before the onset of bad weather a check is essential. The rules are simple:

- Look to all places where water in any quantity could break your defences, including large cockpit locker lids, navel pipes, and the companionway hatch.
- Make certain your pumps are working, and keep a regular check on the bilge.
- Ensure that anything heavy that could take a destructive tour of the accommodation is firmly secured. This should be done any time before going to sea, but it is of obvious importance if a gale seems likely – though lesser wind strengths may be the danger point for a smaller vessel, or one that proposes navigating through an area of exceptional wave activity (Chapter 28). You won't go wrong in this context if you assume that the boat will be turned upside down. There is more about this subject in the Appendix, but it does happen to ordinary people in ordinary yachts, not just to heroes rounding the Horn. Armed with this premise, consider your batteries, cooker, gas bottles, sextant box, dividers and false teeth.
- Double up on all on-deck lashings, and look to your line stowage. If you call upon your engine in an emergency and finish the day with the main halyard round the propeller, you'll wish you'd taken more care.
- You may well feel that now is the time to issue an ultimatum about safety harnesses. Even the helmsman can be lost over the side in a heavy knock-down. Going back for one individual endangers the lives of all hands; harnesses will usually do away with this desperate problem. Use them, and make sure the crew do too.

Sails

We've already noted in Chapter 3 that as the wind hardens, sails need to be flatter so that they do not overpower the boat. In a really stiff blow this becomes of paramount importance. Halyards on small jibs and deep-reefed mains need to be wound up tight, while outhauls and sheet leads should be set to keep any bag out of the canvas. Attention to sail shape helps to keep the boat on her feet as the waves throw her around, which in turn does a lot to maintain helm balance. With an easy helm she will either go straight or steer through the seas more sensitively, whichever you want, and she'll draw far less on the helmsman's reserves as she does so.

Only the finest roller reefing genoas are capable of supplying a flat-enough sail for upwind work in apparent winds up to gale force, so this is the time to deploy your storm jib on its removable stay. Alternatively, if you have a cutter foretriangle, you can roll the jib away altogether and sail on the hanked staysail which you have thoughtfully provided for tough going. Any proper Bermudan cutter should balance under staysail and deep-reefed main.

If your only headsail is a genoa, which becomes balloon-shaped when deep-reefed, you may as well roll it up and motor sail if you have to work to windward. This is a useful option for the average modern cruiser with her big power unit. Keep the reefed main on and steer to maintain it full of wind. You'll point to within 30° or so of the true wind, which should be more than enough for anyone.

When the waves are steep, it isn't worth trying to point high to windward. Crack off 5° or 10° and ease the mainsail down to leeward on the traveller. The yacht will heel less, go faster and not be so inclined to be stopped by seas.

Trysails

Any yacht that wants to be taken seriously must have at least three reefs available in the mainsail. It is philosophical to contemplate the numbers of those that do not.

A yacht that is sufficiently canvassed to sail well in 5 knots of breeze will find herself hard pressed in winds approaching gale force, even with a close-reefed mainsail. The answer is a trysail, which is a triangular sail set from the mast in place of the mainsail. It is hoisted on the main halyard, tacked down by a strop which allows it to set well above the boom, and sheeted home through quarter-blocks to the secondary cockpit winches. The sail has two sheets like a headsail and is entirely independent of the boom. This last feature is particularly important, because if the boom is damaged on passage, the trysail is always ready to take over. It is cut flat and strong and should be considered as a working sail aboard many all-weather yachts below 35ft (10.6m) long.

This yacht still has her storm trysail set after weathering a gale. She's getting moving again by unrolling her full genoa. She'll rehoist the main when the skipper is sure things have quietened down.

Since most mainsails are carried in a groove or track on the aft side of the mast, it is important that the 'gate' that allows the luff or its fittings to enter the groove be sited above the head of the stowed sail. If this is the arrangement, rigging a carefully stowed trysail (still bagged, with just the luff protruding) presents no more difficulty than it need. I won't pretend that doing the job on a freezing dark night in a 20ft (6m) sea is a consummation to be actively sought, but at least the job can be tackled in the reasonable hope of a successful conclusion. If the gate has not been sensibly placed, you are in for a deal of unpleasantness.

Steering in waves

In normal circumstances a yacht should be steered as straight as possible. Any deviation from her course produces extra distance to sail. In waves of significant size and steepness, the situation may change.

Going to windward

Here, the danger is that the boat will fly off the crest and slam herself to a halt as she crashes into the trough behind it. Flat-floored modern cruisers are particularly prone to this nasty habit, but, by happy coincidence, some of them at least are well equipped to deal with it. If a yacht is quick and light on the helm, she should be pointed 'up' towards the crest of a wave. Then, as the top is reached, the helm is brought smartly up so that she bears away down the back of the heap of water. Performed by a skilled helmsman, this technique produces a sort of rhythmic pumping action that will generate worthwhile gains. It is all work, however, and the traditional vessel that carries her momentum straight through the wave crests is easier on her driver. He'll need good oilskins though, because the spray will be flying aft like buckshot.

The beam sea

In many ways this is the worst condition for all boats. As we'll see in the Appendix, the beam sea is the thing to be avoided at all costs for many craft in survival conditions. Before such extremes are reached, however, a beam wind is a fair wind and you won't want to waste it.

The problem of the beam sea is that the big, steep waves pick up your boat and hurl her down into the trough. This is wet, unpleasant, and can cause structural damage on the lee side of the vessel. Large cabin windows are easily stove in on the lee side, bulwarks can be smashed on traditional craft, and spray dodgers rip away (easily, one hopes, lest they carry the stanchions with them).

Intelligent helming can mitigate these horrors, in daylight at least. When you see a beast of a sea coming, bear away and put it on the quarter where it can best be dealt with. After it has passed, try to steer a few degrees above your course for as long as it's safe, in order to make up what you gave away.

Running

When you find yourself running in a strengthening wind, it is vital to remain constantly aware of the apparent wind factor. Forty knots of breeze is a modest gale, but a yacht running before

SAILING IN HEAVY WEATHER

For some yachts, running downwind in heavy weather is just as safe under a well-reefed mainsail is it is under headsail alone, so long as the dangers of a gybe or a broach are fully understood and measures taken to prevent these contingencies.

it experiences only 33 knots or so across the deck. This is no more than a stiff sailing breeze. If she should now find herself having to turn to windward at 6 knots, the apparent wind speed would rise to something in the order of 45 knots. Because wind force increases as the square of its velocity, the force on the sails – from such an airstream – is virtually double. Alarming surprises await those who ignore this rule.

As a result, a yacht's essentially unbalanced hull lines won't be able to cope with the gust of wind. Unless the sheet is eased immediately, your yacht will be out of control.

One feature to be aware of when running downwind in a big sea is the windward roll. As your boat rolls to weather, as roll she will, her natural weather helm changes abruptly to a penchant for lee helm. If you fail to apply the necessary correction promptly, this may result in a gybe-broach. An ordinary broach to windward is bad enough, leaving the boat lying beam-on in the trough, but the dreaded broach to leeward is particularly nasty.

Running under headsail only can lessen any broaching tendency by putting the boat into 'front wheel drive', as it were, though in some craft the loose-footed headsail may not set as stably off the wind as you'd like. Sometimes a yacht will surprise you by running as straight as a gun-barrel with only a deep-reefed mainsail set.

If you are sailing with the wind and seas on the quarter, be ready to run square off on the face of the larger, steeper waves. This will lessen any broaching tendency, so long as you are ready for the roll, and may induce the boat to surf. Surfing lessens the force of the sea still further, as well as being enormously exciting if you are of a sporting turn of mind. It offers you the chance of exhilarating pace in the right direction, but it is emphatically not for the old in spirit. If you get it wrong, the resulting broach is aggravated by centrifugal force generated by the speed of your progress.

THE COMPLETE YACHTMASTER

Survival tactics

The vital question of navigational strategy in hard conditions near the coast will be discussed in Chapter 28, and all survival options must be considered in the light shed by that chapter. Relating the boat handling possibilities to the strategic situation is part of the overall challenge of bad weather, but before you can don your navigator's hat and make a decision about what to do, you need to be aware of the basic survival options open to a sailing cruiser. They are outlined below and, as you'll see, none of them answers all possible circumstances in every boat.

Heaving to

There are two problems attached to heaving to (Chapter 4) as a means of riding out a period of rough weather: there is an upper limit of wind strength for any given boat at which it is no longer realistic, and by no means all boats are suitable for its use.

If heaving to is to succeed in this context, a yacht needs a longish keel and a deep forefoot. Many production yachts have neither. As a result, they fall away beam-on to the seas when hove-to. Some may even tack themselves, but if your boat has been shown to point well up and remain stable in terms of her angle to the wind, heaving to is a wonderful option. For a start, no one need remain on deck except, of course, for lookout sorties. This increases safety

Sailing in heavy seas and a big wind makes sail shape vital. The staysail schooner behind this wave has hers set to perfection. They're so flat they look like knives cutting the wind.

and means that all hands except one can stay in their bunks, proofed against seasickness and conserving their strength. Such a boat should not make more than one knot of leeway. If you think she is doing so, rearrange your sheets so that she is fore-reaching slightly.

The motion on a hove-to heavy displacement craft in a gale is more than acceptable. For those who generally go to sea in such vessels, it will remain the number one choice.

Lying a'hull

Lying in the trough with no canvas set at all is somewhat discredited by modern research. Nevertheless, for a moderately heavy craft with plenty of forefoot it is probably the next thing for a weak crew to do when the gale becomes such that the craft can no longer carry the canvas required to heave to. The danger, of course, is that she will be knocked down, and that is why an understanding of stability is essential to any skipper who contemplates using this option. In principle, light craft should not do it. I've used it myself with great success, but only in heavy displacement working vessels. I would do it again, but not in a short-keeled, flat-bottomed, beamy production cruiser, where the 'para anchor' is a better solution.

The para anchor

Historically, yachts and small working craft used to ride out gales with all canvas stowed, lying to a conical canvas-and-wood contraption called a 'sea anchor'. Successes were certainly recorded, but few modern commentators have much to say in favour of the device. Yet today's lighter yachts, which can neither heave to properly nor lie a'hull safely, need more than ever before to be able to keep their heads up to the weather. One sound answer is the para anchor, which is a parachute-like drogue deployed from the bow and eased away on a long, springy nylon line. The angle at which the boat is lying can be adjusted by a spring line led to the bight of the riding line from the quarter. Numerous reports are filed of the system working well. Chafe is the enemy, and care must be taken to avoid the lines sawing through at fairleads. A para anchor may be very large. It is retrieved by using a trip line.

Running off

This has the advantage that not only does the boat remain end-on to the waves, the apparent wind force is significantly lessened by her own velocity. The important thing about running is to get your speed right. If it is too slow, your steering will be less effective and you also increase your chances of being pooped; sail too fast, and the danger of broaching becomes acute as the yacht surges away in excess of her hull speed.

In most craft, you can tell when you've got it right. You'll settle for something like your best speed closehauled which, expressed in knots, will be approximately the square root of your waterline length. This happens also to be the magic speed above which your fuel economy under power suddenly falls apart. It is the velocity at which your boat makes the best compromise between knots and disturbing the surrounding water.

To maintain your speed at the chosen level, keep shortening sail as the wind rises until you are under bare poles. You would be unlucky to suffer conditions in which the average yacht

THE COMPLETE YACHTMASTER

> **SKIPPER'S TIP**
>
> **The downside of running off**
> Unlike heaving to and lying a'hull, running requires a helmsman, and a good one at that. If your crew is weak, there will be a time limit on what you can expect from this method. It also gobbles up searoom at an alarming rate.

began outpacing herself with no sail set, unless you are off across an ocean. If you do find matters getting out of hand, stream your longest warps in a bight from either quarter. The drag works wonders on boat speed. It also helps you steer by keeping your stern up into the wind.

Working to windward

We have already noted that keeping relatively end-on to the seas is desirable. If you have a searoom problem you won't be able to run. If you can't trust your boat to heave to or lie a'hull you'll have to try to work her to weather. A powerful performer with a good suit of storm canvas may do this under sail alone; indeed, there is precedent that she can, but an ordinary cruising boat may find herself hard-pressed to succeed, usually through lack of headsail drive. The alternative is therefore to motor sail with a deep-reefed main or trysail only.

If your boat has an exceptionally powerful engine you may find that heaving to under power, or 'dodging', works for you. Here, you take in all sail, or leave up a close-reefed main, or preferably a mizzen, and motor slow ahead. Your boat speed should counteract the surface water drift and the tendency of the waves to drive you back, so that you remain more or less stationary over the ground. I know from experience that this works well in a motor fishing vessel of 50ft (15m) or so. I cannot say how it would prove in a yacht, but *in extremis*, it would be well worth a try if her engine were big enough to overcome the windage of her rig and keep her head up despite her lack of forefoot.

Force 9 in the English Channel. Never mind what the anemometer says, if you can stand up without hanging onto something, it's not a full gale.

NAVIGATION – AN INTRODUCTION

11

The *Oxford English Dictionary* defines navigation as 'the art or science of directing the movements of vessels on the sea'. I think that is as good a general definition as we are likely to find, particularly as it reminds us from the outset that the subject may be both empirical and intuitive. This should never be forgotten in an age when navigation has attained a potential for accuracy that would have left even our recent predecessors dumbstruck.

Despite the nuts and bolts of the discipline having been made easier to handle by modern tools, the essential ingredients of the pudding have not changed since Captain Cook's day. To imagine that installing a GPS does away with any need for navigational expertise is a grave mistake, but the revolution it has wrought opens up exciting possibilities for a good pilot to produce even better results.

Navigation breaks down into two essential areas. The first is about determining where you are; the second concerns itself with how to move from there to your destination. The former may seem to be pure science, although the evaluation of results derived by classical techniques may involve a considerable degree of art. The latter requires careful strategic consideration, as well as ongoing monitoring. Not to put too fine a point on it, even when interpreting a GPS readout, informal guesswork is sometimes brought into play. It is this personal assessment of everything from the various tabulated predictions to whether the helmsman steers high of the course on a broad reach that yields the satisfaction available to every skipper who makes a clean track to a landfall. The potential for using waypoints, cross-track error and other electronic functions can help in this process, but if you don't fully understand the questions you are asking it, the computer cannot be blamed if you misinterpret its answers.

It is a mistake to believe that navigation is all about chartwork. People navigated for millennia without charts at all. The average Viking pillaged his merry way around the North Sea adequately enough without troubling the cartographers. He took a pilot with him, though, someone who knew the coasts he hoped to cruise. Much the same was true of the Portuguese in the Age of Discovery, to whom pilots were vital.

Portuguese pilots did keep written notes, some of which were no doubt comprehensive, but these were in no way comparable to the charts upon which we have come to rely. Little more than a century ago, coastal seamen in Western lands often worked a lifetime without charts. They knew their local waters so well they didn't need any. Indeed they were better off without.

In an increasingly electronic world, the compass remains king and should be respected.

A chart is a substitute for lack of local knowledge. When I sail from my home port to the next harbour 15 miles down the coast on a fine day, I don't even open the chart table. I know the way, I understand the dangers that exist, and so long as I am informed about the time and height of High Water, I need no more. Because I am not using a chart, however, this does not mean that I am not navigating. If that were the case, I'd go on the rocks. In fact, I'm doing it by eye, by the occasional depth sounding, and by interpreting my observations in the context of the information preprogrammed into my mind. The chart and all the instruments I can buy are only substitutes for these.

The situation changes when I venture out of my home waters. Then I need a chart and at least a compass, but navigation still takes place on deck as well as down below. It should always be thought of as a three-dimensional affair, part of which may be depicted two-dimensionally upon a chart.

It is of the utmost importance that this is clear in your mind before you read any further. As a Yachtmaster examiner I often see the results of a failure to grasp this essential. An example is a man so obsessed with chartwork that he takes a compass bearing on a buoy only 50 yards (45m) from his current position. Nine times out of ten, to do this is utter nonsense. The buoy is 'at hand' or 'it's just over there'; it certainly isn't 'bearing 235° magnetic, skipper'. It may have been ten seconds ago when you took your bearing, but it won't be now if you are sailing at any speed at all.

Another typical consequence is that the skipper gives the helmsman the course without putting in an appearance on deck. The course may be wrong. If it is, a glance around would usually reveal that to be the case. After all, the skipper should know basically the direction the yacht is headed. If she finds herself steering towards the cliff, all cannot be well. Sales literature on certain electronic navigators would have you believe that you must be constantly informed as to your exact position. This is far from true in a yacht. The proposition is really a classic

NAVIGATION – AN INTRODUCTION

Passing between wall-to-wall rocks like these, an ancient transit of the BYB beacon and the cairn south of it is a lot safer than trying to read a cockpit plotter as you jink along. Not to be used for navigation

wind-up to the sort of navigational insecurity that over-reliance on such equipment breeds. Much of the time in danger-free waters it isn't necessary to make any marks on the chart at all. The criterion is this: 'If I should need to know the yacht's position with a reasonable degree of accuracy at any time, can I do so by immediate observation?' If the answer is 'yes', and you can see where you are going, why spend the afternoon plotting GPS fixes, shaping courses and generally spoiling your day by missing the sunshine? If the answer could conceivably be 'no', then you should be running a plot.

Similarly, when you are sailing a plot, whether electronic or otherwise, you shouldn't be spending more than the minimum of time at the chart table. As we shall see, you will usually be sailing down a predetermined track from one established position towards another. You are satisfied that this will keep you clear of dangers, even if the maximum error reasonably possible creeps in. You have determined that there is nothing to hit and that you are going in the right sort of direction, which is all that should be required for peace of mind. It is not necessary to know exactly where you are at all times, but it is vital that your plot and your log book entries contain enough information to enable you to estimate your position whenever you may want to do so, because even GPS positions require confirmation.

The evaluation of the requirement for extreme accuracy is a constantly recurring question. Tidal predictions and the like seem to promise precision within 10cm, yet any sensible observer knows that real life is often not like that. Storm surges, barometric pressure and local effects all have their little ways of bringing our best calculations to at least some level of grief. So what are you to do? Do you simply accept that your calculations may not produce the correct results on the day, and don't bother to work accurately? You could adopt this policy, then leave huge margins for safety. You would probably survive well enough, but you would be selling yourself short as a navigator. The danger is always that errors may compound. The inaccuracy stemming from your own decision not to interpolate the decimal places may turn out to be additive with a large anomaly generated by conditions existing in the environment, producing a dramatically bad result.

The good navigator makes certain he is so familiar with the various sums that to solve them as precisely as the tables permit poses no problems. He is also aware of the probable effects of circumstances that may affect the relevance of his carefully calculated figures. Beginning from a position of strength based on good simple arithmetic that a 12-year-old could perform, a sound estimate can be made of the more intuitive side of the matter, and a far safer conclusion drawn.

With experience you will come to realise that even using space-age equipment, your results will not always be as perfect as you might have hoped, particularly in the field of tidal heights and streams. One of the arts of navigation is learning to live safely with whatever potential inaccuracies your choice of methods may entail. In terms of position, the variables may only be a few yards so long as your GPS keeps working, but this can soon degenerate to literally miles using only traditional methods.

Perhaps the most basic premise of all is never to rely upon one single method of determining your position where more than one is available. Nothing has happened since the time of Noah to change that. If you are foolish enough to put your money entirely on an electronic navigation computer, only to find it defunct through a short circuit under the chart table just as you are plunging towards a lee shore in poor visibility, it won't help to blame the manufacturers. Neither would there be any justice in your cause.

CHARTS, PUBLICATIONS AND CHART TABLE TOOLS

12

In whatever form it comes – electronically on a screen, or paper on a table – a nautical chart is a two-dimensional depiction of the three-dimensional reality that is the watery face of the globe.

Latitude, longitude and the globe

In order to define positions, the Earth's surface is divided up by the universally accepted convention of *latitude* and *longitude*. Lines of latitude run parallel to one another, and to the Equator, so that in a chart orientated in the usual 'north-up' mode, they run across the sheet. As their organisation might imply, they are often known as 'parallels of latitude'. The vertical, or north/south, division of the world is marked out by lines known as 'meridians of longitude'. Meridians converge at the Poles and so are never truly parallel to one another.

Both sets of lines are labelled as degrees of a circle. The parallels number from 0° at the Equator to 90° at each Pole, and to avoid any possible ambiguity, a line of latitude is always named either 'north' or 'south'. Meridians number from 0° to 180° 'east' and 'west' from Greenwich in the United Kingdom. Over the years, politicians from countries outside 'dear old Blighty' have muttered that this is an unacceptable state of affairs, with all its suggestion of imperial superiority. Sailors, however, have chosen to ignore all their hot air. The so-called *prime meridian* has to be somewhere. Time and longitude are inextricably linked. In the days when these matters were first decided, London was the home of the Royal Greenwich Observatory, which promulgated the best time signal in the world. This suited most people well enough, and so it has remained. The longitude of Greenwich is 0°. So, incidentally, is Accra in Ghana, but no one seems to mind about that. Cape Cod sits at 70° West, while Hong Kong lies at 114° East.

The arrangements for longitude work well unless you are navigating the far reaches of the central Pacific. Here, despite Kipling's assurances that never the twain shall meet, East and West come together at the 180th meridian. This raises the question of what day it is, and the social trials generated by such a ponderous matter have caused the establishment of the rather

Every cruising yacht should carry a full set of paper charts, pilot books and relevant publications in addition to the electronics.

wavy International Date Line, but I am delighted to advise that such paradoxes are no concern of the coastal and offshore navigator.

A position on the Earth is defined two-dimensionally by a latitude and a longitude. Thus, the lat/long position of the mid-Atlantic island of Madeira is given as approximately 33°N 17°W.

The degrees of both latitude and longitude are subdivided into 60 minutes and thereafter into decimal increments. It is a matter of the greatest convenience that one minute of latitude is equal to one nautical mile. In land measurements this is the equivalent of 2,027 yards, or very nearly 2km. One-tenth of a nautical mile is known as a cable, because that was the length of a standard cable-laid hemp hawser in the fighting ships of the wooden wall navies.

Because the meridians converge at the Poles, the distance separating them varies from one parallel to the next. At the Equator, a minute of longitude is equal to a nautical mile, but if you took a stroll around the South Pole, keeping your hand on it as you went, you could cover 45° in a single stride. As a result, if you want to measure distance on a chart, always refer to the latitude scale on the side, not the longitude at top or bottom.

Chart projections

Certain compromises must be made by the cartographer to deal with the inconvenience caused by the world being more or less round, while the chart is necessarily flat. Generally, these arrangements distort the coastline. On world-sized maps, they can give rise to gross misconceptions about the relative size of land masses in different latitudes, but, as we shall see, there are useful trade-offs for these drawbacks.

The *Mercator projection* is the most usual chart form for coastal and offshore work. It is characterised by the meridians of longitude appearing as parallel equidistant lines, while the parallels of latitude are drawn further apart towards the Poles.

The overriding advantage of the Mercator projection for the navigator is that angles on the globe are the same as those measured on the chart. This means that if you draw a straight line on the chart joining your destination with your point of departure, the course to steer will not vary from one end to the other. Such a line is called a *rhumb line*. It forms the basis of the navigator's assumptions for all short- and medium-range passages.

If you extend a rhumb line on a Mercator chart so that it transverses an ocean in an east–

west direction, you will be doing yourself no favours because the shortest distance between two points on a sphere is a *great circle*. This is a section of a line that, if extrapolated round the sphere and used as a cutting edge, would carve it into two exact halves. Because the meridians are all arcing in towards the Pole, a great circle course cuts each one at a slightly different angle. On a crossing from Newfoundland to the English Channel this results in a course to steer that starts off as 069° and finishes at 093°. If you draw the rhumb line course on a Mercator chart it will be straight, but it will be a greater distance in miles because it will not be a great circle.

By now you are probably thinking of throwing this book in the waste-paper basket because it is boring, incomprehensible, and irrelevant. Don't do it. You need not concern yourself at all with this business of projections if it doesn't interest you. Most of your charts will be Mercator anyway. Just remember that if you ever need to work out a great circle course you should procure a *Gnomonic chart* of the ocean concerned. This magic item shows the meridians converging. If you draw a straight line on it, your line is a great circle. All you need to do now is read off the headings at various meridians and alter course accordingly when you get there, if ever you do.

Because Gnomonic charts involve no distortion, they were sometimes used in the past for harbour charts, and may still be found in use. The small scale of harbour charts is such that a heading from one side to the other needs no black trickery to remain straight. For what it's worth, you know if the chart is Gnomonic not only because it says so, but because it will have a distance scale somewhere, to compensate for the fact that the latitude scale may be unsuitable for this purpose.

Fig 12.1 A Gnomonic chart – a straight line on this chart is a great circle. Note how this one cuts the meridians at varying angles.

SKIPPER'S TIP

Mercator projections

The important things to remember about projections are that for short- and medium-range Mercator charts, minutes of latitude equal sea miles, and that a rhumb line is not only as straight as you can rule it, it is also the shortest distance between two points. If you are using a Mercator chart of all but the smallest area, you'll note that the size of a degree of latitude varies as you proceed north or south. In that case, use the latitude nearest your own for distance purposes.

Direction

Having come up with a way of defining positions, the next major requirement is to translate a line drawn on the chart joining two locations into a means of knowing that your boat is travelling in the direction this dictates.

Wherever you are on the Earth, you will be situated on a meridian of longitude, or one of its subdivisions. If you look directly up it, you will be facing the North Pole. Sight down it, and the South Pole will be ahead. Turning from north to south in a clockwise direction you will traverse 180°; continuing on back to north again is a further 180°. That's 360° in all, and this is how a course is designated. If your course line crosses the meridians (all parallel, remember, on a Mercator projection) at 30° to the right of north, your course is 030°. Due south is 180°; while anything beyond south in a clockwise direction is a greater figure still, up to 359°, when you are back to north again.

Thus, a course of due west, which is the cardinal point on the left, straight down your parallel of latitude, will be 270°. Such a course is designated 270° True, because it relates to the True North Pole which is at the axis point of the Earth's rotation.

In practice, you will be steering a compass course. One of nature's sorrier arrangements is that the magnetic pole to which the compass needle points is considerably displaced from the true pole. It moves with measured tread around the Canadian Arctic. Fortunately, its displacement is tabulated and appears on most charts. If you are working on your chart in degrees 'true', you must make the necessary corrections to your final result before giving the helmsman a course to steer, but this is easy to do and will be discussed fully in Chapter 16.

Paper and electronic charts in practical perspective

Many charting authorities, including in the UK, are threatening to stop production of paper charts on the premise that nobody needs them anymore. The truth is that they cost a lot to produce and funds for them, like most things worthwhile, are shrinking. This leaves the responsible small-craft navigator with something of a dilemma. Electronic charts are so useful, and easy to use with a modern plotter, that anybody who argues with their general adoption must be in need of a sanity assessment. However, even if you are currently relying on electronic navigation charts (ENCs) in some form or other for detailed navigation and pilotage, for the time being at least, paper charts remain a vital part of the navigation package. They supply reliable back-up, overview and, in particular, vital passage planning detail at realistic scale (see Chapter 22). Raster electronic charts, which are in effect a direct scan of the paper version of the same chart, offer a substitute many prefer, but even on a sizable PC monitor the issue of screen size inherent in all ENCs still remains.

The paper charts recommended are:

A *passage chart* should be used to determine overall strategy and courses to steer. Ideally you should find one that covers the whole trip, because trying to move a course from one to the next is never easy and can lead to errors at sea.

Landfall charts giving enough detail to approach the coast are required for your departure point, your destination, and any other part of your passage that may bring you close enough inshore to need them. If you are unfamiliar with the harbour of your choice, you'll often need a large-scale *harbour chart* to see you up to the quay.

Clearly, it would be ideal to carry the fullest set of charts available. In reality, questions of cost and space dictate what will be shipped. Only experience can tell you what you can manage without. If in doubt, take the chart. Not having the one required on the day can involve even the most experienced skipper in inconvenience, or considerable defensive navigation. It may even debar him from a vital port in a storm.

At the time of writing (2025), many authorities are issuing dates for discontinuance of paper. These dates have been changed in the last two years and may well change again. When the last paper chart is pulled, its raster equivalent will probably go with it. Work is under foot, at least within AngelNav, to find a solution to this ghastly situation. Imray, who recently announced the cessation of their paper charts, have now published an intention to continue them after all. The only thing I can recommend to responsible navigators is that they hang on to their paper charts as long as they can, bearing in mind of course that they will not be updated, and to treat with caution any suggestion that it is safe to rely on an electronic chart which looks to GPS as its sole arbiter of position. If you can't physically plot on a chart, 'no GPS, no navigation'.

Chart symbols

A great number of forms, symbols and conventions are used on charts. Fortunately, most of the important ones on paper charts can be deciphered with commonsense. For the ones that cannot, or those with a specific technical meaning, you will have to refer to the information published by the relevant chart-issuing authority. The UK Hydrographic Office (UKHO) sell theirs in a booklet called *Chart 5011*. You really shouldn't go to sea without this information. Charts tell you everything from the probable whereabouts of rough water to the material of the seabed. The positions of buoys and lights are noted, together with their flashing characteristics and their colour. Symbols for coastlines, conspicuous hilltops, rocks and off-lying shoals are clearly marked. The depths of the water are denoted by figures known as soundings. All you need is there but you must give yourself access to the symbols.

Symbols on electronic charts vary from manufacturer to manufacturer but are generally far less comprehensive than their paper equivalents. However, a quality chart will have embedded programs which can be interrogated to determine what a symbol may mean. Lighthouses, for

THE COMPLETE YACHTMASTER

example, often do not carry instantly readable details, but a click on them brings up a menu with all the data you need. It's inconvenient compared with the paper/raster system, but it does work so long as you have to time to do it.

Soundings and contours

Depths are marked in either metres or, in North America, fathoms and feet, or simply feet. Metres are subdivided into tenths, where necessary; a fathom is equal to 6ft (1.8m) and in shallow waters fathoms are subdivided into fathoms and feet.

Because the sea is constantly rising and falling with the tide, some fixed level must be found to which soundings will be referred. This has wisely been decided to be the lowest depth likely to be experienced under any normal circumstances. Tidal height is affected by astronomical phenomena, mainly the relative positions of the Moon, Earth and the Sun (see Chapters 14 and 15); it is also pulled around by meteorological conditions, but to a lesser extent. The former is predictable; the latter is not, beyond a day or two in advance. The depth of water is therefore recorded at the height of the Lowest Astronomical Tide (LAT). This level is known as chart datum level. You would be unlucky to find significantly less water than that, except in a few exceptional places.

For your convenience, contour lines are often traced along lines of significant soundings of equal depth. This enables you to establish the general lie of the bottom at a glance. The most important depth contour is the *drying line*. Beyond this are areas that dry out at LAT.

Fig 12.2 A section of British Admiralty chart number 154 – Approaches to Falmouth.
Not to be used for navigation

CHARTS, PUBLICATIONS AND CHART TABLE TOOLS

The soundings have a line underneath them thus: $\underline{0}_9$. This indicates that they show drying height above chart datum. Drying soundings stop when you reach the real shoreline, which is the contour beyond which the sea will not encroach from purely astronomical influences. In areas of large tidal activity, a low drying height may well be covered for most of the time.

Other information on the chart

The scale of a paper or raster chart is shown near the title, as are the units used for soundings (these are normally metres or fathoms, though occasionally they may be in feet). Make sure you take notice of this or you'll have some surprises. Always read any 'cautions' noted on the chart together with information relating to local regulations.

At the bottom left-hand corner of a chart you will find a note of any corrections that have been made, dated and numbered. The chart may also feature a statement concerning the survey from which it has been drawn. The significance of this is greatest in unfrequented areas. If the survey predates about 1930, it would have been made with lead and line rather than an echo sounder. It is possible that this method will not show up an occasional isolated rock, so you should navigate with caution if the topography indicates that such a feature may be a possibility.

Chart datums

Most paper and raster charts carry a statement concerning the horizontal datum to which they are constructed. This is nothing to do with the chart datum for depth soundings referred to previously. It is a convention concerning the pinpointing of position. Because inaccuracies caused by ignoring it are often much less than a cable's length (200 yards), it has only become relevant with the arrival of electronic fixing aids.

Numerous datums are used worldwide. The UK was for many years *OSGB36*. Europe was *ED*, while much of the US worked to *WGS84* (*World Geodetic System*, 1984). Today, most cartographers are lining up with *WGS84*. A chart will often state that this is the datum. If it is not, you will generally see lat/long correction factors for transferring a position derived from a satellite receiver operating to *WGS84* (the general default setting). There may also be a statement about the datum to which the chart is drawn.

There are three ways of dealing with the question of varying datums: the first is to keep your wits about you, check the chart for correction factors and apply them where necessary. The second is to program your GPS to the relevant datum. With a user-friendly set, this is often the easiest option. The third choice is to expect less from your equipment. Even with the datum shifted, GPS often gives far more accuracy than any pre-electronic sailor could have hoped for. The difference is that he expected little, so he was rarely disappointed.

Privately produced paper charts

In addition to the charts produced by government bodies, many areas of coastline are covered by specialist charts, published with yachtsmen in mind. These usually look different from their official counterparts. They are easy to use, with much additional information. In the UK,

> **SKIPPER'S TIP**
>
> ### Half tide
> Most chart authorities mark areas inside the drying line in a different colour to the permanently wet zones.

this service is now almost uniquely supplied by Imray, Laurie, Norrie and Wilson, generally known as 'Imray'. The harbour plans on Imray charts are particularly handy in a limited chart library. Some are issued in book form, or in packs dealing with specific areas, offering a realistically priced way of kitting yourself out. They give ideal back-up for the modern electronic navigator, with all that is needed to produce the safe passage plans which cannot be done on a leisure vector chart plotter. In the chart pack, you also get a key to download a set of Imray's own raster charts for the same area.

In the Scandinavian countries, the USA and others, similar charts are offered for sale packaged like this and priced advantageously.

Electronic charts

Electronic chart plotters, PC navigation programs and tablet/smart-phone programs all use electronic navigation charts. Although many variants exist, these come in two essential formats.

Raster charts

The raster chart is, to all intents and purposes, a scan of its equivalent paper chart. Most authorities are planning to cease production of these excellent charts at the same time as their cessation of paper charts. The reasons will be obvious and the results are to be deplored. In its purest form, the raster chart usually has the same boundaries, notes to mariners and survey data. Until recently, all raster charts in Britain were based on UKHO Admiralty charts. In 2025, Imray are offering the raster equivalent of their paper charts. Whether or not this will continue is unclear at the time of writing.

Raster charts have one huge advantage: they look the same as charts have always done. All their information is visible at any one time and no buttons need be pressed on the plotter to unlock further information. As you zoom in and out on a given chart, nothing changes except the size of the image. In other words, what you see is what you get. And what you see is generally all that most people want. The drawback is that unless the electronic chart 'kit' is 'quilted', which is to say, melded together electronically, you have to decide physically which chart to use, then switch from one to another. For many people – myself included – this presents no problems at all. They even prefer it. Others find it a nuisance.

In most cases, raster charts must be used through the medium of a PC plotter, but certain bulkhead plotter manufacturers and some tablet apps now offer raster chart options.

CHARTS, PUBLICATIONS AND CHART TABLE TOOLS

AngelNav

With all manner of chart plotter apps now available, AngelNav offers raster-chart tablet downloads for many popular areas including all of UK home waters. Uniquely, the software allows users to plot traditional chartwork on the raster charts, so that in the event of GPS being compromised compass bearings can be plotted for an old-fashioned fix. Courses to steer using the inbuilt tidal data for heights and streams, estimated positions and the rest are also readily available. These enable the navigator to hone traditional skills as well as rest easy on the question of what happens if GPS goes down. At the time of writing (2025), no other software on the planet does this. Currently available for Apple iOS products, an Android version which can be driven on a PC is in development.

Vector charts

Vector charts are built-up by vectoring the survey data from which all charts are drawn. The process is quite different from the raster scan and resulting charts don't look at all like the paper version created from the same information. Zoom well out on a vector chart and you'll find no detail at all, save perhaps the line of the coast. On a good one, however, you can zoom in until you have accessed every scrap of data available anywhere within the scope of the survey. The process is seamless and, unless you choose to show the borders of an individual chart, with most programs you will not even be aware of them.

Vector charts are used exclusively on 'hardware' chart plotters (dedicated units), where they are generally issued on SD cards or some other form of electronic storage device, but they may be available via internet download for some PC-based plotter programs.

The main benefit of vector charts is accessibility to all available data, and flexibility about how much of it you choose to show (see Chapter 19). Much of the information remains embedded until you click on an object and enter a menu, so using the charts is not as simple as their raster equivalent. The data is comprehensive, however, and may go beyond the size and nature of a navigation aid all the way to a comprehensive tidal curve for a given port on a given day, any time from the Battle of Hastings until what, for all we know, may post-date Armageddon. The drawbacks are that unless you zoom well in, more details remain hidden than may be convenient, yet when you are zoomed in tight enough to access what you want, the overview is lost. A further downside is that most leisure vector charts offer little, if any, details about shore features, which means any attempt to plot fixes etc are doomed to failure. The only source of position is GPS. While GPS is extremely reliable and phenomenally accurate, it remains a single source. Relying on a single source of data was always a navigational 'no-no', so you must interrogate your own conscience as to how far you are prepared to rely on your GPS-driven chart plotters. Nevertheless, the marvels offered by these remarkable charts are considerable, and explored more fully in Chapter 19.

Chart corrections

The old saying that 'rocks don't move' is, generally speaking, true enough, though sandbanks may shift from one month to the next. Buoys, lighthouses, oilrigs and all the rest of the paraphernalia that civilisation has brought to the seas are, however, permanently under review. They are frequently moved, added to, and expunged. Keeping British leisure charts up to date is very easy today. All you need to do is log on to www.admiraltyleisure.co.uk. Here you'll enjoy the remarkable experience of free downloads for all UKHO leisure charts, plus guidance of where to find updates for other cartography.

Unfortunately, to correct a full set of charts systematically and conscientiously is not a realistic proposition for many people. As a second best, if your chart is known to be not the newest available, you should check the important lights and day marks against the current list in your nautical almanac. *Reeds Nautical Almanac* carries these, as do some of the others. If you find yourself forced into this, you must be aware that it is a poor substitute for a properly corrected chart, and take any measures that seem appropriate to steer on the safe side of danger.

Daily navigation warnings, many of which refer to temporary or permanent alterations in charted information, are broadcast on VHF radio as well as featured in Navtex readouts.

Many electronic plotter suppliers now offer a correction package as a periodic update for all the charts an individual user has paid for. This service is not universal, so if you are equipping a boat with this gear, the question of chart correction will require consideration. For some systems, corrections are available via an internet download, removing one of the greatest logistical difficulties from responsible small-craft management. AngelNav updates its charts automatically every three months when the tablet running it happens to be online. For navigational purposes the app is self-contained and does not need an internet signal.

The Nautical Almanac

If you sail in tidal waters you simply cannot go to sea without one of these. A good almanac is a mine of information on everything to do with seafaring. It covers the tides, the movements of the Sun and Moon, lists of lights, radio aids to navigation, weather forecast information radio stations, first aid, collision regulations in full detail and many other vital subjects. The original *Reeds* even went so far as to offer a step-by-step guide to childbirth, and if you consider this obscure you would be wrong. A number of cases are on record of babies delivered safely at sea using only this remarkable publication, a pair of scissors and some well-boiled string.

If you are only intending short, day-sailing passages you might get by for a while with just a copy of the local tide tables, but you'd be pushing your luck. Sooner or later a question will crop up for which you have no answer. It's odds-on that the almanac will tell you what to do.

Pilot books and sailing directions

Official pilot books are issued by the chart authorities to augment the information on the publications. Different national charts vary in form and content, but the UKHO version is probably as useful as any to the English-speaking yachtsman. It gives comprehensive climatological data as well as describing the movements of currents, while the descriptions of the coastline are extremely full. At first reading, Admiralty Pilots appear rather dry, but on better acquaintance one becomes aware of a definitive style, leavened occasionally with anecdote. If you have room for a copy, you should carry the relevant volume into areas strange to you.

Yachtsman's pilots are far more readable than their official counterparts. They are generally well illustrated and they tell you what you want to know, rather than treating you as a fly on the bulkhead of a large warship. All sorts of pilots are available, to suit most tastes and all but the leanest pockets. Paying proper attention to a well-produced example will make a great deal of difference to how you feel as you approach a strange port in a hard blow.

A tablet or iPad plotter is of huge benefit for close inshore pilotage.

Electronic charts versus pilot books

More and more electronic chart makers are offering additional information at a click, complete with aerial photos, pilotage hints and the rest. As a sometimes pilot-book writer, this ought to have me recoiling in horror, yet it does no such thing. The truth is that an authoritative book is far more psychologically reassuring than data served up by a computer. Furthermore, pilot-book data are generally more comprehensive and are compiled by people who understand the sailor's needs, rather than simply serving them up without a certain amount of subjective sifting. Such information can be useful, but it is no substitute for the real thing. What's more, a lot of sailors still actually enjoy the feel of a book, but it must be written with soul. Simply printing out a list of information is little better than clicking an icon on the chart. Indeed, it may be worse, because there is no excuse for the chart's info not being up to date. A book, like those who read it, has a finite life span.

Crowd-researched data available on the internet are rapidly coming of age. The Cruising Association's CAptain's Mate is a case in point. Members of the association are generally pretty switched-on sailors who enjoy leaving their remarks about ports and other features on the app. It is becoming a worthwhile addition to the pilot book. Indeed, it often delivers more comprehensive and up-to-the-minute information.

Other publications

If you are sailing far afield you may want to ship a list of lights and a list of radio signals. Atlases of tidal streams are available, though the information they contain is mainly duplicated in the almanac. The most convenient answer to these three issues is to buy the Admiralty DVD with Total Tide, List of Radio Signals and List of Lights. It's not cheap but it's the best. Generally speaking, officially published paper tide tables have also become largely redundant for the yachtsman as almanacs have improved. Today, it is more important that you have on board the instruction manuals for your electronics, unless of course you have decided to do

THE COMPLETE YACHTMASTER

without all that. Extracting the full benefit from a modern GPS computer is not something the average person can hope to do without the book in front of him. Just remember while you are achieving computer literacy at your chart table that there is a whole world turning in gloriously organic progress up on deck. How many hundred waypoints you can punch in at a time won't be required knowledge when your inexperienced crew sail you under the bows of a supertanker.

Chart table tools

Dividers are used for comparing the length of a line on a chart, or the distance between two points, with the latitude scale at the side. The one-handed variety (with the loop at the top) is by far the best. While you are at it, buy a long pair, not one of those diminutive affairs that are attractive, but never quite big enough. Most chart plotters have some sort of measuring device in their software, but these are invariably awkward and clumsy when compared with dividers and a paper chart. Use them by all means, but for happiness, invest in the real thing.

Parallel rules transfer lines to and from the compass roses on the chart. The roses are circles clearly marked in 360° notation and strategically situated. They usually feature an extra 'north' pointer, offset, to indicate the amount and the direction of any magnetic variation from True North. Somewhere in the compass rose, you will usually find a written statement of variation, which will also advise you of any predicted changes in its value.

The problem with parallel rules on board most yachts is that they are too cumbersome for the confines of the chart table. They frequently fetch up against the fiddle just as they embark upon the last stride of their walk from course to rose. This knocks them out of true and sends you silly with frustration. It may also be the last straw that results in seasickness. The answer is to use a chart protractor. They were called 'plotters' until the arrival of the electronic chart plotter, but sadly this has confused the issue and the old name has been usurped by the new technology.

Chart protractors come in various patent forms. Which one you use is up to you, but the European 'Breton Plotter' is hard to beat for simplicity, reliability and cheapness. A chart protractor does away with the dynamic aspect of parallel rules. It is placed against a line and its own integral compass rose is orientated so that the heading or bearing can be read off. Some plotters even offer the wherewithal to read out in 'degrees true' or 'degrees magnetic', and they all can take up the slack when working on a chart with no compass roses at all. Such nonsense is proliferating in continental Europe and, while lamentable, it is a fact of life.

A chart protractor can lay off a course or a bearing, even on a chart with no compass rose.

AIDS TO NAVIGATION

13

Traditional aids to navigation such as buoys, beacons and lighthouses are the signposts of the sea. While most of the ones we see today are of modern construction, many are placed on sites so ancient that no one knows when the first cairn of stones was built there in order that it might be identified from seaward. This is particularly noticeable on the rock-strewn coasts of Scandinavia, where the Vardes (black stone towers, often with a white stripe) certainly date back to Viking days.

Originally, lights and daymarks were erected by private individuals or groups either for their own use, or to encourage merchants to navigate in their local waters. Most of these arrangements are now lost in time, but a few are recorded. The original light on the hill behind St Catherine's Point on the Isle of Wight was erected by order of the Pope, who threatened excommunication to the village squire if he failed not only to build it, but also to pay the salaries of the monks who were to stoke the beacon. Being a God-fearing fellow, the squire did the honest thing. If this seems high-handed, it should be borne in mind that the squire's people were notorious wreckers. The Holy Father finally took exception to their behaviour when a large consignment of wine was spirited away from a ship they had enticed on to the shoals. The fact that this was destined for the communion table probably accounts for their undoing.

Nowadays, lights are established in less colourful circumstances. Indeed, with the arrival of electronic fixing systems, light authorities are coming under increasing pressure to cut back their numbers, thus saving shipowners some of the burden of light dues. Practical seamen are resisting this parsimonious approach, however, and will no doubt continue to do so. GPS and the like are, after all, merely one more in the age-old line-up of aids to navigation. Wonderful though they are, they do not render everything else suddenly obsolete.

There are two basic types of visual aid to navigation: solid structures which may or may not be lit, and floating buoys. The former range from sticks of withy wood sunk in the mud of an obscure creek to mighty towers exhibiting lights that could be seen from space with no more assistance than a good pair of binoculars. Buoys include anything moored to the seabed, from lightships offshore down to a plastic can painted red marking a sand-spit off your neighbour's dock. They are all important to somebody. Commonsense will decide whether a particular one is of any interest to you.

Lighthouses

A lighthouse or a beacon is indicated on the chart by a star that marks its accurate position. Your attention is called to the fact that it is highlighted by a magenta 'flash' shaped like a lozenge with one end pointed. The sharp end is hard by the object it refers to. Adjacent to the star is all the charted information about the light. Any further and better particulars, including a physical description of the structure, will be found in the officially published *List of Lights*.

A light is identified by its so-called characteristics, including the period of its cycle. These are usually different from any other light in the vicinity. The sequence may be an arrangement of flashes, it could be isophase (in which light and dark periods are equal), occulting (where the light is generally 'on', and 'flashes' off), or simply fixed 'on' (Fig 13.1). The permutations of these are many, but they are generally easy both to spot and relate to on the chart. Colours are also used for identifying lights. Unless otherwise stated, you can assume that a light is white, but red, green and sometimes yellow are used as well. Details of the various abbreviations used by cartographers can be found in Fig 13.1. These are largely self-explanatory, but notice that 'flashing' is Fl, while 'fixed' is 'F'. The two are often confused by stressed navigators.

The height of a light is charted in metres (as a small m) or feet (ft), and this height is given above the level of Mean High Water Springs (see Chapter 14). Its *luminous range* of visibility is stated in miles (as a capital M). Luminous range is the distance that the light would carry in clear air to an observer unhampered by the Earth's curvature. Whether or not you can see it that far away is another matter altogether, and depends upon the relative heights of the light and your eye.

CLASS OF LIGHT		International abbreviations	National abbreviations	Illustration Period shown
FIXED		F		
OCCULTING *(duration of light longer than dark)*				
Single-occulting		Oc	Occ	
Group-occulting	eg	Oc(2)	Gp Occ(2)	
Composite group-occulting	eg	Oc(2+3)	Gp Occ(2+3)	
ISOPHASE *(light and dark equal duration)*		Iso		
FLASHING *(duration of light shorter than dark)*				
Single-flashing		Fl		
Long-flashing *(flash 2s or longer)*		L Fl		
Group-flashing	eg	Fl(3)	Gp Fl(3)	
Composite group-flashing	eg	Fl(2+1)	Gp Fl(2+1)	

Fig 13.1 Light characteristics (extract from *Reeds Nautical Almanac*).

AIDS TO NAVIGATION

Sea marks vary, from sophisticated light buoys with racon and AIS to historic stone cairns, but they all mean something.

Certain publications refer to the *nominal range* of lights. This is the luminous range as modified by meteorological visibility of 10 nautical miles. Many larger lights will be visible at greater nominal ranges than 10 miles, even in the assumed limited visibility.

Sectors and obscuring lines

Some lights are only visible within certain angles, owing to their being obscured beyond that by a hill, a headland, or some other feature. This is usually, but not always, noted on the chart.

Certain light structures shine different colours into different sectors of their approaches. This is generally used where a specific danger is present whose sphere of influence is defined by a red or a green sector. The coloured sector light may be independent from the main light of the structure, in which case it is noted as such in the light description (e.g. Fl 5sec 25m 15M FR 12m 5M). Lights of this type are commonplace in Scandinavia where winter pilotage through the inner leads is executed by following from the safe sector of one light into the designated sector of the next, and so on, all the way to the Arctic and beyond.

If you see a light charted as having various colours (e.g. Fl WRG 15s), you will see a single flash every 15 seconds. The colour of the flash is determined by the sector in which you are situated. If the sectors are not defined on your chart, you must refer to your list of lights, your pilot book, or your nautical almanac for details.

Coloured sectors are often used as leading lines into harbours. Typically, the white will take you safely in. A red sector warns that you are to port of the line, while green shows you have wandered to starboard. In some areas, a light shows with greater intensity when you are on the safe line. If the chart indicates an intensified sector, you will definitely see this when you are in it. The extra brightness is unmistakable.

Looms

Powerful flashing lighthouses can often be seen below the horizon by virtue of the loom of their light. This sweeps round like a searchlight beam. If conditions are suitable you can identify the characteristics of a loom. Sometimes you can also take a rough bearing, though these must always be treated with caution. Disgracefully, some of the more important British lighthouses have been seriously downgraded in recent years. This is claimed to be because, with the rise of electronics, the mariner no longer requires them to be so powerful, but one cannot help wondering if it is to save money. The looms of such once-mighty lights as Beachy Head will no longer be seen halfway to France on a clear night, as the sweeping flash of Gris Nez fades on the clouds astern. Where a loom can still be found – and mercifully, the French at least seem to have kept their lights at full power – you can sometimes take a rough bearing on it to help confirm your GPS position.

A final warning about lighthouses: you will notice that most structures built within living memory are not situated as high as the terrain immediately behind them might have allowed. On the face of things one would assume 'the higher the better', since the geographic range of the light would thus be maximised. The reason that full advantage is not always taken of this is the prevalence of low cloud, which snuffs a light as effectively as turning off the power. If, therefore, you are looking for a light whose elevation is great and which stubbornly refuses to appear, always bear in mind the possibility that it is lost in the cloud. A classic example of this is landfall in northern Spain, where the lights are often at considerable elevation and low cloud rolls in with surprising regularity.

Major lighthouses like this one usually feature a powerful foghorn.

Fog signals

Many lighthouses and some buoys carry a fog signal, activated when the visibility falls below a critical range. These are highly reassuring to any mariner, particularly a non-electronic one, or one who wisely chooses to seek confirmation of his position from beyond the confines of his 12-volt electrical system.

There are various types of fog signal, listed below. All have their own distinctive sound. They are indicated by type on the chart, which will also show any time sequence, e.g. Horn 60s: one blast on a horn every minute.

Sound travels eccentrically in fog, so that it is sometimes confusing to try to pick up the direction of a signal. When you are motoring, station a crew member on the foredeck if conditions permit, because the engine noise will not help you at all back aft. You might consider stopping the motor from time to time for a listening watch. Taking compass bearings on fog signals is rarely practical, but it is usually possible to home in on one, or to note its changing bearings approximately in relation to the yacht's head.

Wind direction affects the range of a fog signal dramatically. A powerful siren may blow down the breeze for 6 or 7 miles, while a reed trying to penetrate further than half a mile to windward will usually be unsuccessful. These are the fog signal types most usually found:

- Diaphone (Dia) gives a long, drawn-out moan, finishing up with a characteristic grunt. It is often very powerful.
- Horn (Horn) gives a steady-pitched sound, varying considerably from one to another.
- Reed (Reed) produces a weak and high-pitched sound.
- Siren (Siren) is generally higher in pitch than a horn or a diaphone.
- Nautophone (Naut) – electronic – produces a high, penetrating note.

Offshore marks

Lightships are indicated on the chart by a small ship. The exact position is a diminutive circle at the base of the symbol. The characteristics of the light, which is generally 40ft (13m) above sea level, are shown adjacent to this. Light vessels swing to their moorings and carry an anchor light in their forward rigging just as if they were a regular sea-going vessel at anchor. Because of the expense of manning them, these vessels are now almost all automated, and many are being replaced by Lanbies (Large Automated Navigation Buoys) and light floats.

A *light float* is smaller than a lightship and often carries a less powerful light. If it is an important one, the chart will inform you as to its range and elevation as well as its characteristic light pattern.

A *Lanby* is exactly what it says it is. It consists of a circular floating platform 40ft (13m) in diameter on which is raised a trellis mast with a powerful light 40ft (13m) above the water. Lanbies are controlled from shore stations and would seem a sensible replacement for the lightship except that their motion is so extreme that servicing them is an extraordinarily onerous task.

High focal plane buoys are often used to mark offshore dangers, or safe water. These are exactly the same as any other 'pillar' buoy, except that they are bigger than those normally used inshore. Some of them have quite powerful lights but even those whose beam can be seen at 7 miles do not have their range listed on the chart, though they may be found in the relevant *List of Lights*.

In offshore areas of considerable shoaling, ordinary buoys of the larger sizes will be found.

The shape of navigation buoys can vary drastically in different parts of the world, but the topmarks are unambiguous.

Inshore marks

Lateral marks are used to indicate channels. Occasionally one is used singly to show that you must pass to one particular side of it. Colour and shape determine whether a lateral mark is to be left to port or starboard. They may be buoys or beacons, but in either case if they are ambiguous in shape they will have a topmark that is not.

Sadly, all the world does not conform to one arrangement of lateral marks. The North Americans leave red to starboard and green to port going up a harbour, travelling shorewards up a channel or, in the absence of anything more positive, proceeding in a clockwise direction around the continent. In Europe under the IALA A (International Association of Lighthouse Authorities) system, the opposite is standard.

At least it is only colour that is reversed. On both sides of the Atlantic, port-hand buoys are flat topped or can shaped; starboard ones are cones, or 'nuns'. This means that in the US (IALA B), a distant mark with a triangular topmark whose colour is as yet indeterminate should be left to starboard, as in Europe. As it comes closer it will turn out to be red, while under the IALA A system it would be green.

North Americans remember the colour by the mnemonic *Red Right Returning*. So long as Europeans remember that, then reverse it for home waters (*Red Right Returning to Sea*), there is no problem. Starboards are cones in both cases, and ports are cans. 'Have a can of port, old chap!' Personally I like mine in a glass, but there you are.

Throughout the world, special marks are yellow; so are their lights. They can be various shapes, but every effort is made to conform this with the mark's position in relation to other marks, if this is relevant.

Generally speaking, red marks carry red lights; greens carry green; and yellows are always yellow.

Safe water marks such as fairway buoys are universally red and white vertically striped with a white light, but in North America they flash Morse code 'A', while 'IALA As' may be isophase, occulting or one long flash every ten seconds.

AIDS TO NAVIGATION

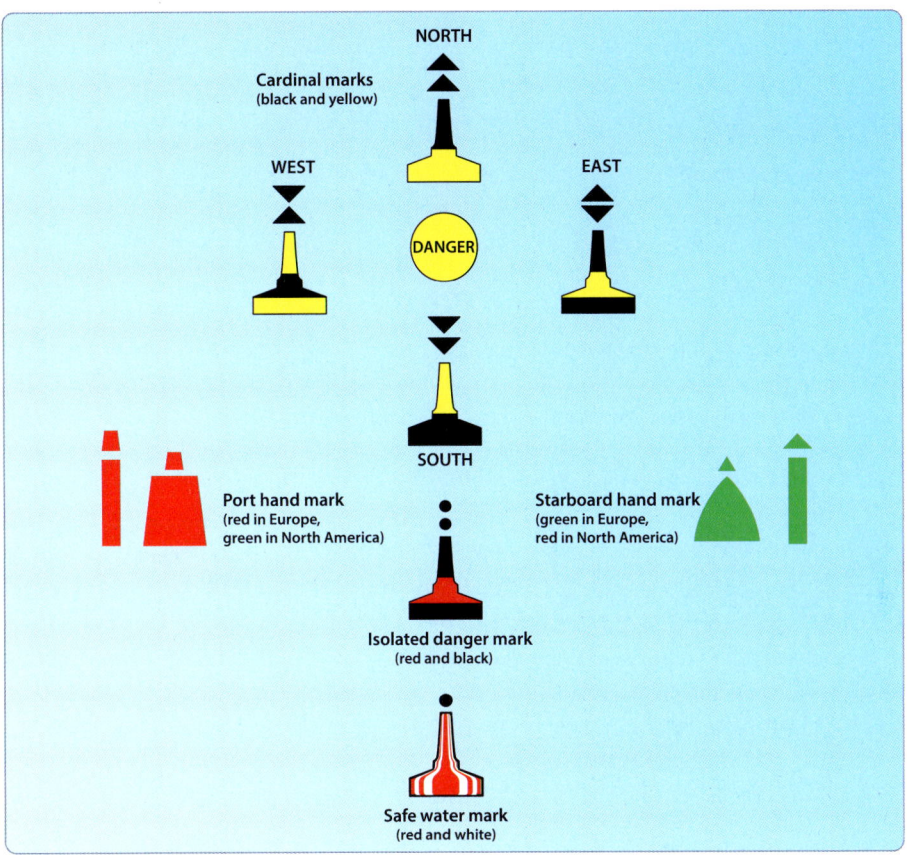

Fig 13.2 Navigation marks.

Isolated dangers are marked in all IALA areas by vertical marks with horizontal black and red bands, with two vertically arranged balls as a topmark. 'Balls-up' is the mnemonic for remembering this, which is certainly what you will experience if you ignore the warning it represents. Such marks are lit with a group flash 2, which corresponds to the balls.

Temporary wreck buoys are laid to indicate the position of recent dangerous wrecks. They are vertically striped blue and yellow, with an unmistakable alternating blue and yellow flash. If the wreck remains a hazard, the authority concerned will buoy it with cardinals in due course. Meanwhile, stand well clear.

IALA cardinal marks are shown clearly in Fig 13.2. A north mark stands to the north of a hazard, and so on. Therefore, if you come across, say, a south mark and you cannot find it on the chart to check its relevance to your life, you will be safe if you pass to the south of it.

At first sight, cardinal marks look complicated to remember. Actually they are very easy indeed. The north mark's topmarks point up, or to the north; the south ones point south. The west topmarks look suspiciously like a bobbin ⧖, so remember, *West Winds Wool*. If you can't get along with the home knitting, just think of a *Wasp-waisted Woman*, which it also looks like if you prefer your ladies without heads. For the classical scholar, the east mark puts one in mind of the letter 'E' in a carved inscription, thus ⟨.

THE COMPLETE YACHTMASTER

> 💬 **SKIPPER'S TIP**
>
> **Learn your signposts**
> Learn your signposts and use them intelligently. We've come a long way since the Norsemen built their cairns on the outer skerries of Norway.

So far so good, but what about the disposition of yellow and black? The answer is that the points of the topmarks point towards the black. Look at the diagram and you'll see what I mean. The black is all at the top on the north mark, all at the bottom on the south, all in the middle of the Wasp-waisted Woman, and at the outsides of the classical ♦.

The lights are white and go round the clock-face: east is at 3 o'clock, and flashes in groups of 3; south is 6 (plus a long one to ensure there is no mistake); west is 9; and north should be 12, but no one could be expected to count that many flashes, so it just keeps going continuously. The IALA cardinal system is one of the greatest bonuses to navigation for many decades. It is easy to operate and utterly unambiguous.

Whether or not you obey the instructions of a marker will depend on your draught and your general intentions, but whenever you see one you should identify its type and check it visually to ensure that it coincides with what you expect from your chart. If you find an anomaly, see it through to the end, or you may live to wish that you had.

Sometimes you can pass the wrong side of a set of lateral buoys in order to avoid close encounters with large vessels, which must treat them conventionally.

The unmistakable form of a safe water mark. These buoys generally, but not always, mark the start of a buoyed channel and can be passed safely on either side.

TIDAL HEIGHTS   14

Depending upon where you are sailing, the importance of tides varies from the critical to being of no significance at all. Navigators in the Bristol Channel, or the waters around south-west Normandy and the Channel Islands, are constrained by tide ranges of powerhouse proportions. These rise to 45ft (13.6m) in St Malo and 50ft (15m) up the Bristol Channel. Sailors in the West Indies take little notice of the movements of the tides, even though the US authorities produce tide tables for San Juan in Puerto Rico. A glance at these shows why – the range rarely exceeds 1ft (0.3m).

Even quite small ranges of tide can generate strong currents. You don't have to be in the Bay of Fundy (55ft/17m range of tide) or the Bristol Channel to be carried backwards by the stream. Poole Harbour has one of the lowest ranges in the central English Channel area, yet I have seen 5 knots on my log while moored to a buoy near its narrow entrance on a full spring ebb.

People unused to tides tend to be intimidated by statistics like these, and by the unfriendly appearance of the average tide table. There is no need for this. 'Don't panic' is my advice. There really isn't a lot to it. For convenience the subject divides neatly into two sections which you can absorb one at a time. These are the height of the tide and the rate and direction of its stream. We'll deal with heights first, but before we do, let's take a brief glance at what is making it all happen.

Tides are produced by the force of gravity. Both Sun and Moon exert a pull on the Earth. Indeed, the Moon's pull is so strong that we and our satellite revolve around one another on a central gravitational axis. The Moon puts in most of the distance work, but its one-month orbit throws the Earth into an oscillation nonetheless. As the Earth turns 'underneath' the Moon, the waters on its face are dragged bodily towards the satellite, forming a 'bump' in the sea that is tiny in global terms but crucial to the mariner. Because of the Earth's own oscillation there is also an equal and opposite centrifugal force that creates a similar bump in the sea on the other side of the globe. The two bumps remain almost stationary, being governed by the Moon's one-month orbit (actually their position advances by about 40 minutes per day), and the Earth turns inside them. This means that an observer standing on the shore at a given spot will be passed by both bumps in a 24-hour period. Thus, there are two tides per day.

The Sun's gravitational pull is also working on the water, and when this lines up with either a Moon-generated bump or its centrifugal equivalent, the force from the Sun will be additive, producing a bigger than average tide. This happens at full moon and 'dark' moon. At half moon, either waxing or waning, the gravities of the two bodies are working against one another. The tides, in consequence, are smaller than average at those times.

In fact, as with all terrestrial effects generated by astronomical forces, a time lapse attaches to the days when the largest and smallest tides occur. In this case it is a couple of days or so, which means that the large tides – known as *springs* – turn up a day or two after full moon and at new moon; ditto with the small tides, or *neaps* (Fig 14.1).

Notice that the term 'spring' has nothing to do with the season of the year. The biggest tides of all occur in spring and autumn because the equinoctial sun is nearest the Equator and exerts its best pull, so perhaps this is the origin of the nomenclature. I can offer no better explanation.

Fig 14.1 The Sun, the Moon and the tide. **a)** Full moon spring tide: gravitational fields in a straight line. **b)** New moon spring tide: gravitational fields still lined up. **c)** Half moon neap tide: gravitational fields in opposition to one another.

TIDAL HEIGHTS

Tide tables

Every maritime nation of any importance works up its own tidal predictions through its observatories. These are made generally available as official publications, but most yachtsmen prefer to acquire them as part of the universally useful nautical almanac, or from the electronic data delivered readily by most chart plotters. If you intend never to sail far from your home port, you may be able to manage with the local tide table booklet issued by most major harbour authorities for a handful of small change. If you are away cruising, you must have an up-to-date almanac.

Tide tables are almost entirely self-explanatory. They normally give the times of High and Low Water at the port in question for every day throughout the year. Heights are given in feet or metres *above chart datum* which, as we have seen in Chapter 12, is also the level of Lowest Astronomical Tide.

Times

Times are worthy of careful attention. If you are operating within a single country these rarely present any practical problems, but if you change from one state to the next, you must remember to reset your watch or you may be an hour out in your workings. British Admiralty Tide Tables, or their almanac equivalent, give UK waters times in Universal Time (UT) as it is now officially known. Foreign ports are stated in the relevant zone time. Always remember to add 1 hour to the tabulated figures in summer for daylight saving time (BST) if you are working with the Admiralty Tide Tables or any of the almanacs derived from these. The English-speaking almanacs even give you the date to change your watch, but they don't advise about continental summer times. That remains a personal initiative test. Some tables issued by local authorities do this job for you and give all tides in local clock time. For example, the *Eldridge Tide and Pilot* on the US East Coast conveniently serves up Eastern Standard Time or Daylight Time as appropriate. Times can be something of a nightmare when dealing with the data flashing up at the touch of a button on an electronic plotter. Often, these do not specify obviously what 'time' they are using. You may find the answer deep in the menus, but even this is not always successful. If all else fails, note the time given, then check it against an almanac. This will show if the electronic time is BST, UT or, in foreign waters, just what the devil it really is. Having made this comparison once, it should hold good for other ports within the same time zone.

Secondary ports

You wouldn't be able to find shelf space for an almanac with a page for the tides of every port. There are too many of them. The problem is solved by the system known as *secondary ports*. Any lesser port is referred to in terms of how its tidal activity differs in detail from the nearest standard port for which the tides are fully tabulated.

Different almanacs give secondary-port data in various ways, but it is normally set out with time differences in one column and height difference in the next. In some areas time and height differences remain constant for a given secondary port. Often, however, they vary depending upon whether the tide in question is a spring or a neap. Differences for such ports are given in relation to MHWS (Mean High Water Springs), MHWN (Neaps), etc.

In the greater tides of northern Europe, the tidal difference is given in relation not only to springs and neaps, but also in terms of the actual *zone* time of High and Low Water. This sounds complicated, but if you study the illustration for differences on London Bridge (Fig 14.2), you'll see that it is really quite straightforward.

In practice, one rarely ends up with a time that is given in the secondary-port information. Normally you want one somewhere in between. In these cases you must *interpolate*. Thus, if you want the time difference at Tilbury and the time of High Water is 0600 (Fig 14.2), you are three hours into the six (0300 to 0900) given at the top of the column. The difference for Tilbury at 0300 is −55 minutes. At 0900 it is −40 minutes. The difference therefore diminishes by 15 minutes in 6 hours, which is 2½ minutes per hour. By 0600 it will have dropped by 2½ minutes multiplied by 3, or 7½ minutes, so the difference at 0600 is going to be −47½ minutes. The negative sign shows that this is subtracted from the London Bridge time to find the time at Tilbury.

TIDES +0252 Dover; ML 3·6; Duration 0555; Zone 0 (UTC)
Standard Port LONDON BRIDGE (→)

Times				Height (metres)			
High Water		Low Water		MHWS	MHWN	MLWN	MLWS
0300	0900	0400	1100	7·1	5·9	1·3	0·5
1500	2100	1600	2300				

Differences TILBURY

| −0055 | −0040 | −0050 | −0115 | −0·7 | −0·5 | +0·1 | 0·0 |

Notes
- +0252 Dover – the Mean HW time difference is 2h 52 mins after Dover.
- ML – Mean sea level.
- Duration – the average time between Low and High Water at Tilbury.
- Standard Port tells you which to use. The arrow shows which way to move in the book to find it.
- Time differences – when a time difference is given as 0115, it means '1 hour and 15 minutes', NOT '115 minutes'.

Fig 14.2 Secondary port tidal differences from *Reeds Nautical Almanac*.

Height differences require similar interpolation in these cases. They are given at springs and neaps, but often you are halfway in between. European tables give mean spring and neap ranges on the tidal curves. If you can't find these, or there aren't any, it is easy enough to run your fingers down a month's tidal heights and see how yours compares with the highest and the lowest. Once you have this information, commonsense can be applied to the problem and a surprisingly accurate answer produced in your head.

I work my secondary port tides by using a simple box diagram that in the days of my freedom I sketched on the back of a cigarette packet. Now that I've kicked the habit, I use a handy ring-bound pad that lives under my chart table. The diagram for the calculation above looks like this: let's say HW London Bridge is 0600 and 6.5m, with LW London Bridge at 1500 and 0.9m.

HW London Bridge (from standard port tide table)	0600 UT	6.5m (half spring/neap)
Difference Tilbury (from almanac via interpolation data)	−00 47.5 mins (Say 48 mins)	−0.6m (from almanac)
HW Tilbury	0512 UT	5.9m

LW London Bridge	1500 UT	0.9m
Difference Tilbury*	−00.55	0**
LW Tilbury	1405 UT	0.9m

The issue of interpolating secondary ports causes more grief than any other item in the Yachtmaster syllabus. It is possible to deal with the matter graphically, and a good method is described in *Reeds Nautical Almanac*. In all honesty, it really is easier in practice to do it as described here, but there is no substitute for repetition. The answer is to set yourself problems to solve. This is not hard to arrange – I just produced one about Tilbury. It can provide a diverting way of passing a winter's evening when a power cut snuffs out the TV, when conversation drags, and you are down to your last candle.

> **SKIPPER'S TIP**
>
> ### Different authorities, different methods
>
> In the USA, but not in Canada, height differences are stated as a ratio. The figure (expressed as a decimal, e.g. 0.91) is multiplied into the tidal height given for the standard port and that is your secondary-port figure for the day. The system is simple to operate and works well for the moderate tides generally experienced.
>
> The French operate on a system of 'coefficients', whereby the number 20 represents a tiny neap, 45 a mean neap, 70 a mean tide, 95 a mean spring and 120, the highest number you're likely to see, an exceptional spring.

*Note that unlike the more typical six-hourly rate of change between the varying differences, in this case the difference in time between the LW figures given in the secondary port for Tilbury indicates only five hours – between 1100 and 1600. This pair is chosen here because our time of Low Water at London Bridge is 1500, which falls between them. The total difference figure of 25 minutes (between 50 minutes and 1 hour 15 minutes) is therefore divided by 5, not 6. Had the time of LW fallen between 1600 and 2300, the total time for the change to take effect would have been 7 hours, so the 25 minutes would have been divided by 7 to find the hourly rate of change.

**A decision must be made whether to go for 0m or 0.1m. You could say, 'Because we're halfway between springs and neaps it's going to be 0.05' and nobody would quarrel with you, but one must work within reasonably practical parameters. I have chosen to apply no LW height difference because that will err on the safe side of less water. Any decisions regarding how to use the information will, if need be, reflect this marginal inaccuracy. On most occasions it will be entirely irrelevant.

THE COMPLETE YACHTMASTER

Tidal definitions

Fig 14.3 shows the various heights of tide that must be defined. Most of these have been discussed already, but *tidal range* has not. The range of a tide is the amount by which that particular tide rises or falls between High Water and Low Water. The *height of tide* at any given moment, including High and Low Water, is the level by which the tide is standing above chart datum. The *rise of tide* is the level that the tide has reached above the Low Water figure for that particular tide.

Elevations and clearances

The charted vertical clearance of a bridge or power cable is now the clearance under it at Highest Astronomical Tide (HAT). The charted elevation of a light remains as it has always been, its height above MHWS (note that this is measured from the lantern itself, not the top of the structure). Lest this apparent complication sound like needless humbug from the cartographer, consider this: the big benefit of working depths from a charted value of lowest astronomical tide is that, even with a worst-case tidal height scenario, the negligent navigator has only to be able to read the numbers and relate them to his draught to stay safe. He will rarely find less water than the chart advertises. Running bridge heights from HAT delivers

Fig 14.3 Tidal definitions.

the same benefit. Even a muppet who can read and knows his air draught is thus guaranteed to avoid disappointment. The careful navigator near the limit of clearance may work the numbers and find he can scrape under. HAT figures are given at the bottom of the standard port tide tables for UK and continental ports.

Tidal definitions

CHART DATUM	Usually, the level of Lowest Astronomical Tide – the soundings on the chart are all referred to this.
LAT	Lowest Astronomical Tide. The lowest level to which tide heights will fall due to the effects of the Sun and Moon.
HAT	Highest Astronomical Tide. The highest level to which tide heights will rise due to the effects of the Sun and Moon.
TIDAL HEIGHT	The height at a specific moment by which the tide exceeds (or very occasionally falls below) the charted depth.
LOW WATER	The lowest level of a particular tide on a particular day. On a chart drawn to LAT in the UK, this will almost invariably be a positive figure, which must be added to a charted depth to find the depth of water.
HIGH WATER	The highest level of a particular tide on a particular day. The value must be added to a charted depth to find the depth of water.
TIDAL RANGE	The difference between High and Low Water for a specific tide.
MEAN LEVEL	Not used in practice very much, this is the average level of the sea's surface.
NEAP TIDE	Small tides occurring twice a month, shortly following half moon.
MHWN/MLWN	Mean High Water Neaps/Mean Low Water Neaps. Essentially, this means the respective heights of an average neap tide.
SPRING TIDE	Big tides occurring twice a month shortly after full moon and new moon.
MHWS/MLWS	Mean High Water Springs/Mean Low Water Springs. Essentially, this means the respective heights of an average spring tide.
RISE OF TIDE	The height of tide at a specific moment above the Low Water of the same tide.
CHARTED DEPTH	The sounded depth below chart datum.
DRYING HEIGHT	The height above chart datum to which a half-tide object or area 'dries' above LAT.
DEPTH OF WATER	Height of tide plus charted depth.
HEIGHT OF AN OBJECT	The height above Mean High Water Springs.
CLEARANCE UNDER AN OBJECT	The clearance height beneath a suspended obstruction or bridge at HAT.

Intermediate tidal heights

Tide tables give only figures for High and Low Water, whether they be for standard ports or as modified by you to give data for secondary ports. This information is of primary value, but you often need to know what is going on at times between High and Low Water.

Electronic chart plotters

One of the hidden glories of the electronic chart plotter is that a good processor will access tidal height information layered into the chart. Typically, a letter 'T', or some sort of self-explanatory icon, appears on the chart at a secondary or standard port for which data is available. All you need do is hover the cursor over this and you will be shown some sort of interrogation box asking if you want to see the real business. Answer 'yes' and, bingo! Up comes a graph, complete with all you need to know about today's tides, yesterday's, tomorrow's or any other day. Often, you can move your cursor around within the box to read out any specific time or height. The accuracy of these predictions is generally not bad, but often the graphs used are a simple sine wave such as would hold good for a port where the Rule of Twelfths works (see p. 135). In many places, this is less than perfect, so a more sophisticated graph is required. The Admiralty Tide Tables and the better almanacs supply these. Some plotters do too, but not all, so make sure you know how good yours is if you intend to rely on it. Amazingly, a really cheap mobile phone plotter app from a firm like Navionics offers full tidal height data as part of the package. Tablets do the same, in more detail. When compared with the miseries of students as late as the 1990s, sweating over a hot chart table and a secondary port calculation in the topsy-turvy world of the Solent, we live in enlightened times indeed.

A Navionics electronic chart with a tidal height icon. When this is activated, the tidal height graph is revealed. Not to be used for navigation

TIDAL HEIGHTS

Tides run to great heights and depths in northern Europe. Working with them enables a seaman to take advantage of all sorts of apparently inaccessible places. This haven near Southampton, England, is seen with the flood just starting to make. In four hours' time all these boats will be afloat and ready to go to sea.

PC programs

PCs and associated plotters can do everything the hardware plotter can, although a dedicated tide program will be required. Admiralty Total Tide does the lot.

These features appear to solve the age-old issue of working out the tides. Indeed they do but, as noted above, the answers they give may vary from the biblical truth according to their Lordships of the Admiralty. On my boat, I carry a bulkhead plotter and a PC plotter, plus apps for my mobile phone and iPad. All operate independently with their own batteries and GPS receivers, so I'm well covered unless the GPS satellites stop sending signals to Planet Earth or someone jams them, yet in a typical tidal situation, all will give slightly different answers to the same question. For this reason, if for no other, we must still be masters of the actual calculations for those times when we need to be absolutely certain. And of course, as always, there remains the not unlikely contingency that the gismo will fail. Show me the experienced sailor who doesn't carry a lead-line in case his echo sounder goes off pop…

The Rule of Twelfths

The ideal theoretical tide rises and falls following the even mathematical progression known as a *sine wave*. What this really means is that starting from its Low Water level, the tide rises by $\frac{1}{12}$ of its range in the first hour of the six that it will be coming up. In the second hour it speeds up, bringing in $\frac{2}{12}$ and giving a total now of $\frac{3}{12}$. The third and fourth hours, the central hours of the tide, show $\frac{3}{12}$ rises each, with the rate easing away to $\frac{2}{12}$ and $\frac{1}{12}$ in the last two hours. The falling tide behaves in a similar manner. The duration of High Water and Low Water is in theory momentary, though in reality little detectable change occurs for 15 minutes on either side of the time in the tables. This is known as the *stand*.

In many places the tide conforms to this ideal, and here the Rule of Twelfths can be confidently employed for tide calculations. All you must do to use this is to work out the range of the tide (HW–LW), divide it into 12 equal parts, then decide how many twelfths you actually need. A useful mnemonic is '1–2–3–3–2–1', which describes the number of twelfths rising or falling in their 6-hour sequences. Here is an example of the Rule of Twelfths:

> LW 1500 1.0m
> HW 2100 5.8m
> What height of tide is there at 1700?
> Range = 4.8m (5.8–1.0)
> $\frac{1}{12}$ = 0.4m (4.8/12)
>
> At 1700, $\frac{3}{12}$ of the range will have risen ($\frac{1}{12}$ in the first hour, $\frac{2}{12}$ in the second).
> $\frac{3}{12}$ = 1.2m
>
> Therefore, at 1700 there will be 1.2m *above* the figure given in the tide tables for Low Water (1.0m). Rise is added to the Low Water figure to find height, so at 1700 the height of tide will be 2.2m above chart datum.

Tidal curves

In the absence of any more accurate method being offered, the Rule of Twelfths can usually be used with moderate success. However, in certain areas (notably the UK, Ireland and northern Europe generally) the tides do not conform perfectly to the sine wave principle. Sometimes the rising and falling of the waters appear eccentric in the extreme. These places are best served by a graph showing accurately what is going on. The graphs and associated tidal data (the best available) are found in *Reeds Nautical Almanac* or the Admiralty Tide Tables (ATT).

Spring and neap curves

Notice the 'mean range' box at the top right-hand corner of Fig 14.4 (p. 137) giving spring and neap ranges, with a firm and a pecked line depicted alongside it. The tide curve with the solid line is the curve for spring tides and that with a pecked line is for neaps. You can ascertain rapidly by inspection whether today's tide is a spring or a neap, or somewhere near. If it falls between the two, you will use an imaginary curve between the solid and the pecked ones. This can easily be done by estimation to a degree of accuracy more than adequate for safe navigation. No interpolation sums are required in practice.

TIDAL HEIGHTS

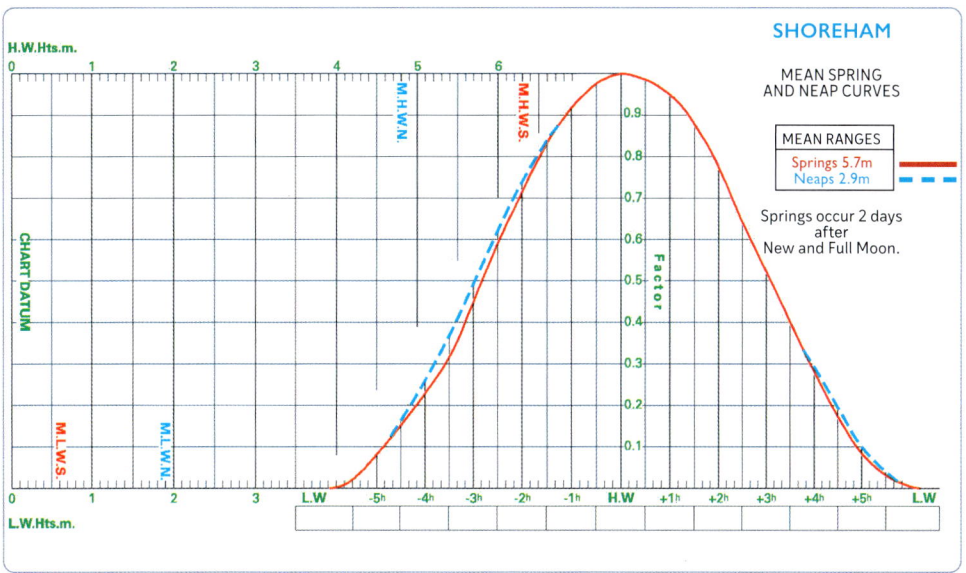

Fig 14.4 Tidal height curve for Shoreham (extract taken from *Reeds Nautical Almanac*).

The 'set up'

Whatever question you want to answer ('question', you notice – there are no more 'problems'), you start out by preparing the diagram for use on a given tide. Suppose we are setting it up for a day when the figures for the morning tide were as follows:

HW	5.6m	0700	
LW	1.6m	1310	range 4.0m

Notice straightaway that today's range, 4.0m, falls between the spring range of 5.7m and the neap range of 2.9m given in the mean range box. Now in order to 'set up' the diagram, draw a line (the 'line of the day') joining the height of Low Water at the bottom of the left-hand part of the picture with High Water at the top, and fill in the boxes beneath the curves for High Water and any other times of interest as in Fig 14.5. Once you have done this, you are ready to ask your question, which will probably be one of the following:

- At what time will there be a given height of tide?
- What will be the height of tide at a given time?

Let us take the first of these and be more specific: at what time on that particular morning will the tide at Shoreham have fallen to a height of 2.8m above chart datum? To find the answer you draw three straight lines, as illustrated in Fig 14.5 (overleaf).

137

THE COMPLETE YACHTMASTER

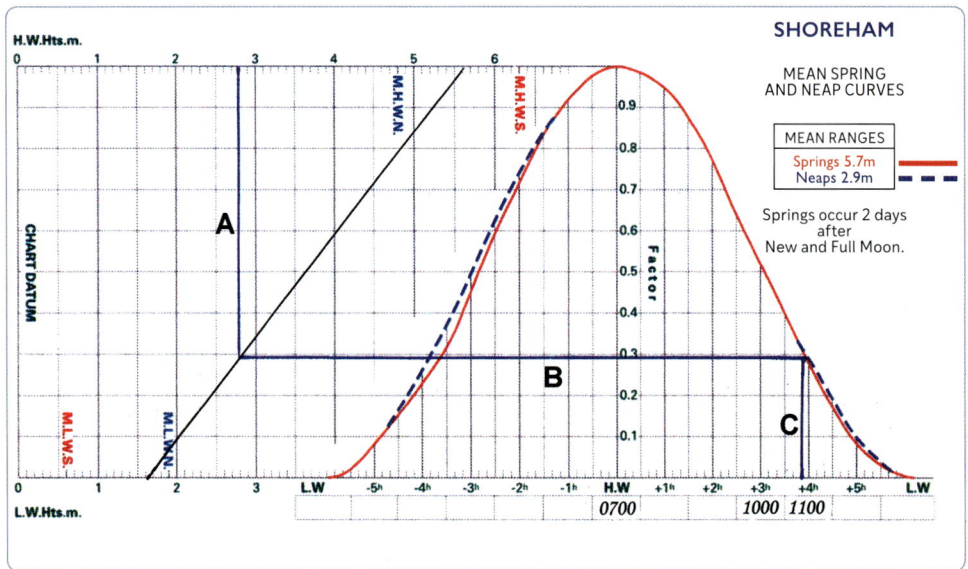

Fig 14.5 Tidal height curve in typical use (extract taken from *Reeds Nautical Almanac*).

1. Starting at 2.8m at the top of the diagram, drop a perpendicular A to your line of the day.
2. From where line A joins the line of the day, draw a line B across to the 'tide falling' side of the tide curve.
3. From where line B joins the tide falling curve, drop line C straight down to the time boxes, and there is the answer to your question. In this case, 1050.

The second question could be posed for the purposes of our example by simply reversing the first, in which case it would sound like this: to what height will the tide at Shoreham have fallen by about 1050?

To answer this, start (having 'set up' the picture as in Fig 14.5) at the other end with the time of 1050. From here you raise a perpendicular (line **C**) to the tide curve. Then draw in line **B** across the 'line of the day' and from there move up vertically (line **A**) to the height of tide scale and read off the height of 2.8m.

You'll have noticed by now that you don't have to do anything to the figure for tide height that you extract from the diagram in answer to the second question. The figure of 2.8m is the actual height of water above chart datum; that is all there is to it. Going in the other way, as in the first question, just enter the height of water required above any relevant charted depth and the diagram gives the time figure you are after. Once the time of day is set up, Low Water does not enter your calculations.

It takes a minute or two to set up the diagram, and thereafter you can find the height of tide within seconds.

TIDAL HEIGHTS

Secondary ports

The one small fly that remains kicking feebly in the ointment is the old favourite of secondary ports. The system for working these out probably can't be improved upon. Just work out the time and height of High or Low Water for your secondary port (see p. 129) and enter it on the diagram exactly as on Fig 14.5.

If you are operating in the areas adjacent to and including the Solent you'll find that, because of the tidal anomalies caused by the Isle of Wight, several extra sets of curves are supplied for the various groups of secondary ports. The only difference between these and all the other curves in the book is that, instead of working either side of High Water, they use Low Water as their point of reference. The time of Low Water is easier to predict in this region than that of the 'double High'.

Non-astronomical factors in tide movements

Published tidal predictions assume a standard barometric pressure and no weather effects. Standard pressure varies between 1017mb (English Channel in July) and 1007mb (Wick in January). If in doubt, use 1013mb. Thirty-four millibars over and above the standard figure will depress both High and Low Waters by 1ft (0.3m). If the pressure drops to 979mb (34mb below 1013mb), an extra foot of tide can be expected. It's more common to find 17mb delivering 0.15m, but it's all pro rata. Conveniently, 1mb of pressure is therefore approximately equal to 1cm of height difference.

Many areas experience their own local tide surges generated by local or distant weather conditions. I remember being told to shift my berth in St Petersburg because of a westerly gale way down the Gulf of Finland. They were right, too. A couple of hours later the dock was under water.

These surges are predictable to those who know the area, but they are rarely written down. Ask, if you are in doubt, but as a general rule, prolonged onshore winds push the tide up, and a protracted period with the wind offshore will drain it away.

The essence of a tidal height question

Because of the various elements of problems involving intermediate tidal height, it is easy to lose your head over them. Then the brain switches off and you decide to sail somewhere else where there is more water, which is a shame. You might also fail your ticket if you were under examination.

The way to succeed is to extract the vital question from the whole situation. As we have noted, this usually boils down to one of two: 'What time will there be so much water?' or 'How much water can I expect at a given time?' You may want to know what time you can safely cross a bar with a predetermined clearance under your keel, or you may need reassurance that you'll still be afloat alongside a drying wall after lunch. Possibly you are feeling your way through the fog near the top of a big tide and you want to reduce your sounded depth to a charted depth in order to relate it to your possible position on the chart. Another favourite query is how to find a suitable depth in which to anchor at half-tide.

All these are best solved by means of a diagram. You can scratch a quick drawing on the

THE COMPLETE YACHTMASTER

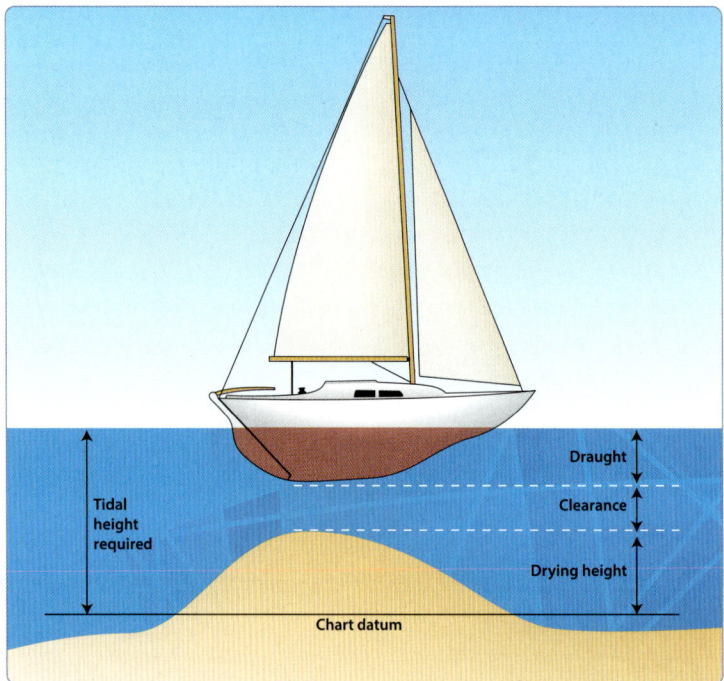

Fig 14.6 Height to cross a bar. Tidal height required = draught + clearance + drying height.

back of a serviette in no time at all, yet the process will do wonders for your clarity of mind. Once you know what it is you are looking for, you have only a simple tidal curve question or a Rule of Twelfths calculation to perform. Figs 14.6 (above) and 14.7 (opposite) illustrate the points.

Anchoring depths

Theoretically, questions arising over anchoring depths are no different from any other tidal height calculation. In practice, however, they are so simple that people tend to make them more complex than they need to.

When anchoring, one is after the maximum available shelter. This is usually so close to the shore that the chart is of little more than overall interest. It cannot indicate soundings every few boat's lengths all round the anchorage, but it will depict the lie of the bottom, how steeply it shelves, what the holding ground may be, and whether there are rocks or other dangers to be avoided. This is the process, once you have determined the general area in which to anchor:

- Fill in the tidal curve for the day, bearing in mind that the next Low Water is the critical factor.
- Decide the depth you will need to remain safely afloat at Low Water. This will be the yacht's draught + the clearance selected.

TIDAL HEIGHTS

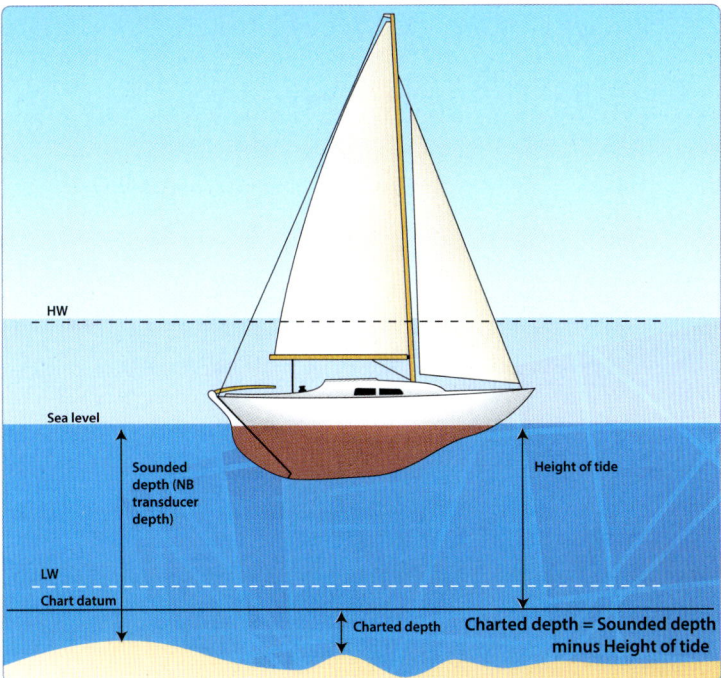

Fig 14.7 Finding charted depth.

- Consult the tidal curve and see how much the tide will fall between now and the next Low Water, even if the tide is rising at the moment. There is no need even to consider such matters as charted depth.
- Add this figure to the depth you have decided upon for Low Water.
- Sail in until you find this depth, then anchor. That is all there is to it.

Having ascertained the depth at which to drop the hook, now is the time to decide how much cable to lay.

- Sort out a suitable scope (usually about three times the depth of water for chain cable), then determine what the total depth will be at the next High Water.
- Consult the tidal curve to see how much the tide will rise by the time of High Water, even if the level is falling when you arrive.
- Add this figure to your anchoring depth. The total will be the depth at High Water.
- Alternatively, you could simply add the range of the tide (High Water – Low Water) to the depth you aim to be floating in at Low Water (Draught + Clearance). The result should confirm your other calculation.

Using tidal height calculations safely

However slick you become at solving tide problems, you should never forget that all your results are based on *predictions*, not established facts. Calculate your figures as accurately as you can, then allow a margin for error. This might be affected by a sensible assessment of the potential risks involved in grounding and upon how near to the truth conditions suggest your calculation is likely to be.

Only a fool believes his calculation to the 'nth' decimal point, but being over-timid is a sign of inexperience. Often I have heard failed Yachtmaster candidates blustering, 'I believe in playing safe at all times,' in circumstances where to sail over a drying patch with a calculated metre under the keel in calm water and a rising tide would be as 'safe' as staying at home.

To start with, take it easy, then slowly begin to sail your boat into areas where the chart says 'not enough water', but the tide tables say there is. Be prudent at all times, then the nasty surprise you will surely receive one day will not be dangerous. Remember the ancient adage: 'If you've never run aground, you're not trying hard enough.'

SKIPPER'S TIP

A time to ground ...

Take no liberties with a falling tide, especially near a lee shore. A rocky bottom will demand a greater clearance than a sandy one if you think things may be tight. You may even be prepared to chance running ashore on soft mud with a rising tide so long as the tide is rising and the wind will blow you off.

Predictions are useful, but a tide gauge tells the truth on the day. However, it must be known whether it refers to depth of water at some point, or to height of tide, which may be very different.

TIDAL STREAMS

15

In areas of strong tidal activity it is absolutely vital that you are aware of what is happening and that you plan to make the most of it if at all possible.

A boat sailing at 5 knots makes a good 8 miles an hour in a fair 3-knot current. With the same current running foul, her net gain drops to 2 miles an hour. If she is beating with a Vmg (Velocity made good to windward) of 3 knots, a similar tide will give her either 6 knots made good or a net gain of zero. Thus it will be seen that it is better by far to beat to windward with a fair tide than to reach against a foul one.

Tidal gates

Even in areas where the currents are generally weak, if there is any rise and fall of tide to speak of, places will emerge where the current becomes a significant factor. Where streams along the coast are strong in any case, salient headlands and narrow channels may produce violent currents for the mariner to contend with. Such places are known as *tidal gates* and it is important to time your arrival at them either for slack water if the sea is known to become dangerously rough, or for the period of fair tide.

In sea areas such as North Brittany, where the current gallops along at 4 knots even well offshore, the whole coast becomes a tidal gate. Fortunately, with such a stream running favourably, a decent boat can make a considerable distance in a fair tide, then anchor up while the stream runs foul. This enables you to take a rest, a meal, a run ashore and be ready for the next fair tide in six hours or so. 'Tiding' along like this is good fun, low on stress, and makes for acceptable progress. It is far better for morale than staying at sea and sailing on the spot for a quarter of a day.

 SKIPPER'S TIP

Deep and shoal water

As a general rule, currents flow more strongly in deep water than in shallow, where their movement is impeded by friction with the seabed. Therefore, if you are working up a shoreline against the tide it will pay you to keep well in, if there are no tactical reasons to do otherwise. If you want to win the full benefit of a fair stream, stick to the deep water.

Knowing the rate and direction of the tidal stream forms a vital part of cross-tide navigation, but this will be discussed fully in Chapter 22.

Tide-induced sea states

Wind blowing with the tide tends to flatten the sea, but wind against current chops it up mercilessly. In strong tides and gale conditions, particularly where the stream is whirling around a headland, dangerous seas can be generated. A shrewd observer offshore can tell when the tide has turned merely by noting the shape of the waves. Look for streaks of foam running down the backs of the short, steep seas. This is the sure sign of a weather-going current.

Tide races sometimes occur due to the shape of the land, and these are usually noted on the charts. If potentially dangerous overfalls accompany the race, small clusters of wavy lines will be grouped around the place in question. You should steer well clear of these in all but the most settled weather. Read your pilot book for more details, because such hazards vary in their intensity, but there are known locations of such notoriety that even on a flat calm day you would enter at your peril. One such is the Race at Portland Bill, halfway up the English Channel.

Information on tidal streams

Tidal stream atlases

The main areas of tidal influence covered by almanacs are featured in tidal stream atlases. The same data are also given in a smaller format in the almanacs themselves. Fig 15.1 is a typical illustration for the Channel Islands. You'll notice the box stating which hour of the tide it refers to. This one is for three hours before HW Dover and is one of a series of 12, covering the whole period of any tide, from LW through to six hours after HW. The information is self-explanatory except to note that, for clarity, the Admiralty chartlet misses out the decimal points in the numbers describing the neap and spring stream rates found in among the arrows. Thus when you see '12,24', you know it means 1.2 knots at neaps, and 2.4 at springs. The arrows show the direction of the tide, giving an excellent overall picture which can be read at a glance. Tidal stream charts are not only user-friendly, however, they are accurately surveyed so that you can lift the direction of an arrow to your navigation chart if need be by using your chart protractor.

 SKIPPER'S TIP

The reference hour

Note that if the tidal atlas, or any other source, refers you to '1 hour before HW Liverpool', it means, 'This information is good for 1½ hours before HW to ½ hour before.' It does not mean from 1 hour before HW until HW.

TIDAL STREAMS

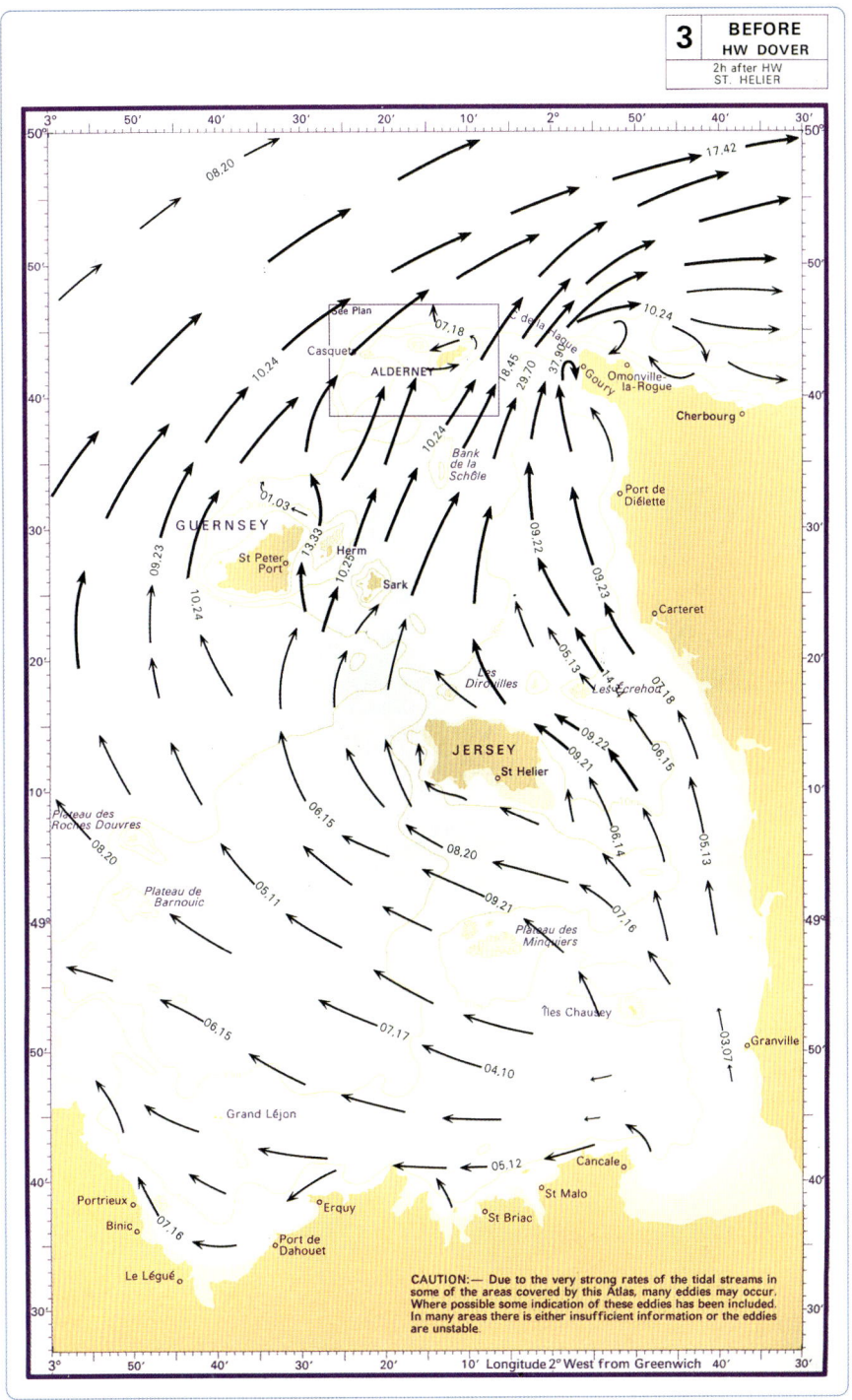

Fig 15.1 A page extracted from the *Admiralty Tidal Stream Atlas for the Channel Islands and adjacent coasts of France*. Not to be used for navigation

THE COMPLETE YACHTMASTER

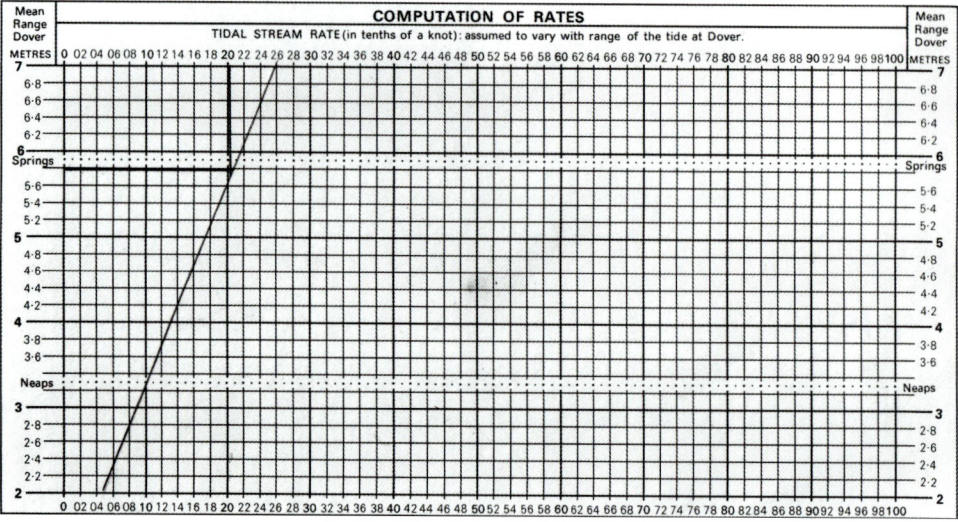

Computation of rates table from an *Admiralty Tidal Stream Atlas*.

Computation of intermediate rates

This can, of course, be done by mental interpolation and in practice it generally is. For examination purposes, or when it really matters to be as nearly right as you can be, use the 'Computation of Rates' diagram in the tidal stream atlas (see above). To get into this, you must first find the range of tide at Dover for the tide in question. Let's say that today's is 5.8m. With this information to hand, check the atlas page for the spring and neap stream rates you want. In this case, the tabulated streams are 'Neap 1.0, Spring 2.1'. Make a pencil mark for the spring rate on the spring dotted line and vice versa for the neap. Join the two dots with a pencil line.

Now enter the table on the left- or right-hand side with the range of tide for Dover you just worked out. Go across from this value until you reach your pencil line, then move up or down vertically and read off the interpolated stream rate at the top or bottom. In this case, mine was 2.0 knots. Hardly worth the trouble? Maybe, but then again, maybe not!

Don't be confused because this atlas is asking for a Dover range when you might be working out a rate off Cornwall. It's just a convenient way of coming up with a 'factor' for the table to work from.

Tidal diamonds

More accurate tidal predictions are to be found on many charts. British Admiralty and USA government charts deliver this in the form of 'diamonds'. Letters of the alphabet are depicted in a diamond-shaped frame (e.g. ⟨A⟩) at various locations. The tidal streams they identify are tabulated in a convenient location on the chart, by reference to 'hours before or after High Water' at a standard port. Some charts have a dozen or more of these diamonds, others few, or none at all. Spring and neap rates are generally given in the table.

Diamonds can be very convenient for plotting vector diagrams (Chapter 20), but bear in mind that the information they give you is good only for the point at which they are sited.

TIDAL STREAMS

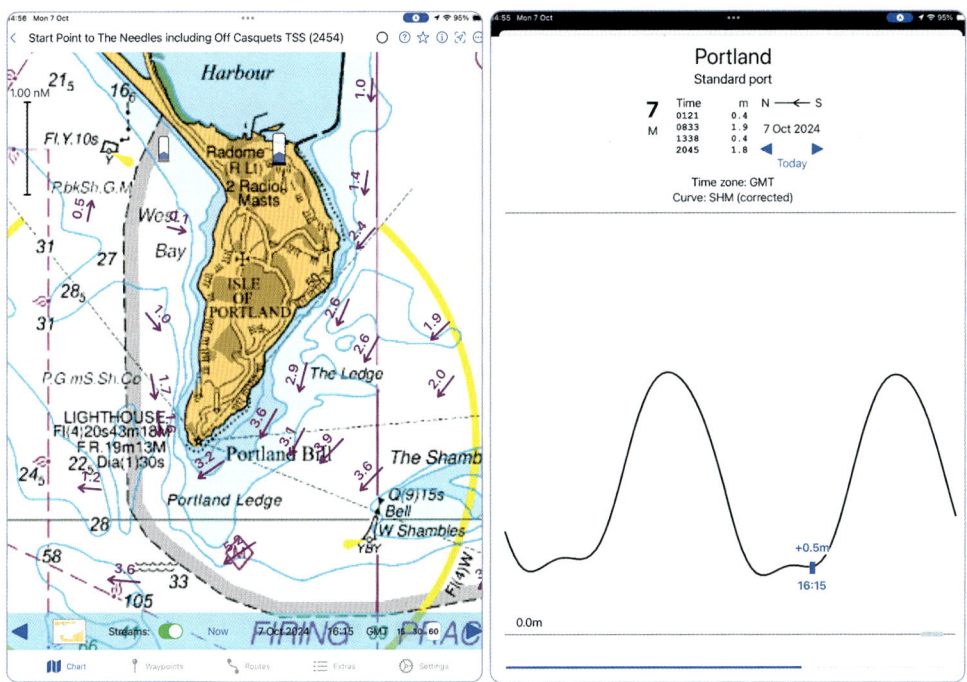

Tidal information on a small-scale chart of the English Channel for Portland Bill. This is an AngelNav raster chart. Note the tidal stream arrows and, at the top of the left-hand illustration, the icon indicating where the tidal heights will be found. A tap on this icon produces the page seen here on the right giving the full Admiralty tidal curve for Portland. Not to be used for navigation

Two cables away, things may be different. Where two or more diamonds are available, study the streams at each and make an intelligent assessment of the overall position from that. A certain amount of interpolation and interpretation may well prove necessary.

Current tables

In the USA, current tables are issued and published in the almanacs. They look for all the world like tide tables, except that they give the time of slack water and the times of the maximum flood and ebb current as well as their rates. Ebb information is given in italic typeface. The similarity with tide tables even extends to the 'differences' pages, where time differences for flood, ebb and slack are given for numerous associated locations. My own favourite is the table for Hell Gate at the northern entrance to East River, New York City. The current differences are offered for such colourful locations as 'Bronx River', 'Manhattan', 'Off 31st Street', and 'Brooklyn Bridge'.

Electronic plotters

Back in 2005, when I first added a section on electronic tidal stream prediction to what was then the latest edition of this book, I noted that much work remained to be done by the

Strong tidal activity near Land's End in the English Channel. The day is relatively calm but in heavy weather this place can become a maelstrom.

software developers. I also remarked that this was a scandalous situation, since a computer, properly programmed, could eat the job for breakfast. In 2025, I am pleased to report that, while some top-of-the-line hardware plotters still cannot compete with a traditional paper chart and the tidal stream atlas for ease of use and an accurate answer, other software companies are now delivering reliable, user-friendly data at the click of a mouse or the tap of a screen. While the stream material dished up by my mobile phone vector-chart app is delivered in an odd sort of format, which is far from friendly, AngelNav offers excellent, easy-to-use data drawn from the same source as the paper atlases.

The bottom line seems to be that while some plotters and apps are offering first-class information, others, which should know better, are no substitute for the paper delivery that navigators have used for over a hundred years. Which you choose is up to you, but when selecting a plotter from the many on offer, if tidal streams are important where you sail, make sure you ask the right questions.

Creative use of GPS in tidal stream deduction

A final source of tidal stream information is your electronic fixing system. The difference between a dead reckoning position corrected for leeway (Chapter 17) and a GPS fix is the set and drift experienced since the last plotted position. Alternatively, you can compare the GPS 'course and speed over ground' (COG and SOG) readouts with the compass heading and logged speed. The on-board data that the latter pair supply can only be measured through the moving water, while the GPS information is equally surely rooted

TIDAL STREAMS

This is not a seal making a good rate of knots; it's a fishing buoy in a strong tidal stream. It gives chapter and verse on what the tide is really doing – never mind the tables...

to the seabed. This time, the difference is your set and drift at the moment you take the readings. A fully interfaced system (Chapter 19) will read out set and drift on demand.

If your on-board information is sound, these methods can give a highly accurate indication of what the set and drift are, or have recently been. Sadly, they cannot peek into the future which, in the end, is more generally what is required. However, comparing the known set and drift with the predictions can indicate whether a particular tide is behaving itself. Sometimes, a tide is larger than predicted and produces faster streams. Noting any regular trend may therefore prove helpful if you have time to handle the rather cumbersome process of deduction.

Personal observation

Tide tables are all right, and GPS can be very helpful, but for accurate information you can't beat your own eyes. Around the turn of the tide, look for direct evidence. A lobster pot marker is the best atlas in the world. If you're moored, don't look in the book; look over the side.

In thick fog, if you come upon a buoy, stem the tide alongside it. When the situation has become stable, read your log and your compass. The log gives you the speed of the stream, your compass offers you the reciprocal of its direction. No tide tables or GPS can beat that, but remember that your information is similar in one respect to that given by a diamond. Two hundred yards away, things may not be quite the same. Look at the terrain on the chart and make an intelligent guess, then plot your next heading, but leave a wide margin for error all the same.

Calshot Spit light float in the Solent. The pilots insisted on keeping the anchor ball in place at the bow because it enabled them to see at a glance which way the tide was flowing.

16 TRADITIONAL NAVIGATIONAL INPUTS

The next three chapters study traditional means of navigation. With GPS, it is theoretically possible to pilot a yacht without reference to these methods, but to contemplate such a policy would be folly. Even setting aside what one might do if the GPS receiver itself or the boat's electrics failed, there can be no check on an electronic fix without a carefully considered estimate of position. Hence, it will be impossible to evaluate a course the computer may be giving to its next waypoint.

GPS-derived information comes to your chart table entirely from sources outside the yacht. In order to perform critical cross-checks on this, a navigator requires input from on board. Unless you are driving an aeroplane with an inertial navigation system, or a supertanker equipped with a gyrocompass, this means employing the three traditional sources of hard information: the compass for direction, the log for distance run through the water, and the lead or echo sounder for determining the depth.

The major difference between these instruments and any satellite input is that they are under your direct and continuous control. They may not be so sparklingly accurate as GPS, but they are – or should be – reliable and understandable. They also boast the feature that only you can turn them off, which is not the case with GPS. The US military establishment that sponsors the satellites retains the right to degrade accuracy, or even shut the whole assembly down if national security demands it. More details of this will be found in Chapter 19, but in the meantime it is true to say that terrorist activity could damage the GPS system. It wasn't made by God either, so the whole system might, just possibly, break down. Apart from radar, which is also self-contained and on board, the tried and trusted friends of lead, log and compass remain the firm foundation on which our navigation is built. For these reasons, they should be understood and treated with the respect they need in order to function at their best.

The compass

Over the centuries there have been various navigational breakthroughs that have provided a huge increase in the security of the mariner. The use of man-made satellites is a recent example, but it pales before the quantum leap offered by the publication of the first charts. Useful though these were, they did not outshine the arrival of the concept of longitude, which took place some centuries earlier. Even these are nothing compared with the compass.

TRADITIONAL NAVIGATIONAL INPUTS

The Vikings may have contrived to cross the Atlantic without one, but to describe their navigation as 'hit and miss' would be less than half right, because they missed far more regularly than they hit.

During the last century or two the compass has become capable of extreme accuracy, so long as it is properly installed and used. A number of factors affect its readings. Some can be removed; others you must live with. The first is variation.

Variation

The theory of magnetic variation was expounded in Chapter 12, but little was said about coping with it in practice. Variation is a factor that we can't change. We must therefore allow for it in our workings by knowing exactly what it is doing to our compass reading. It differs, depending upon where you are. Some areas have east deviation, others west, but it is always charted, so at least you know what is going on.

There will be numerous occasions when you have worked up a course in *degrees true* (i.e. with north and south straight up and down the meridian), but you need to hand it up to the helmsman in *degrees magnetic*. A magnetic heading is the true heading corrected for variation, and if your compass reads accurately, that is the heading you will actually use. Similarly, a bearing taken with a compass will be magnetic, but you may wish to plot it in degrees true. You therefore require a simple, foolproof way of converting one to the other.

The most logical way of doing this, until it becomes second nature, is to draw a small diagram like Fig 16.1a. Here, the variation is 9° west and the heading is 210° (true). By sketching in the lines around the circle from the true north and the magnetic north it is immediately obvious that the magnetic heading is greater than the true by 9°, giving a course to steer of 219°M. Fig 16.1b indicates a 9° east variation, with the angle between magnetic north and the course being that much smaller than that from the true north. The course to steer here would be 201°M.

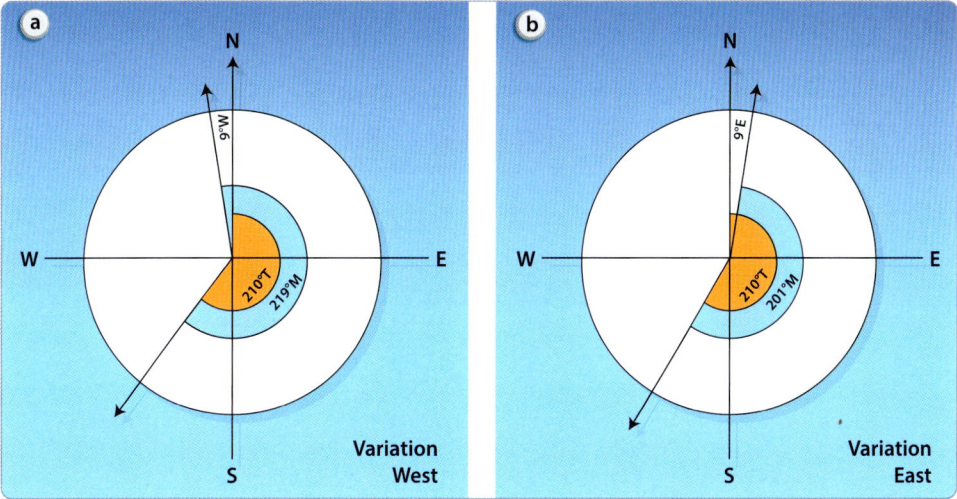

Fig 16.1 Applying compass variation.

If you don't have a pictorial mind, you may prefer one of the standard *aides-memoires*. My favourite is:

> Error West, compass best
> Error East, compass least

For 'best' read 'biggest', and you have a foolproof system that conforms perfectly to the diagram.

If the compass is 'best' with the error on the west side of true north (magnetic greater than true), it follows that the true heading will be less than the magnetic, should you be converting that way. 'Error East, compass least' (magnetic less than true) means also that the true is greater than the magnetic with east variation.

Here are two worked examples:

> 1) Course to steer is 248°T. Variation is 7°W. What is the compass heading?
> 248°T
> + 7°W (Error West, compass best)
> = 255°M
>
> 2) Flashy Point light bears 355°. Variation is 10°E. What is the true bearing?
> 355°M
> + 10°E (Error East, compass least. Error is therefore added back to convert from compass to true)
> = 365°T. This of course is nonsense. The correct way of expressing it is 365°T − 360°T = 005°T

A second mnemonic preferred by some, including my wife, is the creative use of the word 'CADET':

'C' stands for 'compass' (or anything on the magnetic side of the equation), 'T' equals 'true'.

Looking from left to right, if you move from C to T, you walk across the letters A-D-E, which more or less spell, 'ADD EAST'.

> Add East
> CADET ──────▶

Thus, 'Compass to True, Add East'.

It follows that moving the other way – from True to Compass, you will subtract East.

If the error to be compensated for is 'West', the situation is reversed again, thus: 'Because when moving from compass to true (CADET) I add East, I must subtract West', and so on.

Two typical examples would look like this...

TRADITIONAL NAVIGATIONAL INPUTS

> 1) Course to steer is 165°T. Variation is 4°E. What is the compass heading?
> Compass to True = Add East (CADET), so True to Compass subtracts East.
> Compass course is therefore 165° – 4° = 161°M
>
> 2) Grisly shoal light bears 285°M. What is its true bearing with variation 3°W?
> Compass to True = Add East (CADET), so Compass to True subtracts West.
> Bearing is therefore 282°T

Deviation

The other major factor affecting a compass is *deviation*. This is an error originating from within the boat. Any ferrous metal affects a compass to a certain extent. If it is too close (say, either 4 or 5ft in a horizontal direction) the results will be noticeable.

Deviation, unlike variation, is not only undesirable, it can be minimised by your own efforts. Site the steering compass intelligently and don't leave screwdrivers, battery driven appliances, radio speakers and other magnetically active bric-a-brac scattered around it. If you've done this successfully on a GRP production cruiser you may end up with little discernible deviation. On other craft, though, you'll have some left for sure. If your yacht is steel, or ferrocement, there will be plenty.

The first thing to do about deviation is to try to get rid of it. This is achieved by employing the services of a compass adjuster. He will come along with his magic toolbag and work his miracles with compensating magnets. If you want to try this for yourself, buy a book on the subject or go to college, but don't ask me to help. It's a very skilled and specialised job.

The compass adjuster will leave you a *deviation card* which shows how you can now expect your compass to perform (Fig 16.2, p. 154). Look at this and you'll see that, unlike variation, deviation varies with the yacht's heading. This makes sense when you realise that since the boat is effectively turning round under a stationary compass card, the relationship between the 'north pointer' and the boat's ironwork will vary.

Deviation is expressed in degrees E or W *of the vessel's magnetic heading*. Thus, if you dial up your course in degrees true you must convert this to magnetic before consulting your deviation card for the final adjustment to compass. If you are correcting the other way, the opposite process is required, again with magnetic in the middle.

A true heading to which variation and deviation have been applied is called a *compass heading*.

In practice, all this is simple to deal with, so don't be daunted. There's a wonderful mnemonic, beloved of all sailors, which goes like this:

True	=	True
Virgins	apply	Variation (Error West, compass best, etc)
Make	gives	Magnetic
Dull	apply	Deviation
Companions	gives	Compass

THE COMPLETE YACHTMASTER

Fig 16.2 A deviation card.

If you are converting from compass through to true and you happen to be British, 'Cadbury's Dairy Milk Very Tasty' will stand you in good stead. If you are not a native of Blighty you may never have heard of this noble confection, so you'll either have to come up with something else, or reverse your True Virgins.

Note that because deviation is applied to the magnetic heading, you must refer to this on the deviation card, not the true heading. The difference is unlikely to matter in practice, although it might in a steel yacht, but principle is principle, and we may as well get it right.

Here's a full-on 'True to Compass' example, complete with deviation, true virgins and all the fun of the fair. Tackle it step by step and its bark is far worse than its bite.

> Course to steer is 145°T
> Variation is 7°W
> Deviation is 6°E
> What is the Compass Course?

TRADITIONAL NAVIGATIONAL INPUTS

TRUE	VIRGINS	MAKE	DULL	COMPANIONS
145°T	7°W (Additive – error W compass best)	152°M	6°E (Subtractive – ditto)	146°C
TRUE	VARIATION	MAGNETIC	DEVIATION	COMPASS

Totalling up

For a quick result it's possible to 'net' the variation and deviation into a single value. In the above example, this would be 7°W – 6°E = 1°W. Apply this to the True value by either 'Error West, etc' or 'CADET' and your answer will be 146°C – just the same. While this is often a good and easy system in practice, it is wrong in principle, because you have applied deviation to the true and not the magnetic heading. Outside the examination room and away to sea, therefore, you might opt for it, especially where deviation values are small and are changing slowly.

Swinging the compass

Even if the compass adjuster has visited you within the last year, you should still swing your own compass at least once every season or when your cruises take you through a change of latitude of more than 10°.

Unlike compass adjusting, swinging is not a black art. It can be successfully achieved by any two people, given a handbearing compass, a calm sea and an identifiable object at least three miles away. You don't have to know what this actually is, because you'll only be using it as a reference point.

The steering compass is swung by comparing it with the handbearing compass on various headings, having first ensured that the handbearing compass is sited so as to be free of deviation. This requirement is achieved by finding a site where magnetic interference is liable to be at a minimum. It is checked by noting the bearing of the distant object with the handbearing compass as you steer the boat in a slow, tight circle. The change in the yacht's position in relation to the object will be unmeasurable in terms of angle, so if the bearing stays the same you have 'proved' your handbearing compass *in that location*. If the bearing wanders as the heading swings, try again from another part of the deck until you succeed, as you will sooner or later in any but the most difficult of craft.

All that now remains is to steer the yacht on a suitable selection of headings around the whole circle while your mate sights dead ahead with the handbearing compass from the chosen place on deck. He, of course, will be reading the correct magnetic headings. Compare each one with the reading of the steering compass. The difference is the deviation. If the steering compass shows a larger figure than the handbearing compass, the deviation is 'West', and vice versa. When all 16 headings have been noted, plot them on your deviation card and set course for a better landfall. The job can be readily tackled anywhere that you find yourself with a spare half hour.

Given totally slack water and no leeway it is also possible to check a compass against a GPS COG (course over ground) readout. Set the GPS or plotter to give its track in degrees magnetic (dial up 'auto' from the menu to ensure the variation is correct), then steer on the usual series of headings and compare the COG with the compass. Any discrepancies are deviation. Don't assume that it is slack water because the tide table says so. Confirm by observing that a buoy or beacon has no movement of water against it.

Heeling error

When a yacht is heeled, the relative position of her compass and the ironmongery that is deviating it may change enough to affect its reading. This is known as *heeling* error. I have never been on board a yacht, large or small, cheap or expensive, that boasted a table for this. Indeed, to contemplate arranging for one would be totally unrealistic. This does not mean that heeling error will go away. The best way to deal with it is to check it on passage against the handbearing compass.

When you are on a long leg where the compass counts, ask your mate to take the handbearing compass to the site you used for compass swinging and check the yacht's heading. Any difference between the two compasses that is not anticipated from the deviation card is the heeling error. You'll have to hope that the handbearing compass is not being affected by this as well as the steering compass, but that is a fairly safe assumption. The error won't amount to more than a degree or two at most in all normal circumstances. For a video description visit: https://youtu.be/tm7N2E52Y_Y.

Local magnetic anomalies

The composition of the Earth's crust is such that certain areas contain items that disturb its magnetic field. When you are passing one of these, your compass may develop a noticeable error, or it may go completely haywire. However, this should not come as a surprise, because these anomalies are usually announced on the chart – the paper chart or its raster equivalent, that is. You may well not discover any mention of the matter on some leisure vector charts. A magnetic anomaly can have unexpected effects on a yacht steering by autopilot. As the magnetic Fluxgate compass buried deep in the boat's hidden places is affected by the magnetic shift, the autopilot will follow what the compass imagines is the correct course. The ship's head may suddenly swing considerably to one side or the other. This is at best disconcerting. In a tight situation such as may be encountered when passing a dry dock or some other huge heap of ferrous metal close to the shore, it can be dangerous, so be aware.

Compass dip

The magnetic field that determines the direction in which the compass needle points does not always run conveniently parallel to the Earth's surface. In higher latitudes it dives in towards the Earth at a considerable angle, and of course the compass needle tries to follow it. The needle's bearings constrain it from doing this, but the fact that it is trying renders its movements ever more sluggish until, in certain areas, the compass stops working altogether. Sailors in moderate latitudes need not be concerned with this, but if you are planning an epic voyage into the ice, it will be a factor for consideration.

TRADITIONAL NAVIGATIONAL INPUTS

Every boat should carry a handbearing compass, but don't forget the iPhone carries a surprisingly accurate alternative compass. The author has used his when it mattered. It works!

The log

Given that you know the direction in which you have been travelling, the next vital ingredient of 'dead reckoning' classical navigation is how far you have come. This is ascertained by using a *log*.

In ancient times, mariners literally guessed their distance run. Having made a number of ocean crossings myself without using a log, I can testify to the surprising accuracy of a well-tuned observer's eye aboard a ship with which he is familiar.

However, since any instrument should be an improvement over no instrument, it wasn't long before mariners came up with a system of measurement.

The original type of log – still in use well into the 19th century – worked on 'speed per hour', which, multiplied by the number of hours until the next reading, gave the distance run. Except in a racing yacht, distance run is what the navigator usually wants. Speed is only of interest if you are shaping a course and need to predict how far you may travel in the next hour. Your speed *now* in a sailing boat gives no more help with your ETA than how far you ran in the last hour. Speed is merely useful as a means of determining distance. The present fixation with 'we did 8.7 knots today' sounds rather like a schoolboy boasting that his father's car is capable of 103mph, according to the maker's propaganda. Both pieces of information are largely irrelevant in real life.

The original log worked as follows: a fan-shaped 'log chip' attached to a knotted line wound on to a reel was hove over the stern of the ship. The chip, or log, held its position in the water and dragged out the line as the ship sailed away from it. The knots in the line were made at intervals representing 1 nautical mile per hour. If 8 knots ran out in a given time,

157

measured by a sandglass, the vessel was logging 8 nautical miles per hour. Hence the term 'knot' and hence the name 'log', which is still attached to the most sophisticated electronic distance measuring device.

The trailing log

These mechanical devices, still used by some yachts (including my own, as back-up), are a major step up from the old 'log chip' arrangement. They work by towing a 'fish' shaped so that it will rotate at a known rate, from a simple analogue measuring device attached to the aft part of the vessel. Distance run is usually measured, realistically, to the nearest ¼ mile. These instruments are reliable and accurate. If yours over-reads or under-reads it will at least be consistent, so that once this is known, you can correct it as easily as you would a watch that runs fast.

The fact that you must actively stream such a log, and haul it in again, is no nuisance at all. If you are piloting in good weather and you can see where you are, you don't need a log anyway, so you can leave it in the box. Bring it out when land fades away astern, or when the mist thickens. The very act of streaming a trailing log forms a punctuation mark in any passage that says, 'From now on, we take the navigation seriously.'

Don't wrap the log-line around your propeller, watch out for weed on the fish, and beware of its readings if it is in direct line astern of the propeller and you are under power. With these provisos, no better system has yet been devised for the cruising yacht. Inexpensive and reliable, a quality trailing log such as the 'Walker Excelsior' may not supply the data required to run linked functions, but it remains a joy to use.

Electronic logs

Some are better than others, but most are prone to attack by weed and marine organisms. Because they are rarely antifouled, electronic logs on cruising yachts are generally nothing like as accurate as the old trailing logs were. To be in with any sort of chance, they must be withdrawn into the hull at least once a fortnight and thoroughly cleaned. If you don't fancy the water ingress – usually a minor annoyance in these days of non-return valves, rather than the shocking fright it once was – don't expect decimal-point accuracy. In fact, after a month or two, don't expect much at all, and ignore the 'true wind' readout, which is using the log input to make its calculations. If functioning properly, a modern log does give a lovely big dial to announce what you rarely need to know; your water speed. They do read distance in tenths of a mile, though, which is handy. Some of them purport to read in hundredths, which is of no use to anyone except 'electronic man' – who is so misinformed about the real world that he wants to know where he is to the nearest 20 yards (18m) while on passage. Even for close-in pilotage, such promise of accuracy can be a snare. The log can only read distance through the water, so if you rely on it among the rocks in a tideway, you are bilged for certain.

Calibrating a log

Some logs can be calibrated to remove error. If yours cannot, there is no cause for concern, so long as you know what's going on. In either case, you should be empirically aware of its performance.

TRADITIONAL NAVIGATIONAL INPUTS

 SKIPPER'S TIP

Read the instructions
If you have an electronic log, for goodness sake study the instruction book. I could tell you of a number of navigators who have dumped their all-important distance run at the punch of a wrong button. The old-fashioned trailing log was far safer, because the worst that could happen was that a shark chomped off the spinner. At least then you knew where you were when the log stopped turning, because the beast didn't generally flop aboard and zero the dial to complete the job.

The traditional way to calibrate the log is to take a two-way run down a measured mile at slack water. Divide the results in half and compare the answer with the charted distance. The difference is the log error. Either correct it out, or note it in your log book and apply it in the future.

The hard reality is that with the added security of GPS, few yacht skippers actually do this any more, but the subject must not be ignored. The main reason for having a log is to provide data for cross-checking GPS, and to look after us should it fail. In either case, we need to know what it's doing, so calibrate it we still must.

Fortunately, any GPS receiver will read out 'SOG' or 'speed over the ground'. Choose a calm day, wait for slack water (note that no current is running past a handy buoy), motor steadily ahead at a moderate speed, then read the log manual and twiddle the knobs until its reading coincides with the SOG. Nothing is simpler, although some units seem to delight in making this basic task so non-intuitive that one fears for the immortal soul of the maniac who devised it. Perhaps because of this, many people don't take the trouble and some silly boat speeds are recorded as a result.

A final balance is to compare logged passage distances with the charted or GPS distances over an extended period. Having taken due account of any tide or current, does it over-read consistently, or under-read, or neither? Whatever the case, so long as you see a noticeable pattern, you can adjust your future log readings with a confident sense of realism.

Depth

The third essential navigational input is depth. We have already discussed something of the meaning of 'depth' as it relates to tidal height, but the reality of how much water you have underneath you is only truly revealed by some sort of measuring device.

The lead-line
Every boat should have one of these. Not only does it provide vital back-up when the echo sounder goes down, it can also be carted off in the dinghy to sound difficult entrances or to see whether you will swing clear of a shoal while anchored. It also gives an absolutely accurate reading, so when you are alongside a berth that may dry, you can be sure of your ground.

A lead-line need not be an elaborate affair. Traditionally, the various fathoms were marked with pieces of leather, bunting and odd knots you were called upon to commit to memory. Unless you are using it as your primary source of information (and there are still people who do), you don't need to go to these lengths. Just have a line 10 fathoms (20m) long, and knot it at whatever intervals seem appropriate to your needs. One extra knot at the boat's exact draught will prove exceedingly useful.

A traditional lead has a dimple in the bottom which you can 'arm' with tallow or, failing that, engine grease or even margarine. This will bring up a sample of the bottom for your perusal. Fishermen used to find their way round the North Sea with only a compass and a lead, literally sniffing and tasting the samples. For us, it's enough to know what depth we are anchoring in.

The echo sounder

These instruments are, on the whole, reliable and can be cheap. Be aware, however, that varying water densities, passing fish shoals, and sundry other interferences may cause your sounder to give a false echo. This is harder to spot with an analogue or digital readout than with the sort of rotating light emitting diode (LED) instrument now rarely seen. If an LED reading seems ambiguous, turn down the sensitivity (gain) control until only one reading can be discerned. This is more than likely to be the correct one.

Left to themselves, yacht sounders generally read 'depth below the transducer', but most can be calibrated for either 'depth below keel' or 'total depth to the surface'. It is obviously important to know which option is in operation.

If it reads depth below transducer, measure the transducer's depth below the waterline and note it in the log book the first time you see your boat's bottom. All you need do is add this to any sounded depth to determine the total depth of the water. Similarly, if you have said to yourself, 'I must anchor in 4.5m,' and your transducer depth is 0.5m, you will drop the pick when the sounder reads 4.0m.

If you've a mind to calibrate your sounder, note that the true professional will set it up to 'total depth of water'. This saves a step when reducing to soundings in fog. It also instantly relates depth to what the chart says with no more adjustment than adding height of tide. As far as grounding goes, you know the draught of your boat. She goes aground when the sounder reads this figure. Watching the numbers reduce to 1.8m as you wait for the crunch is no more onerous a task than observing it slither down to zero. If you're still worried about grounding, please read the final paragraph of this section.

Many yacht charter companies now calibrate their sounders to 'depth below keel' in order to show novices how close they are to discovering the ultimate truth. Unfortunately for competent charterers, such well-meaning operators often 'add a bit for safety'. This is in fact the deepest insult imaginable. How is one to navigate when one's calculations are based on somebody else's undefined idea of what constitutes 'safety'? Don't be fooled. Safety begins with knowing exactly what the situation is to the limits of the best available data. Armed with this, the proper skipper can make his or her own judgement about how much clearance to allow.

TRADITIONAL NAVIGATIONAL INPUTS

> **SKIPPER'S TIP**
>
> ### The final arbitration
> Whether or not you've had the opportunity to measure the transducer's depth, it's always worth finding a quiet river with a gently shelving weather shore and a rising tide. Gingerly approach the edge and quietly run your boat aground. Note the sounder reading at this critical condition and you will always know the bottom line.

Only a nudge on a friendly bottom can really reveal the truth about a sounder reading.

17 THE ESTIMATED POSITION

Whether we like it or not, the estimated position (EP) marches hand-in-hand with the GPS fix as the core of today's navigation. There is a tendency to think of the fix, whether electronically derived or worked up from other means, as being the centrepiece, but a fix alone is, as my grandfather might have observed, like tripe without vinegar. Contrary to what one might assume, the fix does not arise from a vacuum to reassure the navigator, it follows the EP as surely as the cart rattles along behind the horse.

Most of the time when we are sailing, part of our mind is working up an EP. Whether we are sheeting in the genoa to accommodate a windshift, wondering if we'll lay our objective, or turning in to an unmarked river mouth having decided we've run far enough to clear the shoals in the entrance, we are estimating our position. We may opt for putting nothing on the chart, but the EP is in our minds just the same.

Even when you are sailing waters you know well and never bring out a chart at all, you are still estimating your position. You are aware of the rocks, and you make an educated guess as to whether or not you will clear them. You may possibly know of a defined clearing line, in which case you are halfway to a fix, but mostly you estimate.

On an offshore passage where you have decided to run a plot, you may have chosen to estimate your position on the chart. Having plotted the EP, the next step is to firm it up by means of a fix. However this is derived, the EP still comes first. An experienced navigator using GPS may elect not to plot the EPs, but he is still aware of where he should be. If his electronic plot runs adrift from his mental EP, he jumps on it like a terrier and finds out why. Any fix serves either to confirm or throw doubt on the EP, whether the latter was plotted or not.

If, for any reason, a full fix is not available, the EP is all you will have. You should therefore take it seriously and know how to plot it with all the art and science at your disposal. The first stage is the *dead reckoning position* (DR).

A DR is worked up from two sources only: your course steered, and your distance run from the last known position. It is plotted by drawing a suitable *heading* line on the chart and it is marked with a small cross. A DR should not be used on its own, because it leaves out two vital factors affecting where you have actually been.

THE ESTIMATED POSITION

Leeway

Any boat sailing with the wind on or forward of the beam makes leeway (Fig 17.1). In fact, she makes it all the time except when the wind is dead aft, but it becomes much less significant once the wind is abaft the beam.

How much leeway you make depends on the boat, the wind and the sea. A powerful 40ft (12m) cruiser hard on the wind in force 4 (15 knots) and a calm sea makes only 2° or 3°, while a 22ft (6.7m) bilge-keel yacht trying to hack to windward in force 6 (28 knots) could be sliding off at 20° or more.

The only way of determining your leeway is to look at your wake in relation to the fore-and-aft line of your boat. If it's dark and you can't see it, guess 7° when you are going to windward in moderate conditions for your boat and you probably won't be too disappointed. When you have a good view of the proceedings you might try to measure leeway by comparing a compass bearing of your wake with the reciprocal of your heading, or by holding a chart protractor up to your eye to turn your guesstimate into an empirical assessment.

When the going is rough and danger lies to leeward, *never risk underestimating leeway*. To do so is far too easy and the results of a mistake can be very nasty indeed.

When plotting an EP, you should always apply leeway to your heading. This makes it into a *water track* and shows where you have actually been through the water. The line that appears on the chart with the modified DR at the end of it should be the water track rather than the heading. If you try to draw both, or even part of both, the result could be confusing. Stick to the water track, then you'll always know what you've plotted and there will be no ambiguity. Mark it on the chart with a single arrowhead halfway along its length.

Fig 17.1 Leeway.

The practicalities of this are straightforward. Lay your protractor on the chart against the last known position, indicating your heading. Now imagine the wind blowing across the chart. Swivel the protractor around the point of departure so that it turns *downwind* through however many degrees you have decided. Now draw in your water track along its edge.

THE COMPLETE YACHTMASTER

Plotted vectors

The tide vector

The second factor affecting your estimate of where you are is the set and drift due to tidal stream, or any other current. The information is extracted from the sources described in Chapter 15. It is plotted on to the end of the measured water track. Its direction is that of the tide, and its length is the distance a free-floating object would travel in the time for which the vector is being plotted. The tide vector is identified by three arrowheads. At its measured end, a triangle with a time against it marks the EP.

Ideally, an EP is plotted at the end of a 'tidal hour'. This makes all calculations and constructions as simple as possible. If the boat has covered 5 miles, that is the length of the water track. The tide may be setting at 1.8 knots on a bearing of 250° (any tide directions, like all charted compass bearings, are given in degrees true). The tide vector will thus be 1.8 miles long on that heading. The EP at the end of the hour is on the end of the tide line.

If you need an EP for less than an hour you must make a pro rata adjustment to the length of the tide vector. If the EP is for two hours, or for a period of less than two hours but straddling a part of two tidal hours, it is plotted like this: first draw the water track for the desired distance run. Now plot the first hour's tide on the end of it, or the first pro rata period of tide if less than one hour. Last, plot the second hour, or part of an hour, on the end of the first tidal vector. The EP is at its end.

Fig 17.2 Estimated position when beating.

164

THE ESTIMATED POSITION

If you are beating to windward you will be tacking at all sorts of odd times in order to work your wind shifts (Chapter 21). The last thing you want is to be plotting an EP every time you go about, because you'll find yourself trying to work out some impossible fractions just when you least feel like doing so. Instead, note the times and log readings of all your tacks in the log book, keep a commonsense eye on where you are, then when you are ready, plot a 'compound EP' (Fig 17.2, p. 164). All you need do is plot all your DRs (allowing for leeway), one after the other. When you reach the last one, plot all the tide vectors for the various one-hour periods your run has involved on to this final DR position. Plot the tide vectors one after another also, then lay your EP on the end of the last one. The job can be done very smartly indeed.

The echo sounder

We'll be seeing in the next chapter how an EP should be checked with a fix, if possible, but whether it is or not, you should always hit the echo sounder immediately after reading the log preparatory to plotting an EP. If necessary, make an approximate correction in your head for

A classic EP. UK navigators won't usually insert the numbers on the course and tide vectors. US users may choose to do so. They may also omit the arrow heads. Not to be used for navigation

any tidal height, then check the sounding with the charted depth in the vicinity of the EP. If the two coincide, credibility of the EP is improved. If there is a marked discrepancy, the EP must immediately be treated with some suspicion.

Plotting

It is well worth the effort to take real pride in the neatness of your chartwork. Conventional plotting as described earlier is not only a joy to behold, it is unambiguous, not only for you, but for any other proper navigator who may wish to take over the plot, no matter what his nationality.

It has been suggested that when we come face to face with our first extra-terrestrial aliens, we will communicate in the universal language of pure mathematics, but I believe that it is the navigators who will be the first to break through the silence. I'll bet a forenoon watch to a middle watch that Martian pilots draw three arrowheads on their set and drift vectors as they cruise through the asteroid belt.

The log book

The paper log book is the core of all yacht management on passage. Modern commercial vessels equipped with electronics that would boggle the simple mind still demand their use. Quite simply, the log book, or 'ship's log', is the navigator's bedrock.

In an ideal world, the textbook navigator plots his position every hour during an offshore passage. In reality, you sometimes do it more often, sometimes less, depending on the need of the moment. It is most important that all course changes are logged, together with times and distance log readings. EPs should be recorded; so should fixes, objects abeam, electronic plots and any other significant navigational event. Any fix (electronic or otherwise) plotted on a paper chart must have a time against it to refer it to the relevant log book entry. Even if you've plotted nothing on the chart, there should be enough information stored in the log book to work up an EP at any time.

You might choose to buy a published yacht log book, with entries for all sorts of information, or you may prefer to make up your own from a stiff-backed exercise book ruled off into columns. Professional yachts should have no difficulty in keeping a comprehensive log book. After all, they have plenty of crew and in the event of an inquiry into some incident on board, all manner of information may be required. Aboard a large yacht operating under the MCA Code of Practice, columns should be drawn up for: Zone Time, Log, Distance Run and, perhaps, Distance to Destination. In addition, Course Steered and Course over Ground (COG), Log Speed and Speed over Ground (SOG), Lat/Long, True Wind Speed and Direction, Sea State, Weather and Barometer. These are a suggested minimum. If no dedicated engine log is being run, Engine Hours and Fuel Remaining columns may also be needed. Following all this hard data come the Remarks. One double-page spread per day makes a clear working layout, with the date and voyage details at the top. A crew list is also advisable.

Short-handed yachts running on a more casual basis should at least have columns headed: Time, Log, Course Steered and COG, Weather, Position and a large one for Remarks. Many people sensibly insist on a sixth column to record Engine Hours, which helps to maintain a service schedule.

In an informal group of two people – both competent navigators with absolute faith in one another – the discipline of log entries can be relaxed into 'an entry when it is needed' so long as it is understood that the longer it has been since an entry was made, the worse any EP may be. Depending on circumstances, therefore, when well offshore and clear of danger, one entry every two hours seems a sensible minimum. Where less experienced watchkeepers are involved, a full hourly log entry is a must. It takes little time and ensures that when the skipper needs an EP, or requires to refer back to something else – such as a marked change in the barometer – the information is immediately and accurately to hand, in a familiar, recognisable form.

The end is nigh!

As already noted, at some time in the future, the official charting authorities plan to discontinue issuing paper charts. Commercial shipping and warships now use what is called ECDIS charting. This is built around electronic vector systems corrected weekly and supplied with a full back-up system powered by an independent power source. At the time of writing, back-up can also be supplied by a full set of paper charts, duly corrected up to the minute, but few operators are choosing this route, making it legal for them to put to sea with no paper at all. ECDIS is as near bullet-proof as it is possible to make an electronic system. For reasons of funding and space, such a choice is simply unavailable to leisure users, so it remains vital to maintain the basic skills of traditional navigation. Fortunately, the excellent Imray have no plans to discontinue the production of their fully authorised paper charts, so all is not yet lost.

If ever we should enter a world of total electronics, navigators will have to be taught to work up an EP entirely in their heads. Otherwise, the only input will be a GPS fix. A single source of information, however good it may be, is never enough for the well-trained navigator who, even when surrounded by screens and flashing lights, always seeks corroboration.

SKIPPER'S TIP

Logging on the chart

Some yacht sailors prefer to log their progress on the paper chart rather than maintain a full log book. To be at all safe, a plotted fix must then have more than just the time noted against it. As an absolute minimum it will also have a log reading and the course steered onward from it. This practice may deliver the bones of an EP should one be required, but that is all it does. There is no record of barometer readings, wind shifts that may affect leeway, what the COG was at last count and, for future amusement, what the skipper thought of his breakfast. You can just about get away with 'chart logging', but it has many shortfalls and is not encouraged here.

18 CLASSICAL POSITION FIXING

A traditional fix from three compass bearings. Not to be used for navigation

In the last chapter we noted that the navigator of a yacht is constantly estimating his position, and that this may be done informally, even subconsciously, or formally on the chart. From time to time, the need arises to check the accuracy of these estimates, either because you are in the vicinity of a danger, or because you need a known point of departure for the next leg of the passage. This is done by fixing your position.

There are any number of ways of producing a fix, including electronics, but you should never forget that, at best, a fix tells you where you were when you noted the data. By the time it is plotted, it is already history. The exception is the electronic chart plotter. This produces a 'real-time' position, but even a plotter must be backed up, so it remains vital to maintain a plot by reading the log and noting the time and position regularly. This sound navigational practice defines any fix, however derived, both in time and on the two-dimensional space of your passage across the chart.

For most purposes, fixing offshore or along the coast is dealt with by some form of GPS. The value of the electronic fix will be considered in Chapters 19 and 24, but while it represents the most accurate and convenient answer generally available, it is not the end of the story.

CLASSICAL POSITION FIXING

On occasions, a more direct fix will be appropriate, and the time when a navigator can be so confident in his electronics that there is no need for any back-up skills is still years away. The rest of this chapter therefore concentrates on the classical means of obtaining a fix. It goes without saying that these methods should be practised, not left kicking around in some dark locker of the mind until one day they are suddenly in urgent demand.

The eyeball fix and the position line

Whether or not you are relying on an electronic fixing system for your offshore work, nothing can ever be as good close-in as your own eyes. They remain the best instrument you have by far, and can define distance down to a fraction of a millimetre.

If you are within 100 yards (100m or so) of a charted buoy, you know where you are. In all probability, it will be more than accurate enough to say, for example, 'The buoy bears due north and I am about the length of a football pitch away from it.' You could plot that fix if you felt inclined, or you could note it with a time *and a log reading* in the log book.

As you move further from a known object, using it alone to define your position becomes less accurate, but it still may be good enough, depending upon your current requirements. If you are on a coastal passage with no off-lying dangers in the vicinity and 25 miles to go to your destination, it will sometimes remain adequate in good visibility to note that you are 'abeam of Reassurance Light Structure, distance 1–2 miles'. Such a position is often better than an EP. You could even refine your fix by noting the depth of water (after a rough reduction to soundings done in your head), then relating that to the charted depth, though in the circumstances mentioned this would not be really necessary. To spend five minutes plotting a satellite fix to the nearest tenth of a cable would be a waste of time.

Some navigational philosophers might argue that a fix is a fix and it must always be as accurate as it can possibly be made. I would suggest that for the mature navigator a fix is a refinement of an EP, and it should be as accurate as you need it to be at the time. Commonsense will tell you what sort of definition you require.

At any time when you are using a fix as a departure point from which to steer towards a second point, as opposed to continuing to cruise along the coast, the tighter you can fix your position, the better. If there is no convenient buoy, stake or lightship within the throwing range of a piece of stale toast, you will have to rely on *position lines* (PLs). A position line is a line upon which you are situated at a given time. It can be drawn on the chart and can be culled from all manner of sources. It is labelled with a single arrowhead at the end furthest from the object. As your creativity increases with experience, there is no end to the PLs you can produce. For a good fix, all you need is three.

A single PL defines your position in one direction only. You need to know how far along it you are, and you do this by finding a second PL which crosses it at a useful angle (Fig 18.1, p. 170). If the angle is too narrow, the error in position generated by a small departure from accuracy can be disproportionately large. A good angle of cut ensures only the minimum of position distortion from a small inaccuracy. If the error in one of your PLs is large, however, even a good cut won't help you, and if you only have two lines, you'll never know. A third PL cutting both the first two at a satisfactory angle gives you the

Fig 18.1
Angle of cut.

check you need and produces the classic 'three-point fix' resulting in a 'cocked hat' on the chart. It is rare indeed for all the PLs to intercept at a single point. More normally, there is a small triangle in whose vicinity you are probably situated at the time. Theoretically, a cocked hat is the inevitable result of three position lines being taken, unless they were noted simultaneously by three different observers on board, because you will have moved on between the time of the first and the third PL.

Often a reasonably tight cocked hat is all you need (Fig 18.2). Draw a circle round it with the time noted beside it. Now log it, check it against the depth of water, then shape your next course from it. If you need the greatest possible accuracy because of the presence of a danger either now, or close to your projected course, you should always assume the worst position the cocked hat allows. If one corner of it places you closer to danger than the others, that is where you must assume you are. Any discrepancy of your actual position from this into the safer areas of your cocked hat will thus be a bonus in terms of security.

Sometimes, a cocked hat is so big you just can't get along with it at all, particularly if all the PLs are compass bearings. When this happens, scrap it and take your bearings again, making sure this time that you hold the handbearing compass well away from magnetic influences. These may include your spectacles, the binoculars, and anything else that adorns your person. Now ascertain that you've applied variation the right way, and if you still plot a poor result, start wondering whether you are taking bearings of the right objects. Even if there is no mistake you can still show indifferent results when the distance is great, e.g. 3° error gives rise to 100 yards (91m) lateral displacement of your PL at a range of one mile from the object. At 10 miles this increases to half a mile. It isn't difficult to build in such an error when the boat is rolling around and you are struggling to read the swinging compass card.

CLASSICAL POSITION FIXING

Fig 18.2 A good fix in a tight cocked hat.

Electronic fixing systems work on PLs in a similar manner to any other fixing method. The difference is that PLs derived from GPS satellites are potentially capable of phenomenal accuracy. The cocked-hat work is done for you inside the 'box', so that all you receive is what you want – a position. If you are going to navigate electronically it remains important that you are aware of the classical systems for back-up purposes if nothing else. The traditional navigator used these constantly, so determining how to fix his position on a given occasion was second nature. The danger of always navigating through a computer is that you fail to develop these essential skills. When you need them, it will be too late to start, so study them now.

Sources of position line

Transits or ranges

Depending upon which side of the Atlantic you are sailing, two objects that define a position line are called either a *transit* or a *range*. Since I am from Britain I hope I may be forgiven for referring to them as transits from henceforth. The first type of transit is that set up by the lighthouse authority or a local harbour management. It will usually consist of two conspicuous daymarks and/or lights whose positions are charted. The chart will indicate the exact bearing of the transit in 'Degrees True from Seaward'. This type of transit is found in harbour entrances and in well-frequented areas of critical pilotage. They are also used to indicate measured distances for log checks. Occasionally, they are seen giving a position line indicating the presence of an isolated danger to navigation.

Fig 18.3 Informal transit – a headland lined up with a buoy.

The benefit of these formal transits is obvious. You don't even have to use your plotter to determine the bearing. The chart tells you what it is. When the beacons come into line, a glance at your compass reveals without a shadow of a doubt that you are precisely on the defined PL. I was once at a seminar listening to a manufacturer extolling the virtues of his new 5m accurate electronic plotter. 'Chicken feed!' my neighbour muttered to me, 'I can measure the width of my cockpit with a good transit.'

If there is no formal transit, there is nothing to stop you lining up two conspicuous charted objects and working out your own. A church lined up with a pier end is a wonderful transit, as is the cliff edge of an island brought in line with a buoy (Fig 18.3, above). There is no end to the transits an imaginative observer can find. Buoys drift a few yards around their moorings, so are not quite so accurate as an object ashore or founded upon the seabed, but they are usually better when lined up with a shore feature than used merely to provide a compass bearing.

Always use transits where you can. Nothing beats them for accuracy, including GPS. They are also absolutely free of charge, and no one can ever switch them off.

One final reminder: if you are in the slightest doubt about the identification of your transit, take a bearing on it with your compass. You know what it should be. Even if it seems a degree or two out, the compass will confirm it. If the discrepancy is more than 3° or 4°, take another look.

Compass bearings

In the absence of a transit, a compass bearing is usually the next best way of acquiring a PL. Make sure you are plotting it correctly. It doesn't matter whether you plot in degrees true or

CLASSICAL POSITION FIXING

> **SKIPPER'S TIP**
>
> **Realistic accuracy**
>
> Remember that the closer the object, the better your fix is likely to be. Don't go mad, though. If the object is near enough at hand to guess its distance with enough accuracy for your needs, you only have to take its bearing to complete your fix. Shore objects are generally better for fixing than buoys, which may occasionally be off station. The more important a buoy, the more reliable it is likely to be, but even the finest are moored at the end of a chain whose scope allows some degree of drift.

magnetic, so long as you are clear in your own mind what you are doing. Some plotters make it easy to lay a magnetic bearing on the chart; others do not. If in doubt, keep your chartwork in degrees true, but no one would fail a Yachtmaster examination for doing it the other way, always assuming he got it right.

When noting bearings, or courses to steer, it pays to develop the habit of always using a suffix of T (True), M (Magnetic) or C (Steering compass) after the number of degrees. If you write 'Church bears 035°M', there can be no possible confusion.

Depth soundings

Wherever the bottom is of such a nature that it forms clear contour lines, your echo sounder is a source of PLs. Reduce the depth to soundings, then inspect the chart. Your PL is the relevant contour, none the worse for not being so straight as a transit (Fig 18.4). If your depth places you between two charted contours, you'll have to judge where yours is most likely to be.

Fig 18.4 Use of a depth sounding as a position line: a rough fix is obtained by crossing a bearing with a sounding line.

THE COMPLETE YACHTMASTER

The nature of things is such that contours are rarely so precisely defined as a transit leading mark. Even if your PL is effectively a cable wide, however, it may be all you have to make up the second PL of a two-point fix, so don't despise it.

Every time you take a fix you should hit the button of the echo sounder as a guard against gross error. It isn't usually necessary to reduce to soundings for these purposes. Just have a quick look. If the depth in the vicinity of your fix is seriously adrift from what the chart says it should be, then as with an EP, something is wrong.

Fig 18.5 A circular position line: fix from a bearing plus a distance off.

Circular position lines

There is nothing in the rules that says a PL must be straight. We have just seen how it can be not only meandering, but a hundred yards or more across, as in the case of some depth contours. An extremely useful circular PL can be constructed from a 'distance off' an object (Fig 18.5). Visually, it is possible to determine this in two ways. When the distance off is known, a circle of position can be scribed around the object on the chart. A section of this circle may be used to provide a second PL where it cuts a compass bearing of the object (always at a convenient right angle), and create a fine two-point fix.

The first method of finding a circular PL requires no instruments at all, just an almanac and an assessment of the height of your eye above sea level. If you know the height of a lighthouse (from your chart), you can enter the tables given in the almanac for *lights rising and dipping* to ascertain how far off it you will be when it rises above, or dips beneath, the horizon. This gives you your range. Take a bearing on a light as it first appears, and you have an initial landfall fix. If you are using electronics, this will give you an excellent check on your computer; if not, it may well be the last fix you'll have for some time, until the lesser shore lights begin popping up as you close the coast.

If you're only seeing the light from the tops of the waves, you must make an assessment of the total wave height, divide it by two to give the height of each one above mean sea level, and add this to your height of eye.

The second method of finding distance off and hence a circular position line is by using a *vertical sextant angle*. If you have a sextant on board, it is easy in daylight to measure accurately the angle between the lantern of a lighthouse of known height, and the sea. Correct this for height of tide (unless it is MHWS, you will always have something to add) and enter the tables in the almanac for 'distance off by vertical sextant angle'. Read off your distance. Height of eye is irrelevant.

Cut-offs and sectors of lights

The changing colour of a sectored light offers a useful, ready-charted PL. So long as the sector changes positively it can be used as part of a fix. Sometimes a light is obscured by a hill or headland and the obscuring, or cut-off, line is also charted. If so, you have a useful PL as the light appears or disappears from view. This latter PL should not be treated as the gospel of accuracy, because questions of height of eye (as affected also by tide height) and even whether trees have leaves on them may modify the result. Nonetheless, in rough weather it can prove better than a compass bearing, as it may also do if you are fighting seasickness and want an easily found PL whose perfection is of less than paramount importance.

Transferred position lines

Occasionally, you find yourself in need of a PL that runs in a certain approximate direction and no obvious source presents itself. In these circumstances you can sometimes utilise a PL taken fairly recently by 'running it up' to your current position. This is done by assuming a position on the old PL, then plotting a current EP worked from that assumed position. The PL is now transferred as a parallel line that cuts the new EP. It is labelled with two arrowheads at its end (Fig 18.6).

Transferred position lines (TPLs) are rarely as accurate as a primary PL, but they have their uses nonetheless (see 'The running fix' on p. 176).

Fig 18.6 Use of a transferred position line to find a river mouth.

Preplotting and use of ship's heading

It is surprising how often the chance offers itself to produce a fix on distant objects without using a handbearing compass. Usually, you can predict the circumstances before they arise, so as to preplot the fix. Sometimes, by a minor alteration in course, you can arrange matters so that the yacht passes through a position that has been defined with great precision.

An example of the latter would be if you were running so as to have two objects ahead or astern of you almost in transit, with another transit due to come on abeam. If, by adjusting your heading, you can place yourself so that you are running the first transit when the second comes on, you are fixed as surely as it is possible to be. Plot the transits, note the log, check the depth (you always do, of course, even if you are certain) and carry on.

If you have only a beam transit coming up, but a conspicuous object lies almost ahead or astern, why not steer the boat to bring the object dead ahead just as you pass the transit? The transit gives you one PL; the ship's head, corrected for deviation, is the other.

The steering compass can often be used to give a bearing in this way. If the object won't come conveniently ahead or astern, how about bringing it abeam and adding or subtracting 90° from the ship's head?

The running fix

Once a vital standby when sources of position line were hard to find, the running fix is unlikely to be used in the lifetime of today's typical electronic navigator. However, while satellite navigation has effectively consigned it to the bin for coastal purposes, the running fix still forms the basis of any astro-navigation technique involving a single heavenly body such as the ever-popular Sun. It has therefore been left in this latest edition so that those who plan to set sail on wider oceans already have the concept firmly in hand. Others may enjoy mastering it for its academic interest.

When you have only a single known charted object to go on, and no means of determining your distance off, you can still fix your position with a running fix. A typical situation is when you are passing a singleton lighthouse in the dark (Fig 18.7, opposite). This is the procedure:

> Take a bearing when the light is about 45° on the bow. Note time and log reading and plot your bearing.
>
>
>
> Wait until you have run far enough for a good 'cut', then take a second bearing, noting time, log and depth. Plot the PL.
>
>
>
> Transfer the first PL up to an estimated position, worked out using the technique set out above for transferred PLs (TPLs).
>
> ↓
>
> The point at which the second PL and the TPL intersect is the running fix. It is logged as having been taken at the same time as the second PL, and the charted depth should coincide with the sounded depth, duly reduced to soundings.
>
>
>
> The depth reading supplies an important check on this sometimes rather haphazard means of fixing. Uncertain though it can be, however, it is worth doing if no other method presents itself.

CLASSICAL POSITION FIXING

Fig 18.7 The running fix.

A classic three-point fix, plotted using an AngelNav raster chart on an iPad. The bearings were taken with a handbearing compass and the cut angle is as near perfect as you're likely to get. The size of the cocked hat can be checked against the distance scale at the top left-hand corner of the chart indicating a maximum area of probability for the 'cocked hat' of under a quarter of a mile.
Not to be used for navigation

Evaluation of fixes

The electronic navigator builds his house on foundations of accuracy, and today's satellite systems, if they are working at all, are accurate far beyond the needs of the small-craft skipper. It's easy, therefore, to develop a mindset that assumes pinpoint positioning at all times.

Be aware that while charts are updated for sea marks, landmarks may change and upset things. The War Memorial and the church steeple were once a charted transit. Then someone built a block of flats...

Traditionally, this was far from the case. The main reason for considering classical fixing techniques these days is to back up the boat's safety in the event of satellite failure or the demise of on-board equipment. This can happen for the most unexpected of reasons. I once suffered a crash of my PC chart program because I foolishly opted to update the charts while on passage. It turned out the software was about as user-friendly as a wolf sizing up a lamb for its dinner. Then there was the poor chap whose computer decided to defragment just as he was entering an awkward channel.

Even a GPS or Galileo fix is only as good as the chart it is plotted on, and this may vary depending on the charting authority, the level of survey and how recent this was. We all, therefore, must maintain a 'feel' for working with varying levels of accuracy. Once upon a time, this skill was inherent in every navigator. Today, it must be actively taken on board as a discipline.

Only you know how good a PL is likely to be, because you took it. If you have three winners and the result is a tight cocked hat, you can be confident of your position, particularly if the echo sounder backs it up.

If your input data is not so surefooted, you'll have to treat the results more carefully and plan your immediate future accordingly, always erring on the side of safety.

CLASSICAL POSITION FIXING

> **SKIPPER'S TIP**
>
> ### Multiple sources – the essence of security
>
> The essence of navigational security is to take your information from more than one source whenever possible, so that you are constantly cross-checking yourself. That is why you examine your EP with a fix and, to a lesser extent, vice versa. For the same reason, it does no harm to compare a series of GPS fixes with a high-quality visual fix from time to time. If this is impossible, at least read the sounder.
>
> Don't fall into the trap of believing one source of information all the time, be it ever so good. I have seen GPS fixes plotted by hand checked against radar fixes as a lifeboat scooted through fog-bound rocks at 18 knots. Any error would have ripped out her bottom, and those professionals were not about to trust to any single electronic guide. Even when only electronics would do, they still wanted two inputs using separate silicon chips living in separate watertight boxes. A real navigator always feels uneasy unless he is cross-checking himself, however he is doing it.

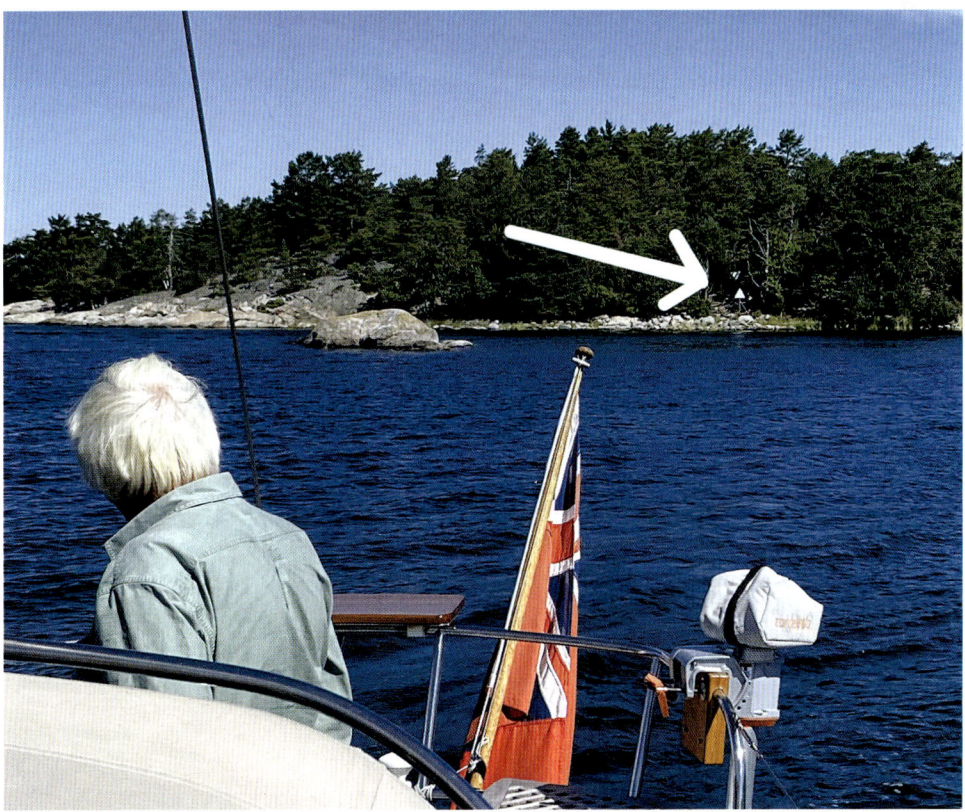

A set-up charted transit gives the most reliable position line of all, so long as you can identify it on the chart. Some are large for big ships; others are tiny and can be difficult to spot like this one in the trees which leads through a nasty set of rocks into a perfect anchorage.

19 SATELLITES AND RADAR

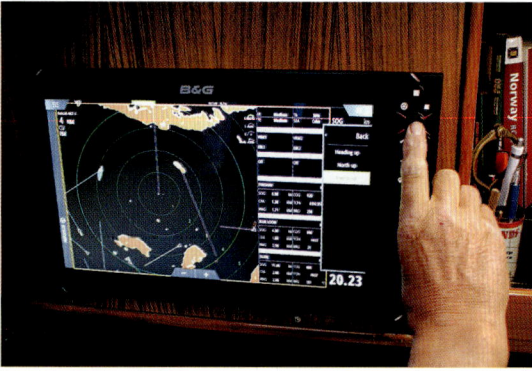

It's worth beginning this chapter by setting satellite navigation into historical context – if you can call it history, it's so recent! The first edition of this book was written in 1993, when the American Global Positioning System (GPS) had been theoretically available to worldwide civilian users for just 12 months. I was probably typical in that I bought my first steam-powered handheld set in 1994, but the revolution was only really completed in the first decade of the 21st century. As late as the second edition (1997), the awful 'doppler satnav' was mentioned, and it was not until the third edition in 2000 that Radio Direction Finding (RDF), a WWII standby that now seems primitive beyond belief, received the final 'chop' from these pages. Even then, column space was set aside for Decca and Loran C, hyperbolic radio fixing systems now superseded in yachts, although Loran C is currently under review as a terrestrial-based back-up system. Electronic fixing became the official basis of navigation with the establishment of GPS and finally came of age with the associated chart plotters.

A number of alternative satellite navigation systems operating on the same principles as GPS are now available. These include Galileo (European) and GLONAS (Russian). Since the wavelengths are similar, it seems that most high-quality modern receivers will switch to the best available with no input from the operator.

Even the most basic marine GPS receivers now offer at least a lat/long fix, full waypoint facilities and route planning, with at least some level of chart plotting virtually a 'given'. So many different instruments are available that it would be unrealistic to give instructions here regarding which buttons to push. The only sensible way ahead is for a skipper to self-educate concerning the specific equipment selected. In the old scholar's phrase, 'Read, mark, learn and inwardly digest' the manufacturer's instructions, and don't rely on the gear until you fully understand what it can and cannot do. Below are some notes that may prove helpful, but they are by no means all you need to know. The same holds good for radar, where any user will be well served by a short course or at least one of the specialist books on the subject.

A sound electronic system, properly installed aboard a well-found vessel, is now the core of many a good navigator's art – and used well, it can make a good navigator even better. If any of these criteria is missing, over-reliance on electronics can lead to serious trouble. Their arrival and acceptance on the scene has transformed the accuracy of offshore navigation and removed much of the stress from a skipper's life, but they have done nothing to change the navigator's basic philosophy that input from one source alone is always to be treated with caution.

The dangers of standing into a tight corner on a lee shore while relying utterly on a navigation system dependent on voltage – even with a back-up hand-held set powered by its own dedicated batteries – speak for themselves. Also, GPS aerials are best sited at or near deck level and so are vulnerable to physical damage. Many an antenna has been kicked off its perch by enthusiastic crew activity. It is also stretching things to place your life at the mercy of a group of satellites, up there primarily for military purposes, which we are permitted to use with the proviso that they may be switched off without warning, and subject inevitably to the potential for enemy activity or mischievous interference. For all these reasons, the first page to flash up on a chart plotter is usually some sort of disclaimer telling you that if you really must use this product for navigation, you do so at your own risk. The same could, of course, be said for the magnetic compass, so we must all make our own peace with ourselves and not be too perturbed by manufacturers whose fear of litigation seems their paramount nightmare.

Global Positioning System (GPS)

GPS supplies accurate three-dimensional fixes 24 hours a day, in all weathers, anywhere in the world, even though for maritime purposes, two dimensions will do very nicely. The system still in general use is operated by the US military. Galileo, the European alternative, is now fully operational and is used by some SAR systems. The US military is 'dedicated to the development and deployment of regional denial capabilities in lieu of global degradation'. In plain speaking, this means that rather than downgrade the signals globally or turn off their satellites completely, sensitive areas can be blacked out from GPS signals.

Fig 19.1 GPS fixes are deduced from the intersection of 'sphere of position'.

To deliver such a system, a constellation of satellites is set in orbit in a 'birdcage' around the Earth, together with stand-by 'spares'. Their extremely high altitude keeps them clear of skywaves and other atmospheric interference. It also guarantees that four or more can be seen from a given location at any time. The system is completed by various control and monitor stations around the world. These maintain system accuracy, together with other forms of monitoring and updating of the navigation message of each satellite.

The satellites' position in space is known. Each one transmits coded data which includes a radio signal timed to mind-numbing accuracy. This enables the receiver to calculate the distance of the transmitting satellite from its antenna, which gives it a position line on the surface of a sphere centred at the satellite.

The receiver chooses a number of satellites offering the best 'cut' of position lines (position spheres in reality) and works out its position from these (Fig 19.1, p. 181).

Control of GPS accuracy

GPS is capable of producing fixes accurate to better than 1m, but this Precise Positioning Service (PPS) is kept by the military for themselves by encrypting the signals. The rest of us must be content with a theoretical potential accuracy of around 5m. In practice, fixes are rarely adrift by more than a boat's length or two. Such discrepancies should be of no more interest to the marine navigator than his altitude, but with so high a degree of potential accuracy it's easy to get carried away, so we end-users must remember that a fix is only as good as the chart it's plotted on. The surveyor's brief may not have allowed for such knife-edge potential, and if the unit is working with a paper chart or the electronic cartographer has committed a *faux pas*, failure to set up the receiver for the correct datum (see below) renders all such niceties a nonsense.

Chart datums

The globe is not a perfect spheroid. Its surface has minor irregularities. In the days before the phenomenal accuracy of GPS, the various charting authorities were content to work within a generally agreed mean latitude and longitude grid. If one nation's convention varied from another's by a few metres, as it did and sometimes still does, no practical navigator was interested. The difference was largely unobservable by conventional means. Because of the precision of GPS, all this has changed.

When any on-board GPS is reading out its fixes to the wrong 'datum' for the chart in use, the plot could be in error by, at the extreme, up to several hundred metres. Datum shifts of a cable or so (0.1M) are commonplace. Fortunately, the majority of receivers will now read out in any one of a variety of datums.

Check the 'title corner' of your paper chart. If it is reasonably modern you will find a statement of datum, e.g. 'WGS84' or 'OSGB (1936)'. The GPS default setting is WGS84, favoured by the US and rapidly becoming the world standard. Some charts do not declare their datum, but give an instruction concerning how to shift 'satellite-derived positions' instead. If this is so, set your GPS to WGS84 and do what the chart says if ultimate accuracy is required. If it isn't, as is often the case, don't waste your time with the extra plotting duties.

SATELLITES AND RADAR

> **SKIPPER'S TIP**
>
> ### Differential GPS
>
> This feature is not relevant to most yacht navigation at the time of writing (2025), but it should be understood lest the current situation change.
>
> Differential GPS (DGPS) upgrades the accuracy of the standard GPS position by comparing the GPS-fixed position of a static, ground-based receiver at any moment with its known geographic position. The ground station transmits signals to all GPS receivers in its vicinity, advising them of any error it has noted. The differential user's receiver then incorporates this data into its fix. Accuracy of a metre or so can be expected.

Most electronic charts have been fine-tuned so that fixes displayed on their associated chart plotters are accurate. Whether this is done by redrawing the chart to WGS84 or by some other computer wizardry is not important to the practical user. Suffice to say that it generally works. However, I have personally seen more than one case where a chart somehow slipped through the net, with a potentially dangerous outcome (see p. 227). The message is obvious: vigilance, and the old standby of input from more than one source.

Modern charts are increasingly being printed to WGS84, but until every chart aboard every boat is set to this, the issue of datums will remain a serious one. Failure to address it can lead to serious errors in a world where so much accuracy is now assumed.

Beyond the fix

Some traditional navigators use GPS for nothing more than fixing their position on a paper chart. This is their choice, but it must be said that in doing so they are not reaping the full value from their investment. The additional functions offered by all GPS receivers have really given rise to what is in effect a modified and much simpler system of passage navigation.

Course and speed

These can be read out from most yacht navigation systems. The machine is, of course, working this up by comparing fixes. These relate to your actual position, so the course and speed are 'over the ground', rather than 'through the water' and the acronyms COG and SOG have entered the vernacular. Do not fall into the trap of imagining that because the GPS reads 9.3 knots, your 28-footer is logging anywhere near this velocity. Check the water log and the tidal stream atlas and re-enter the real world.

One use to which this information can be put is to check your set and drift against that predicted by the tide tables (see Chapter 15). Always remember, though, that any information lifted from the set in this way is, like a fix, passé a second after you have written it down.

THE COMPLETE YACHTMASTER

Waypoints

The idea of the waypoint forms the heart of modern navigation. You may choose to use few or many, but the concept must be understood and accepted so that you can make an informed decision based on the way you think and the circumstances.

It is standard practice to enter a number of predetermined positions along a predicted route into your navigator's computer. The theoretical ideal for a passage of any substance, offshore or along the coast, is to proceed from one of these waypoints to the next. This can be done informally, plotting them as you go, or as a pre-planned 'route'. More information about waypoints and how they should be selected and used will be found in 'Passage Planning' (Chapter 22). Waypoints are helpful on a chart plotter, if for no other reason than that an active waypoint reads out its distance, 'time to go' (TTG), ETA, etc. With a paper chart they ease your task in many ways.

GoTo

By activating the 'GoTo' function, the receiver will lock on to a waypoint, giving a constantly updated distance and bearing to it. Distance and bearing to a known position is, of course, another form of expressing the yacht's position (Fig 19.2). This can often be a more convenient way of plotting a fix on the chart than trying to wrestle with lat/long over the folds of the paper with a chart protractor or parallel rule that is too short and a longitude scale that numbers from right to left in west longitude. As an aside, the concept of defining a fix in terms of lat/long *and* range and bearing is useful when transferring a position from one

Most modern autopilots when linked to a plotter can steer the yacht direct to a waypoint. This can be useful with some caveats (see p. 192).

SATELLITES AND RADAR

Fig 19.2 A position can be expressed either as lat/long or as a range and bearing from a known, charted object.

chart to the next. It is all too easy to make an error over a question of scale, or by reading the longitude the wrong way. If you transfer the position by both means, they should marry up; if they don't, you've made a mistake.

Using GoTo for comparing the bearing of the waypoint and the present track makes adjusting your course to take you to it a doddle, always given that the tidal stream or current is expected to remain reasonably steady. Just steer to keep your COG the same as the bearing and you've cracked it.

Ghost waypoints

Where a leg of your passage looks like passing across a large section of chart without the need for a natural waypoint, it is worth creating a 'ghost waypoint' purely for plotting purposes. If you make this the middle of a compass rose, plotting to or from it will be a breeze. More and more charts are doing this for you by means of so-called 'Plotter Reference Points'. Enter the relevant ones as waypoints and they will be most useful.

Danger waypoints

Where an isolated, unmarked danger lies athwart your direct route and you don't mind which side you pass it, there's much to be said for placing a waypoint actually on top of it. Then, as it approaches, all you have to do is activate it and make sure its bearing keeps changing. You can't possibly hit it then! The hardware plotter on my boat has a choice of waypoint symbols. One of them is a skull and crossbones. Ideal for danger waypoints, although normally I prefer the smiling face option.

Plotting waypoints

Waypoints are conventionally plotted on a paper chart as a small square around the pinpoint of the actual position. They are labelled with a name, a number or a letter:

Cross-track error

Your GPS receiver is aware of the direct track from one waypoint to the next, or from a defined position to a pre-entered destination. It will always be delighted to advise you as to whether or not you are off-track, which side you are off, and by how far, which is sometimes valuable to know.

Many receivers will also offer you a course to steer in order to return to the line, but this must be treated with intelligent caution. If staying on track is crucial to your safety, you should determine whether the recommended heading could lead into trouble from your present off-track position. There may, after all, be dangers in the way, and the GPS will not know about them.

Even if the path is clear, the computer is often so desperate to get you back on to the original track that it demands an alteration so radical as to be irrelevant, particularly in a sailing boat. More often, it is better just to steer 'up' or 'down' by 20° or so until track is re-established. The cross-track information is sometimes sufficiently unimportant for you to ignore the old track and opt instead for a fresh departure to the waypoint from where you are now. Pressing GoTo will generally restart the process. Maybe you can even miss out that waypoint and proceed towards the following one. The processor won't consider any of these options, so don't let it patronise you.

Despite these cautions, cross-track error can be extremely helpful down the last mile or two on to a landfall in thick weather. Under certain circumstances it can also guide you through a series of dangers close by on either hand, but before you consider using it for this, refer to the caveats in Chapter 23.

Except for the fastest power craft, cross-track error should not be considered a substitute for pre-planned course shaping over extended periods, particularly where a turn of tide is involved. Employing it for this purpose will see you steering into the stream regardless of the overall strategic situation. You may well therefore sail considerably further through the water than is necessary. If this sounds like theoretical hot air, take a look at Chapter 20 for the reason.

Man overboard function

This is standard equipment in most GPS receivers. If you suffer a crew member over the side and hit the 'MOB' button immediately, the inbuilt course computer will give a range and bearing back to the geographic location where the casualty was lost. It does this by creating a waypoint marked as 'MOB', then activating the GoTo software to keep you informed of what you need to know most of all – where the casualty lies in relation to you. This can be a life-saver on a dark night, but you must be aware of its limitations. The position given is a position on the seabed. The boat and the casualty are both subject to any current or stream that is running. Their position in relation to one another is governed by the yacht's movements alone, and both are drifting downstream at a constant relative rate. The geographical position given by the computer remains where it was, but any current will be carrying both the yacht and the subject away from it. A mere 2 knots of stream will shift the victim a cable (200 yards) downstream of the waypoint in 3 minutes. Nevertheless, it is generally well worth the 10 seconds it may take to hit that button, so long as you note the time. If you should lose touch with your casualty and are within range of Search and Rescue services (SAR), they will be able to calculate the lost person's set and drift with surprising accuracy, working from the time and the fixed MOB position. Activating the function without glancing at your watch will degrade this accuracy severely in areas of strong current, unless your computer will read out the time as well as the fix, which many do not.

Electronic chart plotters

The electronic chart plotter started life as a computer screen depicting a caricature of a paper chart. Now they deliver full-quality coloured chart coverage with a zoom facility to take the user from global scales down to the local marina pontoons. Some even offer overlaid satellite photographs and 3D charts, although the value for money these represent to serious navigators seems up for argument.

The plotter's computer either interfaces with GPS or contains its own GPS facility, so that the yacht's real-time position is shown on a chart on its screen.

Types of chart plotter

The hardware plotter
This is a single, dedicated instrument incorporating a screen, a processor and a GPS receiver. It will perform all the functions of a simple GPS set with the additional benefit of showing the boat on the chart in a moving, real-time position. Hardware plotters generally use a specific type of chart package so you need to decide which one gives the best deal for the charts you are going to want. It's also important to decide which charts appeal to your eye, because different vector charts vary in appearance. Any rasters on offer may be useful. Some are not what they purport to be and are worse than useless. It is up to you to decide.

Hardware plotters often come as part of a larger package of instruments. These are sometimes known, not as plotters, but as 'multi-functional displays' (MFDs) which can be interfaced in all sorts of directions, such as showing AIS contacts on the electronic chart in real time. Another common interface is with radar, and some can display the radar image as an alternative on the screen. Split screens may be available so you can access both tools at once. Some even overlay the radar image on to the chart, which is of enormous value to the trainee radar operator – a state beyond which few honest yacht sailors progress.

The software plotter
A software plotter is a plotter program installed, together with a chart package, on to a boat's PC. Many people use laptops for this, but an inbuilt PC can be even better in certain applications. The PC is interfaced with an independent GPS receiver via the NMEA data

THE COMPLETE YACHTMASTER

The author's chart table. The B&G chart plotter interfaces with radar, AIS, etc. The PC is running raster charts on its own independent GPS and battery. Note the pilot book and paper log book and the *Reeds Nautical Almanac*. What you can't see is the Imray paper chart pack in the locker under the worktop.

protocol through a serial or USB port connection. The combination is capable of doing most things a hardware plotter can do, and often much more besides. It has the advantage that since most people now have a laptop, the 'hardware' is already in place, so all that need be bought is the software. Another benefit software plotters offer for some of us is that they can use raster charts (see Chapter 12), which many consider to be clearer and more user-friendly. The time was when configuring and interfacing a PC-based system was more of a challenge than a hardware plotter, which in its simplest form you buy, set up the antenna and plug in. As electronics proliferate, this is often no longer the case. Many plotters today are interfaced with all manner of other devices, from autopilots to AIS receivers. The manuals for installing this sort of kit are beyond the capacity of many a university-educated mariner. Whether this is their fault or his is up for debate, but the bottom line is that this stuff is not getting any easier for Jolly Jack the sailorman. Fitting up a PC might seem simple by comparison.

Apps, tablet and phone plotters

The second decade of the 21st century saw the arrival of inexpensive plotter software and electronic charts to use on tablets including the iPad and on smart phones. Most of us now have such a phone in our pockets and to be able to whip it out, hit an app and see the whole picture on a unit entirely unconnected to the ship's systems, using an independent

The author's iPad, on his chart table running AngelNav raster charts. It is capable of controlling the full B&G hardware electronics by interfacing with the multi-functional display. This can all be done from the cockpit if needed.

battery and GPS, is a phenomenal addition to safety. The chart is, of course, too small for a primary navigation system, but as back-up or a quick reference that costs under £20, the value is remarkable. Phone apps generally include full tidal height data and graphs, as well as measuring tools and projected track vectors. Tablet plotters are similar to phone units but have more features and clearer charts. The apps cost somewhat more, but are still less than you'd pay for a decent meal out. Add a waterproof case and you have a cockpit plotter with a screen size that is perfectly usable. Some, such as Raymarine and B&G, can interface with the bulkhead multi-functional display (MFD) via that unit's inbuilt Wi-Fi system with total control. This confers the full benefit of the main plotter wherever the tablet happens to be. Especially for pilotage, this can transform the navigator's life.

When selecting a phone or tablet plotter, make sure it has a projected track feature (see overleaf, and not to be confused with a 'heading' vector). Some do not, and a plotter without projected track is like beer without skittles. One that I have been using is stuffed with software I never use yet fails to address this vital issue. To be able to see instantly where a heading will take you is the best thing that has happened in navigation since Harrison's chronometer. Why a plotter manufacturer would leave it out is beyond me, but I would counsel vigorously to avoid any such product.

General functions of chart plotters

Zooming, panning and overviews

The biggest problem with chart plotters is scale. Where enough of the chart is visible to display an overview, you don't have sufficient detail to see what you're about to hit. This is dealt with by zooming in and out, and panning across the chart. Learning how to do this is not only a physical process, it also requires a jump of consciousness for anyone brought up on paper charts. Larger plotters can actually be used without paper charts by a skilled operator (always given that paper charts are there for back-up and passage planning), but small-screen units really need a paper chart standing by continually to fill in the big picture.

Because vector charts contain too much data to display at all states of zoom, any plotter employing vector charts suffers from the common drawback of data being 'layered out' when the zoom moves beyond some arbitrary range. A vital rock or tidal overfall may disappear at just the scale you have decided is appropriate for your needs at a particular moment. This can be dangerous and numerous cases are on record of vessels coming severely unstuck by falling into this trap. The only safe answer is to check the paper chart or to zoom right in if in any doubt whatever, just to make sure. As world charting improves, this issue has become a greater general danger than datum shifts. Although these can and do occur, they are often localised, whereas the layering out of vital information can happen anywhere. It is of particular importance when planning passages and the use of a bulkhead plotter for this purpose, unassisted by paper or raster charts, is emphatically not recommended.

Vectors and projected track

The projected track vector is the most important single navigational breakthrough since the chronometer. By activating a line projecting from the boat, a plotter can show where she will be after a given time, always assuming that her course over the ground remains constant. In the safe hands of a navigator who understands the variables, this is the most remarkable aid to security because it has, to all intents and purposes, already calculated set and drift, and applied them to your heading. Find out how to activate it, then switch it on!

Ship's heading

In addition to projected track, a good plotter can also indicate your ship's heading with a second vector, perhaps of a different colour. This may well demand calibration and perhaps interlinking to an autopilot, which can lead to difficulties in other than expert hands. If the autopilot is not calibrated to the exact ship's heading in real life as prescribed by the steering compass (and many are not), this vector can be misleading. Once it is working, however, it allows you to see at a glance the extent to which your track and heading are at variance.

A third vector sometimes available is the current, deduced by the processor from the difference between your COG/SOG and your heading/boat speed. In a third colour, this one only works if your heading vector is 'trimmed' correctly. It has its uses, but obsession with such things can lead to failure to look out of the window where real life continues to deliver 'slings and arrows' that are not virtual and which really hurt.

SATELLITES AND RADAR

 SKIPPER'S TIP

Range and bearing from the ship
Click into this feature if the plotter has one, then click the cursor on to an object on the electronic chart. The changing range and bearing of the object will be displayed until you switch it off.

Bearing and distance to cursor
To relate your position to a charted object, you have only to hover the cursor over it and range and bearing are displayed. This gives you an alternative means of recording your position, which is more convenient and often more relevant than a straightforward lat/long. I tend to use this as I approach landfall, keeping to lat/long out of sight of land.

Dividers
Most good plotters offer electronic dividers to measure the bearing and distance between any two points. Very useful for passage planning. On some PC plotters it is possible to use multiple sets of dividers and leave the lines 'active' on the screen. This enables you to plot visual fixes or vector diagrams for tidal navigation, etc. Sadly, few hardware plotters offer this multiple facility. If their GPS goes down, they are therefore useless. A plotter allowing multiple lines to be constructed can be used just like a paper chart, even without GPS. I have even plotted running fixes (p. 176–7) on a PC.

Tidal heights
Many vector chart/hardware plotter programs now allow you to access comprehensive tidal height information at the click of the cursor. PC-based plotters may require additional software for this, but the effect is the same. No more secondary port interpolation nightmares! (See Chapter 14.)

A modern tablet app from Navionics giving tidal height and chart all on one screen. Click on the tidal height symbol for all you need.
Not to be used for navigation

191

> ### SKIPPER'S TIP
>
> **Naming the features**
> Be careful with American-built plotters, which may use different names from European units. Often designed with fast motorboats and low tidal stream values in mind, they may use a faint colour for the all-important COG and a bold one for the far less important ship's heading. They may call ground track (COG) 'course', with no mention of 'over ground' anywhere to differentiate it from 'course steered'. Make absolutely sure your plotter is speaking your language or, if it isn't, that you know what it is talking about.

Tidal streams

As recently as 2007, hardware plotters were not yet offering this data directly, although some could deliver a very crude 'maximum current' figure related to High and Low Water. The more powerful plotters could read out the present deduced set and drift. In 2025, many plotters can show tidal streams in some form which is readily accessed from an arrow or some such indicator on the main chart page. The form of delivery of data may seem odd to the British user, but it is a lot better than in the past. The data offered by AngelNav, illustrated on p. 147, is crystal clear and intuitive. Progress is being made!

Autopilot interface

A fully interfaced yacht has her plotter hooked up to the autopilot. This enables the display to show heading as well as ground track (COG). Such systems can be programmed to have the processor effectively take command. It sets the courses to steer the boat to the next waypoint, then alters to another down the route, and so on until, at some stage, it must be deactivated to pilot into the berth. Sailors may find this a frightening prospect, but many motorboat skippers use it all the time. It goes without saying that such a feature must be treated with more than nominal respect for the potential hazards it can bring to the unwary. Berth-to-berth passage planners are now being offered by the latest software from some manufacturers. This feature literally plans the skipper's passage for him, leaving nothing to do but park and unpark the vessel. Quite what the coroner is going to say when one of these skippers comes unstuck remains to be seen.

The most useful way of benefiting from this type of program without compromising safety is to set the autopilot just to steer from where the boat happens to be to the next waypoint, rather than following a compass course. This can save a lot of fine-tuning as streams and leeway vary, yet nobody is handing over control of the passage to a machine which, when all is said and done, cannot see out of the wheelhouse windows. It's worth noting that different plotters have different ways of executing this function. At last count, a Raymarine chart plotter took you straight to the waypoint as plotted, not to its lat/long. B&G set a corrected course to the waypoint's lat/long, which is all very well so long as the autopilot is set up with pinpoint accuracy. This doesn't always happen in real life, in which case less than perfect results follow. Skippers must be aware of such sophistications if planning on using the plotter to the full.

SATELLITES AND RADAR

Waypoints on a plotter

Inputting waypoints to plotters is extremely simple, sometimes requiring no more than positioning a cursor on the spot and clicking the mouse or 'enter' button. This makes setting up a route far, far easier than on a numeric GPS unit, where you'd think the number punching was going on until the last trumpet. Plotter waypoints can be linked as routes by dragging the cursor from one point on the planned passage to the next, clicking them in as you go. If you leave a line joining the waypoints, you can see at a glance whether the chosen route is safely clear of dangers.

I find this somewhat ironic, because it could be argued that waypoints are less universally applicable to plotter navigation than they are to GPS/paper charts. The plotter shows you the boat. It also projects where she is actually going, so if you want to arrive at a buoy and you can see you're 5° off track, effective adjustment couldn't be easier. You don't necessarily need a waypoint on the buoy as you would have done without the graphic display. If you can't find the projected track function, just pop the cursor over the buoy, note how its bearing compares with your COG and adjust the course accordingly.

Information on the active waypoint is naturally comprehensive on a plotter, often with special 'screens' to display it, so if you enjoy waypoints or if circumstances demand one, you

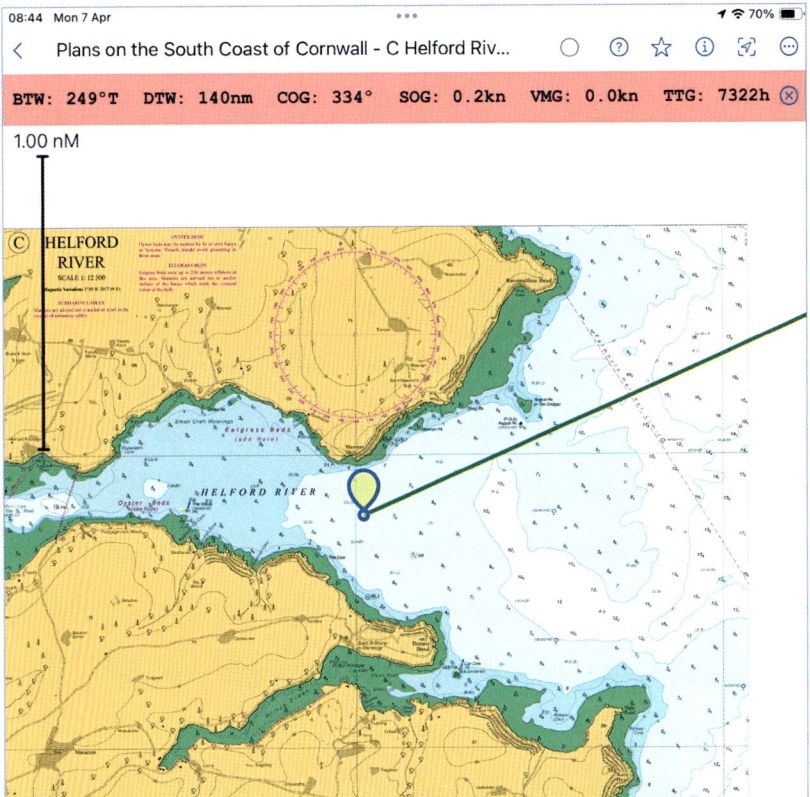

Bearing and distance to a waypoint from a distant anchorage on the author's iPad using AngelNav and a raster chart. Not to be used for navigation

are, as you might say, in the guinea seats anyway. Among certain others I find useful, I always input a waypoint at my destination, if for no other reason than that it shows instantly how far I have to go and an ETA.

Plotting on the screen

Apart from the inevitable shortfalls caused by screen size and the limitations of leisure vector charts, the universal drawback with all chart plotters on the market until 2023 was an inability for the user to plot any traditional navigation lines on the screen. So long as everything is working well and the navigator was not interested in maintaining traditional skills, this presented no problem, but if for any reason GPS should be compromised the system simply could not supply what the ship needed. Vector charts generally do not have enough shore information to enable traditional fixes to be taken from on deck, even if it were possible to plot the position lines. The plotters that use them have no facility for plotting traditional navigation. Fortunately, a new app called AngelNav has become available, which uses raster charts and enables the user to plot fixes, courses to steer and estimated positions. In 2025, the app was limited to Apple products, but it should soon be available for Android as well. The raster charts have all the land features which appear on paper charts, enabling the navigator to take bearings, then plot them easily on the chart.

This is a major breakthrough in navigational safety. As well as providing an instant back-up without recourse to paper charts in the event of a GPS outage, it also enables sailors to keep their traditional skills well-honed simply by using their iPads and the compass, which one hopes has always accompanied their voyaging.

The list of features of the modern plotter is long and growing every year, so the best advice I can give is that we keep our eyes on the ball. Chartwork is not really that complicated and, with the best will in the world, manufacturers and programmers do have a tendency to install features just to show that they can. Explore your plotter thoroughly, decide which bits you want, then become its master. It will serve you well.

Marine computers

There seems little doubt that the long-term future of all but the most frugal small craft navigation lies with chart plotters. For some who grew up before GPS or even Decca, this may be a hard pill to swallow, but the fact that the mind-rattling technology became commonplace within five years of its realistic arrival on the scene tells us how much most of us really want it.

At the time of writing, many 'medium-tech' yachtsmen are using general-purpose laptop computers to run chart programs, but for larger yachts, dedicated ship's computers are already becoming the norm. Among such basics as running major chart plotters, these compact, powerful tools can superimpose weather maps downloaded via low-cost email 'Grib' files on to passage charts. The met data can be processed by the computer to give the best course to steer for speed or comfort, while 'what if' scenarios allow at least a modicum of intuition to be applied to this powerful flow of information. Notices to mariners, conventional weather data, the opening times of your favourite restaurant: the flow of information is growing annually.

SATELLITES AND RADAR

Whether you want it is up to you, but it's getting easier to obtain all the time. Emails and internet go without saying, of course, but you can even watch your favourite DVDs if you finish your handy pocket copy of the *Complete Works of Shakespeare*.

It's a far cry from me setting out across the English Channel in 1971 with an old chart, a pair of schoolboy dividers and a set of parallel rulers I'd won from the dumpster. Strangely enough, I made it to Cherbourg and back. And I saw the sea on the way.

Radar

Radar is the most interactive aid to navigation. Using it properly demands far more expertise than an electronic fixing aid because its readout comes in the form of a moving picture which, to the uninitiated, is hard to interpret, if not incomprehensible. Buying a radar set, therefore, does not solve all navigation problems. Nonetheless, the rewards are great for those who persevere, because radar indicates visually many of those things the navigator would like to see with his own eyes but cannot by virtue of darkness, range or poor visibility. In one sense, it transcends all GPS-based navigation aids, because its signals emanate from the vessel herself and are therefore under the crew's control. GPS comes from outside. It can be interfered with or even switched off, and there's nothing we can do about it. The universal acceptance of the electronic chart plotter has rendered radar largely redundant as a fixing aid for most amateur users, but it remains useful as such in a number of situations, including hand-railing around a headland in an area of known horizontal datum shifts where the safe distance off has been defined, not in lat/long as the plotter would like, but in relation to the land, which the radar can measure reliably and accurately.

The benefits of radar do not end with navigation. The instrument also shows the whereabouts of shipping and small craft so as to form a primary tool for collision avoidance in fog. This capacity will be examined in Chapter 27. In the current context, we are interested in the instrument for its navigational capabilities.

Radar bearings as position lines

Most radar sets have an electronic bearing line (EBL) running from the centre of the screen to its edge. This can be rotated until it touches the image of an object you have identified on the chart. The bearing can be read off from a digital display. If your radar gives a 'head-up' picture (i.e. the top of the screen is where you are headed), this bearing will be relative to your yacht's heading. To convert an EBL reading on a 'head-up' set to a compass bearing, you have merely to add the relative bearing it gives to the compass heading at the time it was taken. For example:

Compass heading	105°M
Relative bearing	080°
Compass bearing	185°M

THE COMPLETE YACHTMASTER

If the relative bearing and the yacht's heading add up to more than 360, subtract 360 from the result to come to a usable answer.

```
Compass heading    195°M
Relative bearing   245°
Compass bearing    440°M
                  – 360°
                 =  80°M
```

More sophisticated radar displays show north at the top, meaning that any EBL bearings will be compass bearings.

Despite their obvious attractions, radar bearings (Fig 19.3, below) do not make ideal PLs. First, they are often less than perfectly accurate because the boat yaws around her heading. Second, most scanners send out a beam width of say, 4°, making a bearing potentially inaccurate to this extent, depending on the skill of the user. Placing the EBL in the centre of a small target will help.

Headlands and other large targets viewed obliquely generally appear a half beam width closer than they are. You can often obtain a more accurate bearing by placing the EBL about half a beam width to landward of the edge of the image (see Fig 19.4). Some sets can adjust their beam width to minimise this effect. If yours cannot, then a width of 4° is a fair assumption unless the handbook states otherwise. If you have no choice but to fix your position by radar bearings only, the same rules apply as to 'visual' PLs. Look out for a good 'cut', use closer rather than distant objects, etc.

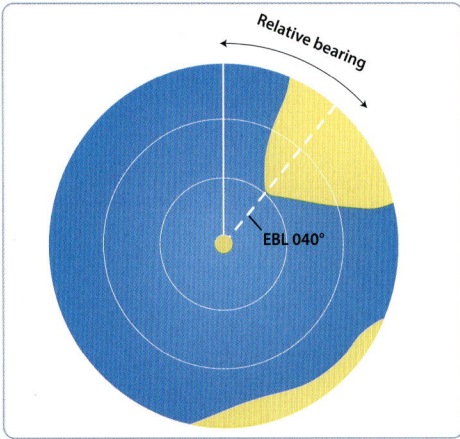

Fig 19.3 The EBL gives a bearing relative to the yacht's head in a standard 'head-up' radar display.

Fig 19.4 The effect of a beam width can be compensated to some extent by placing the EBL about 2° 'inside' a headland that is viewed obliquely.

Radar ranges as position lines

As we have seen, radar bearings may be far from accurate. The capacity of radar to determine range, however, is far more refined. Indeed, it is generally good to within ±1% of the range scale in use.

Most modern radar sets have a Variable Range Marker (VRM) which is adjusted electronically by the user to determine distance off an object on the screen. The distance from an object can be plotted on the chart as a circular PL, just like the distance off a rising light. If you can produce three such PLs you have the elements of a three-point fix, which is likely to be very accurate and whose cocked hat can be evaluated as though it were a visual fix (see Fig 19.5).

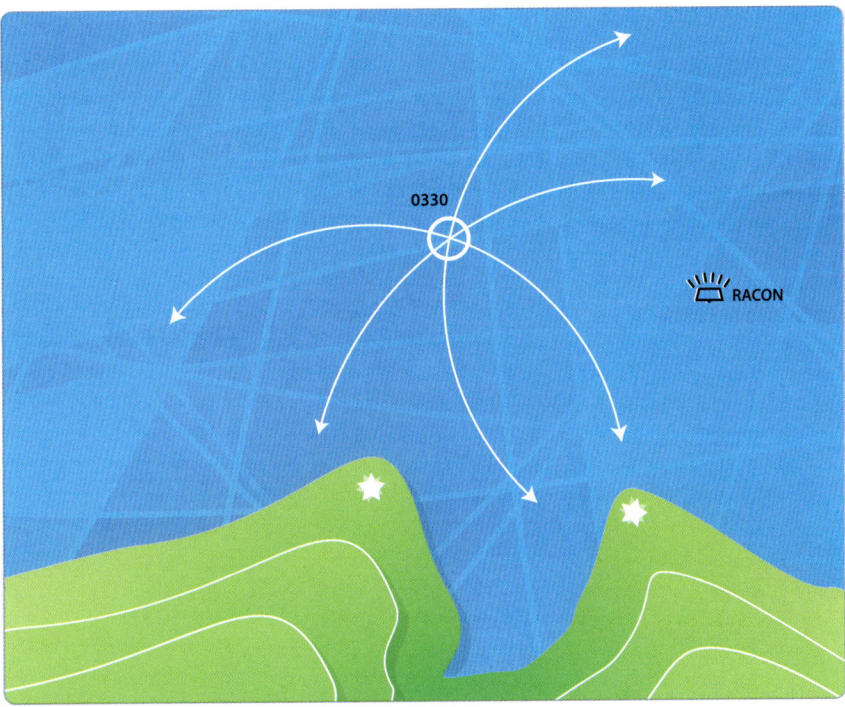

Fig 19.5 The best radar fix is by plotting the distance of three charted objects. Their ranges are read off the screen by means of the Variable Range Marker.

Mixed radar fixes

If you need a radar fix and only a single target is recognisable on the screen, you can use the EBL and the VRM on the same object to generate a fix that is geometrically identical to one worked visually from a rising or dipping light. The fix may not be the finest ever, but it should be a good deal better than its visual counterpart. Plot the distance off as one PL on the chart and the bearing as a second, crossing it at right angles. The resulting fix will be as good as the radar bearing you managed to take. If the range is extreme, this may also be misread because the radar cannot see over the horizon down to sea level. You may be taking the range of high ground half a mile inland from what you thought was the headland.

THE COMPLETE YACHTMASTER

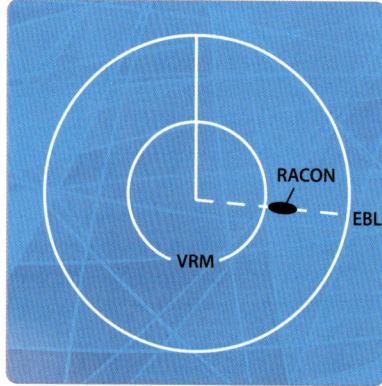

Fig 19.6 A radar fix from a range and a bearing. Note that the racon leaves its 'mark' on the radar screen. The upper illustration carries the following:

Ship's head	335°T
Relative bearing by EBL	095°T
	430°
	− 360°
True bearing	070°T

The illustration below shows the fix plotted on a chart, having extracted the distance from the Variable Range Marker.

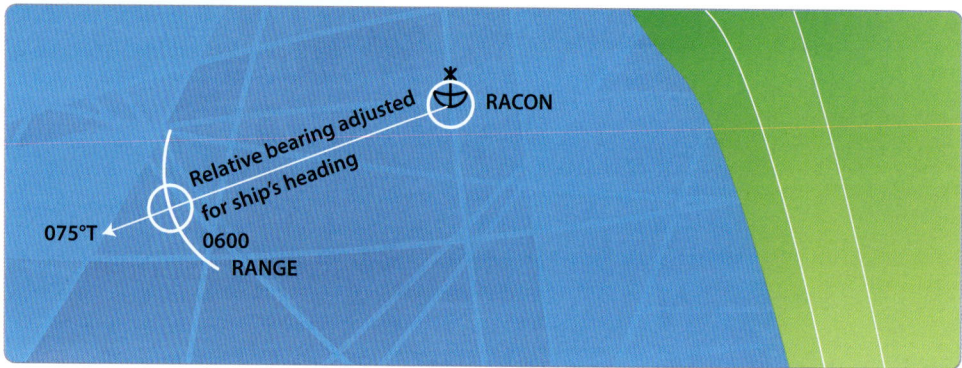

The object in view to the radar in Fig 19.6 has no such problems. It is a racon, which is a radar reactive target marked as such on the chart. This one is a light float. Its compass bearing is 075°T (ship's head + relative bearing), its range is 12 miles and the time 0600. This particular racon identifies itself by a flash running radially out behind the object 'blip' on the screen. Others may show a Morse code.

Had the light float been in sight, a better fix might have been obtained from a visual bearing crossed with a radar range, thus making the best of both worlds. A third PL from some other source, even if it is only the echo sounder, would have further refined the position.

Radar and other fixing systems

If your yacht is equipped with both radar and GPS, it is possible to navigate in poor visibility while subscribing to the essential maxim that one source of information must always be cross-checked against another. If it is absolutely vital that no mistake is made, perhaps in the vicinity of rocks or other dangers, a GPS fix can be checked against one worked up by radar from ranges, or a range and bearing.

Many modern yacht radars will interface with a GPS receiver. Waypoints can thus be displayed on the radar screen, where they appear as a sort of round lollipop on a stick. This comes in handy, and can be a particular comfort when you are trying to work out which of four or five blips is the buoy you are looking for in busy waters on a foggy day. So long as the boat's whole electrical system does not go down, you are now in very good shape indeed because you are using information drawn from two independent sources. The GPS data comes from outside the yacht and is beyond your control, while the radar information is generated by the yacht herself from within her own resources. Where they match up, you can be confident that all is well. If they do not, open your log book and click yourself into 'manual' mode to find out what has gone wrong.

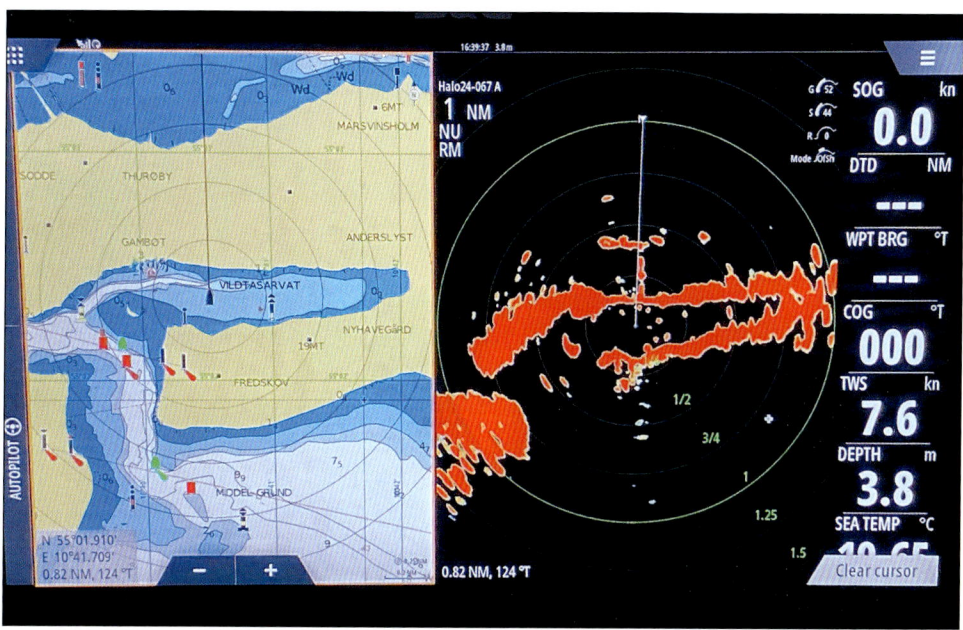

A split-screen display showing the yacht well placed in an anchorage. Note that the radar has been set to read out in 'north up' not the usual 'head up' or 'course up'. This is to make the comparison of the two 'screens' more instantly recognisable than it otherwise would be.

SKIPPER'S TIP

Radar chart overlays

Radar displays can come as part of a chart plotter package, which confers the option of viewing either the plotter or the radar. Split screens allow you to view both at once – albeit at a diminished scale, while the truly sophisticated units allow you to view a full-scale plotter chart complete with boat in situ, then overlay the radar scan on to it. This immediately shows which contacts are buoys and which may be ships, how the land is showing up on the radar, and much more. Perhaps the best thing of all is that you can use the overlay to learn how to 'see' beyond the blips to understand what the radar is picking up. Use the overlay on a fine day and flick between it and pure radar, looking out with your own eyes at the same time. Next time it's foggy, you'll have a far better notion of what your instruments are telling you.

20 COURSE SHAPING

Having now cracked the problem of position, the remaining question for the navigator is how to steer from there to the next destination. In practice, this is comparatively simple, despite the fact that the only time a course turns out to be exactly what an uninformed person might think it would be is when there is absolutely no current and no cross-wind. If you now read between the lines of that statement, you'll see that the two factors that must be allowed for to convert a line joining two places on the chart into a course to steer are leeway and stream.

Fortunately for those of us who are not of a theoretical turn of mind, the situation on the chart is, at its simplest, an exact mirror of what would be happening if the scale of events were small enough for you to watch it all like a god from the clouds. In fact, you can see the correction working if you are rowing a dinghy across a flowing river (Fig 20.2). Under those circumstances the adjustment is usually made instinctively. You eyeball your destination tree on the other side, and start rowing across. As you go, you notice that your tree is moving against the trees behind it, so you choose a big one on the ridge behind the shore, and set your destination up in line with it as a transit. Once you've done that, the rest is easy. You must now head up into the stream so as to keep the two trees in line. If you judge your angle correctly, you'll crab or 'ferryglide' across the river, steering uptide of your destination, yet arriving at it perfectly.

That is the result you are trying to achieve with the chartwork for course shaping, which is really only a pictorial way of depicting the ferryglide of the cross-river dinghy. Let's draw it out (Fig 20.1):

- Suppose you know you are rowing twice as fast as the current. Never mind about knots, just think in terms of units.
- Start out by joining your departure point *a* with your destination *b*. Give the line two arrowheads and call it your ground track.
- Beginning at your starting point *a*, draw in a line *ac*, equal to one unit, to represent the current. Mark it with three arrowheads and call it the tide vector. It is going directly downstream and it shows where you would end up after a given period if you didn't row at all. Let's say you would go that far in one minute.
- Now suppose that at the end of that minute, the current could be switched off, and you have one minute to get back on the rhumb line again, making good as much ground as you can. Obviously, in one minute you will go twice as far as the current carried

COURSE SHAPING

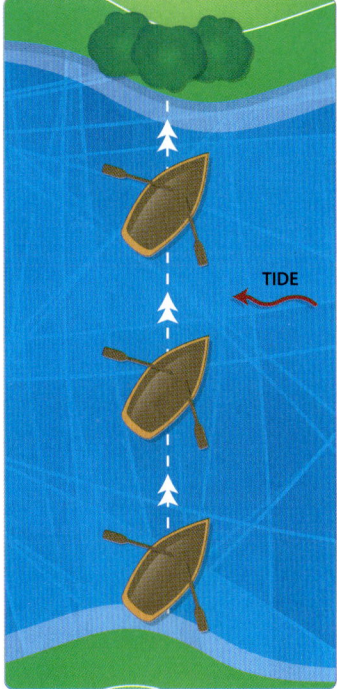

Fig 20.1 Rowing across a tidal stream: the theory.

Fig 20.2 Rowing across a tidal stream: the result.

you, because you are going twice as fast. Take your dividers and extend them to twice the length of *ac*. Put one point into point *c* and scribe across the rhumb line with the other. Make the mark *d* at the intersection.

- Join up *cd* and mark the line with a single arrowhead.
- At point *d* you are back on track. Now switch on the current and do it again.
- Of course, in reality the current runs all the time. The dynamics of the true situation are that the boat starts at *a*, 'steers' off in a direction parallel to *cd* on a line called 'course to steer', then proceeds for the designated period of time towards *b* never leaving the ground track, as in Fig 20.2.

Because this 'velocity triangle' is merely a diagrammatic construction, it doesn't matter what units you use. You could choose nautical miles, but you'd enjoy an equally accurate result if you used milli-cubits as Noah must have done. Even the length of your thumbnail could prove useful in the absence of a pair of dividers.

It is vital that you fully understand this principle. You'll notice that *cd* is a function of your boat speed; it does not join point *c* with the destination. If it did, the diagram would be spurious, and so would your course.

In a factual situation you should size up the picture. Bear in mind that you must draw a vector diagram on the chart and choose units that will fit in acceptably to the scale of things. The bigger, the better, so long as the triangle does not become so large that it runs off the chart, or you run out of chart protractor. Many modern chart protractors have scales scribed along their edges and these can fit the bill excellently. Ideally, you would use minutes of latitude and do the whole job in real knots, but if the scale won't fit, there is nothing to stop you using degrees of longitude for convenience instead.

If the length of the 'leg' is such that you will execute it either in well under, or a little over, an hour, don't worry if your triangle ends up inside or beyond your destination. *It does not matter.* You'll reach the spot just the same, because you never leave the ground track in a simple cross-tide vector.

Obviously, you extract your tide set and drift information from one of the sources mentioned in Chapter 15. Remember that tide booked as 1.3 knots 250° 3 hours before HW Dover means that from 3½ hours before until 2½ hours before HW, you get 1.3 knots at 250°. To get the figure for between 2½ and 1½ hours before HW you need to look up '2 hours before HW'. If your run is going to straddle a change, make a pro-rata adjustment, interpolating in your head if you are not overfussy about the result. If you really care, plot ½ hour of each tide, or whatever you predict the relevant proportions to be.

The same principles apply to legs where you expect to run two hours' tide, or more. In these cases, plot all the tide vectors at the beginning (point *a* in the illustration), then join point *c* (the end of the compound tide vector) with your track by setting your dividers to the distance you expect to run in however many hours' tide you have plotted. Again, you must resist the temptation to join the end of the tide vector to your destination, especially when your dividers are hovering close to it.

Course to steer at the turn of the tide

To take this case at its simplest, let's suppose you have a two-hour leg to run and the tide makes a radical change in strength and direction halfway through it. You have two choices. You could choose to lay off for the first half of the tide in one course to steer, then alter at half time, laying off a fresh course for the new tide. If you do this, you will remain more or less on track throughout the exercise. This could be important if there are dangers to one side of it. However, Fig 20.3a shows that in order to achieve this you have sailed a measurably greater distance than if you had laid both tide lines on at the departure point and allowed the tide to have its way with you (Fig 20.3b). In the latter case, the boat's 'water track' is almost straight towards her destination the whole time. Her 'ground track' drifts with the tide, but she doesn't fight it, because she knows that at the end of the second hour, she will have drifted back to the rhumb line. Her offset is minimal, she has sailed less distance through the water and she is actually further on after two hours than had she fought the tide in order to stay on the direct route.

This example should make clear the folly of using the cross-track error function of a GPS receiver to compensate for set and drift without considering all the implications. In a simple one-hour situation, the technique can be most useful, particularly when homing in on a single-point destination in thick weather, but on a longer passage in a tide due to change it is emphatically not the best thing to do.

COURSE SHAPING

Fig 20.3 Course to steer at the turn of the tide. If you lay off for both hours individually so as to stay on the rhumb line, you will have to sail further than if you lay off both together at the beginning. This is because one hour's tide more or less cancels the other, so to steer into them is in vain.

The longer passage

Identical principles are used when setting up for a cross-tide passage of longer duration. A classic example of this would be an Irish Sea crossing from Anglesey to Dublin. The distance would be in the order of 60 miles. If you expected a reach and reckoned on a speed of 5½ knots, that would be about 11 hours for the passage.

Look up the tidal stream information for all of your 11 hours. Add up the north-going and the south-going streams, take the lesser value from the greater, and you have what is in effect a *net tide vector* (Fig 20.4). Plot this at your departure point, draw in your track, open the dividers to 60 miles (or whatever scale you are using) and complete the triangle. You may drift 15 miles to one side of your track by the time you are halfway there, but the next 5 hours will see you sliding back towards Dublin as surely as you can say, 'A pint of Guinness, please.'

Fig 20.4 The net vector on a passage of several hours.

THE COMPLETE YACHTMASTER

A classical course to steer, plotted on an Imray paper chart. Note the short line at the route of the course-to-steer vector (one arrow). This is plotted an estimated number of degrees towards the wind. It compensates for leeway and is the course logged and handed up to the helm. In this case, seven degrees leeway has been estimated. Not to be used for navigation

Leeway

You'll notice that, after initially noting its importance, we haven't yet mentioned leeway in this discussion. The reason is that, because it is applied to the course to steer, it is dealt with as a final adjustment. If you have understood its place in the estimated position you'll realise how to deal with it for a course to steer.

Depending on her point of sailing, your boat is going to be driven downwind by her leeway at anything from 2° or 3° to as much as 20° in heavy weather. Once you have estimated how much your leeway will be, you must steer upwind by an equivalent number of degrees to counteract it. On the chart you can arrange this by laying your protractor along the course to steer and rotating it 10° (or whatever the leeway angle may be) to windward. On a paper chart it helps to plot this line very short, as shown in the diagram on p. 204. Don't log it full length, as clarity will be compromised, but it should be logged as the course you are steering, after making a note in the log book to remind you about what you have done.

Some log books contain separate columns for course required, leeway and course steered. If you find this helpful, go for it, but don't feel you must if the extra columns seem daunting. It is enough to log what you are really steering. Remember that when you come to plot an EP you'll be applying leeway to the course actually steered, so that is the one that counts.

The question of when to plot a cross-tide vector and when to 'eyeball' it causes considerable misunderstanding among inexperienced sailors. Like most things, the best answer is to eyeball it if you can. In a cross-current, this means being able to identify some sort of transit, perhaps a natural one, either dead astern or ahead, behind your destination. This is often not possible, however, so my recommendation is to practise plotting vectors until it is second nature. Then, when you feel you need a course to steer that will allow for the tide, the job will only take a few seconds. If it absorbs five minutes, you are being a bad skipper. What is more, if you know it's going to take that long you'll be less inclined to do it when you need to. The answer is to follow your commonsense but to be a master of the mechanics of plotting.

Cross-tide sailing with GPS

Some of the more sophisticated plotter programs allow you to shape a cross-tide course using stream information from their own database. The data from which these programs work are not always of the highest quality, so care must be taken not to capitulate to the machine until you are totally confident that it is giving the right answers.

For those with access to iOS electronics, AngelNav will work up a course to steer from data you input. The program uses reliable primary source tidal information.

A classic one-hour, course-to-steer vector diagram, plotted on an iPad using AngelNav software. At the time of writing, this app, which runs independently of the internet, is unique in its ability to do this.
Not to be used for navigation

COURSE SHAPING

Shaping a course to a waypoint with GPS and a paper chart, one has only to inspect the bearing to the waypoint and the course over ground (COG), then steer so that the two coincide. Any cross set is automatically taken care of. It's important to keep checking the bearing, which may change if the boat drifts from the original safe heading. Make sure any new track is not taking the boat across some ghastly danger by noting the bearing on the chart.

The technique with a plotter is even easier, so long as it has a projected track function which has been turned on. All that is then needed is to steer so the vector on the screen is crossing the destination and all will be well. It's immediately obvious if the vector passes too close to a danger on the way.

Using GPS like this is fine for short hops. In a turning tide situation (Fig 20.3, p. 203), it still pays to work out the net vector because most hardware plotters can't do this for you. A good PC will, but working up a few sums isn't much of a hardship and it ensures that you are in charge, rather than capitulating to a machine that may or may not know what's best.

Sailing hard with shipping around like this, nobody feels like taking the trouble to shape a course, but it can matter even more when the going gets rough. If it's just a one-hour vector and you have a chart plotter, you can be grateful that all you need do is steer so that the projected track crosses your destination.

NAVIGATIONAL STRATEGY 21

The next chapter deals with the vital subject of planning a passage, but before you can do this effectively you need to have a grip on the essentials of navigational strategy.

Wind, tide, light and darkness

More often than not, a straight line is not the quickest way for a sailing boat to travel between two points. If you are beating to windward, the timing of your tacks can be crucial. When you are reaching, a wind shift can work for you or against you, depending on where you placed your yacht in anticipation. Sometimes it pays to motor to be sure of a tidal gate. On other occasions it may not matter. Light, darkness, moonrise or moonset can affect your plans considerably, and so the list goes on. The more important strategic and tactical considerations are considered below.

Wind shifts

When you are expecting a wind shift, you ought to decide how it would affect you were you to remain on the rhumb line to your destination. If you are on a tight reach and the shift will free you, well and good, but if it looks like being a header, steer as high as you can before

Fig 21.1 Anticipating a wind shift.

it arrives. Work yourself well to windward of the rhumb line, then when the breeze heads you, follow it round closehauled until it settles down (Fig 21.1 p. 207). You shouldn't risk easing sheets unless you are entirely confident of laying your destination. The instinctive sailor always keeps his destination under his lee as long as the wind remains forward of the beam. When in doubt, work up to windward.

A similar situation occurs when you expect a shift that will put you on a dead run. No one wants a run, so try to adjust your position so that when the wind changes direction you find yourself on a broad reach instead.

Beating in water free of currents

Beating to windward can be enjoyable on a sunny Sunday afternoon with the boat under full sail, heeling firmly in the summer breeze and a gentle pressure on the tiller.

But what about having to beat home to Cape Cod from Nova Scotia in a stiff sou'wester at the end of a cruise? Or a 70-mile thrash upwind in the trades from the Virgin Islands to St Martin? Or the dreaded northerly that always seems to hit you as you come out of Cherbourg homeward bound with 60 miles of choppy English Channel ahead? There's no pleasure in these, or in any other serious beat once the wind rises above force 5.

Mitigation of the pain of windward sailing is one of the great arts of seamanship. In the old days, folk talked of 'working a boat to windward'. Now the buzz is about 'tacking angles' and 'VMG'. The upwind performance of today's yachts is so dramatically superior to that suffered by our forebears that we tend to rely on it alone and forget about the subtleties of tactical beating. In the days when boats struggled to point 55° from the wind and made 10° and more of leeway, people became experts at working to weather, because they spent so much of their time doing it. If a modern cruiser is sailed with a careful eye on her strategic situation, she can make remarkably short work of even the most grisly beat.

The favoured tack

If the wind blew constantly from one direction, there would be no art at all to windward sailing. You could make as many or as few tacks as you fancied until you were able to lay your course to home. Fortunately, the wind hardly ever behaves like this. It fluctuates even when its general direction is not changing, and in most locations it is subject to major shifts from time to time. The way these variations are turned to advantage is the sure sign of a good seaman.

The secret of successful beating is to endeavour always to be on the favoured or making tack. The wind is rarely smack on the nose, although it may sometimes seem that way, and when it is, it doesn't usually stay there for long. One tack will nearly always give you more progress towards your objective than the other. So long as you stay on this tack until you are dead downwind of where you want to be, you can always make the best use of any wind shift that comes along.

NAVIGATIONAL STRATEGY

Unpredicted wind shifts

When you are not laying your course, any shift in the wind either lifts you or heads you. Each time you experience a shift, you should reassess your position, always remembering that the object of your efforts is to try to be on the favoured tack for as much time as possible.

Suppose you are on the favoured port tack, as in Fig 21.2a, and the wind backs (moves anticlockwise). You have been lifted and the tack is now even more favoured. Make the most of it by ensuring that your boat is doing the best speed conditions will allow.

The boat in Fig 21.2b has been headed by a veering (clockwise) shift. She was on the favoured tack, but has been forced to turn so far from her destination that she will make considerable gains by tacking immediately on to starboard, which will now carry her nearer to where she wants to go. Climb on to each successive wind shift like this and your tacks will all bite deeply into the overall ground to be made good on a long beat.

If you still have a considerable distance to make up, the worst mistake is to stay on the losing tack all the way to the 'lay line' in the hope that you will fetch your destination 'in one' after you have gone about. If you are lifted towards the end of the losing tack, the long favoured tack you have worked for will disappear. Were you to be headed near the end of the 'bad tack', of course you could tack on the shift and head home in one with a complacent smirk, but since we are talking about haphazard wind shifts, a 50% chance of success isn't good enough when there is a more certain alternative.

Fig 21.2 Unpredicted wind shifts.

If the wind is blowing directly from your destination, the safest way to organise a long beat is to tack up a cone. You should draw in your rhumb line on the chart, then either sketch or imagine two lines spreading out at a 5° angle on either side. When you have sailed as far from the rhumb line as the outer edge of your cone, you should tack, recross the rhumb line, and so on, given that there is no wind shift. If the wind backs or veers, take a look at things from where you are and see if there is now a making tack.

With the wind on the nose, any shift is beneficial on one tack or the other, so long as you are near the rhumb line. If you are out on a limb, the shift may be a winner or it may be a disaster. The cone keeps you well placed to take advantage of whatever happens.

Anticipated wind shifts

If neither tack is currently favoured but you are anticipating a wind shift to one side or the other of the rhumb line, make sure that you stand to the side that will be favoured after the shift. That way, you will find yourself on the losing tack when the shift comes, headed still further from your destination. Tack when it arrives, however, and your new board will be exceedingly beneficial. You may even make it in one tack, like the yacht *Prudence* in Fig 21.3.

Arrogance has ignored the expected shift and allowed herself to be caught on the wrong side of the rhumb line. For her sins, she is now dead to leeward with a long beat ahead, watching *Prudence* fetch straight in. Both had sailed exactly the same distance from their starting point when the wind shifted.

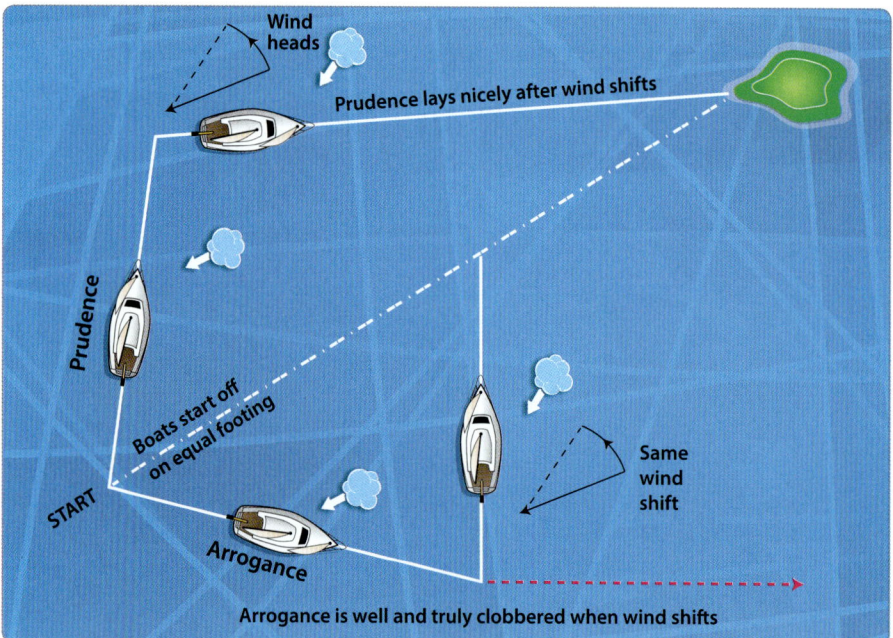

Fig 21.3 Anticipated wind shifts.

NAVIGATIONAL STRATEGY

Beating in a cross-current

If there is a current running when you are beating towards an objective, the favoured tack may not be obvious. Assuming the wind is blowing straight down the rhumb line and the current is running across it, the tack that puts the current on your lee side is the winner. On that tack, the current is lifting you to windward as well as keeping you closer to the rhumb line, so you not only make good more ground, you are in a better position to benefit from any unexpected wind shifts.

Beating in a cross-tide

For these purposes, a tidal stream is distinguished from a current by the fact that it changes its strength and direction every so often. The usual diurnal tide gives us six hours' stream each way. If you are going to complete your beat before the turn of the tide, the stream may be treated as if it were a current as described above. If the tide is going to turn one or more times during the passage, you can take advantage of a hidden bonus if you arrange your tacks to keep the cross-tide on the lee bow.

We've just seen how a weather-going stream will keep you near the rhumb line. If you tack as the tide turns, you'll keep as close to it as possible all the time, but that isn't the end of the benefits. When you have the tide on your lee bow, you are moving in an apparent wind which – unsuspected by the uninitiated – is lifting you by several degrees and enabling you to point even closer to your destination (Fig 21.4).

Here's how it works: if you stopped the boat, took down her sails and were able to switch off the wind, you would drift with the tide at right angles to the rhumb line. As you were

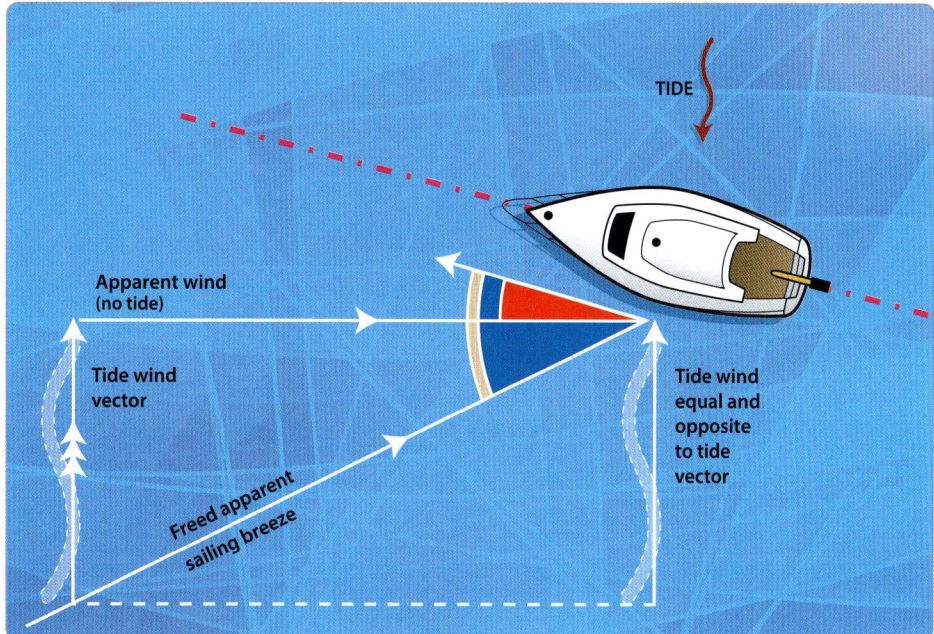

Fig 21.4 The lee-bow effect on apparent wind.

> **SKIPPER'S TIP**
>
> ### VMG
>
> Most GPS receivers offer the user a 'VMG' calculation facility as part of the software package. VMG stands for Velocity Made Good towards a given objective. In this case, the objective will be the next waypoint. If you activate the waypoint, the relevant electronic page will tell you how fast you are actually progressing towards it, as well as your less relevant current speed over the ground. When you are in doubt as to which tack is favoured, note the reading, then come about. If the VMG improves, stay with the new deal. If it drops, tack back again.
>
> VMG is also useful when reaching in a cross-tide. If this has a favourable component, your speed over the ground may appear a good deal better than your actual VMG, so check it out if you want to calculate an estimated time of arrival (ETA).

carried through the still air you would feel an apparent breeze coming from the opposite direction at the same speed as the tide, say 3 knots. This is called the 'tide wind'.

Now turn the wind on again and get under way. The breeze across your deck can be thought of as a mixture of two components. There is the apparent sailing wind from which the average modern cruiser should be pointing 30° or so, and there is the 3 knot tide wind. Because the stream is on your lee bow, this is coming from your weather quarter, so it is exerting a freeing influence on the totality of the apparent wind in which you are sailing.

If the apparent wind is 13.5 knots and 3 knots of that is tide wind, the difference it is causing in the overall direction will be considerable. No change in apparent wind direction can alter your boat's pointing ability but, by lee bowing the tide, you have manipulated the breeze itself so that you are making good more ground towards your goal. Don't ignore the tide, even if it is running at only 1 knot. Every little helps on a long beat.

Famous helmsmen win trophies by using these methods, but there is nothing new about them at all. Successful clipper captains were employing them in the 1850s. Fishermen homeward bound with their catch tacked on every heading wind shift, and the oyster dredger crossing the bay to his working ground did everything he could to work the tide under his lee bow. The techniques pay off for every ship that sails the sea. They have been developed to such a degree of sophistication because, in the end, none of us likes a beat to be any longer than is absolutely necessary.

Tacking downwind

For many people, running dead downwind in a seaway represents one of life's more extreme unpleasantnesses. Poling out the Number 1 as you cream along behind your local island on a summer's evening might be fine, but doing the same thing at sea is worlds away, not only because of the physical difficulty of dancing around the foredeck with the pole, but also because a boat on a run is both slow and uncomfortable. She rolls without the steadying effect of the heeling force from the rig; she is slow because, if the breeze is less than force 4, her own progress will reduce the apparent wind to such a degree that it no longer has any real strength to drive her.

NAVIGATIONAL STRATEGY

Running may be the nadir for sailors, but a broad reach is fast, smooth and safe. So why does the wind always blow from right aft? Sod's Law, that's why. Inconvenience is a fact of the sailor's life, but there is no need to be downhearted. If you can't stand running, why not steer clear of it like the pestilence it is. Don't head directly downwind, however tempting it may seem. Bring the boat up as far as it takes to get her sailing sweetly, then reach away until you have rattled off half your distance. Now gybe on to the opposite tack and reach off the other half. In light or moderate winds you'll probably pick up a knot of extra speed, so, even discounting the gain in comfort, you'll be hardly any worse off in passage time.

Here is a typical example: a 60-mile passage on a run at 5 knots = 12 hours. Come up to the wind by 30°. Your distance is now about 70 miles. If your speed increases by 1 knot, there will be no extension of passage time. If you find 30° is not enough to make the reach really positive, you could come up to 40°, adding 18½ miles to the total distance. You would now be out for 13 hours instead of 12, but what a sail you'd have! You're not racing, so unless there is a critical tide gate to catch, why not enjoy the trip?

Working to windward, a good suit of sails well set is everything.

22 PASSAGE PLANNING

Passage planning is the vital ingredient for a successful cruise. Before I became a sailing instructor I had no idea that it existed as a separate subject. I just did it, and that was that. The result was that it took me many years to organise my ideas so that I remembered everything I needed to consider before setting forth. These days passage planning is a legal requirement, although how far the authorities will pursue the matter for leisure users remains to be tested (2025).

Ill fortune will appear to dog the skipper of a yacht on a poorly planned passage. Fair tides will elude him at headlands, and he will be unlucky with his wind shifts; when the breeze dies, the fuel on board will prove infuriatingly inadequate for the task; while upon arrival, the yacht may spend the night rolling in an open anchorage after missing the tide on the marina sill by just 20 minutes.

A passage plan in an area you know well might consist of no more than a glance at the tide tables and a quick mental calculation about the mileage to be made good compared with the yacht's probable speed over the ground. On a strange coast, preparing for a similar trip could take an hour or more, with detailed study of several charts, careful appraisal of the weather, considerations about what to do in the event of failure to arrive at a particular place before the tide turns foul, and so on.

It isn't always easy to decide how much detail to plan for, but too much rigidity should always be avoided. We are navigating on a rolling road whose movements may prove uncertain. Even motor vessels frequently have to modify their plans to accommodate developments. The chances of a sailing boat being advantageously steered to her destination on some predetermined course, minute in its accuracy, are small indeed. For this reason, time used at the planning stage is better spent on familiarisation with broad topics such as tidal stream, and on unchangeable specifics like the latest time of arrival at a lock gate, than with working out exact courses to steer, which in reality may prove impossible or inconvenient. The measure of a seaman in this context is how easily he is able to look at the overall outline of a passage, decide what he needs to know at this stage, then extract that information from the available sources.

Because of the different types of source material, some aspects of a plan can be worked up at home weeks beforehand if that appeals to you, while others are best addressed ten minutes before slipping the mooring. The subjects to be considered must inevitably vary with the circumstances. Here are some of the more important headings that can come up for consideration.

PASSAGE PLANNING

Even the most meticulous passage plan sometimes requires modification at sea in light of developments.

Charts and overall distances

The first requirement is a paper passage chart. Nothing else offers such a comprehensive overview. Ideally, it will cover both the departure point and the destination. This chart will form the core of the plan, and it will be used to measure off the various distances so as to see whether the trip can be made in one tide, or two, or more, in the conditions you are expecting.

Once you've sorted out this basic information, you'll need to decide if the passage chart contains all the detail required for safe navigation. Often, a larger-scale chart will be essential at the beginning and end of the passage, but you should also pay attention to any areas en route that are of special navigational interest. Suppose, for example, your best course takes you close inshore at a headland where the passage chart shows the presence of off-lying rocks. You are then faced with a choice: either stay well outside the dangers, or invest the price of another round of mixed drinks on the necessary chart for close-in work.

Passage planning with chart plotters

One problem that has become associated with chart plotters as a primary navigation tool is that in many cases they are far from ideal for passage planning. A PC with a good-sized screen running raster charts can work adequately because the charts show all they have to give. This means what you see is what you get. If an overview is required, as it always is for planning, zooming out delivers essentially what would be seen on the equivalent paper chart. The difficulty of zooming and panning a vector chart is that data appears and disappears at the behest of whoever arranged the software. Quite probably this person was not a cartographer of the calibre of those who draw Admiralty or Imray paper charts and their raster partners. Important features may therefore be missed at the planning stage, unless every inch of the route is zoomed in as far as it can go. This is rarely realistic. Indeed, it is often totally impractical because one would also be obliged to check what is happening on either side of the rhumb line. And how far out does one look? When planning with a vector plotter, therefore, it is safer to use a paper chart as well.

Routes

All GPS receivers feature a system whereby the navigator can string a series of waypoints together, forming a planned route. As the yacht travels past one waypoint, the computer automatically gives a course and distance to the next, and so on until the destination is reached.

A route can be a real winner when a large number of course alterations follow within a comparatively short time. A classic example is through the rocks of the Chenal du Four on the north-west corner of France. Tides are rampant in this 12-mile passage with its half-dozen minor but vital course alterations, and sudden fog is common. Given the usual 5 knots of current and a typical 6-knot boat speed, the buoys come up very quickly indeed, so a carefully organised route plan is a source of substantial stress relief, particularly if backed up in practice by radar.

Even if you use a chart plotter with electronic charts, it is better to enter your waypoints at the planning stage in harbour than to click them in at sea where you may be distracted. Choose them carefully and be sure they relate safely to each other.

Alternative destinations

The essence of cruising is flexibility. Most of us aren't out there to wear the hair shirt, so any destination becomes more desirable if it offers workable alternatives on either side of it. If there is doubt about whether you will reach it before a strong tide turns foul, a second choice, either at a shorter distance or a few miles to leeward, could turn a demoralising six hours spent sailing on the spot into a satisfactory arrival and a good night's rest. If it saves you a five-mile slug closehauled in a strengthening foul tide after failing to lay your original choice of port in one, you'll be doubly delighted.

Conversely, when things are going better than you dared to hope, with the yacht rollicking along in the sunshine, you may not want to stop at your official destination. A likely haven ten miles further on would offer the opportunity to extract full value from this rarest of days.

When your track runs in the vicinity of the coast, check for any ports of refuge if there is the slightest doubt about the weather. This does not have to be one of your viable alternatives, but you must ensure not only that it will offer berthing facilities, but that it can be entered safely with the wind in the direction you fear it may take. If you are in any doubt about this, consult your pilot book.

> **SKIPPER'S TIP**
>
> ### Pilot books
> A good yachtsman's pilot is written by us for us and is worth its weight in marine-grade stainless steel. For solid detail of coastal and offshore features, currents, weather, everything else you can think of and more that you can't, the Admiralty Pilots offer the world's finest value. Check them not only for information on harbours at the beginning and end of the passage, but also for the passage notes they may contain.

Waypoints

If you are using GPS waypoints, now is the time to decide where they will be. For paper chart navigation, once you've noted each one and punched them into the machine, 'plot' them into the chart a second time from the co-ordinates in the GPS in order to double-check them. Carelessly entered waypoints are a main source of GPS-induced shipwreck. Only a thorough inspection of the chart for an individual passage can determine where waypoints are going to be useful, but it sometimes pays to have one at your point of departure from the 'pilotage mode'. You will certainly require a second at your destination. Others may be at headlands or offshore shoals along the general route.

Although waypoints are supposed to be positions of real navigational significance, it can be a kindness if you site a waypoint strategically to give the crew a psychological boost. It's reassuring on a long, tedious trip if the skipper can say, 'Things might look grisly, folks, but we'll be at my "Point Misery" in another half hour. That's two thirds of the distance, so it'll be all downhill from there.'

Waypoint lists

Many natural 'corners' are defined by a buoy, a beacon or a light structure with their lat/long positions given in the almanacs, cruising guides or published waypoint lists so that you can enter them directly. This can be valuable where pinpoint accuracy is desired, as it would be if you were using a waypoint in a pilotage plan too tight to plot with pencil and dividers, or to pick out a buoy from other blips on your interfaced radar screen.

Such precision is often irrelevant, however. In circumstances other than those above, I rarely take up the offer of listed mid-passage waypoints because it suits me to make my turns some distance from the charted spot. Steering directly towards an abstract position that serves your particular purposes on the day is simple. Trying to end up some chosen distance adrift from a waypoint predetermined by somebody else can be more tricky. Even an arrival waypoint is sometimes more effective if it is a mile uptide of the breakwater. You can always adjust matters later when you know you're going to make it.

A further reason for plotting your own waypoint positions is that there is always the off-chance the book will get it wrong. While almanac compilers are among the most painstaking people on the planet, I know as the author of a successful pilot book that everyone can occasionally make an error. A notorious error printed in a favourite almanac for the Irish Sea one year could well have led to some classic navigational blunders. You therefore owe it to yourself to double-check. Besides, taking this trouble helps to develop your lat/long plotting skills.

Weather

Whether you are thinking of a two-week cruise plan or a six-hour passage, the secret of making the most of the weather is to be thoroughly informed, but not too rigid in your planning. One of the most genuinely recreational things about going to sea is the confrontation with an elemental force that nothing that can be done or said will ever alter. If you've planned a ten-day cruise with a family crew on a stretch of coast 150 miles distant that turns out on the day to lie full in the eye of an established wind, you'll either have to forget it, or square up for a 48-hour dead beat, or worse. A modern yacht will generally get you there, but the price in terms of discomfort may be higher than you care to pay. It may be a different matter if you and your mates are out for a 'rugby club cruise'. This can be a lot of fun but isn't everyone's cup of tea. If you aren't engaged in yacht delivery, it is usually wiser to have various cruise plans up your sleeve, and to study the internet weather maps, seven-day forecasts and surface pressure charts a week or more before sailing day to avoid ending up with a ferry ride home.

In the shorter term, make sure that you have noted any impending changes in wind strength and direction, and have paid special attention to any likely alterations in visibility. Fog on passage doesn't have to be the end of the world, so long as you have paid due thought to it and planned accordingly. The rules of thumb for fog navigation with and without electronic assistance can be found in Chapter 26.

Tidal streams

After distance, this is the most important item in a passage plan. It is more beneficial to beat with a fair tide than to reach against a foul one, particularly in areas of abnormal tidal activity, such as tidal gates (Chapter 15). There are tidal gates on both sides of the Atlantic that will reduce the progress of a vessel making less than 7 knots to a crawl, while a yacht beating to windward will make no ground at all. It is therefore vital to hit gates when they are open. It can be useful to scribe light circles 'one hour' in radius centred on the gate, which cut the track drawn on the chart and show the latest times the yacht can be at these points if the gate is to be reached before it closes. These marks are of great interest in light going because they can help you decide when to crank up the engine if the latest time to slip through the gate is growing critical. If you can't bring yourself to consider motoring on passage at any price, you'll have to look out for suitable bays in which to kedge to await the next fair tide. Personally I can never understand this point of view from those who have an auxiliary engine. I've done my time without one, and now that I have a diesel I'm all for extracting any benefit I can from that drogue disguised as a propeller that my boat must drag kicking and screaming through every mile she sails.

Tidal stream atlases, or the relevant section in the almanac, should have ship's time pencilled in on each relevant page so as to minimise time spent below. Periods at the chart table can also be axed if High Water at the standard port concerned is noted alongside the tidal diamond key on the passage chart.

PASSAGE PLANNING

If the passage runs across the tide, you will help yourself if you work up in advance the sum of the probable tidal effect in each direction for the initially assumed duration of the passage. Although this information may no longer be relevant by the time you make landfall, it will give you some basic data from which to shape a course after you have been able to ascertain your boat speed in practice.

Traffic separation schemes (TSS)

TSSs are the passage planner's nightmare. We all know the rules, and swingeing fines await any delinquent caught disobeying them. Avoid heavy shipping concentrations altogether if you have the choice.

SKIPPER'S TIP

Dangers

It's well worth familiarising yourself with these before the passage begins, but there is no need to go to the extreme of writing down where they are. After all, you'll see them on the chart as they approach, but if you've spent some time considering their implications, you'll have been able to deal with items such as clearing bearings well in advance. This may save an unseemly scrabble round the chart table later on, when it's heeled 20° and the pencils are flying.

Tidal heights

Some harbours in northern Europe are only approachable at certain states of the tide. If your destination is one of these, calculate the times when this tidal 'window' will be open early on in the planning procedure, so that you can work back from there. As in the case of gates for tidal stream, one or two concentric 'latest time' rings on the passage chart often prove helpful.

Tidal heights above areas of shoal water may also be critical. If a tidal curve is available for the area concerned, fill it in as part of the passage plan. It can then be used for reference, enabling you to work out the height of tide in a few seconds whenever you may require it.

Daylight

The benefits of a dawn landfall are considerable. You can fix your position without ambiguity on the shore lights before the sun comes up. Then you have the whole day in which to work your way into harbour without the additional stress brought on by darkness. You also benefit from being under no end-of-day pressure to find the authorities before nightfall.

If you have to enter or leave a harbour during the night hours, moonlight is a tremendous help, even if the Moon herself is behind the clouds. The approximate time of moonrise and moonset can be found in the almanac. Don't worry if the detailed corrections leave you cold. In most cases, a general idea is all you'll need.

THE COMPLETE YACHTMASTER

With modern navigation, the benefits of a dawn landfall are not so clear-cut, but it still pays to take note of daylight and try not to arrive in strange harbours after dark if there's the option. The aids to navigation may all be in place, but you never know what's going on that you cannot see.

Fuel

Nothing is more frustrating than six hours spent going backwards past a tidal gate because the wind has dropped and you haven't enough fuel to motor. This dismal consummation always happens at 0300, leaving the watch on deck plenty of time to consider the implications of your omission. Most modern yachts have enough fuel capacity for a full 24 hours' running, but you should make yourself aware of what your range is at the extreme, with a sizeable margin for safety. If motoring isn't too traumatic on your boat, a calm spell sometimes gives you the chance to put a painless 100 miles to windward into the bag. It would be a shame to miss the opportunity because you'd decided not to bother filling up.

Courses to steer

These should only be planned approximately, if indeed you consider the trouble worth taking at all. Whatever you precompute will probably be wrong if there is any tide or current, unless you are in a motorboat. If you have worked up a rough heading, however, you can use that, see what speed you make, then determine a proper course to steer using tidal data you have already prepared.

PASSAGE PLANNING

Tactics and strategy

Intelligent anticipation of wind shifts is one of the most important features of planning a passage. This, combined with a creative appreciation of the lee-bow effect, use of the tidal stream to avoid running dead downwind, and a careful avoidance of arriving downwind of one's destination is a mark of a mature, well-organised skipper. Tactics are not a particularly significant part of a motor yachtsman's life; to the sailor they are, all in all (Chapter 21).

Pilotage plan

A plan for entering a strange harbour is essential if the pilotage promises to be of any complexity. There is often time to produce this on passage, but if you are prone to seasickness it is much better done before you set off. The question of whether or not you need a written pilotage plan, and what form it should take, seems still to be a personal one. It depends, among other things, upon how pictorial a memory you have. The matter is discussed in more detail in Chapter 23.

Vitally important in inshore pilotage is a good pair of binoculars with clean lenses.

23 PILOTAGE

Having an electronic chart plotter to hand at the helm has totally transformed the sort of close-in pilotage where traditional navigation methods are rendered ineffective by reasons of scale. Things come up quickly when working into a complicated harbour or jinking through a nasty patch of rocks. With the plotter zoomed to a sensible scale you can literally follow your boat from mark to mark through the dangers in safety. As always with any chart plotter, issues arise because the screen is too small for an overview, but this can be made good by keeping a paper chart available for a quick look to check up on where you actually are. It also plays handsomely to have studied the pilotage area before you get there. This ensures there are no surprises and that you can take the whole process at a relaxed, measured pace.

In reality, most of us will use the plotter for pilotage most of the time. However, all complete Yachtmasters must be familiar with the skills that saw their forebears safely through, so that should GPS suffer interference, they will not be lost.

The essence of successful pilotage is to extract the information from chart and pilot book that will enable you to work through the dangers on a series of positively defined straight lines. Each line takes you past one problem or another, until you either arrive at your destination, or sail safely out into wider waters.

So long as you are on a safe line, or tracking through a defined zone that is obviously clear of danger and that leads you to the next line, you do not usually require to know how far along it you are. Thus, in pilotage, your position is often defined only in the dimension of your desired track. The cross-reference that would constitute a fix is generally absent (see Fig 23.2, p. 225), except at certain important times. Coming to terms with this is vital to competent pilotage. An examiner can always tell a tyro because of the way he is constantly trying to fix his position, even when to do so is not only unnecessary and a waste of time, it is also nigh on impossible.

Because of the presence of cross-currents in much pilotage, it is rarely sufficient simply to steer so that the yacht's head points towards the next object. Fortunately, there are a number of wrinkles for making sure that the boat remains on the desired line without having to resort to fixing.

PILOTAGE

Safe track

Two types of line are essential to the business of pilotage (Fig 23.1): the safe track, which is the straight line leading through a particular set of dangers; and the clearing line, defining the edge of a danger area. Keep on the right side of a clearing line and you are safe; venture across it, and you are stranded.

The best way to establish the whereabouts of either type of line is with a transit. As we have seen in Chapter 18, the line joining two known objects, projected seaward, is the most reliable position line of all. When used to mark off a safe track you can work along it with no difficulty, and you can see straight away if you depart from it by as much as a cockpit's width. A transit works equally well if you are steering directly towards or directly away from it and it makes a fine 'leading line' for entering or leaving a harbour. For this reason, many authorities set up transits using posts and lights in crucial places. These are charted and noted in all relevant pilot books.

In addition to indicating safe tracks, transits also make fine clearing lines. If the two markers remain 'open' on the correct side, all is well; if they close, you are on the clearing line; and if they open on the wrong side, instant action will be required if you are to continue having a happy day.

Fig 23.1 Safe pilotage. Above: a safe track. Below: a clearing line.

THE COMPLETE YACHTMASTER

When identifying distant marks, particularly after dark, it really pays to stand up as high as you can for a better look.

We have looked at many forms of transit in Chapter 18, but in pilotage you can be especially creative. If no 'official' transit lends itself to your needs, inspect the chart carefully for two recognisable objects that, when in line, will give you the safe passage or the clearance you are seeking. It will surprise you how frequently something will show up. It could be the end of a pier and a conspicuous hotel, two islands with their edges just 'closed', the right-hand side of a building 'on' with a light structure, etc. The best method of finding them is to lay your protractor along the desired track on the chart, then see what you can spot along its edge. You may have to shunt it around a little, but there is frequently something that will serve.

If you cannot make up a transit to lead you from one mark (a buoy, perhaps, or a post) to the next, your second line of defence is to use a compass bearing. This is an indifferent substitute for a charted transit, but you can still use natural transits to make the best of the situation. Immediately after rounding the first mark, steer the boat directly for the second. If you cannot instantly identify it, ask all hands to look for it dead ahead. As soon as you have it, glance astern at the first mark to ensure you have not already been set off the safe track. Now line up your goal with anything immediately behind it that is not going to move. A fisherman mending his nets will do so long as he doesn't walk off. Keep the buoy and the fisherman in transit, and you can only be on the direct line from the first buoy to the second.

If you cannot find two objects to line up, you will have to use your handbearing compass, which is a pilot's last resort. When you are sailing away from a known object down a safe track defined by a compass bearing, you can keep on track by using a *back bearing*. Watch the object over the compass as its distance increases, and make sure that its bearing remains constant. The preferred technique for achieving this end is to hold the compass at the desired

PILOTAGE

Fig 23.2 Straight line pilotage. The pilot only knows his exact whereabouts when one of his straight lines intersects with another at a point-of-course change.

bearing and see if the object moves to the left or right. When the boat wanders from her track it is easy to decide which side you have slipped if you are using the compass like this. If you sight the actual bearing of the object and try to work out which way you have drifted by doing sums in your head, you can easily come unstuck.

Always remember that the best compass you have is the ship's steering compass. If you are sailing *towards* a specified object on a safe track – or if an object whose bearing defines a clearing line is almost ahead – you have only to read the compass when the boat's head is exactly on the object to determine its precise bearing, given, of course, that you correct for any deviation. If the object lies more than a few degrees off the bow, you can always 'twitch' your heading every so often to check its bearing on the steering compass. This technique can save considerable trouble trying to use a handbearing compass when there is no need.

If an object defines a safe track and you are steering directly towards it, the trick for remaining in line is the same as that used for a back bearing with the handbearing compass. Keep your heading constantly on the safe bearing. If the object drifts away to one side, it should be easy to decide which way to correct so as to set you back on track. Make a positive 'jink', then put your ship's head back on the safe bearing. Note the relationship of the object to your heading, and retry if necessary until you get it right.

There will be occasions when your only useful source of input is the echo sounder. Don't despise this. We've already looked at how it can supply a position line of a sort, and there are many occasions when you are rounding a shoal that is not steep-to when a depth is all you need – and indeed all you have – to ensure safe passage.

Sometimes a particular track will remain safe until you have run to a given point at which you must alter course. In these situations, always look for an unambiguous visual definition to tell you when you have arrived. This could be a transit closing abeam of you, or an object coming on to a certain bearing. It might be a depth on the echo sounder, or, less accurately, a single object directly abeam. The time when something is exactly abeam can best be judged by looking down the mainsheet traveller. It is as good as a primitive gunsight.

If no visual cut-off point presents itself, see if you can work in an easy-to-use GPS position line. GPS reads out in latitude and longitude, both of which are no more than lines of position. Sometimes you can define the point to leave a safe line as the moment you pass a certain meridian or parallel. A typical instruction would be: 'Stay on the transit of Brown Cow Rock and Farmer Giles' gable end until the latitude racks up to 50° 43.15N´'. So long as the safe track is making a reasonable cut with the chart grid (see Chapter 18, Position Fixing) this technique is convenient and accurate, but you must check your GPS datum.

Often, a safe track is broad and straight, but surrounded by ghastly nasties below the surface of the water. Try to think of such a track as a safe corridor. Define both walls of the corridor with clearing lines of some sort, keep inside them, and you have nothing to fear. Where no clearing lines can be found, and you can be absolutely certain of the position of a suitable single waypoint plotted smack in the centre of one end of the corridor, you might in extreme circumstances venture into the corridor on the safest track to the waypoint. Now work towards or away from it (straight down the middle) using cross-track error to fill in the shortfall. This means committing to a course of action with your colours nailed to a single source of information that cannot be cross-checked, so you have chosen to break the first law of navigation. If the GPS should fail halfway along the line, you may have little choice beyond anchoring or trusting in the Lord to find you a safe route out.

In larger-scale pilotage, GPS can also supply a clearing line where no visual object can be discerned. If a distant beacon is too small to see, even with binoculars, plot it as a waypoint and note its changing bearing just as you would a visual compass bearing. If no beacon exists, plot an 'abstract' waypoint at the most suitable place from which to run a safe bearing.

Three general caveats apply to pilotage with GPS:

- Make sure you have an instant contingency plan for electronic failure.
- Triple-check everything you pre-plot and double-check your datums, because this close to danger these become critical.
- Determine whether your GPS is reading out in Magnetic or True degrees, because most have the facility to deliver either and the difference can spell disaster.

Further thoughts on piloting with a plotter

On the face of things, an electronic chart plotter delivers all the answers to inshore pilotage. You can actually watch the boat as she jinks among the rocks to a safe haven. Very nice in theory. One danger is that an over-zoomed electronic chart may be a fool's paradise, and it is easy to over-zoom without noticing because unless you do so there may be insufficient scale to see what's really going on. Furthermore, while you can rely on a set-up transit because it was put there by pilots who certainly knew what they were about, trusting the plotter is putting your faith in everything on the chart. Among the reefs, it is possible that the survey may be less complete than a zoomed chart suggests. In any case, if the GPS is not agreeing with the

PILOTAGE

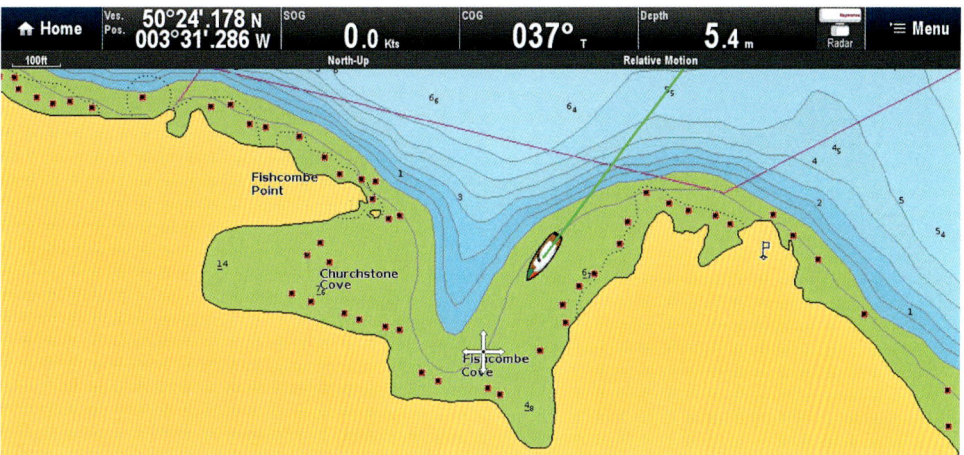

It should be impossible for a chart plotter to get its datums wrong, but it isn't. Sometimes a datum shift will show a yacht 330ft (100m) or more from her actual position. Such an error is usually obvious. Smaller errors are not so clear cut and can have drastic consequences. Fortunately, in this case, the relatively minor error less than a mile from Brixham, did not end badly since the yacht was anchored and comfortably afloat with the crew enjoying lunch while their plotter showed them hard aground.
Not to be used for navigation

chart survey to the tune of a couple of boat's lengths (which can still happen), following the silver screen could lead to your Nemesis.

In a tight passage defined by a transit, it is generally better to rely on this than to peer into a plotter screen showing every rock in the vicinity. All you need to know is that you are on a safe road. The transit gives you this without any distractions. Also, for the record, it was probably set up hundreds of years ago by pilots who risked execution if they got it wrong…

If you do decide to use the plotter, make sure you have a ready exit strategy in case of sudden failure.

Having delivered such a catalogue of dire warnings, I must say that I often use a portable plotter in the cockpit to back up what I am seeing with my own eyes. Very reassuring it can be, too. These days, in intricate situations strange to me where set-up transits are scarce or non-existent, I generally use a paper chart in the cockpit with my iPad plotter on hand to check exactly where I am. The combination of the two makes for safer pilotage than at any time in my life.

Forward planning

Because your affairs may develop rapidly when you are engaged in this type of work, it is helpful to prepare a plan in advance. Your pilot book will sometimes do this for you, but more usually you must deal with the question yourself. The form taken by these plans is highly individual, but they should contain such information as courses, bearings and approximate distances from one mark to the next. It may also be useful to know how much tide has risen above chart datum at any given moment, so fill out your tidal curve and keep that handy as well. The information will stand you in good stead, particularly if you have to modify your

Piloting with a paper chart backed up with a tablet plotter can offer the best of both worlds.

plan during its execution, so that you end up somewhere you did not intend to go. If you have a well-thought-out plan at hand when the action starts, you are under far less pressure to dive below and start fumbling around with the plotter.

Ideally, you should ask someone else to steer while you are piloting. Your sole task is then to con the vessel using your plan and the chart. This way it is easy for you to call the shots on the sailing of the boat, as well as keeping her off the bricks and the putty.

> **SKIPPER'S TIP**
>
> ### Instant position lines
>
> The one thing you won't have time for when things are developing fast is fixing your position on the chart. Even if you could manage to bang one down, you are usually moving so rapidly relative to the scale of your surroundings that a fix is yesterday's news by the time it has been plotted. In these circumstances, the less you use the handbearing compass the better.
>
> Fortunately, there are numerous sources of instant position lines close to the shore. There's the steering compass for observing objects directly ahead, astern or abeam, and there's nothing to stop you pre-measuring all sorts of angles on the deck of the boat, then adding or subtracting these from the ship's head. Note the angles of, say, the forward shrouds, the aft shrouds, a particularly useful stanchion, and so on, from the steering position or the companionway. Bearings thus obtained will be rough, but they are always ready.

Always remember that you have much less control over your boat's direction of travel relative to the seabed with a following tide than you have with a foul tide. When the current is strong and foul, small course alterations bring you a big dividend in terms of sideways tracking. At night particularly, you must be doubly vigilant about these effects.

Take your time, and never hesitate to stop altogether if you become disorientated. Once you are anchored, or hove to, or simply not going anywhere any more, you can shed the stress, then plot an accurate fix before collecting your thoughts for a fresh start.

Cockpit-mounted plotters

I fully expect to be vilified for the following remarks, but since honest readers are paying for my opinion, here it is:

The proper place for a chart plotter is at the chart table or, if there isn't a chart table, down below wherever the formal navigation takes place. The only sensible reason for siting the plotter on a pedestal in front of the wheel is that it should make piloting in close quarters a breeze. So it does, as long as the various caveats mentioned in this chapter are noted. At all other times, the thing is a distraction. Screens hold a fascination for all of us. Give folks a screen and they will peer into it. It's human nature and it's the last thing we ought to be doing for the great majority of our time on the water. Skippers should be looking at the sails, the run of the sea, the horizon for shipping, the birds of the air and Cousin Cuthbert to see how his seasickness is progressing. We need the plotter and all its data when filling in the log book, so why not keep it where the log book lives? It's often hard to read in sunlight anyway, but it's crystal clear down below.

There are of course exceptions to this. One area where having a plotter in front of the helm makes complete sense is in the Baltic Sea archipelagos, particularly those of Sweden and Finland. Among these islands total concentration is required virtually all the time, because of the rocks that lurk under the surface and on either side of the safe passages. Traditionally, one referred to the chart almost constantly and it was easy to lose track of your position since one island looks pretty much like the next. The cockpit plotter has changed all this. Because I do not have one, I use my iPad in the cockpit and find this to be a perfect substitute.

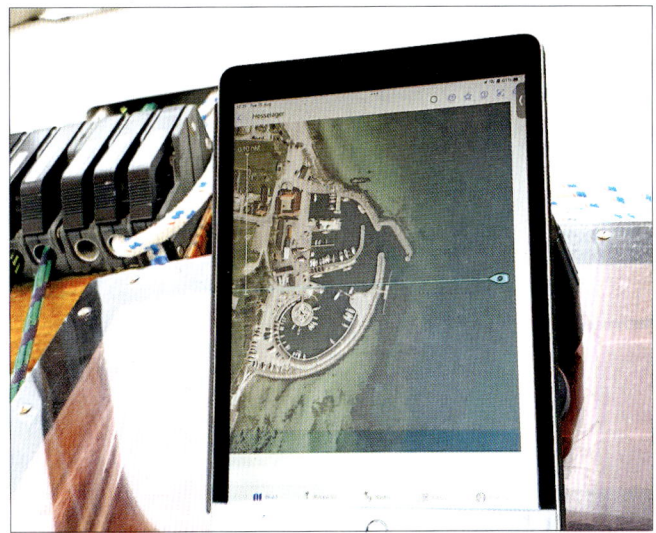

A geo-referenced satellite chart can be worth its weight in gold for pilotage. This one was produced on demand by AngelNav, and assisted in entering a strange harbour where pilotage information was in short supply.

24 PASSAGE NAVIGATION

This chapter describes three different ways of making a typical 12-hour passage in a sailing boat, much of which is out of sight of land. Most people make such passages choosing GPS as their main fixing system. Many will also use waypoints in conjunction with a paper chart, while chart plotters are gaining rapidly in acceptance and popularity. Electronic navigation is here to stay, and mostly we are glad of it, but I would be selling readers short if I did not describe a system of sound practice using no electronic aids whatever. It's not so long since we all had no option, and there will come a time for every one of us when circumstances throw us back on the basics. Besides, I believe that a skipper who can find a foreign port in indifferent visibility after 60 miles or more of dead reckoning will be able to extract far more benefit from a plotter than one who cannot. I am going to describe a passage from Yarmouth, Isle of Wight, to Cherbourg in northern France. First, I'll take it from the standpoint of a navigator unassisted by printed circuit boards. Second, I'll look at it as though I were using GPS and a paper chart. Last, I'll switch on the chart plotter and see what difference that makes.

You'll notice that in each case, I keep up my log book religiously. The reason is simple. Whatever system I am working to, I must retain the capacity to produce an EP within an hour of my last known position. If I'm navigating by the 'Four Ls' of 'lead, log, lookout and trust-in-the-Lord', the information is of primary importance. If I'm using GPS and plotting on paper, I need an EP of some sort to check my GPS fix, even if I don't plot these hourly in their entirety. This is not really to cover me in case the instrument is wrong, because this is highly unlikely. It is to supply a second opinion to my own workings. I know how easy it is to err while plotting a fix or to misread all those numbers when I'm tired, so I keep an old-fashioned plot running just to make sure. And of course, if I lose my GPS, I'll be in a strong position to carry on regardless.

Even with my brain in plotter mode I must keep up my log book so I can step seamlessly into paper-chart navigation if one facet of the interfaced system goes on the blink and drags the rest down with it. This has happened to me before, as it has to many others, but so long as there's a recent lat/long position with a course and distance recorded between it and now, there's really no problem. I just produce the chart, plot my last position, work in an up-to-date EP, then lay off a new course. Easy. If the log book's staring at me blankly, I might as well be on the Moon!

PASSAGE NAVIGATION

The passage plan

The wind is forecast westerly, about force 4, and it's spring tides. A quick look at the passage chart on p. 235 reveals that the journey breaks into two parts. The first will be a 5½-mile beat down to the buoy labelled 'Bridge' just west of the Needles light. I might get lucky and be able to lay this in one, but the frustrations of a lifetime suggest that I shan't. I'll therefore definitely need fair tide for that section because I can see from the atlas that streams run strongly. The paper chart for the Needles Channel is reproduced below.

From the Needles, it's about 60 miles almost due south to Cherbourg. A study of the tide tables tells me that streams off the French coast run like an express train, so I'll plan to arrive uptide of my destination, even if that means I'm a bit downwind. Making up ground with a 3-knot tide under you is easy. Trying to fight back against it after a long day is brutal. I don't need that, so I'll make sure right from the outset that it doesn't happen.

The tide will be ebbing west past Yarmouth from 0300 until 0900, which will get me off to an early start. It's August, so dawn is around 0530. I'll turn out at 0500 and chuck some bacon in the pan to make butties; my shipmates will soon smell it and wake up slavering.

An Imray chart of the passage from Yarmouth to the Bridge buoy. Not to be used for navigation

Far more civilised than booting them out of their bunks. Our boat is 35ft long and I expect we'll be out and under sail by 0600. We'll have the early-morning forecast under our belts, and if nothing has changed, we'll go for it. No need for any alternative heavy weather harbours in force 4 – a good thing, because there aren't any mid-Channel!

Our velocity made good to windward (VMG) should be around 3½ knots, but with 2½ knots of tide we'll be out by the Bridge in an hour or so – could be less if we get a slant. Then we'll set course straight down the rhumb line and see how fast we're going. The likelihood is we'll make 6 knots. If we don't, we want shooting. That'll be around 10 hours to Cherbourg. If so, and we're at the Bridge by 0700, we'll have the last 2 hours of the west-going tide, then we'll receive the full 6 hours of east-going, followed by a short, stiff shove to the westward at the end. I'll add up all the east-going and subtract the west-going from it. I'll also make up a little table showing what the tide will actually be doing at my probable hourly positions, assuming 6 knots or so. That will be useful for plotting EPs and will save trouble on passage.

I'll expect a net tide vector of around 5 miles to the east, so I'll steer initially for a point 3 or 4 miles west of the rhumb line. There are two entrances a couple of miles apart, so we'll head for the eastern, or uptide, one. That'll give us an extra 2 miles in the bag if need be.

I'll have plenty of time to work up a pilotage plan for my arrival on the way.

There's one final issue. A note on the chart advises me that although the central Channel is not officially a Traffic Separation Scheme (TSS), I am told to cross the shipping lanes as nearly as practicable at right-angles. East- and west-bound big-ship traffic can be expected in the area I will be crossing and the lanes are shown on the chart. Complying with this instruction will be easy with this wind and weather. It will also place me even further uptide when I reach the other side, so I'll do it to the letter. If I were closehauled and unwilling to bear away, or otherwise hampered, I might stretch the wording of 'as nearly as practicable' a little, but I'd make sure that I hit that right-angle if any shipping looked like coming close enough to be interested in me. In fog, I would cross at right-angles like a shot, even if I had radar, and I'd make sure it was my course that made 90°, not my track, because that is what the regulations specify. If the area were a full-on TSS, there would be no discussion at all. Right-angles it would be.

The passage without electronics

Setting sail from Yarmouth with the rising sun behind me, I'll stand out on the port tack to get clear of the rock off the harbour, then eyeball it down to the Bridge, tacking as dictated by commonsense. There are plenty of buoys and they should be visible. I'll stay out of Colwell Bay (rocks), and I'll take special care to tack in good time as I approach the Shingles Bank marked by red buoys. Once I'm clear of the Needles, there's plenty of water before I reach the Bridge buoy to set course early, but I don't know what the sea conditions will be like, so I'll take that as it comes.

The log book might look like this:

TIME	LOG	COURSE	WIND	BAROM	REMARKS	ENGINE
0600	–	P (pilotage)	W4	1018	Beating down to the Needles. Full main and genoa. Nice morning.	Off
0700	00.0	184M	W4	1017½	Bridge Buoy at hand. Beam reach (true); one more yacht out here going our way; sea moderate; kettle on. Log to zero.	Off
0800	6.3	184M	W4/5	1016½	Fix on chart. Sea a bit steep. Hanging on to full sail for now.	Off

A position of some sort every hour is sound policy, and since I can see the land clearly I should take a fix. In any case, right now it's easier to do that than to work up an EP. I'll cross-reference it against my course steered and distance run, but I won't physically plot the EP. So long as it all stacks up, I'm happy. At 0920 the land is fading from view and I take a departure fix, which gives me my last certain position before I sight France. After this, it's all EPs.

TIME	LOG	COURSE	WIND	BAROM	REMARKS	ENGINE
0920	14.9	184M	W4	1016	Departure fix. Vis about 15M. EP and fix on chart. Yacht falling astern!	Off

Notice that I have plotted my EP this time. That's to make sure the tide is behaving as expected. If it hadn't been I could have modified my course to steer. It was, so I haven't. It also gives me a confirmation of this important fix.

Things now proceed systematically. I go off watch, leaving instructions for the hands to record the log each hour and to call me as we approach the shipping lanes. They can manage without me until then and I need to stay fresh, so it's down to the bunk for me with my favourite book. If I don't do this, I'll just sit up there with things going round and round in my head. Far better to take a break.

TIME	LOG	COURSE	WIND	BAROM	REMARKS	ENGINE
1100	24.0	180M	WNW4	1015	EP on chart. Alter course.	Off

This course alteration is for the shipping lanes. The wind has veered a touch, freeing us, and I have no compunction about giving away a bit of ground to windward. I make up the plot now I'm awake, and place a fresh EP on the chart.

TIME	LOG	COURSE	WIND	BAROM	REMARKS	ENGINE
1405	42.2	200M	WSW5	1014	EP on chart. Out of shipping lanes, but so far east that we've altered well to the west, just to make sure.	Off

This next EP shows that my keenness to comply with the traffic regulations has left me well to leeward and the wind has backed unkindly. Things aren't looking so good and we're really going to need that westerly set.

Here's the next log entry:

TIME	LOG	COURSE	WIND	BAROM	REMARKS	ENGINE
1450	47.0	210M	WSW5	1013½	Fix on what can only be Pte de Barfleur and what I take to be C Levi. EP and depth confirm, but suggest we're a mile or so to leeward of the fix. Motorsailing now. Cone hoisted.	On

Note how keeping the plot going has enabled me to make the right decision about motorsailing and has helped me identify my landfall with confidence. We went so far east looking for the first of the west-going tide that we'll end up beating at this rate.

TIME	LOG	COURSE	WIND	BAROM	REMARKS	ENGINE
1600	52.5	215M/P	WSW5	1012½	Cherbourg Fort de l'Est in sight. Altering course to bring it into transit with its background. Rolled in genoa.	On

But fortune is kind, and my landfall fix indicates that I've found the tide earlier than I expect. Deteriorating sea conditions as the stream begins to set against the tide have already suggested that. I've logged my positions and even if the fog came in now, I'd stand a good chance.

PASSAGE NAVIGATION

TIME	LOG	COURSE	WIND	BAROM	REMARKS	ENGINE
1735	60.4	P	SW5	1011	Fort de l'Est abeam. Pilotage plan activated. Good thing we motorsailed.	On

A safe arrival. Note how the plot was maintained throughout.

The passage chart of the central English Channel. Not to be used for navigation

The same passage using GPS and a paper chart

Planning

My plan for this trip using GPS would be very similar to the non-electronic equivalent, except that I'd plot a number of waypoints. They'd be punched into my receiver and double-checked the night before. I wouldn't use a formal GPS route for this passage in a sailing boat because I'll be beating to start with and couldn't possibly stay anywhere near it. Crossing the Channel, the tide may well force me to modify my plan to suit boat speed, so sticking to a route might do me no favours.

235

THE COMPLETE YACHTMASTER

Instead, I'll place my waypoints as follows:

- One at my departure point (the Bridge buoy). This will be a useful plotting aid in the early stages.
- A second at the projected EP where I leave the shipping lanes. I could put one at the beginning of the lanes, but there really wouldn't be much point because I'm obliged to cross them at right-angles wherever I actually fetch up. However, the point at which I leave them is a good position from which to shape a new course for Cherbourg based on where I really am at that time. By comparing this waypoint with a GPS fix, I'll be able to assess what the tide has actually been doing and adjust my new course on that basis. Note, however, that the waypoint exists purely for planning reasons. I don't have to go to it. Indeed, if I try to do so, I may end up forcing the boat to offset more for the tide than she needs.
- My third waypoint will be at Cherbourg, Fort de l'Est. Some people might find it useful to place one 5 miles out and uptide. The reasons would be obvious and I'd have no quarrel with this. For myself, the arrival waypoint will suffice.

Notice that even though I'm using GPS, I plan to allow the boat to drift with the tide to a controlled extent. I could use the instrument's cross-track error (XTE) function to keep her smack-bang on the rhumb line all the way, altering course to compensate for the tide, but if I did I'd end up sailing many miles further than I need. If you're puzzling over this concept, take a quick look back at Chapter 20, where all will be revealed.

Executing the passage

Piloting
The early part of the passage is carried out in much the same way as if there were no GPS. It's pilotage down to the Bridge buoy, then I set course just as before.

On passage
Once clear of the land, I use the fixing power of GPS to plot an hourly position of known accuracy, double-checking each lat/long fix against bearing and distance to one of my waypoints. My log book looks like this:

TIME	LOG	COURSE	POSITION	WEATHER	REMARKS	ENGINE
0800	6.3	184M	Needles 6.5M 193T	W4/5 (1016½)	Sea a bit steep, hanging on to full sail for now.	off

Note that I now have a column for position. Previously, I plotted this on the chart, because it was inevitably somewhat imprecise for numerical definition to the second decimal point. Now, however, I know where I am and it makes sense to log the position as well as plotting it.

PASSAGE NAVIGATION

This not only allows a back-check, it also means that unskilled crew members can jot down a lat/long on the hour if the navigator is off watch. Working back from these positions, he can then see exactly where he's been, and if the GPS fails, he knows where he was at the last reasonable moment before the lights went out.

Having an accurate fix to compare with my projected 'EP waypoint' when I come out of the shipping lanes helps me quantify how far east I'm being set. I can therefore alter course with more confidence. The tide has yet to turn, however, so I will continue to shape a course rather than follow a GPS bearing to my destination waypoint.

Nearing the destination

Round about the time I make landfall, I'll begin using GPS to compare my COG (course over ground) with the bearing of Fort de l'Est. I'll also be logging my position as 'Fort de l'Est 14.9M, 211T' in preference to my mid-Channel lat/long.

Knowing that the tide will strengthen, I'll initially shape for a point uptide of the waypoint's bearing, but as I come within an hour or so of the fort, I'll begin steering to have the two figures coincide. If it were foggy, I'd refine the arrival waypoint to be in a very safe place after double-checking datum one more time. Then I'd reactivate the GoTo function and follow the XTE screen 'right down the middle' for the run-in. If 'vis' is good, as it is on this passage, I'll forget the GPS once I'm absolutely certain about what I am seeing. I'll switch into eyeball mode a few miles out and use natural transits to home in as before.

Paper chart for overview, chart plotter to confirm the position, and a paper log book so that if all fails we know where we were no more than an hour ago. Makes total sense.

The passage with a plotter

The plan

Unless I have a PC with raster charts running, I plan the passage on paper before transferring it to a bulkhead plotter to make sure I haven't missed any hidden rocks that might have been layered out by the vector charts. Depending on the machine, I might plot the same waypoints as before, but if it has the capacity to pre-plot a cross-tide passage by predicting the streams, the only one I'd enter would be the arrival waypoint. While my own hardware plotter doesn't have this capacity, I also ship out with a PC plotter that does. I'll use this to draw a curving electronic line on the electronic chart showing where it expects I'll be along the route at 6 knots. It won't work out perfectly, of course, because these things never do. For one thing, I won't make exactly 6 knots. Neither will the tide behave precisely as the computer predicts, but the line will at least show approximately where I ought to be as I work my drifting track. This can be handy as reality develops and course changes are demanded.

The graphic display may also prove useful if I'm being set way off track even before I reach the shipping lanes. It helps me to modify my course visually without having to read and input numbers. Theoretically, of course, I could do all this using GPS and a chart by pre-plotting all my EPs, but the hard fact is that few people would want all that trouble, especially if they're feeling a touch 'Tom and Dick' down below at the chart table with the boat lurching along. The plotter makes it easy.

Even using a plotter, I still plan an arrival waypoint because it enables me to read quickly how far I have to go and how the bearing is shaping up numerically as well as graphically. The ETA it so boldly projects will be a load of nonsense until the tide has settled down at the end of passage, because not even my present PC plotter can crunch the numbers for the turning stream, but no doubt this will be possible as well in due course. Sooner or later, we'll be able to sail our boats from the spare room at home…

Executing the passage with a plotter

Piloting

We've said very clearly in the pilotage chapter that plotters may be of limited use here, but it doesn't do to make too many hard-and-fast rules at sea. The initial part of this particular passage is a classic case where the plotter is just what the bosun ordered. Even if the buoys are hard to spot, keeping an eye on that little boat tracking across the chart tells me exactly when to tack as I bash down the channel outside Yarmouth to the Bridge Buoy. I don't get silly about it and go zooming in to the last 50 yards because I don't have to. I just use the electronics to remove any vestige of stress that might be left if the passage were unfamiliar to me. Lovely!

On passage

Although I'm using a plotter, I'll still let the boat slide away to the eastwards just as before, and my log book contains exactly the same items as if I were on 'GPS and paper chart'. If I've a big-enough plotter screen, my chart might even stay in its locker, but I'll have it ready in case

PASSAGE NAVIGATION

Often the most dangerous time of a passage is when the boat is almost there. Harbour mouths tend to be active places, and it's important not to let concentration slip until securely berthed.

I need it. If I do and I've ignored my log book, my last known position may well be Yarmouth Pier. What I need is reassurance about exactly where I was an hour ago at worst, so hourly log entries are the order of the day and night. Why not? We aren't exactly busy out there for much of the time, are we?

I'll probably have the plotter's projected track switched on from the start, because it'll be handy in the pilotage. It won't help a lot for a few hours after the Bridge buoy, because it will show me ending up further and further to the eastwards, so I'll carry on more or less as if I were using a paper chart until the boat is homing in on Cherbourg. Once the tide has settled into its final west-going mode and I've reached the point where I'd be adjusting my course to steer on the basis of the arrival waypoint bearing and my COG, I steer so as to put the projected track line on to Fort de l'Est, and keep it there. It's just like running an XTE screen really, but it's a whole lot easier.

25 DOMESTICS OF A PASSAGE

In the previous chapter we considered the navigational aspects of passagemaking. Of almost equal importance are the domestic arrangements made for the welfare of the ship's people, who will see her through whatever may betide. If they are not properly looked after, they will fail in their duties, be they masters or cabin girls, just as surely as an engine will stop if its fuel filters clog up. The skipper must therefore consider his crew at all times, and this emphatically includes himself, because if he should become sick, tired or otherwise inefficient, everybody suffers as a direct result. Navigation is important, looking to the sail combination helps a great deal, but thought for the 'hands' should never be far from the skipper's mind.

This subject divides conveniently into five main subheadings: food, sleep, warmth, space and seasickness. The importance each adopts on a particular passage will depend upon conditions, upon whether it be night or day, and on the overall length of the trip between ports.

Food

The most important items for crew morale are food and drink. Whatever horrors are coming to pass, if the team know that they will be fed and watered appetisingly and on time, you are at least halfway to a happy ship – and a happy ship is usually an efficient ship. The galley should be set up so as to make this requirement realistic to fulfil. On passages of more than 12 hours, this becomes vital, but

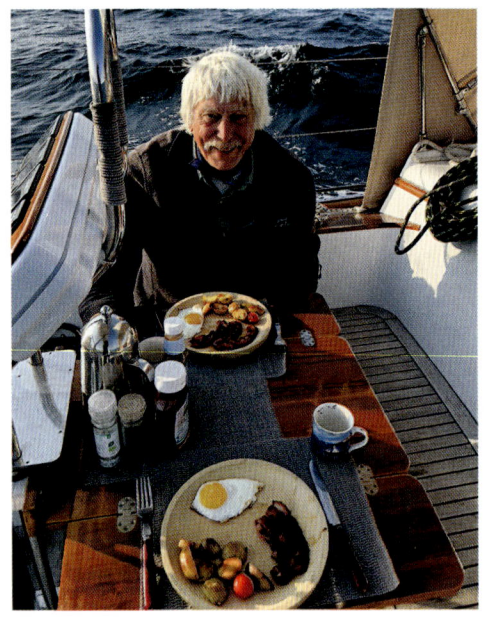

Whatever happens, keep the food coming. Here, the skipper is sitting down to a full English on a broad reach, with the sea smooth enough for him to chance his luck at the cockpit table. At the other end of the scale, a couple of rounds of cheese on toast hit the spot very well, but you do need a grill on your cooker.

even with poor cooking arrangements, there are certain precautions that can be taken to make the cook's life (if cook there be) more tolerable:

- For a short daytime passage that promises to be rough, make up some solid sandwiches before you slip your mooring.
- Always cook a serious stew, chilli, curry, or whatever suits your tastes, before setting out on an overnight passage. Ideally, this should be left on the stove with the pan lid on, well secured against a proper fiddle rail with serious pan clamps to prevent an unscheduled trip to the cabin sole. Then a hot meal is guaranteed, even if the boat is standing on her ends and volunteers for the galley are 100% absent.
- Keep the tea and coffee coming, and don't go mad washing up the mugs in bad weather. Each person should have their own, clearly labelled, so that you only need commit them to the suds if you are feeling virtuous and conditions make the sink an attractive proposition.
- Small boats' crews are well served by the provision of Thermos flasks containing drinks or hot soup.
- Keep plenty of instant food handy. Biscuits, cookies, chocolate, pies and the like may be officially 'junk', but they won't kill anybody in the short term, and they do wonders for keeping up a crew's spirits.

Sleep

Keep everyone properly rested. This may not involve a watch system on a short trip, but you should take active notice of your crew's condition, nonetheless. It is often difficult to persuade people to go below, but if they start to look tired, that is where they should be, lying down in their bunks (see p. 242 for seasickness).

On passages of over 12 hours, and in any case overnight, you must devise a watch system. I refuse to be drawn into suggesting what form this ought to take. There are almost as many arrangements as there are yachts. All I would say is, keep it simple, and stick to it. You don't want any martyrs, and that includes yourself. There are two reasons for this: first, the person who does more than his fair share will become tired. Second, anyone 'helped out' with his watch will feel obligated to his benefactor, which is precisely the sort of inequality that leads to tension and, ultimately, trouble.

Exceptionally, a key individual such as the skipper or the cook can be awarded an extra hour or two in the sack if they expect to be up for a long or inconvenient period later on, possibly for strategic reasons.

Don't expect to sleep like a baby on your first night out. Most people's experience is that they are too excited or unsettled to sleep properly. It's the second and third nights, as tiredness begins to take hold, that one begins to resemble a felled tree. Even if you don't feel tired, you should make a point of getting your head down. You don't even need to undress if it doesn't seem appropriate. The respite from staring at the horizon is worth it in itself.

Warmth

Nowadays, keeping your crew warm and dry is less of a problem than was once the case. I remember many years ago crossing the English Channel at Easter with no oilskins, simply because I couldn't afford them. To own a yacht as well as a sailing suit seemed a height of hedonism to which only the prodigiously wealthy could aspire. Modern gear, while not cheap, is remarkably effective and most sailors seem at least tolerably well equipped in these more prosperous times.

Watch out for hypothermia, particularly in those who fancy that a spell below will bring them down with seasickness. The result of this irrational fear is that folks sit in the corner of the cockpit, sometimes with the sea literally washing over them, rather than face a period in the warm. As soon as they begin to go quiet and lose interest, you should do something about them, otherwise exposure will take its toll. How you persuade different people to do what is surely best for them is entirely individual. The job may tax your interpersonal skills to the utmost, but act you must, and sooner rather than later.

Space

Among other things, modern yachts are notable for the large number of berths they supply within comparatively short overall lengths. However, filling all these for extended passagemaking is not always a good idea. Stuffing a vessel full of personnel as a means of defraying the expense of a bareboat charter might have its financial appeal, but if human beings are to enjoy a degree of contentment, they need a little space they can call their own, especially when very young or very mature.

Even if it is only a bunk that remains private, the difference to an individual's morale after a few days can be quite noticeable.

Seasickness

There is no easy answer to the ancient problem of motion seasickness. On a short trip, sufferers or potential sufferers will undoubtedly fare better on deck than down below, but as time passes, fatigue and exposure become an issue and people simply must take a watch below.

The difficult period then comes between entering the companionway and being flat on one's back. Once in the latter state, nausea rarely wins the day, so the trick is to waste as little time as possible getting there.

If you are feeling really rough, don't squander valuable minutes climbing out of your oilskins. Dive below, hit the bunk, pull your sleeping bag over you and try to sleep. Unless you are sure you can cope, don't even undress. The benefits of undressing are well publicised, but they hardly apply if you are seasick in the attempt. Sure, you'll make your bunk cushion wet, but that is a small price to pay for three hours' rest without throwing up.

People tend not to believe that the bunk is the best place until they've tried it a few times, so all your powers of leadership will be required to persuade your crew to help themselves.

It's the skipper's job to keep an eye on seasick crew. In extreme cases, send the victim below with a useful bucket to crash out 'all standing'. Getting undressed is often the final straw.

But they'll thank you in the end, especially if you've been thoughtful enough to give them a bunk that holds them in and is sited well aft.

Of the various proprietary remedies for seasickness, the most effective seem to be those that work directly on the balance organs in the inner ear. Whether taken orally or through the skin, these drugs offer a reasonable degree of immunity, or at least relief, to the majority of people. My experience as a sailing instructor confirmed this proposition beyond a shadow of doubt. The vital thing is not to wait until nausea sets in. If it's pills like Stugeron, start them the day before as per the instructions. For wristbands and the like, follow the data sheet.

As skipper, you'll have to make an assessment of the real condition of your seasick crew. Anyone who loses interest in life altogether should be sent to the bunk, encouraged to take water to ward off dehydration, and issued with a bucket. For the rest, it is surprising how most folk perk up after a while, or at least manage to remain useful. Try to give any members of this group something active to do while they are on watch. Helming is often best. Look after them as well as you can; they in their turn will look after the ship and will derive great satisfaction from having done their share in the face of one of life's more debilitating disorders.

For further thoughts on seasickness, visit my YouTube channel at www.youtube.com/watch?v=1jtpNzrBxtY

26 FOG

No one born of woman likes fog at sea. It strikes us more or less blind, which the sighted majority are unable to come to terms with. A sharp summer gale may be grist to a sailor's mill, but whoever he is, fog causes the gnawings of unease deep in his vitals. At the worst, it can frighten him into irrationality.

These anxieties are akin to fear of the dark. Just as the growth of adult reason dispels this childhood horror almost completely, education and experience go far towards neutralising fear of fog, though for most of us, the ghost of doubt always remains.

There's nothing inherently lethal about fog. It's the same stuff as that magic mist that creeps across the fields on late summer evenings. It doesn't even make you ill, but at sea it means you can't see where you are going and neither, in all probability, can anyone else. Radar helps, of course, but many of us don't have a set, and some who do cannot use it to its best advantage. The result is that we are liable to collide with vessels unknown, and while, with sensible use of GPS, we are no longer in doubt of our position, we are still thrown entirely on to our instruments if we are to keep out of navigational difficulties. Without GPS, we are not necessarily lost, but we are undoubtedly exposed to substantial additional danger.

The best thing to do about fog is to listen to the forecast before you leave harbour and give the whole project a resounding miss if fog is predicted. Most of us suffer from the besetting sin of hoping for the best, however, so for those walloping bravely on regardless, here are some useful policies to adopt.

Maintain your plot

The most important single action to take when your eyebrows start getting dewy, when the navigation lamps develop a halo and when damp begins to drop from the mainsail even if it's not raining, is to determine your position. If it's not foggy already, with signs like these it soon will be. If, by any chance, your GPS is not working, make sure that you fix your position visually at the last possible moment. If this proves impossible, work up a current EP. It is from this position that all your tactical decisions will stem, so it needs to be as accurate as you can make it. If you've been careless about running your plot, you'll regret it now. Even if you have a GPS receiver, a solitary unconfirmed electronic fix sitting self-consciously on a clean chart does little to dispel the anxiety of a prudent mariner.

Fog seamanship

As soon as you have serviced your primary need by plotting your position, you can attend to the immediate well-being of ship and crew.

Double the lookout

This is always worth doing if possible. The collision regs demand it. Furthermore, if visibility is 164ft (50m) or less, and your converging speed with another vessel is a boat's length per second, as it often is, one lookout is just not enough. Ideally, the extra lookout should be stationed on the foredeck where he will be comparatively undisturbed by engine noise if you are motoring. He'll be listening for fog horns, engines and even bow-waves. Knocking the engine off every few minutes will help enormously. On some vessels it is also useful to contain the drone of the machinery by keeping the hatches closed.

The direction of sound is often distorted by fog, so be circumspect about leaping to conclusions. It is, however, unusual for a fog horn on the port bow to sound as if it is coming from the starboard quarter. If a sound is repeated at regular intervals it's often possible to detect a pattern in its direction that will prove useful. For example, homing in on a siren at a harbour mouth can usually be achieved successfully, given a reasonably wide safe path of approach.

Listen out for unexpected sounds and use them creatively. I once navigated along the north coast of Norfolk on a mixture of echo sounder, compass, wild-fowlers' guns and dogs barking on various bathing beaches.

Be seen

Hoist your radar reflector, if it isn't already aloft; it is your number one protection against collision. Turn on your navigation lights, as required by the Colregs, and begin sounding your fog horn if it seems remotely possible that anyone may hear it. One long blast if you are under power (here I come, sounding one); one long and two short blasts if you are sailing.

Leave your mainsail hoisted if you are motoring. Not only will it dampen your tendency to roll, it will also increase your prominence to a lookout high up on a ship's bridge.

Prepare for the worst

Regardless of a skipper's private views on lifejackets, wearing them in fog makes unarguable good sense. If you were run down you could sink virtually without warning. If all hands have their 'lifers' round their necks, there will be no unseemly scrabble for them in a rapidly filling cabin, or subsequently in the water for the only one that bobs up after the bubbles have stopped rising.

Don't let anyone fall overboard in fog. This may sound obvious, but even so, it does no harm to remind the more boisterous of your crew that if they go over the wall, they may be lost to view and to everything else. If in doubt, clip on.

THE COMPLETE YACHTMASTER

Fog tactics

Having prepared your ship and crew (a matter of minutes) and plotted your whereabouts, you are now in a strong position to decide what you should do.

The first consideration is not to be run down. If you have a radar set, it will be warmed up by now because the Colregs specifically oblige you to use it in restricted visibility. Plot your contacts, take the relevant avoiding action, but don't forget that the fishing boat that may sink you is out there in the real world, not lurking in your glowing tube. In other words, use your radar by all means, but don't neglect your lookout.

If you have no radar, clear yourself right away from the remote vicinity of any avoidable areas of shipping concentration. Having done this, you can decide where to go next, if anywhere. While you are inspecting the chart, the watch on deck can make an informed guess at the range of visibility. Try to relate this to the scale of known visible objects as they appear: buoys are best, seabirds come next and waves are last but are still better than nothing. If it's oily calm, good luck to you. Without birds, buoys, passing seaweed or convenient flotsam you've nothing to go on but your wake and the length of your yacht, so unless you are very rich, your guess is unlikely to be accurate.

Should you be well out at sea and clear of shipping, you will undoubtedly plump for *option number one*. This is simply to press on with caution at a safe speed and maintain your plot. A variant of option one, when no better possibility presents itself, is to stay at sea and heave-to, even if your passage is not advanced by doing so. At least you are safe from rocks and shoals out there. Options two and three involve the shore.

If there is no convenient safe harbour, you might choose *option two*. Work your boat into water too shallow for commercial vessels, then either anchor or stooge about until visibility improves.

Motorsailing into fog, the watchkeeper is wearing a lifejacket and sounding one long blast. Under sail, it's 'Dah dit-dit'.

Early one morning... Hoping that this is land fog, not sea fog and that it will burn off as the sun rises higher.

A ferry boat materialises out of dense fog, sounding one blast every two minutes. If the fog's this thick, you'll hear the bow wave before you see the vessel, unless your engine is making too much noise.

There is much to be said for this tactic, particularly if the wind is offshore. So long as you can find an area clear of dangers, it involves little navigational finesse and gives you a good chance of keeping out of trouble. If you have no GPS, you can still use your sounder and work a plot from your starting point. This will give you an approximate position, which may well be good enough to be safe.

The big negative feature of option two is that it leaves you at sea. You'll be more popular with your crew if you can manage to get in somewhere.

Option three is to go looking for a harbour. Once secured alongside, you are as safe as you can be, so long as you can enter this happy state with minimal risk of stranding in the search. GPS and radar, if you have them, make the whole proposition infinitely less stressful than it was even in the 1980s. However, since nothing under heaven can be absolutely relied upon, we'll first consider the business from the viewpoint of Natural Man, unassisted by anything but traditional systems.

If, by any chance, you find yourself with no electronics working save your echo sounder, one thing *not* to do is aim straight for the harbour of your choice. Unless visibility is within the error of your EP, you will almost certainly miss. You won't know whether to turn to port or starboard when you see the beach or come on to soundings, and you will then be officially lost.

Fig 26.1 Finding a harbour entrance in fog.

Well offshore, with no dangers near by, in good visibility, you shouldn't mind at all if you are uncertain of your position to a mile or so. As soon as visibility deteriorates, however, paranoia sets in and we feel we must know our exact whereabouts. If we could see where we were going, we would be content to squirt our boats in the general direction of our destination, then refine our course as we come closer in. In fog, we can do exactly this, but one extra factor is required. Without the far-seeing eyes of electronics, we must ensure that we miss our destination, and we must miss it by far enough to one particular side, so that there can be no possible ambiguity.

Choose the side with a safe depth contour running up to the harbour mouth (Fig 26.1). If there isn't one on either side, forget the harbour, even if you have a GPS, unless either it is cross-checked by radar, or you are prepared to take the chance that it will not let you down at the crucial moment. Your electronics are going to be used to assist the classical approach mentioned below. They don't change anything radically unless you are equipped and confident with radar. They merely make the job easier and even more certain. If you rely on them implicitly and they go down or misread, you're in real trouble.

If a good, clean contour presents itself, run in until your sounder picks it up, then turn along it towards the harbour. In areas of big tidal rise you'll have to reduce your depth to soundings, but that is the only complication. Steer inshore across the contour until depths shoal, then come out 40° until you are to seaward of the line. Now come in again, and so on until you find your landfall buoy, or harbour wall, or even the suddenly deep water of your river mouth.

The technique is simple and, given suitable topography, it works every time.

A wise skipper, with GPS but no radar to supply a second source of electronic position finding, does well to adopt this policy. By refining his position and reassuring himself with the electronics, success will be assured. If, on the other hand, GPS alone is used to steer direct for the harbour, unless a fortuitous line of soundings can continuously confirm the position, the only other source of input would be what may prove a fairly dubious EP. While the EP for a sailor running in for a depth contour well to one side of a harbour entrance demands only minimal accuracy, to achieve the pinpoint precision of a direct hit in 50 yards' visibility it would need to be phenomenal. The GPS would therefore be an unconfirmed source of data. If it went down, all might be lost, so unless a sure-fire route of retreat is available, stick to the old ways and augment them with GPS accuracy. If it fails, no problem! Shrug your shoulders and take more notice of the echo sounder. If you are really confident of your GPS receiver or plotter and have a spare tucked away ready for action, there's no reason not to steer directly for a destination in fog. However, a contingency plan is important, lest the GPS satellites be jammed at some critical moment. This is unlikely, but the contingency is becoming more common. The plan will either be to aim off and go into a traditional 'contour-running mode', or just to turn around, sail back out to sea and wait.

 SKIPPER'S TIP

Buoy hopping

Sometimes in fog it's helpful to run from one buoy to the next, when there are enough of them to make success probable. Buoy hopping with GPS – and especially radar – presents few difficulties, and it can be most reassuring to see the metalwork loom out of the gloom. Without these aids, it should only be attempted when to fail would not be catastrophic. Miss one buoy and you've had it, so don't rely on the technique exclusively if in doubt.

If visibility is sufficient to be certain of finding the 'visibility bubble' around the next buoy without electronic assistance, you are in good shape, but if the fog is thick, the buoys far apart and the currents strong, you may be backing a lame horse. Always remember that you can take a personal observation of set and drift with great accuracy (see Chapter 15).

27 COLLISION AVOIDANCE IN POOR VISIBILITY

As stated in the Introduction, the nuts and bolts of the Colregs (International Regulations for Preventing Collisions at Sea) are so well covered in official files and dedicated booklets that it is not appropriate to spell them out again here. In previous editions, therefore, nothing was said about the subject. It was straightforward, and was best taught in practical situations at sea. Today's electronic advances in this area have moved things on from this basic proposition, and it has become appropriate to consider certain aspects of the subject here.

Yachts are not obliged to be equipped with anything more than the eyes and ears of the watchkeepers, augmented by applied commonsense. Many, however, now carry the latest in radar and AIS. The latter is fairly straightforward to operate. The former, rather less so, especially if the display offers choices beyond the traditional 'Head-up' screen.

None of this changes the essential 'flow-chart' (Fig 27.1) that keeps us out of trouble. That remains as it always has. The basic rules for stand-on and give-way vessels *in sight of one another* are assumed knowledge for anyone reading this book.

In an eyeball situation, it should be obvious to anyone with a sense of self-preservation that passing close under the bows of another vessel is a bad idea. There are exceptions to this for yachts racing, but in all other cases, whether you are the stand-on or give-way vessel, being close ahead of someone else under way is not where you want to be. If that someone is a container ship logging 25 knots, the policy becomes emphatic.

In fog or poor visibility, the rules change. Where ships cannot physically see each other, there is no stand-on or give-way vessel. To cross the bows of another vessel of unknown size may then be literally suicidal. Without electronics, nobody in their right mind who can see what's happening would put himself in such a position. Where electronics are relied upon in poor visibility and the operator has not thought things through, that is just where he may end up. Hence, this chapter.

Responsibility for lookout

Rule 5 of the Colregs clearly states that every vessel must at all times keep a proper lookout by sight, hearing (including sound signal or marine VHF radio) and all available means (e.g. radar, MARPA, AIS and GMDSS) in order to judge if risk of collision exists.

COLLISION AVOIDANCE IN POOR VISIBILITY

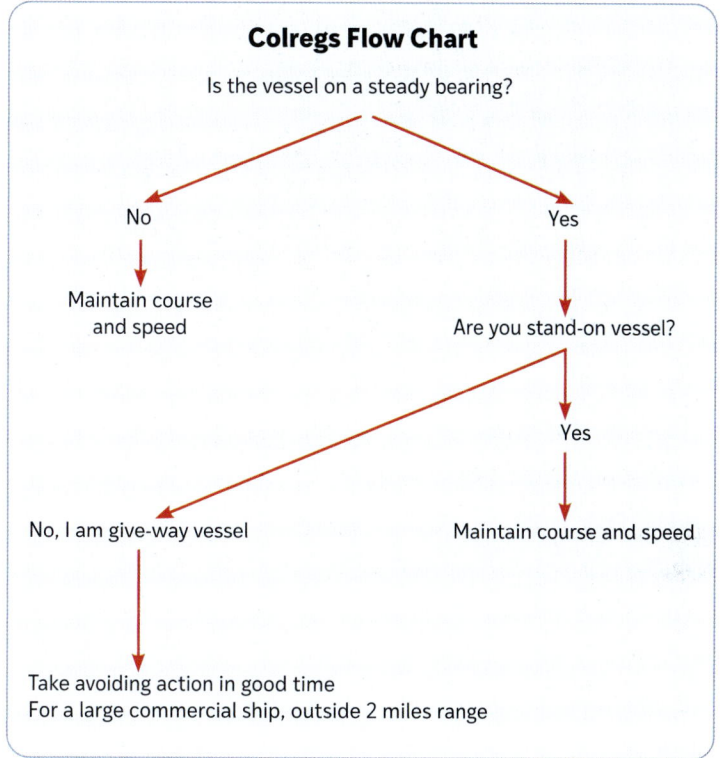

Fig 27.1 The basic rules for stand-on and give-way vessels in sight of one another.

So that's it then. No argument. If you have radar, AIS, etc, you are obliged to use it. In fair weather, it is sensible to assume that small sailing craft with limited battery capacity will not necessarily turn on all the electronics, so long as good visual lookout is maintained. In fog, everything changes. A yacht involved in a collision that had not behaved 'according to the Act' would find little sympathy in a court of law. It is therefore everyone's active duty to learn about our gear and be ready to make full use of it when it counts.

AIS

AIS stands for Automatic Identification System. Every SOLAS ship over 300 tons going foreign must carry it, as must anything at all over 500 tons and all passenger ships. They are also obliged to have it switched on, so as to transmit data to any vessel within VHF radio range that has the kit to process it. There is no rule against anyone fitting AIS even if not in these categories. Bearing in mind the low cost when seen in the big picture for a commercial vessel, it is surprising that all do not do so or, even if they have it, don't choose to use it. Many fishing vessels do not transmit their data and most naval vessels stay quiet also. AIS transmitters may also be found today on certain major navigational marks, now known as 'Atons' (Aids to Navigation). Some buoys and aids have disappeared altogether, to be replaced by a sort of virtual Aton which appears on the plotter screen as such and gives the position and nature of the mark it has replaced. Needless to say, while theoretically a great money-saving idea, this is not to everyone's taste.

Jargon-buster

AIS	Automatic Identification System
COG	Course Over Ground
Colregs	International Regulations for Preventing Collisions at Sea
CPA	Closest Point of Approach
DSC	Digital Selective Calling (for VHF)
EBL	Electronic Bearing Line
GMDSS	Global Maritime Distress and Safety System
IMO	International Maritime Organization
MARPA	Mini-Automatic Radar Plotting Aid
MMSI	Maritime Mobile Service Identity (radio 'phone number')
ROT	Rate Of Turn
SOG	Speed Over Ground
VRM	Variable Range Marker

A transmitting commercial ship uses 'Class A AIS'. This gathers data from on-board instrumentation, including GPS, and transmits 'dynamic information' about position, SOG, COG and ROT. Also, broadcast is 'static information', which includes the ship's call sign, name, MMSI number (unique IMO identification), and dimensions. Even voyage-related material is included with cargo, draught, destination and ETA. A good deal of this is of little direct use to yachts, although it could be of great service to a pilot vessel. The dynamic data can be solid gold.

Private yachts, unless operating commercially and over 300 tons, are neither required nor encouraged to fit the expensive Class A AIS, but Class B AIS is readily available at steadily decreasing prices. In its most basic form, it does not transmit, so it doesn't help ships 'see' the yacht, but it processes AIS data from every transmitting vessel within VHF range. It can immediately give the CPA (Closest Point of Approach), and the time this will occur. Accuracy levels are far higher than would be achieved by radar plotting aids such as MARPA but, at the time of writing, many units do not commit themselves as to whether the target will pass ahead or astern of you. This is no problem if the distance predicted is a couple of miles, but if it's substantially less and the vessel is large, you may end up too close under her bows. Take no chances, therefore, even if relying on a predicted track vector.

AIS data can be displayed either on a dedicated unit with a small, radar-like screen, or overlaid on the chart of a compatible PC or bulkhead chart plotter. Most systems feature a menu that activates projected track vectors. AIS targets can also be displayed on compatible radar screens, making target identification unambiguous. Targets appear as 'ship' icons. Land your cursor on one of these for full data. If it's a Class A transmission, the only thing you won't know is what video the third mate is watching. Raymarine offer software that delivers 'predicted areas of danger' emanating from an AIS target on the plotter screen. This shows a hatched red area on the vessel's heading vector. If your own vector passes through this, a collision risk exists. If your vector cuts the target's ahead of the box, you are passing clear ahead. If astern, she will pass safely ahead of you. This represents real progress as, at last, one can see if an AIS target

COLLISION AVOIDANCE IN POOR VISIBILITY

will be close ahead or close astern. You are in no way exonerated from the Colregs, but this excellent initiative helps a good deal in making sound decisions.

More and more yachts are now fitting fully enabled Class B AIS, which transmits data about the yacht as well as receiving info broadcast by others. Typically, these units send out the name and type of the vessel, her call sign, SOG, COG, heading, position, dimensions and MMSI number.

Fitting a Class B AIS might sound like a sure-fire guarantee against collision with anything of serious tonnage. Sadly, this is not the case. Some merchant vessels, while obliged to run their AIS, do not monitor it methodically. A further issue arises in areas where so much Class B data is being hurled around that electronic charts become cluttered with what, to a large tanker who is 'stand-on vessel' by virtue of being constrained by her draught, are mainly irrelevant targets. Class A units have a switch that filters out Class B transmissions, leaving only the Class A broadcasts from vessels big enough to interest her. Activating this is entirely understandable, but it means that relying on transmitted Class B AIS as a suit of armour may be misplaced optimism.

This ship looks too close for comfort. Actually the channels are narrow and the yacht is in the process of steering away to give her clear water to overtake. The message is, 'Look behind you!'

It's critical to understand that AIS is not a substitute for radar. Although very accurate as far as it goes, the system only displays targets that are broadcasting AIS information. Vessels and objects not transmitting won't appear. These may include other yachts, small commercial craft and fishing boats. They may even be large commercial vessels or fighting ships keeping a low profile. AIS remains the biggest advance in collision avoidance in decades, especially for non-specialist operators, but non-transmitting vessels still make a big dent if they hit us.

💬 SKIPPER'S TIP

Making contact

Note that ships equipped with DSC radio are no longer required to monitor VHF Channel 16 (calling and distress). They may still do so, but they are more likely to be listening out on Channel 13, the 'bridge-to-bridge' frequency. Remember that with AIS you can identify a target vessel by name. In ambiguous situations where you cannot, or do not choose, to get out of the way, it makes sense to call up and talk with the officer of the watch. You may also be able to attract a ship's attention on VHF by DSC, via her MMSI number as displayed on the AIS data screen.

Digital radar

The first radar I used was the size of a fruit machine. It was on the bridge of a coaster way back in the 1970s. To see the cathode-ray screen, your head had to be inside a huge sight guard. Other than changing the range and various other controls, including gain, tune and clutter, there was no choice about what you could see. The glimmering green display was 'Head-up or nothing'. Today's digital, daylight sets are far more sophisticated, but a potential nest of confusion lurks under the 'display options' button, where 'Head-up', 'Course-up' or 'North-up' are generally on offer.

A radar overlay on a Navionics chart image delivered by a Raymarine E-series plotter. The following illustrations showing Head-up, Course-up, etc, were taken with the boat in this area.
Not to be used for navigation

Display options

Head-up

The line representing the ship's head (the heading line) runs from the centre (your position) to the top of the screen. Nothing is fed into the computer other than radar input, so it works on its own, assuming itself to be stationary with all other objects moving around it. Its reference point for bearings is the bow of the boat. These are therefore always relative. Distances or ranges are all taken from your present position.

COLLISION AVOIDANCE IN POOR VISIBILITY

The same chart as on p. 254, shown in raster form for clarity. Note that the dock head which appears on some subsequent radar images is just off the screen at the top. The position of the boat in the image on p. 254 is marked with an arrow. Not to be used for navigation

A Head-up radar image. The boat is travelling south-eastwards but straight up the radar screen. Note the clearly defined square corner of Hythe Marina over her starboard quarter, and the long jetty on her starboard bow. As in all radar images, the boat's position is at the centre of the rings.

Benefits

The picture corresponds with what you see when looking straight ahead from the cockpit. This means that an object off the starboard beam appears halfway down the right-hand side of the screen, and so on. As long as nobody changes course, this makes orientation with the outside world intuitive.

Drawbacks

If your course changes, the whole screen rotates with you. This means all targets, whether or not you have been following their progress, change position. Their relative movement will also change immediately. In addition to this, it can be tricky or impossible to tell at a glance what another ship's aspect may be. All you can be sure of is where she is and, after a while, what her movements are – but only in relation to your own.

Because a small sailing craft yaws around her course, targets sometimes appear to zig-zag, especially in rough weather, which renders straightforward Head-up radar less than ideal for collision avoidance.

North-up

Paper charts are generally drawn with north at the top, which makes them 'North-up' in radar terminology. To deliver a North-up picture, the radar works with data from a fluxgate compass, usually from the autopilot. The radar picture is stable with north at the top, while the heading line follows your direction of travel. If you are steering 270°, the heading line points to '9 o'clock'.

The same radar screen as is shown on p. 255, but this time with the instrument set to North-up. The dock head is clearly visible to the north of the long jetty. In this mode, the radar image is immediately comparable with the North-up chart, also on p. 255.

COLLISION AVOIDANCE IN POOR VISIBILITY

Benefits

Comparing the screen with the chart is easy, and because the picture remains North-up, if you change your heading, any targets you are monitoring do not alter theirs. Linking the display to the compass rather than the ship's head stabilises the picture, so that the yawing and pitching that upset the Head-up display are largely neutralised.

Drawbacks

North-up is sometimes awkward for comparing the screen directly with the outside world. If you are steering south, the top of the radar screen shows what is happening astern of you. Unless you're used to it, this can be disconcerting for people whose minds work in such a way that they occasionally hold a road map upside down.

Course-up

At first glance, this appears the same as Head-up, but the compass is used to stabilise the picture. Short-term yaw is thus removed, just as with North-up. In this mode, the top of the screen represents your course. Usually, the heading line wavers from side to side of it, indicating where you have yawed to right now.

Different manufacturers use varying systems to define what they call 'course'. This is likely to be something other than what was on the compass in the previous two seconds. Think of it as the course you are trying to achieve. The usual solution is for the processor to look for the answer in a number of places, typically in a defined order.

The Course-up radar image. Note the similarity to the Head-up image on p. 255. In the real world, the difference is that the course-up display is stabilised, whereas the head-up equivalent will rotate slightly as the boat yaws on her course.

A typical list, in order of preference, might be:

i) Bearing from origin to destination (i.e. between waypoints)
ii) Locked heading from autopilot
iii) Bearing to active waypoint
iv) Instantaneous heading (i.e. the course you are steering by hand)

Benefits and drawbacks

These are similar to Head-up, with the important exception that because the image is stabilised by the sampling of compass data, the collision avoidance potential is more reliable.

Simple collision avoidance

Head-up

The first action on identifying a new target should be to place the Electronic Bearing Line (EBL) on it. This line emanates from the centre of the screen, which is your ship. If the target stays on it and closes its range, it is obviously on a steady bearing. If the bearing isn't changing, you are in a potential collision situation.

If you could see the other ship, by night or day, you'd tell at a glance what her aspect was, which would indicate clearly what action, if any, to take. Without going into the laborious process of paper plotting, which isn't often practical for a single operator who is also skippering the boat, Head-up radar will not tell you this. All you know is that she is tracking towards where you will be. It's natural to assume that the other vessel is heading towards you, but this may be far from the truth. For example, a vessel on your port bow which you assume to be closing and showing you a green light may in fact be one that you are overtaking. However, at least the collision risk has been identified.

If you alter course, the whole picture changes. If you take off way and allow the yacht to drift, perhaps losing steerage altogether, confusion may well follow.

North-up

If the screen is set at North-up, a target's heading will not change on it as you alter course. This helps you to see what is happening. The stabilising effect of the compass input also makes things a lot clearer than the Head-up ambivalence.

Course-up

This confers the benefit of stabilisation on the intuitive orientation of Head-up radar. The picture holds solid while the boat wanders, making life very much easier all round. If way is taken off, the computer will usually maintain the display on the last course steered or made good.

North-up or Course-up?

Generally, either is safer than the unstabilised option of Head-up. For some people, the advantage of Course-up over North-up is that the picture is more recognisably orientated while way is on. However, it can certainly be argued that with the boat drifting and the course stabilised to the last continuous heading, Course-up might confuse an inexperienced operator. The answer is that anyone using radar should know what these options are, understand what they mean, and remember which has been selected. Above all, he must understand the EBL and VRM, and use them – see below.

The fix and the lollipop stick

Checking a target's bearing using the EBL can be augmented to fix its position on the screen with the Variable Range Marker (VRM). The VRM is an adjustable range ring centred on your ship, manipulated in a similar way to the EBL. Move it so that it's on the target, and the two lines fix the target's position at that moment, just as though they were bearings plotted on a chart. The fix will stay put until you move one of its component lines.

As the target steams away from the fix, its closest point of approach to you at the centre of the screen can be estimated with a lollipop stick, or some other straight edge that will be kind to the glass. Hold the stick between the target and the fix left behind it. The target is effectively moving along the edge of the stick. To see where it will end up in relation to you is now just a matter of visual, straight-line projection.

A second 'instant plotting' aid is to use a whiteboard marker pen to drop a dot on to a moving target every so often. You then have a history of its recent activity and can 'join the dots' by inspection to see whether or not it is bound for a collision. If it looks critical, lay any convenient straight edge across the dots to extrapolate.

MARPA

MARPA stands for Mini Automatic Radar Plotting Aid. Inbuilt into many plotter/radar set-ups, it plots a target's movement electronically and delivers data both in numbers and by way of a projected track vector.

When a target is selected with the cursor, the MARPA program comes to life, always assuming it is switched on. A minute or two later, once the radar and the processor have synchronised, a symbol appears on the target indicating its course, speed (potentially to ± 1 knot) and CPA. Fuller data are available via a further click, including the time to go to CPA. How useful this information really is depends on how the operator has set up the radar, and whether or not he is aware of such issues.

True and Relative Motion

Down in the depths of the radar menu lie the alternative displays of 'Relative Motion' and 'True Motion'. Which is selected is always important. If you are running MARPA, the choice is critical.

THE COMPLETE YACHTMASTER

Relative Motion

Relative Motion is what you might call the old-fashioned default position, where all targets move in relation to your ship, just as they do in Head-up, where only Relative Motion is available. Trying to assess a Relative Motion target if you are changing course is notoriously awkward. The job is made a lot easier if you can relate it to another target you know to be

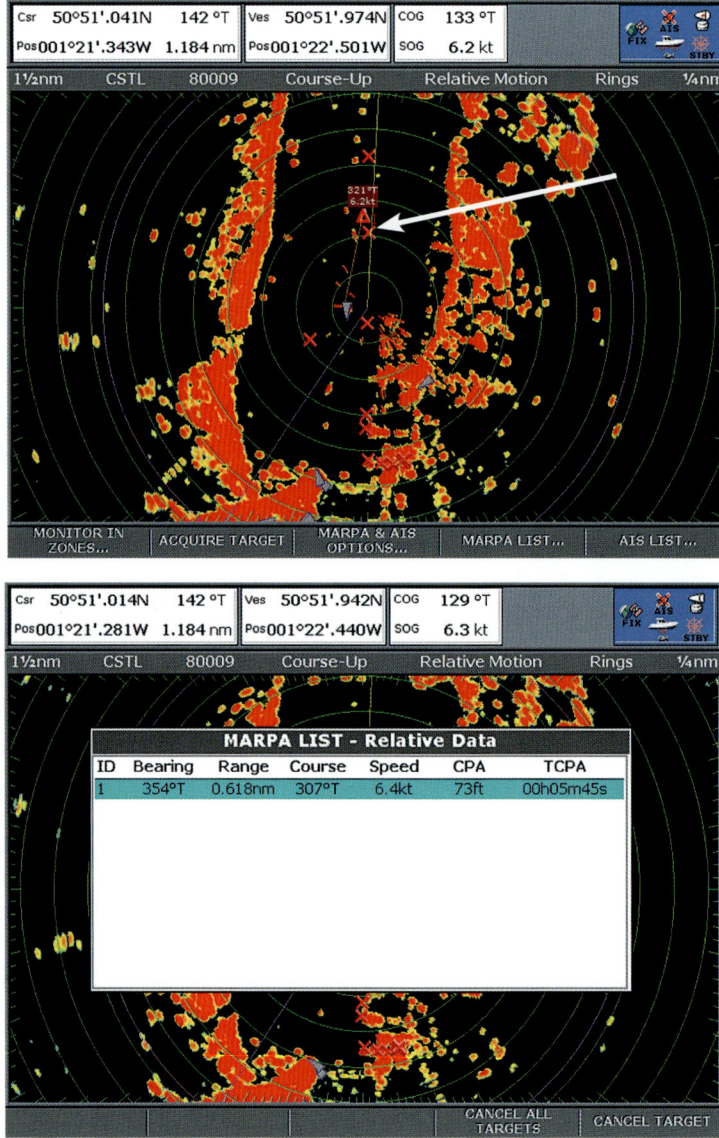

Relative Motion and MARPA. The radar is now scaled out somewhat. Note the AIS targets which will also appear on the chart page of the same plotter (MFD). The triangle, marked by an arrow, is a buoy identified by MARPA as a target. Because the radar is set to relative motion, the MARPA data (lower image) shows the buoy travelling towards the vessel at around 6 knots, which is the vessel's own speed.

COLLISION AVOIDANCE IN POOR VISIBILITY

stationary, such as the short pier in the illustration (at about 2 o'clock from centre-screen), rather than to yourself in motion at centre-screen.

With MARPA engaged and Relative Motion selected, all the courses and speeds it gives are relative values. A buoy securely tethered to the bottom will therefore be given as cruising along on a reciprocal course and speed to yours, so long as there is no current or tidal stream. If this is the case, always clap the EBL on to the target to make certain that a collision risk doesn't exist.

For a ship heading across your track, the computations are more complex, but the bottom line is the same. The CPA may be accurate – or as accurate as it can be if your radar is on unstabilised Head-up – but it won't tell you what the ship is doing, except in relation to you. Therefore, any attempt to use unassisted MARPA to determine the aspect of the other ship will be doomed to failure.

True Motion

With the radar set to the stabilised options of Course-up or North-up, its readout can be further clarified by opting for True Motion. This uses the processor to show targets as they really are, rather than as they appear in relation to you. The movement of targets is independent of your ship's motion.

The effect on MARPA is immediate: a container ship is shown ripping up-channel at 25 knots, the buoy is stationary, and a yacht running parallel to you is making the same speed that you are on the same course. The stabilised heading removes most of the problems of yaw so that, suddenly, this remarkable piece of equipment starts to earn its keep.

True Motion and MARPA. The target is the same buoy as the one shown on p. 260, but the radar has been switched to True Motion. The buoy now appears as it really is – virtually stationary. For purposes of MARPA, anything around 1 knot or less can usually be taken as zero.

Whether you opt for True or Relative Motion, many authorities prefer to set the radar on North-up when using MARPA. Whatever you make of all these options on the day, it is vital to have a firm grasp of what they mean, to choose in light of what you want to know, and to remember which mode is active.

MARPA vectors

MARPA sets a vector (a line) on the screen. Its length is proportional to the target speed. The direction shows where the target is going. In the set-up menu the operator can decide how many minutes of travel the vector will show. Six is often a good choice, because 6 is $^1/_{10}$ of an hour, so everything is conveniently decimalised. Whether the radar motion is true or relative is vital. If it's relative, the vector will show relative direction and the length will be relative speed. If the vector points to the centre of the screen, there is a potential collision situation. In True Motion, the vector will point to the actual direction of travel of the target and the length will represent the actual speed. A vector of 1 mile length is a vessel doing 10 knots if set to 6 minutes. True motion also shows a vector for your own vessel, pointing ahead of you with the length showing your speed. A collision situation is not so obvious as it is in Relative Motion, but it is indicated if the end of the target's vector touches, then crosses the end of yours, like crossed swords.

COG and heading

Radar inputs can, on some units, be linked to your vessel's course and speed over the ground (COG and SOG) or her heading and speed through the water. Which is chosen has substantial effects on MARPA. If a fishing boat were steaming at 8 knots through the water with a following tide of 4 knots, her vector would indicate 12 knots if set to the COG option. You and your target are all subject to the same tidal effects, so the figure you are interested in is the 8 knots at which she is closing with your own heading and speed. If this option is available and you are using radar for collision avoidance, it is better to switch it to 'log'. For navigation purposes, the opposite may well apply. The important thing is to understand the options, and to use them intelligently.

Split-screen radar

The obvious benefit of Relative Motion is that you can see at a glance which targets are a collision risk – so long as you use the EBL. Using a split-screen display with True Motion on one and Relative Motion on the other can offer the best of both worlds. Relative (with EBL) shows any targets heading for centre screen and draws attention to them. The EBL cannot be used with True Motion to determine collision, because 'collision targets' are not usually heading for centre screen. The importance of the True Motion picture is that it allows you to work out the aspect of targets, thus providing data enabling you to decide what action to take.

Wakes

Most of today's radars can display an electronic wake, apparently 'astern' of a target. The usefulness of this in Head-up, unstabilised Relative Motion is questionable, because of the risk

COLLISION AVOIDANCE IN POOR VISIBILITY

Split-screen display to clarify True and Relative Motion. Note that for True Motion the processor has moved the centre-screen position further down. The target on the port bow is in fact stationary, but only the True Motion display shows this clearly at a glance. It could be deduced by more extended observation, but often for a single operator doing the job of skippering and piloting, this is not practical.

of confusing it with the actual wake created by the vessel in the water. Change course yourself, and all the wakes take on a kink. They may even be coming out of the bow of a vessel being overtaken. In True Motion, they indicate where the target is actually heading. You have only to lay the lollipop stick along the wake so that its extrapolation crosses your heading line to see what is going to happen, and whether this should concern you.

Top tips for radar collision avoidance

- **Rule of thumb** – Rule 19(d) states that all vessels should take early and substantial action to avoid collision if detecting another vessel by using radar alone (not in sight). Note that:
  a) any change of course to port for a vessel forward of the beam should be avoided except for a vessel being overtaken (e.g. determined by radar plot).
  b) any change of course towards a vessel abeam or abaft the beam should be avoided.

Fig 27.2 Target closing, on or near a steady bearing. Photograph this page and paste it into the logbook for instant reference!

COLLISION AVOIDANCE IN POOR VISIBILITY

In plain terms, this means the following:

- **Slow down** – Don't forget that if a target is on a steady bearing on the EBL, you always have the option of slowing down. This should move the contact off the EBL in due course, but it does more than this. Because you can lose way so rapidly, a ship's operator can tell you aren't a big vessel. The target on his screen may not show him this and it helps if he knows what you are. A motor yacht can lose 10 knots in 100 metres, whereas a ship may take half a mile or more. Even a sailing yacht under power can cut her way from 7 knots to 2, which will do the trick nine times out of ten.
- **Go 'Ground Stabilised'** – The best view any radar operator gets is the one enjoyed by the guys running shore stations. Because their scanner is literally set in concrete it can't have any motion. Everything else literally moves around it. Working out what the various targets are doing is thus a simple matter. If all else has failed, or perhaps just because you want a totally unambiguous view of the world, you can always simulate a shore station by finding a buoy or some other stationary object, and stemming the tide so that your speed relative to it becomes zero. If you can see the buoy close at hand through the gloom, so much the better. In this state, your radar is said to be 'Ground Stabilised'. A happy condition indeed.

Here, the author is in thick fog using an iPad depicting the main plotter screen by tuning to the boat's Wi-Fi. The screen is split showing chart and radar. For boats whose plotter is down below, this system offers a perfect solution.

28 TACTICS AND NAVIGATION IN HEAVY WEATHER

In Chapter 10, we considered the main survival options open to the average yacht caught in deep water by weather of sufficient severity to demand a change of voyage plan. To recap, these were heaving to, lying a'hull, running off and working to windward under power-assisted sail. Which, if any, of these you choose to adopt on a given occasion will depend upon your position in relation to land or any other relevant danger, the type of craft you are sailing, and the strength of your crew.

At the onset of heavy weather at sea, or as soon as it is forecast, you should check that your plot is systematic and up-to-date by making sure the plotter is behaving and noting your latest log entry so that if all else fails, there is a solid known position from which to begin a new plot. There are then two main options: stay at sea or seek shelter. The questions to ask when it becomes clear that a change of plan is necessary, either for reasons of safety or to avoid the extreme unpleasantness of being at sea in a gale, are these: 'Can I bring the yacht safely to a suitable haven either before conditions become heavy, or in conditions as they may develop? If I succeed, can I negotiate the entrance, and will a snug berth await me after I have done so?'

Should all these boxes be ticked, there is no need for further heart-searching. Sail into shelter. If the response is either 'no', or 'I'm not sure', you must stay at sea and either press on regardless or adopt a survival tactic.

If shelter lies to windward and you have the power to work up to it under sail, motor, or both, your situation is not at all grave. Always bear in mind, however, that you may be in for a wind shift. There are a number of harbour entrances on the south coast of England, for example, that are secure with the weather coming from west of south, but as soon as it begins to hook round south-easterly, they become death-traps, especially on an ebbing tide.

You must be far more circumspect if running to leeward to escape worsening conditions. It takes no imagination to realise that a narrow entrance with a storm blowing straight into it, with seas to match, is to be avoided. Any lee shore should be treated with the greatest possible respect, but there are often areas where a broad deep entrance will lead you to a corner you can safely work round to find shelter. Sometimes it is acceptable to approach the extreme end of a long lee shoreline, knowing that a protected roadstead lies behind it. There are all sorts of circumstances in which you can run or broad reach to escape staying at sea, but all must be viewed dispassionately in the light of a developing 'worst case scenario'.

TACTICS AND NAVIGATION IN HEAVY WEATHER

Looks like a nasty squall coming through. Time to check the safety harnesses!

Navigation in poor conditions

In good weather, navigation should be one of the skipper's more enjoyable duties. When the going is rough, the situation in a small vessel is reversed. Any idea of precision from sources other than the electronics goes out the porthole as the yacht leaps round like a bronco. The log sheds much of its reliability, leeway becomes alarmingly difficult to estimate, visibility often deteriorates, compasses swing so wildly that the helmsman can only attempt to keep the course, and anyone taking a bearing goes cross-eyed as the card swings 20° either side of the target. To add to the sum of this craziness, it is more than likely that you'll be feeling seasick. Even if your stomach is performing well on deck, you may succumb if you have to spend more than the absolute minimum of time at the chart table.

The temptation to rely on the chart plotter alone becomes even greater at times like this and, indeed, GPS used sensibly has transformed the heavy-weather navigator's lot. We have noted already that under easy circumstances it may be practical to keep a plot going in your head while checking it against regularly plotted electronic fixes. This becomes far more difficult when your body is stressed by cold and wet, and is staggering to hang on at 30° of heel, so you must exercise the maximum of self-discipline and keep your log book up to date.

Commonsense will dictate what 'up to date' means. If you are in deep water with no land for 100 miles and every probability that things will clear up within five or six hours, you could be forgiven for doing no more than making hourly entries. Should you be running down to shelter with dangers to leeward it may be necessary to monitor your position every ten minutes. At times like this you'd be crazy not to make full use of the plotter, but take note of any easily recognised clearing bearings, transits, objects abeam and all the other instant position lines discussed in Chapter 18. If all goes well, you can use them to confirm your reading of the electronics, and if the plot should go pear-shaped, you will have a back-up system of traditional pilotage already in place. You won't be sorry you've taken the trouble when your crewman tumbles onto the GPS antenna at a critical moment. You may not have time to start from scratch.

Position fixing

GPS and the chart plotter are a life-saver for the sailor in big waves. Any position line derived from a magnetic compass in a rough sea was likely to be of poor quality in a small craft. There was little to be done about this, other than to watch the card swing either side of the object you were sighting and mentally average out the difference between the two extremes of its movement. If it careered around between 135° and 160°, you'd plot the bearing as 147°, hoping for the best but assuming the worst in a seamanlike manner. The resulting enormous cocked hat was more akin to an area of position than a fix, and you would assume yourself situated in the most dangerous part of it. If none of the triangle lay near a danger, the course from it still demanded close inspection. Did it pass near rocks, shoals or overfalls? If so, the track was worked up by laying a safe course from the corner of it nearest to the danger, thus covering the worst-case scenario.

Unless you suffer an electronic meltdown, all this is mercifully now history, but you should still keep a clear eye on transits if you possibly can, maintain an interest in your surroundings to keep estimating where you should be, and always double-check your plotter's fix with the echo sounder.

Course steered and estimated position

While GPS positions are in theory always to be confirmed by an EP, ideally formally plotted but at least guesstimated, it must be understood clearly that, in heavy going, the helmsman's hourly report on course steered could prove to be the wildest of guesses, even if he is experienced. A further factor must now be added to the equation of diminishing certainty: leeway.

Leeway can increase out of all proportion in gale conditions. On the wind, 20° is by no means uncommon, while a beam sea and the increased surface drift associated with the wind that made it can knock you literally miles 'downhill' in an hour. If you make an exaggerated allowance for leeway, then at least you are less likely to be disappointed as the projected track line on the screen sags off to leeward. If you don't, you'll find that things always turn up on your weather bow. This is demoralising and can result in a failure to arrive at all. The best solution today is to make sure the plotter's projected track feature is switched on. You'd be surprised how many skippers don't bother or don't even know about it. Keep an eye on this. Ensure you are going where you hope you are going and all will be well.

Even if you are working towards a waypoint, which makes much sense in bad going, it is prudent for the paper-chart navigator who has to operate without a projected track vector,

TACTICS AND NAVIGATION IN HEAVY WEATHER

Fig 28.1 Course plotting in heavy weather.

to sketch a line on either side of the plotted course to steer, which assumes a 10° or 15° error (Fig 28.1). So long as the conical course this produces carries the yacht clear of dangers, all is well. When it does not, you will need to make an alteration to the heading or, should this prove impossible because of dangers on the other bow, watch the bearing of the next waypoint carefully to make sure you are not drifting into danger.

The same 'techniques for uncertainty' can usefully be applied to plotting the tidal vector. Bear in mind that the strong winds may be affecting streams in a manner you are unable to predict. Your distance run may also be in doubt, because your carefully calibrated log, be it a trailing spinner or a through-hull impeller, may well be spending part of its day out of the water registering either airspeed, or nothing much at all.

THE COMPLETE YACHTMASTER

Very pretty, but it's the sort of dirty sunrise that a sailor ignores at his peril.

The result of all the uncertainty engendered by bad weather is that, while GPS helps enormously, entering any area where precise navigation is of the essence may still be imprudent. The precision of electronic fixing can lead to a sense of overconfidence in deep water that is rapidly dispelled when the boat broaches her way into a narrow harbour entrance swept by breakers. Harbours of refuge must have easy, unambiguous approaches. Wide but sheltered roadsteads suddenly become seductively attractive, even if you do roll at anchor. Trying to spot a flashing buoy rising and falling on 15ft (4.5m) waves in the dark is not a reliable way to save your ship, so if a plan depends upon this to confirm the position, abandon it if you have an option to go somewhere else.

Keep your chart table tidy, look after your plotter and, above all, your log book which is your only hope of salvation in the event of the unthinkable contingency of the screens going blank. Fight the natural tendency to let navigational discipline go to pieces and never allow a box full of printed circuits, chips and tiny wires to take over the responsibility that remains yours alone until the vessel under your command is securely in her chosen berth.

DAMAGE CONTROL   29

The subject of damage control is more one of philosophy than of having a yacht stuffed full of expensive gear to be used in case of calamity. The secret of real safety lies in seamanlike forethought, sensible caution and a cool head. The first two can keep you out of trouble for a lifetime but if, owing to a momentary lapse of vigilance or a stroke of genuine bad luck, you find yourself with a pending emergency, the third item is the only thing that can save you from having to put Chapter 30 (on dealing with emergencies) into practice.

Most large problems start out as small ones. If handled successfully at the outset with a policy of prudent self-help, the matter will usually rest there; if not, the end may be a call for assistance.

The way in which difficulties are avoided before they ever happen is the hallmark of the successful skipper. His galley is equipped with proper gas taps so that the cooker can be made safe, but there is also a fire blanket handy to douse any fire without mess and with a minimum of drama. If he finds himself manoeuvring near a lee shore or in a confined space under power, there is always an anchor ready for action in the event of an engine failure. The careful skipper doesn't lose folks overboard because his crew are always clipped on when they should be. Should his engine stop because of a fill of bad diesel, there is a spare filter element aboard and the tools required to bleed the system. He never suffers a flat starter battery because his engine electrical system is carefully isolated and is always off when the engine is not running. He doesn't frighten his crew by overpressing the yacht under sail and no one ever notices him doing much in the way of navigation because his well-organised system runs like clockwork.

Some skippers achieve all this and much more so that passages come and go in a relaxed atmosphere; others are so insecure that heavy stress is placed on 'store-bought safety' when the yacht is navigated into danger. Every Yachtmaster examiner has seen numerous sailors like the latter. The problem arises from too much book learning and not enough seafaring. The answer is to spend as long as possible out on the water, so that the boat becomes as much an extension of yourself as your motor car. Then, just as you know you shouldn't be driving at 70mph 10 yards from the next vehicle's exhaust pipe, you'll know a dangerous lee shore when you see one, and you'll be nowhere near it on the wrong day.

Even with the most seamanlike approach imaginable, however, the unforeseeable may still occur to the fabric of the yacht, but a fully equipped vessel should be able to cope with most circumstances, without requiring the search and rescue services. Her resources begin

Here's why every boat should carry at least one spare drive belt for the alternator. Turn a belt 'inside out', like this, and you'll soon see if it's got any life left in it.

with the basic tool kit, without which the smallest irregularity can leave the finest craft totally disabled.

Tool kits and spare parts

Every boat must carry spare parts, both specific and general, as well as the tools to make feasible repairs when she is beyond the reach of outside assistance. What you carry will depend, to a certain extent, upon your personal technical capacity, but your best plan is to think the boat through from stem to stern, decide what is likely to go wrong, and make sure that you have the necessary items to fix it.

Generalisation is difficult, but the lists below concentrate on the home-water yachtsman rather than the world cruiser. Any item marked with an ☑ can be considered essential; 👍 = worthwhile piece of gear; items marked with ⚓ = inessential – but whatever a tool's grading under this system, it should be appropriate to the size and current needs of the boat.

DAMAGE CONTROL

ENGINE TOOLS

- ☑ **Comprehensive spanner or wrench kit** (including large and small adjustables) of high quality
- ☑ **Allen key set** as required
- ☑ **Screwdrivers** – large (square-shafted to accept wrench, if possible), medium, stubby, small, and electrical. Cross-headed as required
- ☑ **Pliers** – general purpose and sharp-nosed
- ☑ **½in drive socket set** – plastic boxed variety, of medium quality
- ☑ **¼in drive socket set** – can be bought cheaply and junked if they become rusty. Often extremely useful
- ☑ **Sump-oil pump**

ENGINE SPARES

- ☑ **Fuel filters**
- 👍 **Oil filter**
- ☑ **One complete engine oil change** in case sump-oil is dumped in error
- ☑ **Water pump impeller and gasket**
- ☑ **Spare drive belts**
- ⚖ **Cylinder head gasket** – even if you aren't competent to lift the head yourself, you may have to employ an engineer who does not have a gasket on his shelf. Any upper engine job will require its replacement
- ⚖ **Spare injector**
- ☑ **Gasket goo**

ELECTRICAL TOOLS

- ☑ **Various screwdrivers** including one with a 12v test lamp
- 👍 **Simple test meter**
- 👍 **12v soldering iron, flux and solder**
- 👍 **Crimping, cutting and stripping tool**
- 👍 **Needle-nosed pliers**
- ☑ **Insulating tape**

ELECTRICAL SPARES

- ☑ **Selection of spade and ring terminals**
- ☑ **Ditto useful wire**
- ☑ **Fuses as required**
- ☑ **Light bulbs as required**

THE COMPLETE YACHTMASTER

PLUMBING SPARES

- ☑ Spares kit for heads
- ☑ Ditto for bilge pumps
- ☑ Spare terminal fittings for the favoured plumbing system in the boat and a few metres of appropriate piping
- ☑ Check around the boat's systems and stow a set of spares for any of these whose failure could affect safety
- ☑ Assorted odd lengths of piping, armoured hose etc.

GRP HULL REPAIRS

- ☑ **Underwater epoxy putty** – extremely useful for all sorts of applications because it cures in the damp
- ☑ **Gel-coat, GRP resin, hardener, and fibreglass cloth**
- ☑ **Scraper, putty knives, and throw-away paint brushes**
- ☑ **Life-caulk** or another brand of stopping that cures in the damp

RIGGING

- ☑ **Winch spares** – pawls, springs and a circlip, if required
- ☑ **Bulldog grips** for standing rigging
- 👍 **Rigging terminals and spare rigging wire**
- ☑ **Self-amalgamating tape** for 100 uses
- ⚖ **Swedish fid and braidline splicing kit** for those who will make the time
- 👍 **Wire cutters** or bolt croppers
- ⚖ **Nut splitter** – often useful for jobs other than removing rigging lock nuts
- ☑ **Battery-driven grinder** – better than any bolt croppers yet devised
- ☑ **Split pins, etc**
- ☑ **Spare rigging screw** to replace any that may be bent in an accident. Bent screws cannot be relied upon
- ☑ **Clevis and cotter pins** – as required
- ☑ **Bolt stoppers**

SAIL REPAIRS

- ☑ **Palm**
- ☑ **Selection of needles** stowed in an oil-filled tube
- ☑ **Waxed sail twine and whipping twine**
- ☑ **Spinnaker repair tape** for all 'get-you-home' repairs to any sail
- 👍 **Spare sail cloth** for more serious jobs
- ☑ **Contact adhesive** for sticking patches to sails before stitching around them

DAMAGE CONTROL

GENERAL

- ☑ **Hacksaw, junior hacksaw and blades**
- 👍 **Baby spanners**
- ☑ **Mole, or vice grips** – medium and very small. Baby versions are exceedingly useful – you can even tune pianos with them on a one-off basis
- ☑ **Twist drill, hi-speed metal bits, and centre punch bits** to be kept in a screw-top jar, well oiled
- ☑ **Hammers** – medium claw, heavy 'lump', and a soft 'combination hammer' for hitting threaded ends
- ☑ **Set of soft-wood tapered bungs** to block off damaged seacocks
- 👍 **A few hard-wood blocks** to use as drifts, anvils, etc
- 👍 **Soft brass or bronze drift**
- ☑ **Saw** with at least an 18in (45cm) blade, smaller for GRP craft
- ☑ **2 chisels** 1in (25.4mm) and ½in (12.7mm), as required
- 👍 **Portable vice or 'Work-Mate'** and a site designated for it to be mounted. Vices are available that fit into the top of a winch-barrel
- ☑ **2 files** – one large, and one triangular 'thread file'
- ☑ **Selection of lubricants and greases**
- ☑ **Stilson or pipe wrench** also efficacious on extremely large nuts
- 👍 **G-clamps** particularly important if no vice is carried
- ☑ **Emery paper, or wet-and-dry sandpaper** for cleaning electrical terminals, etc
- 👍 **Miner's head-torch**
- ☑ **Good torches or flashlights, and batteries**
- 👍 **Old driving mirror, or 'dentist's mirror'**
- ☑ **Seizing wire**
- ☑ **Wire coat-hangers** as purveyed by dry-cleaners – vital when you need to improvise hooks, probes, etc
- ☑ **Sharp knife**
- 👍 **Sharpening stone**
- ☑ **Araldite, superglue and Vaseline (for battery terminals)**
- 👍 **Epoxy repair kit**

BITS BOXES

Ideally, these should be watertight containers of the type now favoured for packed lunches.

Their contents and extent will reflect their proprietor's character, but remember the important maxim, 'If in doubt, take it with you'.

No boat should put to sea without a good supply of screws, bolts, odd nuts, washers, spare blocks, shackles, pieces of inner tube, threaded rod, coach bolts, gasket material, undefinable items and things that go bump in the night. If the weight is a problem and you are cruising, you've chosen the wrong boat.

Fire prevention and fighting

Like first aid and radio operation, firefighting is a specialised subject. Short courses are offered to sailors in various countries. If you ever have the opportunity to attend one, make use of it. You'll be highly enlightened.

Fire is mercifully rare in yachts at sea, but when it does take hold, its effects can be terrible. An intelligent, defensive attitude to everything that can cause combustion is the only real answer to fire, be it throwing the petrol (gasoline) engine over the side or avoiding deep-frying at sea, no matter what gastronomic temptations it may offer. Nonetheless, there will be occasions in every long-term sailor's life when fire occurs, and that is when only preplanning and precautions can turn a potential disaster into an alarming inconvenience.

All but the smallest boats should have two exits continuously available. If there is a serious flare-up aft, someone trying to get out from the fo'c'sle will be in trouble unless there is a forehatch that can be opened from down below as well as from the deck. Similarly, yachts with seductive aft cabins from which there is no emergency exit should be given a careful inspection, particularly when access to the cabin is gained via the galley. Imagine what would happen if a person were asleep when the cooker turned into an inferno. It has happened, so there is no shortage of precedent.

A fire blanket by the cooker is the best primary protection against fire. Every boat should have one so that a burning pan can quickly be starved of air before it develops into something serious. Suitable extinguishers, as recommended by national authorities (US Coast Guard, or RYA, for example), should be sited at each exit from the accommodation. In the event of a fire emergency all hands should be evacuated safely before the skipper or his deputy reach down for the extinguishers and attempt to fight their way back in. In this context, a large extinguisher in a cockpit locker can be a boat-saver.

If a fire is making ground, you should take all possible steps to decrease the draught fanning it. Once everyone is on deck, close one hatch if you can, then turn downwind.

In a substantial vessel with a full crew, it is advisable to make a PAN PAN radio call (see Chapter 30) while attempts are being made to put out a fire. This may prove impractical in a smaller craft, but it should always be borne in mind that the search and rescue people prefer to rescue living souls than to pick up charred remains.

Jury rigs

Standing rigging

The stainless steel wire standing rigging favoured by most modern cruising yachts is immensely strong and stable. The fittings by which it is attached to hull and spars are cunningly contrived and, considering how much is expected of them, they are extremely reliable. Even so, rigging failure has not been entirely eliminated from the list of sailors' headaches. Be aware that many insurers ask for standing rigging to be replaced at ten-year intervals. This is a very broad-brush approach to which commonsense may be applied.

Rigging wire rarely breaks halfway along its length. Fractures almost invariably occur where the wire joins the terminal fitting, especially if there are no proper arrangements for

DAMAGE CONTROL

'universal movement'. Inspect your rig regularly, aloft and at deck level, because its working life is not indefinite. The first sign of failure in a 1 × 19 stainless steel wire will probably be the parting of a single strand. Immediate action is then imperative, not only because of a strength loss, but since where one strand has parted, more are liable to follow.

Shroud failure

Rigging failure does not always mean instant dismasting, so long as you tack immediately when you see a shroud on the windward side fail or begin to strand. Better still, heave to on the opposite tack. Both actions relieve the damaged wire, which can be either repaired, replaced, or jury-rigged. Split seconds count here. There is no time to waste admiring the banana-shaped mast.

Forestay or backstay failure

A mast may be in dire straits following the loss of a shroud, but when a forestay or a backstay carries away it will be lucky to survive. There is, however, a slim chance that if the backstay lets go, the combined effect of the lower shrouds and the leech of a closehauled mainsail will hold it up long enough for the crew to act. Similarly, a damaged forestay may be covered for a few moments by the luff of the jib, or a halyard stowed on the pulpit combined with a baby stay, but the only real hope lies in an immediate manoeuvre to relieve the injured wire. There is not a watch-tick to lose.

Getting you home

If a shroud has failed it may be unwise to drop the sails, because they are steadying the boat. Once the damage is on the lee side, having tacked if necessary, the first thing to do is to set up the most convenient item of spare running rigging in place of the lost stay or shroud. The main halyard, for example, may well prove the most effective jury backstay. If a cap shroud carries away, extra 'spread' can often be supplied by passing a jury shroud – which will probably be the spinnaker halyard – through the beak of a solidly set-up spinnaker pole before winching it tight.

 SKIPPER'S TIP

Semi-permanent repairs

All yachts venturing seriously offshore should carry a long length of Spectra or Dyneema rope for standing rigging repairs. Ideally also a length of rigging wire a little longer than the longest shroud or stay, and of similar gauge to the heaviest. Add to this half a dozen bulldog grips and a selection of thimbles. If your boat uses patent end-fittings, it may not be possible to replace them on board. If you can, a few spare terminals and the necessary vices and wrenches may save the mast; if you cannot, the spare shroud should be longer still, and be equipped with one fitting at either end. Where two forms of terminal are used, one of each should be fitted to the wire. Careful cutting of both the broken shroud or stay and the spare wire will allow the replacement fitting to be installed while the attached length of wire is bulldog-gripped to what remains of the original. Yachts have crossed oceans with their rigging splinted like this. The secret is forethought.

Ropes around the propeller

Of all the avoidable disabling horrors lurking in wait for the modern mariner, this is perhaps the most common. You might be really unlucky and foul a length of ropey flotsam in the dark, but more usually the incident occurs as a result of carelessness.

Other than being caught by a length of free-floating rope, there are two main ways of allowing a propeller to become ensnared: the first occurs when part of the yacht's gear falls over the side; the second comes along when you snag a mooring line, or some other unseen horror.

If the engine is running when a rope goes into the vortex, your reaction should be spontaneous. If the motor has not already stalled, throw it out of gear immediately, just as you should whenever there is the slightest suspicion that a rope may have been kicked overboard, or that the boat is passing a submerged line. If the propeller turns out to be foul, the first step is to try and get a hold on the rope. If you can, there is a possibility that the problem can be solved with a minimum of fuss. You know the rope went on with the propeller driving ahead. Reverse that direction of revolution while maintaining a firm pull on the line, and you have at least a chance of winding it back off again. This is best achieved by decompressing the engine, engaging astern propulsion and then winding the engine round (with the 'stop' button on) using the starter motor or, better still, the handle, while your mate pulls on the offending line.

If this doesn't work, you are left with the knife and two choices: either you hack through the rope and leave the tangle on the shaft, or you clear it completely, which probably means someone going into the water. Should this be required but you don't fancy it, you'll just have to face up to sailing without an engine until you reach a calm haven. Loss of engine in these circumstances is emphatically not a cause to call for help. Boats have been sailing without power since the time of Noah, and most of them were far more unwieldy than ours are.

With ropes and propellers in mind, you should always carry a diving mask. A snorkel is also of great value. As for cutting tools, there is no doubt that serrated edges are best for this job. It is occasionally possible to reach the problem zone with a hacksaw or stout breadknife lashed to the boathook, particularly if the operator is in the dinghy, and you should certainly give this a try. Otherwise, it's the cold plunge for somebody.

Where the water is dangerously frigid, you ought to be carrying aboard at least a wetsuit singlet. If you have no such gear, but nature has provided a useful tidal range, you'll have to opt for the less convenient but more comfortable solution of sailing the boat to a suitable wall or scrubbing pile. There, you can wait for Low Water before strolling down to clear the line at your leisure.

Steering failure

It is a statistical fact that loss of steering is one of the most popular reasons for yachtsmen to give up the struggle for self-reliance and call for help. Losing your rudder, or the means of controlling it, is undoubtedly a serious matter, but it does not usually present an immediate threat to life. The ship is not about to burn to the waterline, and unless she is among rocks or in seas of exceptional severity, she will continue to swim indefinitely. Losing your primary steering system will normally allow you time to reflect, and given a well-equipped tool-locker and plenty of bits and pieces, it is surprising what an inventive group of sailors can contrive.

Some wheel steering failures are readily repairable at sea; others are totally impossible. If all attempts to fix the system meet with frustration, it will be necessary to rig the emergency tiller, which should be conveniently accessible and be tried before it is ever needed. These items are not always as ideal as they would appear, and you don't want to find out how impossible the thing is to use when you are seasick and in danger.

A really good emergency tiller. Note that this skipper has taken the trouble to try it out and make sure it works!

Rudder loss

Rudders, in particular spade rudders, will always be vulnerable, not least to yachts heading from northern Europe to Gibraltar due to orca activity.

No one can call himself a Yachtmaster until he has a thorough understanding of rig and hull balance, and their effects upon steering. These are always important, but when the rudder is lost they become vital, because no jury rudder is as effective as the real thing, so it needs all the help it can get.

There are numerous possibilities for rigging a jury rudder, including making full use of any wind-vane steering system and its attendant servo or auxiliary rudder, but the most commonly effective method is to press the spinnaker pole into service.

The spinnaker pole rudder

This system has been proved to work. A dinghy paddle, or something larger, is securely lashed to the pole, which is itself lashed loosely but safely to the pushpit so that the paddle blade is well submerged and the inboard end can be manhandled. Using the steering oar thus formed is largely self-explanatory, but there are some predictable problems. The biggest difficulty is keeping the business end down in the water. As the boat moves ahead, water flow tends to float the pole up. This effect can be neutralised in some cases by weighting it down with, for instance, an anchor, which offers the added advantage of increasing the pole's water resistance.

The other usual difficulty is that actually pushing the inboard end of the pole from port to starboard and back again can become very tiring. Control lines rigged through quarter blocks to the sheet winches can help.

Dismasting

It is surprising how rarely crew personnel are injured in a dismasting. The greatest threat presented by the broken or dismounted spar is to the ship herself. A significant weight of aluminium tubing, rope, wire and sailcloth slamming alongside a thin hull can do terrible damage. It can even sink the yacht.

As soon as you have checked that your crew are safe, or have arranged first aid if they are not, your first priority is *not to start the engine*. If you do, a fouled propeller is virtually guaranteed with all that rubbish in the water. And a fouled propeller will rob you of your most obvious means of arriving at a safe haven without troubling the search and rescue services.

The motion of a boat deprived of the roll inertia of her mast is terrible in a rough sea, so you may find it necessary to advise deck workers to clip on to the jackstays, particularly if the guard rails have been carried away.

Your choice is now whether or not to cut away the mast. If you were in mid-ocean, you would be well advised to try to secure the wreckage, because it is from those remains that you would have to fashion a jury rig. Within engine range of a harbour, the question becomes rather different. The gear over the side could be badly damaged and it is probably insured. While the underwriters may be unhappy about an owner committing his rig to the deep, they would presumably be even less pleased if he gave it a chance to hole the yacht herself, taking their whole risk to Davy Jones's Locker.

Once the mast is either gone or fully secured, and you are absolutely certain that there are no stray ropes or wires under the water, then, and only then, can the engine be started. If the mast has been saved, great care must be taken that nothing is loose, and so long as the boat is under power with the spar alongside, ceaseless vigilance will be required to make sure the propeller is not fouled. Many a simple dismasting has been transformed into a disaster by the propeller grabbing the one halyard that was left trailing.

Loss of electronics

While the loss of navigational electronics undoubtedly creates a sickening feeling in the pit of the stomach, so long as the yacht has been navigated and equipped responsibly, it really is not the end of the world. The last known position will be in the log book at the most an hour ago, and a suitable paper chart will be under the lid of the chart table. Make a new log entry, work up an EP on the paper chart from the last known position and plot a course to wherever it is you are going. You are then no worse off than any sailor ever was before the mid-1990s, and most of us lived to tell the tale...

EMERGENCIES 30

Having considered damage control and self-help in Chapter 29, we must now turn our attention to the sort of emergency that you cannot deal with using your own resources. Man overboard is an emergency by any definition, but it is one that, primarily at least, you can tackle yourself. It therefore does not form part of this section, but is considered separately in Chapter 31.

There are many reasons that yachts find themselves having to call out the Search and Rescue (SAR) services. Some are obvious; others are surprising. Fig 30.1 (p. 283) shows a breakdown of the reasons for lifeboat call-outs in the UK and is fairly typical of worldwide circumstances. Studying this will build up an awareness of the things that usually go wrong. To be aware is to be on guard, so take notice of the figures.

- Stranding usually follows a failure of navigation or pilotage, though it may occasionally result directly from adverse conditions.
- Machinery failure aboard a sailing craft should only be a true emergency on the rarest of occasions.
- Adverse conditions can often be avoided, and no vessel should intentionally be exposed to weather that she may not be able to handle.

And so on down the list. Think about each heading, and be aware of its implications for any boat you may be skippering, under any given set of circumstances.

Speak to any SAR personnel and you will be surprised at how comfortably they live with the messy business of human frailty. 'There but for the Grace of God, go I,' is their philosophy. I once criticised a sailor who had called out a lifeboat under circumstances that, in my opinion, went no way towards warranting it. The cox'n of the lifeboat was a friend of mine, and he put me firmly in my place.

'Listen,' he said, 'the truth is that a person is in danger at any time when he thinks he is in danger. What is no problem for you might be a cause for panic in someone else.' His message is absolutely clear. 'If in doubt, call them out.' SAR crews would far rather return home after what proved to be a false alarm than arrive ten minutes too late and have to bring bodies back to shore. This is not only the private view of my chum the cox'n, it is also the official position. It is therefore very important that you take the time to consider your own views on self-sufficiency.

If you are within radio reach of help when things begin to go badly wrong, don't forget that there is such a thing as PAN PAN (urgency) call. Let the coastguard know what your problem is and what you are doing about it. This will enable him to make sure that SAR services are on stand-by should they be required. The time saved in the event of your ultimately issuing a MAYDAY broadcast could be vital.

The other important use of the PAN PAN call is the PAN PAN MEDICO. These are used to prefix calls to coast radio stations requesting medical advice. Should you have a medical problem on board that requires urgent attention beyond your immediate knowledge, a doctor will talk to you free of charge via this service. If it is decided that the casualty requires evacuation from the yacht, either the lifeboat will be launched or an SAR helicopter scrambled.

Lifeboat rescue

Time spent waiting for the lifeboat is emphatically not to be considered as a period of inactivity. The call for help is no capitulation of your responsibility, nor is it necessarily a cause for humiliation. With the best will in the world, anyone could be dismasted, for example. The lifeboat crew know this and are not thinking any the worse of you for your predicament.

Probably the most important single item is to communicate with the lifeboat if you possibly can, as early as you are able. This will achieve a number of things: in the first place, you can tell the cox'n where you are. As a competent skipper you can, at worst, offer him an EP. At best, you should give him an electronically derived position.

When you see the lifeboat approaching (flashing blue light if in the dark), advise the boat of her position relative to your own by radio, because you may see her before you yourself are noticed. At night, if you can discern her navigation lights, let off a red pinpoint flare if you think she may not have seen you. If her running lights are in your line of sight, your flare is visible to her crew.

Another reason for talking with the lifeboat cox'n is to tell him more about your vessel, the nature of your problem, what you are doing about it, and the form of assistance you require. The information is useful in itself, but in fact it goes beyond this. The way you are communicating tells the lifeboat people a great deal about your emotional condition and about how able you might be to cooperate in the rescue. Whatever your state of mind or overall competence, the SAR services are better able to help you if they are aware of it.

If you are hoping for a tow, you should do all you can to prepare your boat. Decide where a line will best be attached. Look round for ways of relieving the load on a bow cleat, if that is to be used, and be ready.

Have all your crew wearing their lifejackets and harnesses, and clear away any debris, particularly ropes that may be hanging over the side. Even lifeboats can foul their propellers.

Never shine a powerful light in the direction of a lifeboat. The lifeboat carries searchlights and will supply such extra illumination as circumstances may warrant. Be ready for this flood of light, and resist the temptation to look straight into its source.

Remember that you remain in command of your own vessel. Where there is no need to transfer personnel, don't attempt it, because if the lifeboat comes alongside in a seaway, you could sustain structural damage. A yacht's best emergency fenders are well-stuffed sailbags. If the sails inside are neatly folded, take them out and bundle them in willy-nilly. You'll be surprised at how little damage even the bags sustain during a short encounter.

EMERGENCIES

RNLI statistics – sailing craft only			
Cause of service	Launches	Lives saved	Rescued
Machinery failure	440	4	959
Stranding or grounding	270	10	330
Thought to be in trouble	184	0	45
Fouled propeller/impeller	108	0	215
Capsize	102	6	55
Sail failure/dismasting	85	8	124
Adverse conditions	60	1	63
Vessel abandoned, derelict or adrift	51	0	4
Steering failure	50	1	115
Illness	41	2	46
Leaks/swamping	40	2	50
Vessel dragging anchor	30	0	26
Man overboard	27	5	12
Injured	23	0	16
Out of fuel	23	0	47
Fire	19	0	23
Vessel unsure of position	18	0	9
Person to be taken ashore from a vessel	16	0	20
Collision	5	0	6
Grand total	**1592**	**39**	**2165**

Lives saved are included within the people rescued category.

Fig 30.1 Lifeboat launches to sailing yachts in a typical year. Figures supplied by RNLI. They make interesting reading.

Helicopter rescue

It should always be borne in mind that helicopters have a limited flying time, which means that there is not a moment to lose during a rescue. It is therefore vital to prepare yourself and your boat while the helicopter is on the way.

Location

You will probably spot the helicopter before its crew identify you. Keep a good lookout and when you see it, use any available means to attract its attention. Ideally, this might be a smoke flare or red pinpoint (*not* a parachute flare, with aircraft in the vicinity – shooting down the helicopter is a poor start to the proceedings), VHF or a homing beacon. Alternatively, you can use a lamp or a mirror, and wave the ensign, a brightly coloured lifejacket or even a coloured shirt. As with the lifeboat, communicate with the SAR crew. 'I am behind you on your left side,' etc.

A helicopter is a noisy machine. Talking with crews on VHF is not easy. Be aware of this and always be ready to ask radio operators to 'say again' their message.

Survivor rescue

No two rescues are the same. You will be asked to comply with requests of the helicopter crew, and this you should do, to the letter if possible. However, regardless of the operation, you should endeavour to prepare your boat as follows:

- Secure all loose gear on deck, or place it below. Unsecured covers, ropes, litter, etc are easily lifted by the downdraught of the rotors. If they are ingested by the helicopter's engine they can, quite simply, cause the aircraft to crash.
- Provide a clear place for transferring personnel up and down. In most sailing yachts the best area is the cockpit. If possible, drop the mainsail (headsail too if your engine is working), lower the boom to the deck on the starboard side and take the topping lift to the mast. The winchman is going to board you on the port quarter because the pilot sits to starboard in the aircraft and he needs to see you, so clear away everything movable from that area. All danbuoys, aerials and the rest must be removed from the stern.
- Stand by to receive instructions. Be ready to operate at the course and speed the pilot asks for. This will probably be as fast as you can comfortably motor in an upwind direction. At night, the helicopter may survey you for some time with searchlights to locate obstructions. Be ready to turn your deck lights on or off as required.
- Whatever you do, maintain a steady course and speed during the transfer. Designate a reliable helmsman and don't let him be distracted by the temptation to 'watch the show'.
- The racket of a helicopter overhead at low altitude is dreadful. Brief your crew about this and don't let it alarm either you or them.

The lift

Under ideal conditions it is possible that a helicopter crewman will be winched straight down to you. He will bring with him either a lifting strop or a stretcher, and will take off either a casualty or all hands one at a time, whichever is required.

It is important when you are being lifted that you only help when asked to do so. Once you are in the strop, keep your arms by your side. When you are up alongside the helicopter, do nothing until instructed. If a stretcher is being employed, you'll probably have to help the winchman to place your casualty in it. It is the winchman's responsibility to oversee the transfer, so you must obey his instructions.

Hi-line transfer

When the weather or the cluttered landing environment likely to be offered by a yacht makes it difficult for a winchman to be lowered direct, a Hi-line transfer may be used.

The Hi-line is an extension line attached by a weak link to the hook on the winch cable. Its weighted free end is lowered to the yacht and used for guiding the rescue device (a strop, a stretcher or, more probably, a winchman) down to your deck. Here is the usual order of events:

- Helicopter lowers the Hi-line to you.
- Let the line touch the sea or the yacht before you grab it, otherwise you may receive a shock from static electricity. That is the 'official word', but there is some discussion about this, and I have been aboard yachts where the line has been lowered straight into the cockpit without ill effects.
- Take in the slack on the line. Flake it down safely, but under no circumstances make it fast. If you allow a 'tug of war' situation to arise, the weak link in the line will break.
- The helicopter will now move away so that the pilot can take visual references. Keep working the slack on the Hi-line.
- A winchman or a rescue device (strop or stretcher) will now be lowered. Use the Hi-line to steady this and guide it, or him, on board. The job may require a hefty pull, so choose someone strong to handle the line.
- If a winchman is sent down to you, he will take charge. If not, secure evacuees as appropriate and signal to lift with 'thumbs up'. Note that lifting strops have a toggle that should be pushed down towards the evacuee's body as far as possible for maximum security. Keep your arms by your sides when you are on the wire.
- Ease out on the Hi-line as the lift is in progress, using it to dampen any swinging. Keep it in hand, however, as it may be needed again.
- Release the Hi-line only when no further lifts are needed and when you are instructed to do so.
- If the helicopter crew decide that even Hi-lining is too dangerous, they may ask you to stream the casualty astern in a dinghy on a long painter.
- In order to facilitate rapid evacuation of more than one casualty, the helicopter can send down two strops so that two people can be lifted at a time, under the winchman's supervision.

First on the scene

Occasionally, a situation arises where a private yacht is the first vessel to arrive when another craft is in distress. If this should happen to you, there are certain duties of which you should be aware, as well as exercising a normal seamanlike care for other mariners.

If you sight a red flare or hear a MAYDAY, or notice any other signal indicating distress, you are obliged to render assistance. If the distress signal has not been acknowledged by a shore authority, you should relay the message yourself by MAYDAY RELAY procedure.

The same applies to a PAN PAN call. Here is a list of actions you may find useful:

- Make your intentions clear to everyone by calling on Channel 16.
- Do what you can to assist.
- If you were first to arrive you will automatically become 'on-scene commander' if further craft show up. You remain in charge until a larger or better-equipped vessel arrives. Typically, this would be a commercial craft, an SAR helicopter, or a lifeboat. You then hand over command. Keep the coastguard informed at all times.
- If you are on the scene of rescue and are not immediately involved, stand well off and monitor progress on Channel 16.
- Should you find yourself co-ordinating with a helicopter, you may discover you cannot hear the radio because of its noise, which can be a problem up to 437 yards (400m) distant. Helicopter crews may use sign signals under these circumstances, or even chalk instructions on a blackboard held up in the doorway. These are best read from a position of 3 or 9 o'clock from the helicopter as it hovers head-to-wind.

Taking to the liferaft

What follows may sound like a trite observation, but the more you think about it, the more sense it makes. The best life-saving vessel at your disposal is the yacht herself. Unless she is terminally burning or in a sinking state, stay with her. She is bigger than the raft, so she is easier for SAR crews to see. She is also more comfortable, better equipped and, if she is still afloat when the danger is past, she has a better chance of carrying you in the direction you want to go – like home, perhaps. Once aboard the raft, you have abandoned all hope of navigating to safety. Your survival is entirely in the hands of others.

There is precedent aplenty to back up the statement that you are safer on the boat so long as she swims. One of the more dramatic manifestations of this was in the gale-struck Fastnet Race of 1979 in which a number of people died either in or trying to reach liferafts whose parent vessels were subsequently found floating and intact.

Launching the raft

It is important that you stop the yacht before heaving the liferaft into the water. This may appear obvious, but it is worth noting that incidents are on record in which rafts have been seriously damaged by the drag of their own stabiliser drogues.

Always check that the painter is secure before pulling on it to inflate the raft. Do the job on deck if this seems a realistic option.

The liferaft's painter is long, so you may find you have 30ft (9m) or more to pull out of the pack before you come up against the 'rip-cord' action that will fire the gas bottle. Sometimes, a sharp jerk is needed before the whole affair hisses into action.

If the raft inflates upside down, right it as soon as you can, to minimise water ingress. If you are unfortunate enough to have to board the raft from the water and it is inverted, send your most agile crew member round to the gas bottle and tell him to right the raft by standing on that while pulling on the handles provided.

EMERGENCIES

A casualty's-eye view of a rescue helicopter. Note that the Hi-line is dangling beneath the stretcher. The winchman has already boarded the yacht and he will use the line to guide the stretcher as it is lowered.

The painter on most rafts is secured near the door. This helps you to board from the yacht.

The windage on a liferaft with its canopy up is considerable. Once inflated in a gale, the device is likely to blow away like a supermarket bag, fetching up a boat's length or more away at the end of its tether. If you allow this to happen, you could well find yourself unable to heave it back to the yacht's side, leaving you no option but to swim for it.

Obviously, all hands will by now be kitted up in lifejackets, but they should also be wearing their harnesses. Before entering the water to work across to the raft, clip on to the painter. If you don't, you could well be cast adrift and find yourself with a long swim to safety.

Remember that in temperate conditions cold is the enemy, so make sure everyone is fully clothed. Damp will aggravate the difficulties so if you can keep the inside of the raft dry from the outset, so much the better. If possible, take extra clothes aboard the raft.

Always enter the raft immediately after launching it. The longer it remains alongside, the greater are its chances of suffering damage or being swamped.

The raft contains minimal survival gear and some pyrotechnics, but the more you can throw aboard at the last minute, the better. Chuck in your 'grab bag', if you have one, also any flares remaining on the yacht, ready-use food, a few containers of water, and all your torches or flashlights; it is also worth taking the boathook with you from which to wave a distress signal. In even a moderate sea, rafts can be surprisingly difficult to spot, and a red shirt an extra six feet up in the air could help a great deal, especially if you have no hand-held VHF radio.

Your last action on leaving the yacht, if at all possible, is to broadcast a final MAYDAY and make sure you've remembered your EPIRB (Emergency Position Indicating Radio Beacon). If you are sailing near the coast or on densely used shipping lanes, this last item may be less vital to your survival, but if you are far from civilisation, a liferaft without an EPIRB is like a yacht without a sail. In the words of my friend, the lifeboat cox'n, 'You haven't survived until you have been rescued.'

Having boarded the raft, find the equipment and particularly the safety knife which you will use to sever the painter, then make yourself comfortable. You may have a long wait.

Pyrotechnics

Flares are expensive to buy and since you hope never to use them, it comes hard to spend more than you must. Traditionally, the answer for the thinking boat-owner was always to ship a complete outfit of up-to-date flares and smoke signals, but to keep the previous issue aboard as well. Unless they came from HMS *Victory*, there was a good chance that they would work and, although technically past their sell-by date, they could still save your life.

Times have changed, however, and these days anyone sailing with out-of-date flares is due a finger-wagging from the safety industry who will assure him that the additional precaution, instead of giving the crew a second chance, represents a clear and present danger. How true this may be when viewed in the balance of percentages is not for me to say. Skippers of non-professional yachts will make up their own minds.

However, it is now a hard fact that any yacht going to France is advised not to pitch up with older flares because they are illegal in the Republic and fines have been levied.

While pyrotechnics and Channel 16 VHF Mayday broadcasts remain the traditional means

Do all you can to become natural on the VHF. There's nothing worse than someone sounding as if they've never used radio before.

of summoning assistance, it doesn't do to forget how effective the mobile phone has become in recent years. If you aren't confident about talking on the VHF there's something to be said for keeping the local coastguard's number in your phone so you can call him up if in doubt.

Red rocket (parachute) flares are used to indicate that there is a vessel in distress. They may not show exactly where you are, but they will attract attention if they are seen. Should your parachute flares be in short supply, do not blaze away willy-nilly. If you can, wait until you see a ship's lights on the horizon, unless you are near an inhabited coast.

Rocket flares should be launched pointing skywards, but slightly downwind. They will then recurve to windward and burst overhead. If a flare fails to fire, don't peer into the top to find out what is wrong. It may just be a slow starter.

Red rocket flares should ideally be used in pairs, because if somebody sees one out of the corner of his eye, he will turn and look at it, musing, 'That looked like a red flare. I wonder if it really was…' When he sees the second one, which you send up half a minute after the first has died, he knows what's what and reacts. If you only have four rockets, save the second pair as long as you can.

Red pinpoint (hand-held) flares are used to indicate your exact position. If you can see the side lights of a small vessel, she will certainly be able to make out your flare, because although you may be lower and partially obscured by waves, it is a hundred times brighter than her steaming lights. Always hold a pinpoint flare to leeward.

Smoke canisters are used to indicate your position in daylight. Launch or hold them to leeward.

White rocket flares can be of inestimable value when searching for a man overboard, or in any other emergency that requires a general lighting-up of the scene. Hand-held whites are your final defence against being run down. When all else fails and you can't get out of the way, ignite a white flare. The ship's lookout, if there is such a person on the bridge, will see that for certain.

Flares are dramatic items that have been known to cause injuries to users who have not read the instructions carefully, or are just unlucky enough to have acquired a faulty one. Super high-powered red electric 'flares' are now available which are easy to use and seem to be free of hazard. You may feel it worthwhile to ship one of these in addition to the flare pack because it will keep going long after the pyrotechnics have run out of steam.

31 MAN OVERBOARD

The most effective way of dealing with this terrible hazard is to have a positive policy on safety harnesses so as to ensure that it never happens at all. Every crew member should be issued with his own equipment, so that it can be adjusted to size before it is needed. It should then be worn and used as a matter of course at any time when either you, or any of your crew, might feel it necessary. If you are looking for guidance as to when this might be, the following may prove helpful:

- If you are wondering whether or not to clip on, do it.
- When you are sailing in open water and conditions are such that you would consider reefing the mainsail, clip on at any time you leave the cockpit.
- In gale or near-gale conditions when a knock-down seems even a remote possibility, everyone on deck or in the cockpit should be clipped on.
- Clip on when approaching an area of tidal disturbance. It may be worse than you expect.
- Even in fair weather, clip on at night.

If, having taken all these precautions, you do lose someone, man-overboard recovery is a two-stage operation. The first part is to bring the boat close to the casualty and keep her there for long enough to be able successfully to execute the second, which is assisting him back on board.

Whatever is happening, the most vital aspect of phase one is never to lose eye contact with the casualty. As soon as he goes over, throw a lifebuoy and danbuoy after him, then designate someone to watch him continuously even if he is carrying a radio homing device. Even a few seconds' slackness can result in your crew member being lost to view among the waves, quite possibly for ever. On a short-handed cruiser, this requirement can be a tall order, but nonetheless it must be followed. If you are left alone on board, you will have to do your best, but always remember the danger of losing touch.

There are two basic systems for bringing a boat to rest close by, or even alongside, a crew member in the water. Which you choose will depend on your yacht's characteristics, the sea conditions, and how you rate your own competence.

MAN OVERBOARD

The reach-turn-reach

This method works well in a moderate-sized, manoeuvrable yacht with an expert in command. It is successful in any conditions and has the benefit of not requiring any recourse to the engine. Here is how it goes, step by step (see also Fig 31.1):

- Immediately sail the boat away, properly trimmed, on a true beam reach. Now you should hit the MOB button on your GPS and mark the time, if appropriate.
- As soon as you have enough room to manoeuvre (how much this is depends on many factors; only practice can give you the necessary expertise), either tack or gybe. Bear in mind that tacking will take you further upwind. Gybing will lose you ground. Either may be what you require.
- You want to approach the casualty on a close-reach, because no other point of sailing gives you such control over the boat's speed. So steer directly for him, release your sheets to see if all sails will spill wind on demand, and determine whether or not her attitude to the wind is to your satisfaction.
- If she is on a close-reach, lose way just as if you were picking up a mooring with no tide running (as in Chapter 5).
- If she's 'below' a reach (i.e. to leeward of the desired heading, or too hard on the wind), make all the ground you can closehauled, 'above' the target, before bearing away and spilling wind on your final close-reaching approach. Fail to do this, and the boat will stall into the windward sector as soon as you try to slow down.

Fig 31.1 Man overboard: reach-turn-reach pick-up (note the close-reaching approach).

- If she's 'above' the desired heading (you'll see this immediately because the mainsail will refuse to spill wind), bear away sharply, run downwind for a few yards, then shape up for the casualty once more, reassessing your angle to the wind.
- You sailed away from the casualty initially in order to gain the searoom to execute either of these last two manoeuvres, should they be required. Do not waste that ground through indecision.
- In moderate conditions, you'll discover that if you stop to windward of the man with the breeze well out on your weather bow, the stalling boat will slide down towards him, particularly if you put the helm hard 'down' to luff off the last of her way. You will now be able to pick up amidships. Watch out for flogging jib sheets and if you've a roller genoa, furl it before you go out on the deck.
- In hard weather, you may prefer to stop a few yards away from the casualty and heave him a line so as to avoid any possibility of running him down. When it's really blowing, there is a respectable school of thought that says you should stop to leeward of the man so as not to be driven down on to him.

Finding that close-reach in the heat of the moment requires judgement of a moderately high order. Don't be disheartened if it seems hard going when you begin to practise, and always remember that in a genuine crisis there is nothing to stop you having your engine turning over – check round for ropes over the side first! – to give the boat a last shove up to windward if need be. Try the manoeuvre again every so often and see if you are improving, but stick to the 'crash stop' method described below if you are in the slightest doubt.

Reach-turn-reach is said by some to be the best way of coming back to a casualty in the water, but it has two drawbacks. To be sure of pulling it off, boat handling of a high standard is required, and it involves taking the boat away from the casualty while working up the searoom for the pick-up approach. At night, you may well be uncertain that the victim has caught hold of the flashing light you threw him; the light may even have failed to function – such occurrences are all too common – so you may feel that the risk of losing touch with him in the dark is too great. Even so, it is well worth taking the time to practise the method, especially if your engine is unreliable, non-existent, or lacks the power to deliver the punch needed in heavy seas.

Crash stop

The crash stop method offers the huge benefit of keeping boat and man overboard close together throughout the affair (Fig 31.2). This is what you do:

- As soon as your man goes over the side, push the helm hard down, regardless of your point of sailing. This will normally tack the boat.
- Leave your headsail sheets made fast so that the jib and/or staysail come aback.
- The yacht is now effectively hove to. The reality in a seaway is that this is often a messy manoeuvre, with ropes and sails flailing around in disarray, but in spite of this discomfort, the boat will often settle down close enough to the casualty to pass him a line. If this isn't the case, it may well be worth trying to work the boat across to him by juggling sheets and tiller.

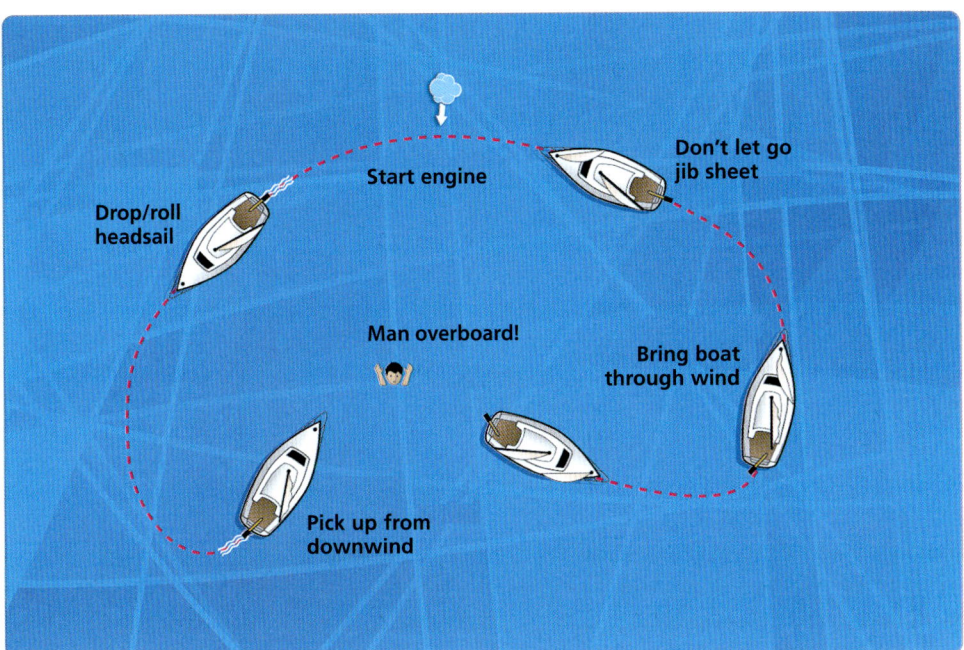

Fig 31.2 Man overboard: crash stop.

- If it looks as though you will not come close enough to effect a rescue, you will have to motor sail. This is where the modern yacht with her powerful, reliable auxiliary scores over her predecessors, but first you have a job to do. Unless you have a spare person to detail for the duty, nip below, press the MOB button on your GPS – assuming it is running – and note the time. Now carry on with the main task.

- Motor sailing from the hove-to mode is the favourite means if you entertain secret doubts about your capacity to make the grade as a boat handler. It is also the best way to teach your crew to cope in the event of the real catastrophe of falling overboard yourself.

- Keeping a constant eye on the victim, drop your headsail or roll it away. Now work the boat to a point downwind of the casualty and start the engine after double-checking, then checking again, that no rope of any description can find its way into the propeller. The pick-up is made with the boat approaching from slightly off dead downwind with the mainsheet pinned amidships. The sail steadies the boat while the propeller maintains control, but it is important to keep the person in the water towards the 'shoulder' of the boat. A propeller can inflict traumatic injuries on a swimmer, which, in his already shocked state, could render the object of the whole exercise somewhat futile.

- With a conscious and uninjured casualty it is always better to lose the last of your way five yards from him and toss him a line, than to risk injuring him by direct contact in a seaway.

Probably the most difficult man-overboard scenarios occur when you are on a run, either with spinnaker set, or with a headsail poled out. There are a number of ways to deal with these undesirable situations depending upon the boat, the skill of her crew, her size and various other factors. It is therefore impossible to generalise. The only responsible answer is to consider deeply what you would do under these circumstances, then try your theory out in practice using a bucket and fender tied together as a dummy victim. If it doesn't work, think again until you find something that does.

Bringing the casualty aboard

If the casualty is reasonably fit and the sea state not abominably rough, the first option would be to use a boarding ladder of the type fitted to many modern yachts or carried by them. So long as its steps reach well below the surface, a fully clothed swimmer has a good chance of climbing back aboard by timing his efforts to coincide with the boat's movement in the waves. If the ladder is rigged aft, it is easier to climb with the yacht rolling in the trough than if she is held head-to-wind, pitching violently.

There are two schools of thought on boarding by stern ladder in a seaway. Some people's experience is that the technique is surprisingly effective, but you should be aware that certain boats are apt to bring their sterns down with a wallop on anyone manoeuvring in the water.

If you have no ladder and your casualty is in good shape, the first thing to try – assuming you cannot simply manhandle him over the rail (always the premier option if there is enough muscle on board) – is to lower a bight of line into the water. The tail of a jib sheet is ideal. The swimmer steps in this and, as the boat rolls, heaves himself up as best he can while you take up the slack around a cockpit winch. After two or three bursts of effort he is usually high enough to roll under the top guard rail. The lower rail should be let go to make the job easier, which is a very good reason for lashing the ends rather than tensioning them up with a rigging screw. A lashing can be quickly cut in an emergency.

In some circumstances, a bowline to put a foot in is better than a bight of sheet. It depends on the shape of the boat, the height of the lift, etc.

If the man overboard is unconscious or injured, the first priority will be to secure him alongside. As usual with seamanship, methods will depend on circumstances, but a serious option to consider if the yacht has high freeboard is as follows: attach the lightest crew member to a spare halyard, sitting securely in a bosun's chair in a deflated lifejacket. Lower him over the side with the topping lift in hand. He secures the topping lift to the victim via whatever lifting system is to be applied (see below). Be ready to give the crew member plenty of slack in case he has to swim a few yards, but do not let him become detached. Winch him back on board with the most powerful winch available, then transfer the topping lift to the same winch and hoist the casualty with care.

For this to work, the boat must have at least two lines that can be made available from aloft. I have suggested the topping lift as one of these as it is pretty typical. If you are serious about real safety on board and are intending to sail out of reach of SAR, then perhaps you should consider making sure these are rigged and ready.

With any but a fit person in full possession of all faculties in the water, you will now have to devise a lifting arrangement of some sort. As mentioned above, the ideal is to go straight to an electric winch in the cockpit. While by no means standard equipment, power foredeck windlasses are now becoming the norm on larger yachts. If you have one of these, it is vital that at least one halyard or the topping lift is long enough to be led to it via snatch blocks to recover a casualty from the water. Failing power assistance or a winch big enough to wind up by manpower, a tackle must be employed.

The purchase must be at least 4:1 ratio. When overhauled it should be sufficiently long to reach the water comfortably, allowing for wave action, when its upper block is raised well above the level of the rail by a halyard. The halyard is shackled to the upper block and the lower block is attached to the swimmer, either to his harness, or to a bowline passed under his arms. The fall of the purchase is now led, via any necessary turning blocks, to a primary winch. The resulting power will enable a ten-year-old to lift a wrestler.

It is often suggested that the boom vang (or kicking strap) will serve well enough for this purpose. On some vessels it may, but generally speaking it is more sensible to carry a 'dedicated' tackle stowed somewhere convenient. It won't cost a lot, you will find other occasional uses for it, and there will be no doubt that on the night when it might save a life, you'll be glad you carried it.

Research on both sides of the Atlantic indicates that an unfit or badly debilitated casualty may be at risk from heart failure either during or shortly after being lifted from the water in a 'standing' attitude. It is far safer to hoist in a prone position if this is at all feasible. At least one commercial device is available that achieves this by means of a triangular 'parbuckling sling'. One side of the triangle is tied to the toerail while the opposite angle is attached to a halyard. The casualty is manoeuvred into the bight of material thus formed then hoisted out.

The whole business of bringing an MOB casualty back aboard once 'safely' alongside can sound glib in a textbook. The reality is very different and many lives have been lost from crews' inability to manage it. The only sure route to confidence in your planned system is to try it out on a summer's day when a volunteer feels up to a swim.

Search and rescue

When you are sailing a large, fully crewed yacht within radio range of help, there is no doubt that you ought to designate a competent person to call for assistance immediately someone goes over the side. This does not mean that you are capitulating your control of the situation, but it enables you to concentrate more fully on retrieving the casualty in a situation where every minute, indeed second, may count. However, if a helicopter or lifeboat scrambles and your attempts fail, they will be with you that much sooner, which is very definitely what they prefer.

Where your boat is short-handed, especially two-handed, leaving you alone, the situation is not so clear cut. It is up to you whether you risk losing sight of a casualty while you radio for assistance. My own feeling is that under these circumstances a competent sailor should do all in his power to effect his own rescue, but remain aware that assistance can be called should matters turn ugly. The point at which you take time out from your efforts to call the search and rescue people will demand the coolest judgement you will ever have to make.

If you have GMDSS radio, it may well make sense to crash stop, deploy your safety gear, then nip below very quickly to activate the red button and note the time before returning on deck to go into your recovery routine. Don't stop to fill in the details of your distress. Just send the automatic broadcast, then get back out there and stay in touch with the casualty. Grab the hand-held radio, but only so long as you can do it quickly, because you simply must not lose sight of your shipmate. As a rule of thumb, you should be seriously considering further radio procedure (or initial MAYDAY calls if you've no GMDSS) after two failed passes or a first abortive attempt to hoist a casualty you have brought alongside. If you have thought through your drill, however, and have practised it thoroughly so that you know it works, the question will probably never arise.

A halo like this with a dropping barometer and a backing wind is a sure sign of trouble.

WEATHER   32

The two most important variables in yachting are the tides and the weather. Tides we can predict, years ahead if need be; weather is different. With the exception of the trade wind belts of tropical and subtropical latitudes, we are down to comparatively short-term weather forecasts and informed personal observation when we need to know what the wind is going to do (and who doesn't?).

For coastal and offshore sailing, we can find most of what we require in the numerous commercial and free public sources of meteorological information. These range from VHF coastguard bulletins or US VHF round-the-coast broadcast forecasts via 'weather radio', to TV, Navtex and Weatherfax. Then, there's the great community feeling that comes with the wind-swept group of wet sailors peering at harbourmasters' noticeboards. The most common source today is undoubtedly the internet. A choice of half a dozen different sites for marine weather forecasting in any given area are often available. One maybe better than another, some sailors will swear by this and others by that, but they're all useful, but never forget the surface pressure chart. These can be downloaded from the UK Met Office site for the whole of Europe and a fair bit of the North Atlantic too. Following these day by day gives a mature feeling for what the weather is actually doing. If the little arrows on the Internet sites coincide with what you think may be happening from the synoptic chart, you have a solid foundation for making decisions. If not, then as in all diagnostic situations, something is wrong somewhere. As time goes by, learning to read the charts and, above all the sky and the sea, is a source of enormous satisfaction.

The trouble is that forecasting has become so sophisticated that there is a growing temptation to rely upon it implicitly and ignore the old ways. A red sky in the morning and even the manner in which the cows are sitting in a riverside field are useful sources of data to those with the knowledge to use them, and sometimes the official weather predictions are out of reach when more primitive signs are plainly manifest.

The true answer to enjoying the weather and not being caught napping by it is to make informed use of forecasts where they are available, and to temper the information or, if need be, substitute it with what your senses are telling you. However, you can do neither if you do not understand the basis of air movements. For our purposes at least, this is not a complicated subject, and the essence of what the temperate waters' Yachtmaster needs to know is set out below. The explanation revolves around the anatomy of the most common wind-inducing weather system of middle and high latitudes: the depression.

If Erik the Red could take a stroll down a modern marina pontoon on a stormy day, there would be little that he could recognise except the rain. Bad weather is the same now as it was in the good old days and it stems from exactly the same causes. Nowadays we can predict it, draw computer models of it and build ships so huge that they are not unduly bothered by it, but so far we haven't made it go away.

The frontal depression

A depression is a free-moving cell of air whose central pressure is lower than that of the surrounding atmosphere. A system can vary in magnitude between a young 'low' only a hundred or so miles across and a mature system stalled on the eastern side of an ocean, affecting conditions 1,000 miles from its centre. Depressions are a primary cause of high winds and of all forms of precipitation, including fog. They can produce storms of hurricane violence, or pass by virtually unnoticed. They are equally common both north and south of the Equator, but for convenience we will consider the northern version first.

Mutually exclusive air masses

The machinery of a depression depends entirely upon the fact that air masses originating in different climatic circumstances are unwilling to mix. Wherever you are situated, your local air arrives in enormous packages, the nature of which is governed by where they have come from and what has been happening to them on the way.

A parcel of warm air, for example, is capable of holding more water vapour than an equivalent quantity of comparatively cold air. If a mass of air moves northwards up the Atlantic from the tropics it will therefore be rich in moisture by the time it reaches the temperate zones. This type of air is referred to as *tropical maritime*.

Air originating in polar and subpolar zones is obviously much colder, and hence is inclined to be drier and denser. In the North Atlantic the enormous mass of Greenland's two-mile-thick ice cap together with the Canadian Arctic supplies a powerful source of so-called *polar maritime air*. 'Polar' for obvious reasons; 'maritime' because it has come across enough water to take the edge off its dryness.

The convergence line of these two global air masses is known as the *polar front*. It is nowhere near the actual Pole, but meanders seasonally between the 35th and the 60th parallels (north and south). Occasionally, it can be found even outside these rough limits.

Air circulation

A person standing at the Equator is actually moving very quickly relative to the space above him, with the turning of the Earth. An explorer stationed at the Pole isn't moving in any direction at all. Instead, he is pirouetting like a skater in a slow spin, executing one revolution every 24 hours. If the sun-lover careering round at the Equator could hurl a ball far enough to get anywhere near the polar explorer, it would not arrive because it would carry with it a component of its original lateral movement and would curve off to one side long before it reached the Pole. Similarly, if the deep-freeze merchant threw a ball from the Pole towards his chum on the Equator, by the time it reached the 0° parallel, its target would have been carried smartly eastwards, leaving the ball to fall into the ocean at a point way to the west of where he was standing when it was thrown. If you could trace its route on the Earth's surface it would appear to curve away westwards as it left the higher latitudes.

The same is true of any free-moving item in the atmosphere with a north–south component in its direction of travel, including an air mass. In the northern hemisphere this tendency causes air to circulate clockwise around a high-pressure area and anticlockwise around a centre of low pressure, rather than flow directly from 'high' to 'low' as would otherwise be the case.

Depression formation

At the polar front in the northern hemisphere, the high-pressure centre of the cold polar air lies to the northwards, so as air tries to flow southwards towards the low-pressure centre it is displaced to the westwards along the front, setting up the clockwise circulation of the system.

Down in the Horse Latitudes (somewhere in the 30s), the other side of the low-pressure zone, lies the mid-oceanic 'high'. This is typified by the 'Azores high' in the North Atlantic, which is funnelling tropical maritime air up its western leg towards the polar front. By the time this air has reached the front, it is moving to the eastwards and is still part of the main clockwise circulation of the oceanic system (Fig 32.1).

Fig 32.1 Oceanic air circulation: eastern North Atlantic.

Cirrus clouds like this, in the upper sky, usually herald the arrival of a weather system. If the barometer is falling as well, there'll probably be a warm front by morning.

Where the two air masses are actually colliding, the warm air will tend to rise as the dense, cold air tries to slide underneath it like a wedge. As this happens, the moisture in the tropical maritime air condenses in the form of clouds, and rain.

The situation is inherently unstable. Two independent air masses trying to overlap one another while they travel in opposite directions doesn't encourage peace on Earth. It takes little disturbance to produce an eddy in the airflow at the front. Such a 'kink' on the front may result from a local area of extra warming, which causes the warmer air to rise slightly faster and the cold air to try to push in behind. It can also result from the presence of a mountain (Pico in the Azores creates amazing eddies in the air) or just a particularly heavy inrush of one type of air into the space of the other.

Once a wave has formed on the front, things take on a life of their own. Fig 32.2 shows how a package of warm, moist air moves up into a 'salient' in the cold air to the north of it. As it does so, cold air moves down behind it from the north and tries to undercut it. The warm air is rising, causing precipitation that releases what is known as *latent heat*. This extra heat helps to energise the system and set up the cyclonic circulation.

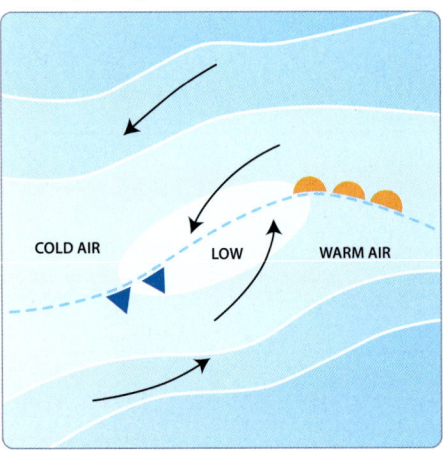

Fig 32.2 Depression formation.

Within 24 hours the eddy will have developed into a young depression showing a warm front (a front with warm air behind it, overlapping the cold air it is displacing), a cold front (followed by colder air which undercuts the warm air) and a complete anticlockwise aircirculation. It will then set off on its life's journey.

WEATHER

With a weather front like this approaching fast, something dramatic is about to happen. Be ready!

Depression tracks

The movements of individual depressions do not conform to a tight stereotype. However, by studying averages over a period of years it is possible to draw some general conclusions. In its first day or two of life, the vertical development of a depression is comparatively modest and is unlikely to penetrate the *jet stream* wind systems of the upper atmosphere. Because it is not interfering with these, the young 'low' will tend to move along their general direction, which more often than not is north-easterly. As it matures, the system extends its influence higher and higher until it is distorting the upper winds. It will probably then slow down and may turn from its straight track usually, but not always, to the left. Ultimately, as we shall see, the circulatory mechanism stalls and decays.

Frontal anatomy

The boundaries of the *warm sector* of a depression are marked by a warm front on its leading edge and a cold front behind (Fig 32.3). As a warm front moves along, it pushes across the upper cold air first and gradually comes down to sea level over a width of anything up to 200 miles.

The first visible evidence of a warm front arriving is the presence of high 'mare's tail' clouds known as *cirrus* (Fig 32.4, p. 302). These are followed by a layer of thin *cirro stratus* cloud, which often begins by generating a halo round the Sun or Moon but ends by obscuring the sky completely as the cloud base falls and thickens up. This is accompanied by a falling

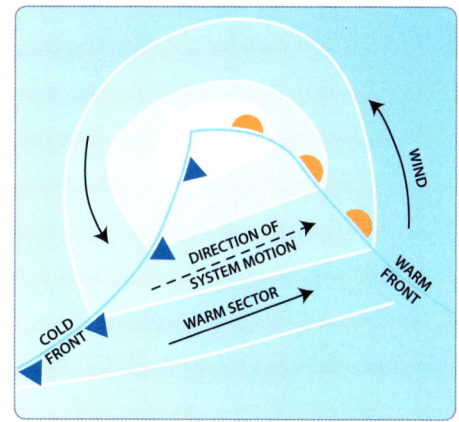

Fig 32.3 A frontal depression.

301

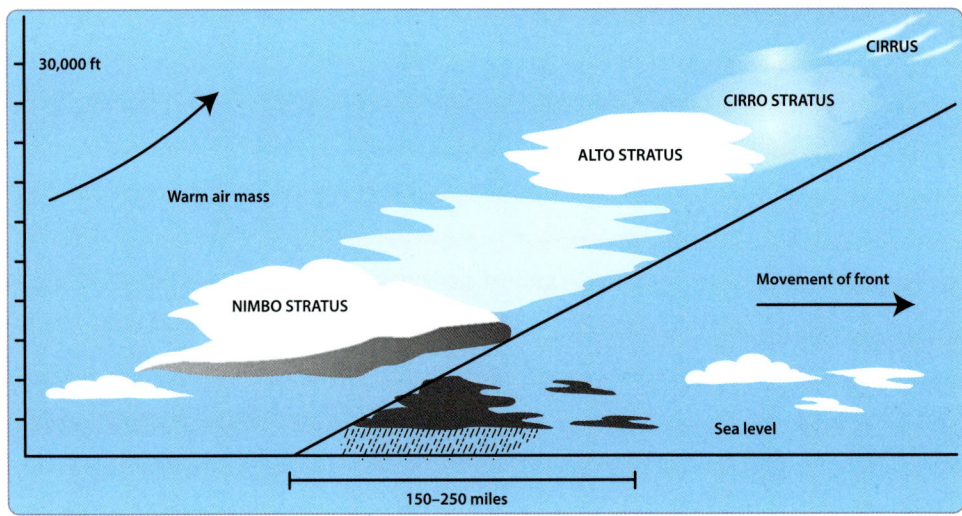

Fig 32.4 A warm front.

Fig 32.5 A cold front.

barometer and the wind will be backing (shifting counter-clockwise), generally to the south or the south-east.

The breeze, which is now strong if the depression is built on a sharp pressure gradient, will veer (shift clockwise) as the front goes through. The barometer will probably stop falling. Rain is now intermittent and visibility remains moderate or poor with fog a possibility. The wind will typically be from the south-west.

You are now in the warm sector. How long you stay there will depend upon the size and rate of progress of the weather system, but 12 hours would not be uncommon. As the cold front approaches, the wind may back a little and pressure often drops. Rain will fall more heavily and conditions generally deteriorate.

The arrival of a fully paid-up cold front can be one of nature's more dramatic atmospheric events. Because the cold air is heavier than that in the warm sector, it pushes along at sea level first, with its wedge of air rising to great heights astern of it. You don't get a lot of warning, but you can't miss it when it comes (Fig 32.5, p. 302).

Classically, the wind veers sharply into the north-west with a ripper of a squall to accompany it. The barometer climbs rapidly and visibility suddenly opens up as the cold, clear air streams down from the Arctic. Huge *cumulonimbus* clouds tower up to 30,000ft (9,144m), sometimes with anvil-shaped tops flying off to leeward in the thin upper atmosphere. As the advancing cold air drives the moisture upwards, convection in the clouds may be so powerful that the raindrops are carried aloft until they freeze, to rattle back to earth as hailstones. Blue sky reappears as the front moves past, and the wind moderates gradually.

Occlusions

As the pair of fronts chase one another across the ocean, the depression is doomed from the outset because the cold front always moves faster than the warm. When the cold air behind the warm sector finally overtakes the cold air in front, its advancing wedge lifts the warm air off the sea, forming an *occlusion*. For a while this hangs around at a moderate altitude, producing varying degrees of unpleasantness, and although the writing is on the wall for the depression once this happens, the system may still remain active for quite some time as the occlusion spirals in around the centre. It is usually at this point in its life that a depression, if it is not to perish without issue, gives birth to one or more secondaries.

Secondary depressions

When a depression slows down, generally but not always on the eastern side of an ocean, it frequently trails its long cold front out behind it. The front, which is in effect once again a part of the polar front, is in a susceptible condition for the formation of a wave that will result in a new depression. These secondary depressions are often more violent than their parents. They can also develop with unforecast rapidity. For this reason it always pays to watch the western sky and the barometer carefully for a while when things seem to have cleared up. A belt of cirrus, a halo round the Sun, a dip in the air pressure, and hold on to your hat! There's more where the last one came from.

If a low-pressure system passes to the southward you may well avoid the frontal systems; the wind pattern will also be very different. Beginning in the south-east, the breeze will back to the east as the centre passes. It will then work round to north of east and may finally merge with the north-westerly airstream behind the cold front. Weather conditions on the north side of a depression are often less violent than in the frontal department down south, but there is still plenty of wind and rain about. In winter, the north-east winds can be particularly severe.

Locating a low-pressure centre

If you are sailing coastwise, the forecast will keep you aware of what weather systems are bound your way. In mid-ocean you'll have to work things out for yourself, unless you have access to modern forecasting.

Fortunately, it's hard to mistake an approaching 'low' as it marches up out of the west. To find the approximate location of its centre, stand with your back to the wind and extend your left hand (right hand in the southern hemisphere) at 90° to the way you are looking. 'Buys Ballot's Law' states that you are then pointing to somewhere near the middle of the system. You can make a fair guess at which way it's heading if you do this every couple of hours. Once you've sorted that out, all you need to do is decide how you are going to handle it.

Wind strengths in depressions

The windspeed around a 'low' is dependent upon how tightly packed are the isobars that indicate its depth. If you are at sea, as soon as you fancy a depression is approaching, you should plot the barometer readings every hour, whatever your normal routine. If the barometer tumbles at a rate of two millibars per hour for at least three hours, stand by for gale-force winds. You may suffer these even if the barometer is less active, but two millibars per hour is a sure sign of grief.

Cyclonic winds

Conditions for the luckless mariner caught in the centre of a depression are grim in the extreme. If the system is vigorous, the windspeed could well vary between zero and force 8 in as many minutes, and the blast can come from any direction. Precipitation is highly probable and the sea state will be a shambles, with steep seas hurling themselves around in total confusion, looking for the discipline of an honest wind.

Depressions in the southern hemisphere

Depressions in the southern hemisphere behave exactly like their northern relatives, except that they are the other way up. The air moves clockwise around southern 'lows', but the winds in the warm sector are still westerly and the mechanism of the systems is exactly the same.

Land distorts depressions and can render their behaviour far less predictable than at sea. To appreciate their organisation to the full, you need to tackle them in mid-ocean. You don't have to like them, few of us do, but there is a straightforward gutsy character about them that you might just find yourself missing if ever you slope off to the tropics for a year or two of trade-wind sailing.

High pressure

Generally speaking, high-pressure circulations are larger and more slow-moving than 'lows'. They often bring settled weather, though at certain times of year this may be accompanied

> ### SKIPPER'S TIP
>
> **The isobar squeeze**
>
> It's not unusual in summer months to find yourself in an area of strong winds, with no particular weather system in the offing. This may be caused by a squeeze of isobars. It's most likely when you are situated between high- and low-pressure centres, neither of which is going anywhere particularly quickly. The winds generated can be strong and stable, giving near-gale conditions which continue for days out of a maddeningly clear sky.

by poor visibility or even fog. High-pressure weather typically favours the formation of sea breezes (see p. 306).

Fog

Two types of fog are of interest to the Yachtmaster. The first sort, which creeps into harbours overnight in spring and autumn, may well turn out to be land fog. This forms over chilled fields and river valleys under cold, clear skies during the hours of darkness. Usually, the sun 'burns it off' soon after it rises, and even if it doesn't, there is every chance that the fog will not persist far out to sea.

Far nastier is the sea fog generated by warm, moist air meeting colder seas. The classic example of sea fog is created when the tropical maritime air brought up the North American coast with the Gulf Stream meets the arctic Labrador Current in the vicinity of the Grand Banks of Newfoundland. The cold water lowers the temperature of the moist air until some of its water vapour precipitates out in the form of fog. Depending on the consistency of the water temperature and air condition, such fog can form in seemingly endless banks, or it may appear only in occasional patches. Often, it fades out in the lee of a headland and sometimes it can even be affected by the turn of the tide.

A synoptic chart downloaded on to an iPad via the Met Office website. Scotland and Ireland have had a reasonable day. For the English Channel things seem to be finally looking up as the cold front sweeps away the warm sector that has spoiled a late-season's day on the water.

Sea breezes

Land warms up more rapidly than sea for a given heat input. It also cools down faster. As a result, on a hot, sunny day, in quiet 'gradient' wind conditions, hot air will begin to rise over the land towards lunch time. Cooler air moves in off the sea to take its place, creating as it does so a *sea breeze* over inshore waters. If there should be a light or moderate onshore gradient wind in addition to the conditions described above, the sea breeze will add itself to this, making up a strengthened wind for the period of its duration. Should the gradient wind be running offshore, the sea breeze will be subtractive, possibly knocking the airflow out altogether.

Sea breezes in temperate zones are usually at their most noticeable in spring and early summer, when the ocean temperatures are substantially lower than those built up during the day ashore.

A converse effect to the sea breeze is sometimes caused by the land cooling rapidly at night while the sea maintains a more even temperature. If the land falls below the heat of the sea, air rising over the water is displaced by cooler air flowing off the land. Such effects are generally less dramatic than the sea breeze of the daylight hours, but it can still produce some fine gusts off steep headlands with high ground behind them.

Sea and land breezes are essentially local affairs. They can sometimes be felt five miles or more offshore, but they may fizzle out within the first thousand yards. They are, however, predictable to the local sailor with his eyes open. Many is the time I've drifted in the west Solent around 11 o'clock on a May morning, waiting for the fine south-west breeze that I knew would carry me as far as Cowes. Whether it would hold into the east Solent and on towards Ryde was another matter altogether, but if I could work down as far as Hayling Bay before the sun set, I could safely bet there would be wind aplenty being poured off the open Channel to cool the suntrap of the hot, flat fields around Chichester Harbour.

Significant local winds

While winds in northern Europe and the north-east and north-west coasts of America tend to be fairly random within the framework of the weather systems described above, other zones are notable for significant local winds. Many of these have colourful names, and it is a negligent sailor indeed who navigates the coasts of Western Australia without a nodding acquaintance with the character of 'The Fremantle Doctor'. The Mediterranean specialises in spectacular winds of considerable force that can make or break a passage, a holiday or a charter business. All Yachtmasters operating in such areas owe it to themselves and their crews to know about their local winds, what triggers them, how long they are likely to last and what actions to take when one is imminent. An example is the way in which the 'North Wind Sector' of a circulating low-pressure system in the Gulf of Genoa is likely to crank up a Mistral, which comes thundering out of the mouth of the Rhône to command the whole attention of the western Mediterranean for five days or more.

Appendix 1
Stability in Sailing Yachts

The question of stability in yachts should always be seen in light of the fact that very few are actually 'knocked down' while cruising in coastal waters. Some of us venture further afield, however, and become involved with conditions from which, for us at the time, there can be no escape. Even for coastal sailors, the chance of encountering heavier seas than were expected, in a tide-rip, for example, remains a real one. Stability therefore concerns us all. Nonetheless, working stability in active situations is awkward to define, slippery to calculate, and dangerous to pontificate about.

The GZ curve

Under theoretical conditions, a vessel's ability to stay 'on her feet' arises from two basic forces: the *form stability* that she possesses by virtue of her beam, and the pendulum effect of her ballast. The results of form stability are noticeable at relatively small angles of heel, while the righting effect of a ballast keel is at its greatest when the boat is on her beam ends. For a yacht to be properly seaworthy, her stability must stem from a healthy combination of the two.

When a yacht heels, her centre of buoyancy shifts to leeward as more of her volume is immersed on the downwind side (Fig A.1, p. 308). Her centre of gravity (G), however, stays more or less where it was. This means that as her ballast is pressing down, the buoyancy is pushing up. Both are trying to return the boat to an even keel, and an equilibrium is reached with the sails, which are attempting to do the opposite.

The length of the 'lever arm' between the centre of gravity (G) and the moving centre of buoyancy (Z) varies with the angle of heel. It is known, logically enough, as GZ. A graph of the length of GZ (which, for a 35-footer with good stability characteristics, may rise to between 2ft and 3ft) against heel angle gives a useful indication of a boat's range of stability in flat water. It demonstrates, among other things, the angle at which the value of GZ becomes negative, and at which the yacht's stability vanishes.

Fig A.2 (p. 309) shows clearly that the moderate-shaped Contessa 32 remains positively stable until she is virtually inverted at almost 160°. The flat-floored 'fin-and-spade profile' yacht of similar waterline length becomes negatively stable if she is rolled to just under 120°. Should she be knocked down to that angle, she will actually try to float upside down, because her centre of buoyancy will have passed on to the 'wrong' side of her centre of gravity.

It is important to understand that while a boat's range of positive stability provides a vital clue to her potential safety in heavy weather, it is by no means the whole story. Her actual

THE COMPLETE YACHTMASTER

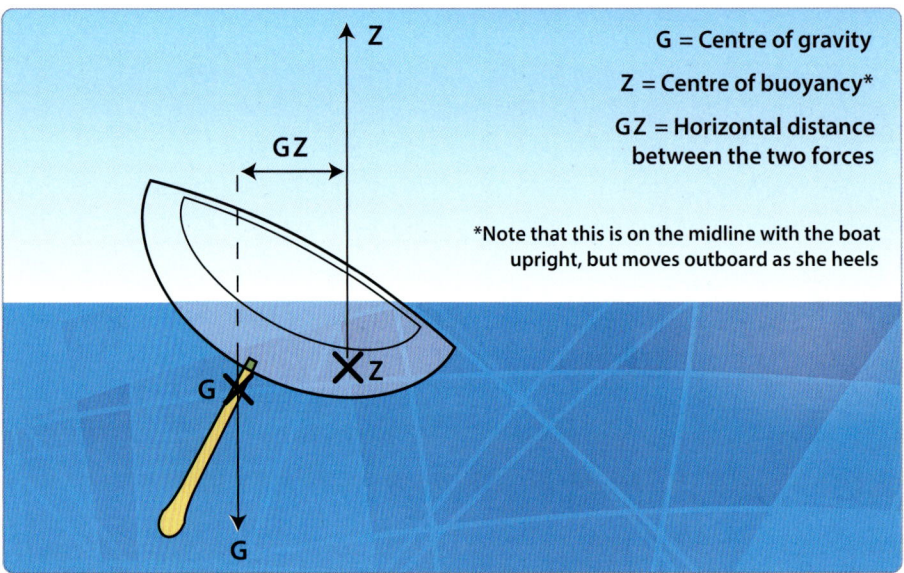

Fig A.1 Stability of heeling yachts.

ability to resist capsize depends directly upon her displacement. A big boat with the same range of positive stability as a small one will be more likely to remain upright in a given set of circumstances. Similarly, if two boats are the same length while one is of greater displacement than the other, she may well have greater resistance to capsize, even if her GZ curve were to prove less advantageous.

So far, we have considered stability only in a static sense. We have looked at yachts in a flat sea and have measured performance in relation to a steadily increasing heeling force. The sea rarely delivers such ideal circumstances. The wind does not generally capsize 30ft yachts. In nearly every case, it is the waves. A wave is a moving force. It arrives in the yacht's vicinity and, especially if she is beam-on, it causes her to roll and rise, or be knocked down if that is what circumstances warrant. After a brief encounter, it continues on its way.

If a yacht can generate enough short-term resistance to a wave's efforts, her angle of vanishing stability is less likely to be put to the test than would otherwise be the case. Resistance of this type is offered by a yacht's inertial unwillingness to begin rolling, which is determined, among other things, by her *roll moment of inertia*. How effective this is depends upon her weight and its distribution. It is, for example, ironic that if she has a heavy mast, the force needed to start her rolling is greater than for a lightweight equivalent. Yet a massive metal spar would have an entirely negative effect upon the yacht's GZ curve. A wooden one has buoyancy characteristics of its own which cannot be discounted should it hit the water, and so on. A dismasted vessel has a far worse roll moment of inertia than an intact one. Ask anyone who has lost his stick in rough water. The sparless yacht's range of positive stability as plotted on a GZ curve will appear greater than before, yet she is undoubtedly less seaworthy.

From these comments about masts alone, it will be obvious that however important the dynamics of capsize may be (and in the USA they are considered extremely important), they are difficult, expensive, and often unreliable to assess empirically. It has also been

APPENDIX 1

Fig A.2 Two contrasting GZ curves.

said with some justification that a big enough breaking wave will knock down any boat afloat. A GZ curve is an excellent starting point for making an assessment of a yacht's likely performance in potentially capsizing conditions, but it is never more than that. This is why some traditional working craft have such a remarkable record for seaworthiness, despite unimpressive static stability predictions.

If you anticipate ever being at sea in really bad weather, your assessment of a boat's chances if she meets a big breaking wave beam-on will affect your choice of survival options deeply. It is therefore important that any serious seafarer studies this matter as fully as he may. There are a number of excellent books specialising in the topic. It is wise to read and consider at least one of them. In the final analysis, however, the experienced, unprejudiced seaman can tell a great deal by the way a yacht looks and feels. There are few surprises lying in wait for the sailor with sensitive 'gut reactions'.

Recreational Craft Directive

The European Recreational Craft Directive (RCD) sets out standards for, among other things, ranges of operation for yachts. While these may be superficially helpful, like all specific rules dealing with imprecise subjects the results sometimes leave much to be desired. Boats are being categorised as ocean-worthy that no sane skipper would take across the North Atlantic north of 40°. As in all seafaring, the final decision must be down to the skipper. If you don't like the feel of a boat that the paperwork says is up to the job, trust your judgement. It's your crew who are on the line, not some bureaucrat sitting in a nice warm office. In the UK the Recreational Craft Regulations (RCR), or UKCA, work in exactly the same way and are similar in all respects.

Appendix 2
Commercial Endorsement of the RYA/MCA Yachtmaster Certificate

While a Yachtmaster certificate is an end in itself for many, to those occupied in professional yachting it represents an entry requirement to the commercial world of the professional seafarer. Instructors, skippers and crew are all involved, whether running a classic racing yacht, crewing aboard a 150ft (45m) motor yacht, delivering a 40ft (12m) family cruiser or running a workboat with lifting gear. As many as 4,500 people apply to the RYA for a commercial endorsement annually. Whatever your job is on board, you are no different from the captain of a cruise liner in terms of your duties of care. If things go horribly wrong you will be held to account. The author can testify from his own work as an expert witness that this is no idle warning.

Commercial qualification empowers a Yachtmaster Offshore holder to skipper yachts up to 200 GRT and 197ft (60m) length overall. In order to qualify commercially, holders of any relevant ticket, which includes Yachtmaster Offshore, must be in possession of in-date certificates as follows:

- First aid, which lasts three years and must be updated on pain of invalidation of all other commercial qualifications
- Radar
- Firefighting
- Sea survival
- In-date medical certificate. This is either an 'ML5' via a GMC-registered doctor which must be 100% clear, or an 'ENG1' via the MCA
- 'PPR' certificate – see opposite
- Marine Radio SRC Certificate or other acceptable GMDSS Marine Radio Operator's Certificate
- You may also require an STCW (Standards of Training, Certification and Watchkeeping for Seafarers) endorsement for some jobs

This sounds a demotivating list, but the RYA have simple courses for them all and only the medical and the PPR involve serious examinations. The medical is what it is. If your vision or heart fall below the standard required, there is little you can do about the matter. The PPR does not represent an enormous challenge and is generally agreed to signify a major step forward in safety.

APPENDIX 2

Professional Practices and Responsibilities (PPR)

This is awarded after an online course organised in the UK by the RYA. It is broken down into four modules:

- **Commercial environment** – This gives a useful perspective on how professional yachting fits into the larger world of professional seafaring.
- **People** – Here, the manning rules are spelled out. It also clarifies how to keep your own skills up to date and discusses techniques for the safe management of vessels going to sea commercially.
- **Vessels** – Issues involving codes of practice and compulsory carriage and maintenance of safety equipment are dealt with here. This module also initiates students into the mysteries of risk assessment and control, as well as operating procedures.
- **Purpose** – A rather strange title which includes ensuring a vessel is suitable and legally qualified for any proposed work. It also takes in such questions as obligations in environmental protection and the catch-alls of appropriate planning and situational awareness.

These instructional modules are followed by a 'mock' assessment that gives students the opportunity to see how they are doing before moving on to a graded online assessment.

It is possible to manage the whole process in a day, but it might be more sensible to allow a day-and-a-half or two days, especially if English is not the first language. The course and exam do not require you to memorise large tracts of technical data. All that is asked is that you know where to look it up when you need it. The course supplies all this information and it will be examined on this understanding. Finding one's way around the files online can be less easy for non-English speakers, so they should be aware and allow as much time as they can for familiarisation.

You cannot apply for a commercial endorsement until you have passed the PPR course. If you already have an endorsement but no PPR, you'll have to acquire one before your next update. The course is not expensive and can be organised via the RYA website.

A Yachtmaster certificate endorsed commercially. The author and publishers are pleased to report that Captain Kidd has now retired and will not be working as an instructor.

INDEX

aerofoil effect 8–9, 10
a'hull, lying 101
air 297–300
AIS (Automatic Identification System) 251–4
almanacs 116
anchoring 42, 73–87
   cable types 76–7
   depths 140–1
   fouled anchors 83–4
   holding ground 74
   kedging off 86
   laying an anchor 79–82
   selecting an anchorage 78
   stern- or bow-to 85–6
   storm anchoring 86–7
   types of anchor 74–6
   weighting the cable 77
apparent wind 13–14, 36
apps 134, 147–8, 188–9
astern, motoring 48–9
atlases, tidal 117–18, 144

backing off 82
batteries 88, 90
beam sea 98
beating
   in a cross-current 211
   in a cross-tide 211–12
   to windward 12, 208
berthing 42–3, 49–58
bleeding an engine 92–4
blowing off 44–5
bow thrusters 59
bow-to mooring 50
box berths 50–1
breakdowns and breakages 271–80
Bruce anchor 75
buoys
   buoy hopping 249
   cardinal marks 125–6
   high focal plane 124
   Lanby (Large Automated Navigation Buoy) 123
   temporary wreck 125

cable types 76–7
cardinal marks 125–6
chafe 69
chain 76–7, 87
chart datums 113, 182–3
chart plotters
   electronic 134, 147–8, 187–94
   general functions 190–4
   passage navigation 238–9
   passage planning 215–16
   piloting with 226–9
   types of 187–9
charts
   corrections 113, 115–16
   electronic 114–15
   passage 215
   passage requirements 110–11
   projections 108–10
   scale 113
   symbols 111–13
   table tools 118
   using on passage navigation 235–7
clearance 132–3
clearing line 223–7
cleats 66–7
closehauled sailing 11
'Code Zero' sails 22
coiling rope 67
collision avoidance 250–65
coming alongside 54–8, 68–70
commercial endorsement 310–11
compass 150–8
   bearings 172–3
   deviation 153–6
   dip 156
   heeling errors 156
   magnetic anomalies 156
   swinging the 155–6
   totalling up 155
   variation 151–3
contours 112–13
course shaping 200–6
course to steer 202–3
CQRs 74, 75

crash stop 292–4
cross-tide sailing 203, 205–6
cross-track error 186
cruising chutes 22
current tables 147
cut-off lines 174–5
cyclonic winds 304

damage control 271–80
Danforth anchor 75
darkness, navigation strategy 207, 220
daylight 207, 219
dead reckoning position (DR) 162
depressions, weather 298
   formation 299–300
   frontal anatomy 301–3
   secondary 303
   southern hemisphere 304
   tracks 301
   wind strengths in 304
depth of sea 111–13, 159–61
deviation, compass 153–6
digital radar 254–65
dinghies, towing with 72
direction of travel, establishing 110
dismasting 280
dividers 191

echo sounder 160, 165–6, 173–4
efficient sailing 13–22
Electronic Bearing Line (EBL) 195–6, 258
electronic chart plotters *see* chart plotters, electronic
electronic charts 114–15
electronic logs 158–9
elevation 132–3
emergencies 281–9
ends, rope 65–6
engines 88–94
estimated position (EP) 162–7, 268–70

INDEX

eyeball fix 168–71
eyes, rope 65–6

fire prevention and fighting 276
fisherman anchor 75–6
flares 288–9
fog 244–9, 305
    fog signals 123
food and drink 240–1
Fortress anchors 75
fuel 92–4, 220

genoa
    poling out a 26–7
    twist 15, 16
Global Positioning System (GPS)
    accuracy control 182
    chart datums 182–3
    course and speed 183
    cross-tide sailing with 205–6
    differential 183
    extra functions 183–7
    navigation 150, 181–2
    passage navigation 235–7
    position fixing 181–3
    tidal stream deduction 148–9
    waypoints 184–7, 217
GMDSS 295–6
Gnomonic charts 109
goose-winging 26
great circles 109
ground track 191, 200
gybing 24–5
GZ curve 307–9

half-tide 114
halyards, wire 61–2
hand-starting engines 90–1
harbour charts 109
heading, ship's 175–6, 190
headsails
    changes 33
    shaping 14–17
heaving to 28–30, 100–1
heavy weather sailing 95–102, 266–70
heeling error 156
helicopter rescue 283–5
high focal plane buoys 124
high pressure 304–5
hull balance 19

IALA cardinal marks 124–6
in-boom mainsails 32–3
in-mast mainsails 32
inshore marks 124–6

instant position lines 228
isolated dangers 125

jury rigs 276–7
    spinnaker pole rudder 279–80

kedging off 86
keel 9
knots 62–6

Lanby (Large Automated Navigation Buoy) 123
landfall charts 111
latitude 107–8
lead-line 159–60
lee-bow effect 211, 212
lee helm 18, 19
leech-line 15
leeway 163, 204–5, 268
lifeboat rescue 282–3
liferafts 286–8
light floats 123
lighthouses 120–3
lights, navigation 120
lightships 123
log 157–9
log book 166–7
longitude 107–8
lookout, responsibility for 250–1
looms 122
low-pressure centres 304
luminous range 120–1
lying a'hull 101

magnetic anomalies, local 156
mainsails
    in-boom 32–3
    in-mast 32
    sailing only under 37
    shaping 17–18
making fast a rope 66
man overboard 186–7, 290–6
marine computers 194–5
MARPA (Mini Automatic Radar Plotting Aid) 259–63
MAYDAY 285–6, 288
Mercator projections 108–12
mooring
    leaving a 42
    Mediterranean stern-to 50
    under power 49–50
    under sail 38–42
moving ahead 47

Nautical Almanac 116
nautical miles 108
navigation 103–6

aids 119–26
    in poor conditions 267–8
    strategy 207–13
    traditional means of 150–61
    see also passage navigation
neaps 128
nylon rope 60–1, 77

obscuring lines, lighthouse 121, 174–5
occlusions 303
offshore marks 123–4
oil spills 89
overheating engines 91–2
oversheeting 38

PAN PAN call 282, 285–6
para anchor 101
passage charts, paper 110–11
passage navigation 230–9
    using GPS and paper chart 235–7
    with a plotter 238–9
    without electronics 232–5
passage planning 214–21, 231–2
PC programs 135, 187–9
phone plotters 188–9
pile moorings 51–3
pilot books 116–18, 217
pilotage 221, 222–9
pivoting 44
plotted vectors 164
plotting 166
plough anchors 74
polyester rope 60
polypropylene rope 60
position fixing 168–79, 181–3, 197–9, 268
position lines 168–75, 195–7
power, boat handling under 44–59
preplotting 175–6
propeller
    effects of 46
    ropes around the 278
    publications 116–18
pyrotechnics 288–9

radar 195–9, 254–65
rafting manners 57
ranges 171–2
raster charts 113, 114
reach-turn-reach 291–2
Recreational Craft Directive (RCD) 309
reefing systems 20, 30–2
rhumb line 108–9

rigging 274
rollers 28, 33, 34
ropes/ropework 60–72
   around the propeller 278
   for anchoring 77, 87
   handling rope 66–7
   hi-tech materials 61
   types of rope 60–1
rudder
   effects of 45
   loss of 279
   spinnaker pole rudder 279–80
Rule of Twelfths 135–6
running 98–9
running fix 176–8
running off 101–2

safe track 223–6
safe water marks 124
sailing directions 116–18
sailing theory 7–12
   aerofoil effect 8–9, 10
   closehauled sailing 11
   running 10–11
   windward sailing 11–12
sails 8–12
   balance 20
   basic trim 9
   camber 9, 13, 14–15
   combinations 18
   efficiency 13–14
   in heavy weather 96–7
   painless reduction of 28
   repairs 274
   shortening 19–21, 37
   twist 14, 15, 16
satellite navigation 180–99
scandalising 38
sea breezes 306
Search and Rescue (SAR) 281–2, 295–6
seasickness 242–3
secondary ports 129–31, 139
sectors, lighthouse 121, 174–5
short turns 47
single-line reefing 32

skipper 4–6
sleep 241
slow sailing 37–8
soundings 112–13
space on board 242
spade anchor 75
spare parts 272–5
splices 62–6
springing off a berth 58–9
springs 128
stability in yachts 307–9
steering
   at turn of tide 202–3
   failure 278–80
   in waves 98–100
sternboarding 43
stern-to mooring 50, 55
stopping 35–6, 70
storm anchoring 86
survival tactics 100–2

tablet plotters 188–9
tacking 23–4, 208, 212–13
temporary wreck buoys 125
tides
   atlases 144
   awareness 36
   curves 136–9
   definitions 132–3
   diamonds 146–7
   electronic plotters 134, 147–8
   gates 143–4
   GPS use 148–9
   heights 127–42, 191, 219
   intermediate heights 134–6, 146
   navigation strategy 207
   non-astronomical factors 139
   personal observation 149
   safety 142
   sea states 144
   secondary ports 129–31, 139
   steering through 202–3
   streams 143–9, 192, 218–19
   tables 129
   times 129

vectors 164–5
   when mooring 40–2
tool kits 272–5
towing 70–2
traffic separation schemes (TSSs) 219, 232
trailing log 158
transferred position lines (TPLs) 175
transits 171–2
traveller safety 26
trysails 97–8
turning 44–8
tying up 68–9

Variable Range Marker (VRM) 259
variation, compass 151–3
vector charts 115
VMG 212

wakes 262–3
warmth on board 242
water track 163
waves, steering in 98–100
waypoints 184–7, 193–4, 217–18
weather 218, 297–306
   see also fog
weather helm 18, 19
whippings 62–6
wind
   apparent 13–14
   awareness 36
   cyclonic 304
   navigation strategy 207
   shifts 207–8, 209–10
   significant local 306
   speed 13
   spilling 37–8
   strengths in depressions 304
   when mooring 40–2
windward sailing 11–12, 98, 102, 208
wire halyards 61–2

Other books by Tom Cunliffe:

Bosun's Bag
The Complete Day Skipper
The Complete Ocean Skipper
In the Wake of Heroes
Hand, Reef and Steer

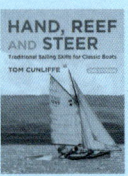

Visit www.bloomsbury.com/uk/author/tom-cunliffe to find out more